Contemporary Approaches to Second Language Acquisition

AILA Applied Linguistics Series (AALS)

The AILA Applied Linguistics Series (AALS) provides a forum for established scholars in any area of Applied Linguistics. The series aims at representing the field in its diversity. It covers different topics in applied linguistics from a multidisciplinary approach and it aims at including different theoretical and methodological perspectives. As an official publication of AILA the series will include contributors from different geographical and linguistic backgrounds. The volumes in the series should be of high quality; they should break new ground and stimulate further research in Applied Linguistics.

For an overview of all books published in this series, please see
http://benjamins.com/catalog/aals

Editor

Rosa Manchón
University of Murcia

Editorial Board

Volume 9

Contemporary Approaches to Second Language Acquisition
Edited by María del Pilar García Mayo, María Junkal Gutierrez Mangado and María Martínez Adrián

Contemporary Approaches to Second Language Acquisition

Edited by

María del Pilar García Mayo
María Junkal Gutierrez Mangado
María Martínez Adrián
Universidad del País Vasco (UPV/EHU)

John Benjamins Publishing Company

Amsterdam / Philadelphia

The paper used in this publication meets the minimum requirements of
the American National Standard for Information Sciences – Permanence
of Paper for Printed Library Materials, ANSI z39.48-1984.

Library of Congress Cataloging-in-Publication Data

Contemporary Approaches to Second Language Acquisition / Edited by María del Pilar
     García Mayo, María Junkal Gutierrez Mangado, María Martínez Adrián.
pages cm. -- (AILA Applied linguistics series, ISSN 1875-1113 ; v. 9)
Includes bibliographical references and index.
1. Second language acquisition. 2. Language and languages--Study and teaching.
     I. García Mayo, María del Pilar, editor of compilation.
P118.2.C655   2013
418.0071--dc23   2012048059
ISBN 978 90 272 0525 4   (Hb ; alk. paper)
ISBN 978 90 272 7222 5   (Eb)

John Benjamins Publishing Co. · P.O. Box 36224 · 1020 ME Amsterdam · The Netherlands
John Benjamins North America · P.O. Box 27519 · Philadelphia PA 19118-0519 · USA

In memory of Teresa Pica (1945-2011),
outstanding researcher and warm friend

Table of contents

Acknowledgments

We are grateful to all the colleagues who have contributed to this volume, without whom the book would not have been possible. Special thanks go to Florence Myles, Jason Rothman and Bill VanPatten for their willingness to write the foreword and afterword, respectively. Thanks are also due to all those colleagues who have helped with the detailed evaluations of the different chapters that comprise the volume. They are (in alphabetical order): Eva Alcón Soler, Marta Antón, Teresa Cadierno, Robert DeKeyser, Veena D. Dwivedi, Robert French, Ulrike Jessner, James Lee, Anne McCabe Ana Martín, Wang Min, Catrin Norrby, Anne O'Keefe, David Stringer and Bill VanPatten. Very special thanks should go to Alison Mackey and Jenefer Philp who, due to Teresa Pica's untimely death, finalized her chapter in her memory. We are also grateful to the AILA Series editor, Rosa Manchón, and to Kees Vaes at John Benjamins for their advice during the preparation of the volume.

The editors also gratefully acknowledge support from the Department of Education, Universities and Research of the Basque Government (Grant IT311-10), University of the Basque Country (UPV/EHU) (Grant UFI11/06) and the Spanish Ministry of Education (Grants FF12009-10264 and CSD2007-00012).

Foreword

Florence Myles
University of Essex

This is an ambitious volume: Second Language Acquisition (SLA) research has grown exponentially in the past decade or so, not only in terms of the number of empirical studies investigating an increasingly wide range of phenomena and languages, but also in terms of the theoretical approaches productively used in the field. As a result, SLA researchers have become more sophisticated in the kind of questions they are asking and in the methodological tools they use in order to investigate these questions. This has led to the emergence of a range of new approaches, some thanks to technological advances (e.g. in neurolinguistics or psycholinguistics), others to borrowing from neighbouring disciplines (e.g. dynamic systems theory).

This volume covers all the main theoretical approaches, from the best established to the most recent newcomers to the field. This complements in a timely fashion the plethora of recent very lengthy handbooks, as, rather than attempting to provide a comprehensive treatment of all aspects of the various SLA theoretical approaches which are currently productive, it focuses on providing a situated illustration of some of the current work within the various paradigms. It thus gives an up-to-date and non-technical account of some of the ways in which influential theories are used in this field, for the relative newcomer to SLA theorising as well as the SLA researcher working within a specific paradigm but wanting to keep abreast of development in neighbouring approaches. It also enables SLA researchers from a range of perspectives to gain an insight into complementary approaches, thus facilitating interdisciplinary crossovers. Additionally, many of the chapters make it a central concern to outline the links between a particular theory and its pedagogical applications and implications.

Not only is the volume comprehensive in terms of its coverage of old and new theories or approaches, it is also wide ranging in terms of its breadth of coverage, inclusive of the linguistic as well as the cognitive, social and pedagogical dimensions of SLA theorising.

The first linguistic theory introduced is the *generative* perspective (Slabakova, Chapter 1), still one of the best established and most prolific approach within SLA. However, rather than attempting to review it comprehensively, which would be impossible given the scope of the volume, the approach adopted is to give an illustration of one way in which it has been conceptualised within SLA research recently: in this case, Slabakova outlines her *Bottleneck Hypothesis,* in which she argues that the main source of difficulty for second language learners is functional morphology, whereas syntax and semantics are relatively straightforward.

Other well established SLA paradigms reviewed in the volume include *Processability Theory* (Håkansson, Chapter 6), with its focus on how processing constraints shape development, and here again, the emphasis is on illustrating from recent work which has extended the range of typologically different languages this approach has been applied to (German, Swedish and Arabic in this chapter), as well as its application to the diagnosis of language impairment in bilingual children.

The contribution on the *Interactionist* approach (Pica, Chapter 3), after tracing the evolution of this long standing tradition, focuses on its more recent links with psychological constructs such as noticing or attention, as well as its strong pedagogical basis and applications, making a concluding plea for its application to the study of new computer-based communicative patterns.

Also preoccupied with the role of input and of processing in SLA, is the *Input Processing* approach (Benati, Chapter 5). The focus here is on its precise contribution to the field of SLA, in terms of a better understanding of how learners relate forms to meanings when exposed to an L2, and the pedagogical applications of the strategies they employ in so doing.

Firmly focused on the classroom and the role of contextualised practice within it, Lyster and Sato apply *Skill Acquisition Theory* (Chapter 4) to the analysis of the proceduralisation of knowledge in SLA, through providing awareness-practice-feedback instructional sequences to enhance learner performance.

The classroom is also an important player in the *Sociocultural* approach (Gánem-Gutiérrez, Chapter 7), as the locus for mediated activity which is claimed to drive the acquisition process. The focus of this approach, however, is on the social rather than cognitive processes involved, with language seen as a culturally created means of mediation for mental activity, rather than as a separate cognitive faculty.

A model of language which is also very different from the generative perspective is applied to the understanding of classroom processes by Llinares (Chapter 2), who adopts a Hallidayan Systemic-Functional model to investigate EFL and CLIL – Content and Language Integrated Learning – classrooms. In this view, language cannot be separated from the meanings it encodes nor the context in which it is used; language is seen as both process and product.

Yet another conception of language underpins both the usage-based and connectionist chapters. In the chapter adopting a *Usage-based* framework (Weinert, Basterrechea & García Mayo, Chapter 8), the focus is on the need to base SLA analysis on spoken grammars rather than the grammar of traditional reference textbooks. This is demonstrated through the lens of an investigation of subordination in native and non-native spoken language.

Connectionist models (Li & Zhao, Chapter 9) argue that the emergence of human cognition, including language, is the outcome of large networks of interactive processing units operating simultaneously. They review the progress that this relative newcomer to SLA has made recently in designing increasingly sophisticated computational models of bilingual acquisition and processing.

A complete newcomer to the field of SLA research is the application of the *Dynamic Systems Theory* (de Bot, Lowie, Thorne & Verspoor, Chapter 10), originating from applied mathematics, to the study of second language development, conceptualised as a complex adaptive system undergoing constant changes. This approach emphasises the crucial importance of both spatial and temporal dynamics in second language development (both acquisition and attrition), and the authors explore its potential complementarity with other SLA approaches such as sociocultural theory and usage-based theories.

Last but not least, recent technological advances have enabled great strides to be made in the application of neurolinguistics to SLA research. The use of event-related brain potentials (ERPs) to measure cognitive brain activity is enabling researchers to isolate differences in the nature of processing in L1 and L2 populations of different kinds. And although results of studies to-date are rather inconclusive, this approach enables very fine grained investigations to be carried out on the role of e.g. proficiency and age of onset of acquisition on the organisation of language in the brain, as explained by Sabourin, Brien and Tremblay (Chapter 11).

This book offers a good reflection of the growth of SLA theorising in recent years. The end result could have been a volume lacking in coherence, making it difficult for the reader to get a comprehensive overview of this complex field. This is not the case, however, as each approach is clearly situated within the field as a whole, before being exemplified and illustrated with relevant empirical studies.

Florence Myles
Essex, October 2012

Introduction

María del Pilar García Mayo, M. Junkal Gutierrez Mangado
and María Martínez Adrián
Universidad del País Vasco (UPV/EHU)

Second language acquisition (SLA) is a field of inquiry that has increased in importance since the 1960s. Early research was descriptive and mainly tied to language teaching pedagogy, but the interest in the nature of learner language changed this direction of inquiry. Currently, researchers adopt multiple perspectives in the analysis of learner language, all of them providing different but complementary answers to the understanding of oral and written data produced by young and older learners in different settings. After all, and as acknowledged by researchers in the field, SLA is a multi-faceted phenomenon that needs to be considered from multiple perspectives in order to gain insights into the complex process of acquiring and using a new language.

In May 2010 some of the contributors to this volume converged in Vitoria-Gasteiz (Spain) to participate in a seminar entitled 'Multiple Perspectives on Second Language Acquisition', organized by the research group *Language and Speech* (http://www.laslab.org), to which the editors of the book belong. One of the aims of the seminar was to make both young researchers in the field and second/foreign language practitioners aware of the latest developments of this exciting field of research and, above all, to convey the idea that SLA research provides informed answers to some of the problems that practitioners face in their classrooms.

Following the seminar, we contacted several colleagues and asked them to write state-of-the art chapters on the perspectives within which they develop their research and illustrate the claims made with relevant empirical findings whenever possible. Thus, the main goal of this volume is to provide the reader with updated reviews of the major contemporary approaches to SLA, the research carried out within them and, wherever appropriate, the implications and/or applications for theory, research and pedagogy that might derive from the available empirical evidence. The volume, therefore, features a selection of current approaches to SLA and, as Rothman and VanPatten point out in their Afterword, it presents "[...] a snapshot in time of the historical progression of [the SLA] enterprise".

There are several clarifications that need to be made regarding the choice of some of the words in the title of the volume. We have used the adjective *contemporary* in its literal meaning to refer to approaches that are contemporary in that they are currently being employed in SLA research to shed light on second language (L2) processing and L2 language use as well as to analyze learner language. We have also chosen the noun *approach* as an encompassing term to refer to the different theories/models/perspectives/frameworks that are represented in this volume. We are well aware of recent work where an effort is made to characterize different proposals offered to explain the SLA process on a number of dimensions (see Hulstijn 2012; Ortega 2007). However, given that assessing whether or not each of those proposals qualifies as a theory, model, or framework is beyond the scope of this volume, the term *approach* has been chosen. As for the term *SLA*, we understand it as encompassing both the simultaneous and the sequential acquisition of an L2. It is not our intention to use SLA and bilingualism as synonymous terms.

The book is divided into eleven chapters. The first two focus on two well-established linguistic theories. Slabakova (Universal Grammar) and Llinares (Systemic-functional approach) consider the relevance of those theories for the analysis of learner language and both offer implications for research carried out within their respective approaches and for pedagogy. The next five chapters by Pica (the Interactionist model), Lyster and Sato (Skill Acquisition theory), Benati (Input Processing theory), Håkansson (Processability theory) and Gánem-Gutiérrez (Sociocultural theory) present the main tenets of well-established SLA theories/models and also implications for theory and research as well as for pedagogy (Pica, Benati). The last four chapters feature more recent approaches to the study of SLA: Weinert, Basterrechea and García Mayo (Usage-based approach), Li and Zhao (Connectionist approach), de Bot, Lowie, Thorne and Verspoor (Dynamic Systems theory) and Sabourin, Brien and Tremblay (electrophysiology of second language processing). The afterword by Rothman and VanPatten presents an epistemological reflection on SLA theory on the basis of the different issues raised in the chapters that comprise the volume.

All the contributors to this volume were provided with a set of guidelines about the internal organization of their chapters. Following this common set of guidelines, each chapter starts by informing the reader about the main tenets of the approach in focus and about the manner in which each approach addresses L2 processing, L2 use and the analysis of learner language. In addition, contributors were asked to provide a review of the empirical research carried out within the different approaches, draw theoretical implications stemming from that research, provide implications and/or applications for pedagogy whenever possible and suggest future directions in the field.

The book is intended for SLA researchers as well as for graduate (MA, Ph.D.) students in SLA research, applied linguistics and linguistics, as the different chapters will be a guide in their research within the approaches presented. The volume will also be of interest to professionals from other fields interested in the SLA process and the different explanations that have been put forward to account for it.

During the preparation of the manuscript, Teresa Pica (University of Pennsylvania) unexpectedly passed away on November 14th, 2011. Tere was very excited about contributing her chapter on interaction. She had visited the Basque Country back in 1998 and since then she had advised the first editor of this volume and collaborated with her on several projects. Tere also participated in the 2010 workshop and was planning a visit scheduled precisely for November 2011. An outstanding researcher and a warm friend, her work and her contribution to the field will not be forgotten. This book is dedicated to her memory.

References

Hulstijn, J. H. 2012. Is the second language acquisition discipline disintegrating? Language Teaching. Available on CJO2012 doi:10.1017/S0261444811000620.

Ortega, L. 2007. Second language learning explained? SLA across nine contemporary theories. In *Theories of Second Language Acquisition. An Introduction*, B VanPatten & J. Williams (eds.), 235–250. Mahwah NJ: Lawrence Erlbaum.

CHAPTER 1

What is easy and what is hard to acquire in a second language

A generative perspective

Roumyana Slabakova
University of Iowa

Explaining why some linguistic features and constructions are easy or difficult to acquire in a second language has become a prominent current concern in generative second language acquisition (SLA) research. Based on a comparison of findings on the L2 acquisition of functional morphology, syntax, the syntax-semantics and syntax-discourse interfaces, the Bottleneck Hypothesis argues that functional morphemes and their features are the bottleneck of L2 acquisition; acquisition of syntax and semantics (and maybe even the syntax-discourse interface) flows smoothly (Slabakova 2006, 2008). The chapter presents recent experimental studies supporting this view. A pedagogical implication of this model is discussed, namely, that an enhanced focus on practicing grammar in language classrooms is beneficial to learners.

Introduction

In recent years, there has been increased interest in examining and explaining the differential difficulty of acquisition of language modules, operations, and constructions. Within the Interactionist approach (Mackey, Abduhl & Gass 2012 – see Pica, this volume), researchers are interested in what linguistic structures benefit the most from classroom interaction, and more specifically, interactional feedback (Jeon 2007; Long et al. 1998). DeKeyser (2005) has argued that a number of linguistic elements are hard or impossible to learn through mere exposure in the sense of communicating in the target language, because these elements have low frequency or otherwise lack salience, especially where form-meaning mapping is concerned. Therefore his practice approach (DeKeyser 2007) recommends systematic and deliberate practice in the classroom with the goal of creating explicit knowledge and skills in the L2. The generative framework of second language acquisition (SLA) has taken a somewhat different slant to the issue: it identifies the harder and easier to acquire properties based on their inherent characteristics as defined by linguistic theory. The goal of the present chapter is to endorse, justify and promote such an approach.

Generative theory argues that the linguistic competence of speakers can be described as a highly abstract and unconscious system, a grammar, that allows them to produce and comprehend language. The structure of sentences (syntax), the sound of sentences (phonetics/phonology) and the meaning of sentences (semantics) are components of this unconscious system, or Universal Grammar (UG). Some properties that pertain to syntax, semantics and pragmatics are universal to all languages; some other properties, however, mostly pertaining to functional morphology encoding the universal grammatical meanings, are language specific and are described as subject to parametric variation. Since its inception in the 80ies, this approach to SLA has inherently been interested in how UG facilitates and constrains the process of acquisition. Universal properties such as principles of UG can be transferred from the native language; parameter values different from the native ones but available from UG have been discussed as potential sources of L2 knowledge.

As generative SLA theory has evolved, the fundamental issue of how UG aids acquisition has been augmented with scrutiny of concrete parameter values and the composition of features within these values. For example, Lardiere's (2005, 2009) Feature Re-assembly Hypothesis recently argued that morphological competence should be accorded a special status and highlighted its difference from syntactic competence. In a nutshell, the hypothesis postulates that learning a second language involves figuring out how to reconfigure the formal features of the native language and those available from UG into new or different configurations in the L2. It is precisely this assembly and re-assembly of formal features (which is almost never straightforward mapping) that is at the core of language acquisition. White (2003, Chapter 4), asked the question of whether knowledge of functional morphology drives learning the syntax, or the other way around: knowledge of syntax comes before knowledge of functional morphology. She dubbed the two views *morphology-before-syntax* and *syntax-before-morphology* (see more on this below). Slabakova (2006), building on the insights of White and Lardiere, and viewing the issue from the point of modular critical periods in SLA, argued that there is no critical period for the acquisition of semantics; that is, meaning comes for free if functional morpho-syntactic competence is already in place.

It is crucial that we use principled distinctions, well understood in linguistic theory, and solid bodies of data in assembling this relative delineation of linguistic processes and modules. The ultimate goal of this endeavor is, of course, to explain the cognitive process of language acquisition. However, it can also inform language teaching by applying the insights achieved by generative SLA research and theory in the last thirty years. It makes practical sense that if teachers know what is hard to acquire and practice it more in the classroom, they will be in a more favorable position to help learners achieve better fluency and higher accuracy in the second language.

Presenting the first of the multiple perspectives on SLA in this volume, this chapter will make the case that generative SLA research findings are eminently applicable to the language classroom. In this chapter, I will argue for the Bottleneck Hypothesis as a partial answer to the question of the title: what is easy and what is hard in second language acquisition. I will show that it is functional morphology that is the bottleneck of L2 acquisition; acquisition of syntax and semantics (and maybe even pragmatics) flows smoothly (Slabakova 2006, 2008). The hypothesis is based on a comparison of findings on the acquisition of functional morphology, syntax, the syntax-semantics interface, the syntax-discourse interface, and the semantics-pragmatics interface. I will summarize findings from representative studies in these areas to make the main point: Functional morphology is the bottleneck of acquisition.

Language architecture and the location of functional morphology

In order to understand how the SLA of various linguistic properties proceeds, we need to have a clear idea of the various units that make up the language faculty and their interaction. The architecture of the language faculty is important because it directly bears on what has to be learned or not, and what comes for free in acquiring a second language. I will assume a widely accepted model of grammar following Reinhart (2006), which is illustrated in Figure 1.

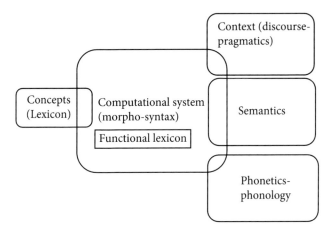

Figure 1. Modular design of the language faculty, modified from Reinhart (2006)

What is to be learned and what comes for free, keeping in mind the language architecture in Figure 1 above? Lexical items are drawn from the language-specific lexicon into the computational system. The latter can be imagined as a working space where syntactic operations like Select, Merge, and Agree combine lexical items into phrases, and then into bigger phrases. Syntactic operations continue until all of the lexical items in the numeration are exhausted and all formal features are checked. Both visible and invisible movements take place here. Principles and language-specific parameters (leading to different grammatical rules in every language) reside in the computational system. The complete syntactic object (a tree) is then passed on by means of Spell-Out to the phonetic-phonological system for linearization and pronunciation and to the semantic system for interpretation. Context, for example the discourse-pragmatics of the message or the dialog, also impacts semantic processes and interacts with the computational system.

Two types of formal features are relevant to the grammar-meaning interface: interpretable and uninterpretable ones. Interpretable (semantic) features are legible in the semantic component and contribute to the interpretation, so they cannot be eliminated. Uninterpretable features, on the other hand, should be eliminated before Spell-Out, since they do not contribute to meaning.

(1)   My daughter often take-s the bus.

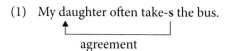

For example, in the sentence in (1), the interpretable feature [singular] on the subject phrase nominal head survives into the semantic module. The uninterpretable feature on the verb, which ensures agreement, on the other hand, is eliminated by the interface with semantics, though it may survive until the acoustic system to be pronounced as /-s/.[1] Which feature is interpretable and which is not is subject to language variation, so this attribution is predicted to pose a problem for L2 learners. (See Adger 2003, Chapter 2, for more examples of features across languages).

The set of functional categories constitutes a sub-module of the computational system, namely, the Functional Lexicon. Each functional category is associated with a lexical item, or items, specified for the relevant formal features. Parameterization is a blueprint made up of a finite set of features, feature values, and properties (e.g., whether a certain feature will induce phrasal movement or will move on its own, what we call *strength of features*). Acquisition of L2 functional categories involves the functional properties of a set of lexical entries, but is manifested in

---

1.   It may seem contradictory that a feature can be eliminated and survive at the same time. This is only seemingly so. After Spell-Out, the linguistic message divides into meaning and form. The feature is eliminated from the meaning, but survives in the form; that is, it can be pronounced or written.

syntactic reflexes superficially unrelated to these lexical entries, like displacement of a phrase away from its position of merging. For example, linguistic theory postulates that the presence of overt agreement morphology on the verb in (1) signals agreement with the subject, but the formal features present in this category also capture Tense (present), the necessity of an overt subject in English as opposed to some null-subject languages, the case of the subject (Nominative), and the fact that the verb stays in the VP in English, thus appearing after the adverb *often*. There is a lot more information in a simple third person singular *-s* than meets the eye.

While the content of meaning (the concepts and relations between them) is arguably the same for all languages, different linguistic forms map different natural groupings of meanings. Let me illustrate such a mismatch with Spanish and English aspectual tenses. While the English past progressive tense signifies an ongoing event in the past, Spanish imperfect can have both an ongoing and a habitual interpretation. The English simple past tense, on the other hand, has a one-time finished event interpretation and a habitual interpretation while the Spanish preterit has only the former.

(2) a. *Guillermo **robaba** en la   calle*   (habitual event)
         Guillermo rob-IMP in the street
         'Guillermo habitually robbed (people) in the street.'

     b. *Guillermo **robó**   en la   calle.*   (one-time finished event)
         Guillermo rob-PRET in the street
         'Guillermo robbed (someone) in the street.'

     c. *Guillermo **robaba** a alquien en la   calle   quando llegó*
         Guillermo rob-IMP someone in the street when   arrived
         la   policía   (ongoing event)
         the police
         'Guillermo was robbing someone in the street when the police arrived.'

(3) a. Felix **robbed** (people) in the street.   (habitual event)
     b. Felix **robbed** a person in the street.   (one-time finished event)
     c. Felix **was robbing** a person in the street (when the police arrived).
                                                        (ongoing event)

Thus, the same semantic primitives (ongoing, habitual, and one-time finished event), arguably part of universal conceptual structure, are distributed over different pieces of functional morphology. When learning Spanish as an L2, a simple mapping along the lines of "English simple past is similar to Spanish preterit" is at least partly misleading. A speaker may be confronted with different mappings between units of meaning on the conceptual level and units of syntactic structure.

To recapitulate this section, we will assume the Minimalist premise that the functional lexicon is where most language variation is encoded, while meanings (the content of thought) are universal. It follows logically from this language architecture that learning a second language entails learning the new configurations in which the various interpretable and uninterpretable features are mapped onto the target language functional morphology. In what follows, each section will correspond to a building block of the Bottleneck Hypothesis.

Syntax is easier than functional morphology

White (2003: 182–184) describes two views of the morphology-syntax connection, which she labels *morphology-before-syntax* and *syntax-before-morphology*. On the morphology-before-syntax view (Clahsen, Penke & Parodi 1993/94; Radford 1990), lexical acquisition of functional morphology actually drives the acquisition of functional categories, as mentioned above. The syntax-before-morphology view, on the other hand, argues that L2 learners who do not have perfect performance on functional morphology can still have engaged the functional categories related to that morphology and have the abstract syntactic features represented in their interlanguage grammar. Evidence comes from several studies of child and adult L2 production (Haznedar 2001; Haznedar & Schwartz 1997; Ionin & Wexler 2002; Lardiere1998a, b). White (2003: 189) summarizes the data of four studies as follows.

What is especially striking in the data presented in Table 1 is the clear dissociation between the incidence of verbal inflection (ranging between 46.5% and 4.5%) and the various syntactic phenomena related to it, like overt subjects, nominative case on the subject, and the verb staying in VP (above 98% accuracy). But knowledge of all the properties reflected in Table 1 is purportedly knowledge

Table 1. L2 English suppliance of functional morphology in obligatory contexts (in %)

V in VP	3 sg. agreement	Past tense on lexical verbs	Suppletive forms of *be*	Overt subjects	Nom. case
Haznedar (2001)	46.5	25.5	89	99	99.9
Ionin&Wexler (2002)	22	42	80.5	98	–
Lardiere 100 (1998a,b)	4.5	34.5	90	98	100

Reprinted with permission from White (2003: 189, her Table 6.2)

related to the same underlying functional category, IP, and its features. In view of such data, it is hard to maintain that morphology drives syntactic acquisition.

In order to illustrate the difficulty of functional morphology, I briefly summarize the results of a recent study, Slabakova and Gajdos (2008), which investigated the L2 acquisition of the different forms of the German copula *sein* in the present tense. Beginner and intermediate learners of German, for the most part undergraduate students, participated in the experimental study. The learners' proficiency levels were established based on the number of class hours of exposure to German instruction at a US university. At the time of study, the beginners were exposed to roughly 40 hours of German classroom instruction; the intermediate learners to 140 hours. The test contained simple sentences with missing subjects. Participants had to choose which subject (out of four options) went well with the provided sentence. They could choose more than one option and they were provided with an example that showed more than one correct choice. See an example test item in (4). It was considered that the test participant made an error if she chose an unsuitable subject for the pronoun, for example *Moritz* in example (4), but also if she neglected to choose a correct subject, that is, if she did not choose *du* 'you'.

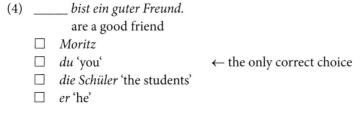

(4) _____ *bist ein guter Freund.*
            are a good friend
     ☐ *Moritz*
     ☐ *du* 'you'   ← the only correct choice
     ☐ *die Schüler* 'the students'
     ☐ *er* 'he'

As the reader can determine from Table 2, errors in choosing correct pronouns persist even in the second year of classroom instruction. Error rates in choosing DP subjects are stunning, if one considers how easy the test is and the fact that the copula forms are the first thing the learner hears in the language classroom. Slabakova (2009) looks at various linguistic accounts of morphological knowledge development and argues that two feature-based accounts, the Morphological Underspecification Hypothesis (McCarthy 2008) and the Combinatorial Variability Hypothesis (Adger 2006) were largely supported by the experimental findings. Slabakova (2009)

Table 2. Percentage errors in all forms of *sein* depending on type of subject Slabakova and Gajdos (2008)

Type of error	Beginners	Intermediate learners
Errors in choosing correct pronoun subjects	7.5	4.5
Errors in choosing correct DP subjects	20.2	29.8

argues that only accounts looking at mental representation of features adequately explain the type L2 morphological variability exemplified in this data.

However, using functional morphology to comprehend grammatical meanings is hard for some native speakers, too. The research program of Dąbrowska offers support for such a claim. For example, Dąbrowska and Street (2006) test comprehension of pragmatically plausible and implausible passives by English natives and L2 learners. The researchers tested four subject groups: highly-educated native speakers with more than15 year of education, typically with MA/PhD degrees, low-educated natives with no more than high-school education, highly-educated non-native speakers with MA or PhD degrees, and low-educated non-native speakers who had not studied beyond high-school. Participants were asked to listen to the experimental sentences and then to answer the question of who was the doer of the action (the agent). They heard sentences in four conditions: plausible and implausible actives and passives as in (5). Accuracy of comprehension and standard deviations are given in Table 3.

(5) a. The dog bit the man.   (plausible)
     b. The man bit the dog.   (implausible)
     c. The man was bitten by the dog. (plausible)
     d. The dog was bitten by the man. (implausible)

It is clear from Table 3 that all experimental groups were quite good at comprehending plausible sentences, that is, when knowledge of the world could be used to help them identify the agent of the action. However, low-educated native speakers had trouble comprehending implausible actives, while their understanding of implausible passives went down to 36% (see percentage in bold). These results suggest that the speakers were not using the passive inflectional morphology to process these sentences. Dąbrowska and Street concluded that native speakers sometimes process sentences non-syntactically, relying on simple processing heuristics such as an Agent-Verb-Patient template. This suggestion is not new, it has been proposed by a number of psycholinguists: Townsend and Bever's (2001)

Table 3. Accuracy and SD (%) on active and passive sentences from Dąbrowska and Street (2006)

	Plausible actives	Implausible actives	Plausible passives	Implausible passives
Hi Ed natives	100 (0)	100 (0)	100 (0)	96 (13)
Hi Ed non-natives	98 (6)	100 (0)	100 (0)	98 (6)
Lo Ed natives	98 (6)	**64 (30)**	98 (6)	**36 (26)**
Lo Ed non-natives	94 (13)	90 (11)	98 (6)	94 (10)

two-tiered processing, Clahsen and Felser's (2006) *shallow* processing, Ferreira, Bailey and Ferraro's (2002) *good-enough* representations.

The results of Dąbrowska and Street's (2006) study, however, also suggest that some non-native speakers process syntactic cues such as functional morphology much more reliably than less educated native speakers. In this respect, they surmise, the second language may even give an advantage to these speakers. Bilingualism may actually enhance attention to formal cues in language processing. Furthermore, input or exposure to a particular construction is not a completely decisive factor in comprehension, since the low educated non-native speakers did better than the low-educated non-native speakers on processing plausible and especially implausible passives. Interestingly, Street and Dąbrowska (2010), who tested and then trained a similar low academic achievement native speaker group on the same passive sentences, showed that, after a brief training session on the passive, test performance improved dramatically: from a mean accuracy of 48% to 94%. Delayed post-tests indicated that the increased recognition of the passive morphology persisted for at least 12 weeks after the training. The authors attribute the findings to the speakers' previous lack of sufficient exposure to the passive.

While most studies looking at acquisition of functional morphology have relied predominantly on off-line measures, there has recently been an increased interest in studying the processing of morphologically complex words with on-line measures such as comprehension and production latencies, eye-tracking and event-related brain potentials (see Clahsen et al. 2010 for a recent review). One influential view stemming form the work of McDonald (2006) is that L1-L2 differences in processing functional morphology are explainable in terms of domain-general processes (memory, attention, etc.), L2 processing being slower and more memory-demanding than L1 processing (McDonald 2006). However, it is also established that processing demands over and above the task requirements are reflected in a similar way by native and L2 speakers. McDonald (2006) compared the performance of native speakers and that of L2 speakers on a variety of linguistic structures. In a second experiment, the native speakers performed the same task under additional stress. The differential accuracy on the various constructions was remarkably similar for the natives under stress and the L2 speakers, with articles, regular past tense and subject-verb agreement being affected the most, while SVO word order remaining unaffected.

Furthermore, there appear to be correlations in emergence and error rates in the processing of functional morphology versus syntax across adult native speakers, children and L2 speakers. For example, McDonald (2008a, b) looked at a wide range of grammatical constructions and general cognitive measures in the grammar of 7 to 11 year-old children and adult speakers. Half of the adult participants in McDonald (2008b) processed the test items under additional memory load (memorizing numbers), thereby reducing the processing resources they could allocate to linguistic processing. When relative construction difficulty for the children was compared to that of unstressed and stressed adults, it was found that children resembled adults under increased memory load. The latest features to emerge and the hardest to process were subject-verb agreement and regular past tense: not even the oldest group (11 years) had reached adult levels. McDonald concludes that later acquired and less resilient grammatical properties impose higher working memory and phonological demands on children as well as adults.

Why would these particular functional morphemes pose the most problems? Relative salience and frequency of the morphemes, factors proposed by DeKeyser (2005), go only some way in explaining the discrepancy. From the perspective of linguistic theory discussed in this chapter, the grammatical information (expressed in the number of features and syntactic effects) that subject-verb agreement and past tense marking carry is much higher as compared to plural, for example, and affects the syntactic analysis of the whole sentence. If this is the case, then the fact that the same morphemes are hard for children, stressed adults and L2 learners makes perfect sense.

Summarizing my main points about functional morphology, I have argued that it is by definition the sticking point of acquisition because it encodes all the formal features of the grammar; it is hard not only in production but also in comprehension and it is hard for native speakers who do not pay attention to syntactic cues. Processing studies confirm the differential difficulty of functional morphology not only for L2 learners, but for children and native adults as well. Functional morphology posits a higher cognitive load in processing because it carries higher syntactic information. The next issue we look at concerns the differential difficulty of functional morphology and narrow syntactic properties.

Relative difficulty of syntax for native and non-native speakers

In the previous section, the relative difficulty of subject-verb agreement and past tense was compared to that of word order, indicating that the latter emerged early in the grammar of children and was not adversely affected in processing by additional memory load. In this section, I will speculate on the relative difficulty of syntax. According to the linguistic theory I have espoused here, apart from limited language-specific parsing strategies, processing syntax involves universal, therefore transferable, operations. Once the features encoded in functional morphology and the lexical items of the L2 are acquired, learners should have no trouble understanding complex syntax. This prediction actually follows from the language architecture discussed above and from the assumption that differences between languages are captured by formal features reflected in functional morphology. This prediction is largely supported and has been amply documented in the work of Dekydtspotter, Sprouse and colleagues (e.g., Dekydtspotter, Sprouse & Thyre 1999/2000 among many other works; see Slabakova 2006, 2008 for review). However, it is a less known fact that processing complex syntax such as multiple embeddings or long-distance *wh*-movement may be affected by lack of experience with specific constructions as well as working memory or processing limitations. Is what is difficult for non-native speakers easy for all native speakers? Next, we shall look at one study that points to a negative answer.

Dąbrowska (1997) tested 5 groups of native speakers differing in levels of education: cleaners, janitors, undergraduate students, graduate students, and lecturers at the same UK university. She tested them on the comprehension of two types of parasitic gaps, complex NP, and *tough*-movement constructions. I will illustrate here with just one example in (6). Sentences were presented visually and aurally.

(6)   Paul noticed that the fact that the room was tidy surprised Shona.
      Then participants were asked the following comprehension questions:

(7)   What did Paul notice?
      What surprised Shona?

What the accuracy results in Table 4 point to is the fact that complex syntactic structures, as exemplified here by the complex NPs, are not inevitably processed problem-free by native speakers.[2] Furthermore, a speaker's accuracy on comprehension was highly correlated with the amount of schooling the individual had received. This finding highlights the importance of exposure and input for the linguistic performance of native speakers. One more study should be mentioned in this connection. Chipere (2003) tested complex NP comprehension again, following Dąbrowska (1997), with the same experimental design. This time, subjects were graduate student native speakers, high-school-only native speakers, and highly-educated non-native speakers. Chipere found that the highly-educated native and non-native speakers had the exact same behavior, while the low-educated

Table 4. Accuracy percentage on complex NP comprehension from Dąbrowska (1997)

Cleaners	Janitors	Undergrads	Graduates	Lecturers
29	14	38	66	90

2.   It is possible that the low educated participants in Dąbrowska's studies show task effects; specifically, lack of familiarity with test environments. Since criticism of this body of work is beyond the scope of the present chapter, I refer the interested reader to the *Linguistic Approaches to Bilingualism* epistemological issue on this topic, particularly the comments therein.

native speakers had an error rate higher than 90%. This situation is of course reminiscent to the results of the Dąbrowska and Street (2006) study discussed in the previous section. While functional morphemes may be comparatively harder to process than simple syntax, complex syntax poses difficulties of its own, certainly affected by exposure to a construction, construction frequency (Street & Dąbrowska 2010) as well as working memory limitations.

We can tentatively conclude, indeed, that what is difficult for non-native speakers is also difficult for low-educated native speakers who have had little exposure to complex syntactic constructions or little exposure to test environments. After they learn the formal features, non-native speakers roughly pattern with their native speaker education peers in processing complex language. In processing syntax, as well as in the processing of morphology, learning an L2 may afford some advantages in terms of attending to syntactic cues in processing.

The syntax-semantics interfaces

In discussing properties at the syntax–semantics interface, Slabakova (2008) divides them into two qualitative types. The first type is dubbed *simple syntax – complex semantics*. These L1-L2 learning situations involve some meanings that are denoted by seemingly similar morphemes, such as the English past simple and past progressive aspectual tenses compared to the Spanish preterit and imperfect tenses. Examples of this syntax-semantics mismatch are given in (2) and (3) above. In this case, the learner is initially tempted to map L1 morphemes onto L2 morphemes: simple past onto preterit, past progressive onto imperfect, based on the similarity of some meanings. However, this initial assumption is only partially correct, since not all meanings encoded by the simple past are rendered by the preterit. The habitual meaning (2a and 3a) is denoted by the English simple past and the Spanish imperfect. This is a classic morphosyntax-semantics mismatch, which understandably takes time to learn.

I will illustrate the same situation with another contrast and then discuss its L2 acquisition. The linguistic properties whose acquisition Slabakova (2003) investigates have to do with grammatical aspect. English differs from German, Romance, and Slavic with respect to the semantics of the present tense. It is well known that the English bare infinitive denotes not only the processual part of an event but includes the completion of that event in a perceptual report structure.

(8) a. I saw Mary cross the street.   (completion entailed)
     b. I saw Mary crossing the street.   (no completion entailed)

In trying to explain the facts illustrated in (8), many researchers have noticed that English verbal morphology is impoverished (Bennett & Partee 1972). Slabakova (2003) adopts Giorgi and Pianesi's (1997) proposal. English verbs, they argue, are "naked" forms that can express several verbal values, such as the bare infinitive, the first and second person singular, and the first, second and third person plural. Giorgi and Pianesi (1997) propose that verbs are categorially disambiguated in English by being marked in the lexicon with the aspectual feature [+perf], standing for *perfective*. Thus, children acquiring English can distinguish verbal forms from nominals, whose feature specification bundle will exclude the feature [+perf]. In Romance, Slavic, and other Germanic languages, in contrast, all verbal forms have to be inflected for person, number, and tense. Thus, nouns and verbs cannot have the same forms, unlike English, in which zero-derivation abounds. The Bulgarian verb, for example, is associated with typical verbal features as [+V, person, number] and it is recognizable and learnable as a verb because of these features. Bulgarian verbs are therefore not associated with a [+perf] feature. Consequently, Bulgarian equivalents to bare infinitives do not entail completion of the event, as (9) illustrates.

(9) *Ivan vidja Maria da presiča ulicata.*   (no completion entailed)
     Ivan saw Maria to cross   street-DET
     'John saw Mary crossing the street.'

Thus, Bulgarian and English exhibit a contrast in the present viewpoint aspect.

The property itself, if Giorgi and Pianesi (1997) are correct, is the [+perf] feature that is attached to English eventive verbs in the lexicon. How can this property be acquired? The trigger of this property is noticing the fact that English inflectional morphology is highly impoverished, lacking many person-number-tense verb endings. Knowledge of this property will entail knowledge of various aspectual interpretations, among which the fact that bare verb forms denote a completed event. This is a syntax-semantics mismatch that relates a minimal difference between languages – the presence or absence of a feature in the lexicon – to various and superficially unconnected interpretive properties. All of the properties are not attested in the native language of the learners. Even more importantly, of the four semantic properties related to this parameter, the aspectual meanings are introduced, discussed, and drilled in language classrooms. The bare verb interpretation, however, is not explicitly taught.

Participants took a production task to ascertain knowledge of inflectional morphology and a Truth Value Judgment Task with a story in their native language and a test sentence in English. Complete and incomplete event stories were crossed in this condition with bare verbs or present participles, see (10) for an example.

(10) Matt had an enormous appetite. He was one of those people who could eat a whole cake at one sitting. But these days he is much more careful about what he eats. For example, yesterday he bought a chocolate and vanilla ice cream cake, but ate only half of it after dinner. I know, because I was there with him.

I observed Matt eat a cake.   True   False

Results on the acquisition of all four semantic properties pattern the same way. On the three instructed properties (habitual interpretation of the present, progressive needed for ongoing interpretation, states in the progressive denote temporary states), both successful acquisition as well as native transfer was observed. Figure 1 presents the results on the untaught property. Advanced learners are as accurate as native speakers in their knowledge that an English bare verb denotes a complete event, and should be rejected in the context of an incomplete event story (see first group of columns).

After establishing that it is *possible* to acquire semantic properties in the L2 that are not manifested in the native language, let us now turn to the impact of the instruction variable. Is it the case that instruction is a significant variable and learners were more accurate on the taught than on untaught properties? The short answer is "no," since all groups perform equally well on all conditions. Even un-taught syntax-semantics mismatches are learnable to a native-like level.

In the other learning situation identified by Slabakova (2008) and dubbed *complex syntax – simple semantics*, the properties to be acquired involve intricate and less frequent constructions such as double genitives, discontinuous constitu-ents, quantifiers at a distance, scrambling, etc. As mentioned above, acquisition of

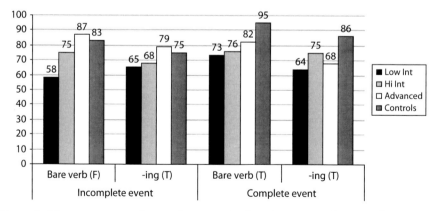

Figure 1. Mean accuracy on bare verb versus -*ing* form in perceptual reports from Slabakova (2003)

this type of property was pioneered and developed in the work of Dekydtspotter, Sprouse and colleagues (e.g., Dekydtspotter, Sprouse & Thyre 1999/2000). Very often the native speakers in these experiments show far lower than the acceptance rates we are used to seeing in the L2 literature. In a lot of cases, alternative ways of articulating the same message exist, making the tested constructions dispreferred (that may explain the fact that learners sometimes have higher rates of acceptance than native speakers.) In most cases, the properties under scrutiny present Poverty of the Stimulus situations to the learner. However, at the syntax-semantics interface, these same properties do not present much difficulty, as there are no mismatches. If learners have acquired the relevant Functional Lexicon item and have constructed the right sentence representation, the presence or absence of semantic interpretation follows straightforwardly without any more stipulations. In most cases (see Slabakova 2008, ch. 7) learners demonstrate that a contrast exists in their grammar between the allowed and the disallowed interpretations.

Scrutinizing the combined findings of the already vast literature on acquisition of the syntax-semantics interface, we can safely submit that it does not present insurmountable difficulties to L2 learners. The two learning situations discussed in this section may present differential difficulties to the learners: complex syntax may take longer to learn to process, while a complex semantic mismatch may take longer to notice and sort out in its entirety. In both learning situations, however, successful acquisition depends on the effective knowledge of the functional morphology.

The syntax-discourse interface

The syntax-discourse interface may be qualitatively different from the syntax-semantics interface. There is a growing body of research suggesting that *external* interface properties (those that are at the interface of linguistic modules and other cognitive systems such as syntax-discourse) are especially difficult to acquire and subject to developmental delays, as compared to *internal* interface properties (those that are at the interface of different linguistic modules) (Tsimpli & Sorace 2006; White 2009). The most well researched property at the syntax-discourse interface is the Null Subject Parameter, since it involves both syntactic and pragmatic constraints (Belletti, Bennati, & Sorace 2007, Rothman 2009, among many others). I will compare here two studies that investigate another property: clitic doubling. Clitic-doubling in Bulgarian (a syntactic property) is sensitive to which argument is Topic (old information, based on the current discourse), Topics are clitic-doubled whether they are fronted as in (11A) or in situ as in (11B). In (11C), # stands for 'infelicitous'.

(11)   Q: Has anybody seen Ivan?

    A: *Ivan go*   *vidja Maria.*   O-Cl$_{obj}$-V-S
       Ivan him-CL   saw   Maria

    B: *Maria go*   *vidja Ivan*   S-Cl$_{obj}$-V-O
       Maria him-CL   saw   Ivan

    C: #*Ivan*   *vidja Maria*   #O-V-S
       'Maria   saw   Ivan'

In Spanish, a very similar construction is known as clitic-left dislocation (CLLD): a fronted topic is doubled by a clitic, but only when it is specific:

(12)   *El libro, lo   lei*
    the book, it-CL read-1SG
    'The book, I read.

(13)   **Un libro, lo   lei*
    a   book, it-CL read-1SG
    'A book, I read.

Valenzuela (2006) studied knowledge of this semantic-pragmatic constraint in the interlanguage grammar of near-native speakers of Spanish with English as their native language. She employed an oral grammaticality judgment task, an oral sentence selection task, and a written sentence completion task, all targeting knowledge of the same property. Oral presentation of the experimental stimuli is crucial in such studies, as the intonation should include a pause between the fronted object and the rest of the sentence, but not a very long pause (Valenzuela 2006: 291). Results of all three tasks indicate that near-native speakers do not distinguish between specific and non-specific topic constructions to the same degree as the monolingual controls. However, the differences are really a matter of degree, as all the choices of the near-natives are in the right direction. Note also that examining individual results may point to a somewhat different conclusion.

    Ivanov (2009) also investigated knowledge of clitic doubling as a marker of topicality, but he compared it to knowledge of the fact that the clitic is ungrammatical when it doubles focused constituents. He employed a grammaticality judgment task and a context-sentence evaluation task: a situation described in English and a short dialogue in Bulgarian where the participants had to evaluate four options on a scale from 1 (totally unacceptable) to 5 (perfectly acceptable). Test items were presented both written and aurally. Here is an example of a test item from the context-sentence evaluation task. Table 5 gives the mean acceptance rate in the accusative condition.

Table 5. Mean acceptance rate (out of 5) in the accusative condition

Participant group	O-Cl-V-Adv Felicitous	Adv-Cl-V-O Felicitous	O-V-Adv Infelicitous	Adv-V-O Infelicitous
Bulgarian controls	4.82	4.52	1.72	2.7
Advanced Bg learners	4.73	4.32	2.62	3.2
Intermediate Bg learners	3.7	3.33	3.79	4.41

(14) Mr. Jordanov, the manager of Doublestream Ltd., runs into the office looking for one of the company employees, Ivan. Ivan is nowhere to be seen but
there are several other employees working in their cubicles. Mr. Jordanov
asks them:

Q: Has anybody seen Ivan today?

A: *Ivan **go**   vidjah   tazi sutrin.*   Felicitous
Ivan him-CL saw-1SG this morning
'I saw Ivan in the morning.'

B: *Tazi sutrin **go** vidjah Ivan.*   Felicitous

C: *Ivan vidjah tazi sutrin.*   Infelicitous

D: *Tazi sutrin vidjah Ivan.*   Infelicitous

Note that knowledge of clitic-doubling in these learners' interlanguage cannot
come from English since English lacks clitics. The discourse-marking function of
clitics is not taught in Bulgarian classrooms but clitics marking topic are extremely frequent in every-day informal Bulgarian. Intermediate learners as a group are
not sensitive to the discourse properties of clitic-doubling, although on the whole
they are aware of their syntactic properties. All 10 advanced learners exhibit
knowledge of the syntactic as well as the discourse requirements of clitic-doubling,
and 8 of them are statistically indistinguishable from native speakers in recogniz-
ing the pragmatic constraints.

While the jury is still out on L2 acquisition at the syntax-discourse interface,
some studies indicate that acquisition of constructions integrating knowledge of
the discourse is extremely difficult, while other studies including the ones summarized in this section, show no such mismatch. It is essential in the future to expand the range of properties and languages that we investigate at this interface.

The semantics-pragmatics interface

Finally, we will review some recent work on the acquisition of properties on the
interface between semantics and pragmatics. Work on L2 acquisition of such

properties is in its very early stages, but there is already a considerable body of findings on the child knowledge of such properties. An ideal property to study at the semantics-pragmatics interface is scalar implicature. It involves additional calculation of meaning over and beyond what compositional semantics brings. For example:

(15)   Some professors are smart. → IMPLICATION
(16)   Not all professors are smart. BUT NOT
(17)   All professors are smart.

Logically speaking, *some* means *some and possibly all*. For pragmatic felicity, however, *some* means *some but not all*. Thus the sentence in (15) actually implies the meaning in (16) but not (17). The logic goes like this: If the speaker wanted to say that *some and possibly all* professors are smart, she would have uttered (17), being maximally informative. Since she did not, she must really mean (16), *not all* professors are smart. Understatements of this sort in human speech are regulated by Gricean maxims, and more specifically, the Maxim of Quantity: Make your contribution as informative as is required; do not make your contribution more informative than is required (Grice 1989). Lexical items that induce such calculations are arranged on a scale: <*some, most, all*>, <*start, finish*>, etc, where uttering the lower-placed item implies that the higher placed item is not true. Since the scalar implicature computation mechanism is universal, the learning task in L2 acquisition involves transferring this purportedly universal mechanism from the L1. Therefore, we expect L2 learners to be accurate in scalar implicature derivation once they know the scalar lexical items, but that processing resources may have an impact on accuracy and speed. Findings from child language acquisition (e.g. Papafragou & Musolino 2003; see also Reinhart 2006) point to processing resources being essential for the calculation of implied meaning.

Slabakova (2010) tested knowledge of scalar implicatures by English and Korean native speakers, advanced and intermediate Korean learners of English. The two native speaker groups were intended to ascertain that the scalar implicature calculation mechanism is indeed universal. In Experiment 1, subjects read 8 universally true sentences (*All elephants have trunks*), 8 sentences infelicitous with *some* (*Some elephants have trunks*), 8 sentences felicitous with *some* (*Some books have color pictures*), 8 sentences false with *all* (*All books have color pictures*), and 8 absurd fillers (*All/some garages sing*). Percentages of logical responses across participant groups are given in Table 6.

The results in Table 6 confirm that English and Korean adult native speakers give roughly 60% logical answers and 40% pragmatic answers. In addition, individual results reveal that these participants fall largely into two groups: people who consistently give logical answers and people who consistently choose

Table 6. Percentage of Logical Responses across participants groups in Experiment 1

Groups	True *all*	False *all*	Felicitous *some*	Infelicitous *some*
English controls	75.5	98.9	96.7	55.4
Korean controls	88	98.5	99	61.2
L2advanced	82	98	98	39.2
L2intermediate	78	97	90	41.8

pragmatically felicitous answers. Importantly, Korean learners of English attribute more pragmatic interpretations to scalar implicatures without context than they do in their native Korean, and significantly more than English native speakers. When asked to judge sentences with *some* in context, they offer pragmatic judgments around 90% of the times (Experiment 2). These findings suggest that L2 learners observe Gricean maxims even at an intermediate level of attainment, and probably right after they learn the scalar lexical terms. Much more research on properties at the semantics-pragmatics interface is necessary before we come to any solid conclusions. However, it is safe to say at this point that the first findings point to no real difficulty at this interface.

Taking stock

Concluding the theoretical part of this chapter, let me reiterate the main points of the argument. I have argued that narrow syntactic knowledge comes before accurate knowledge of morphology in production and comprehension (Slabakova & Gajdos 2008; White 2003). Functional morphology is harder for low-educated native speakers than for non-native speakers (Dąbrowska & Street 2006). In processing complex syntax, low-educated native speakers who have had little exposure to complex constructions may be at a disadvantage compared to non-native speakers (Chipere 2003; Dąbrowska 1997). I have also argued that once the functional morphology is learned, learners are aware of all its semantic consequences, taught and untaught (Slabakova 2003). Even at the syntax-discourse interface, acquisition of properties unavailable from the L1 is possible (Ivanov 2009). At the semantics-pragmatics interface, L2 learners transfer universal properties like Gricean maxims (Slabakova 2010).

The rationale of the Bottleneck Hypothesis is as follows:

1. Functional morphology reflects syntactic and semantic differences between languages;
2. Narrow syntactic operations and meaning calculation are universal;

3. In order to acquire syntax and meaning in a second language, the learner has to go through the functional morphology;
4. Hence, morphology is the bottleneck of acquisition!

Implications for teaching

It is fairly common to assert that the generative approach to L2 acquisition does not really have any predictions to make about how we should teach language. As a cognitive discipline with a theoretical perspective inherently not interested in the process of learning (as opposed to the process of acquisition), this approach has frequently turned its attention to the L2 acquisition of subtle phenomena that are never discussed in language classrooms, and language teachers have no explicit knowledge of these properties. Subjacency, the linguistic constraint that regulates how far a *wh*-phrase can move away from its original position and how many other phrases it may jump over, is one such example among many. Generative studies of L2 acquisition rarely incorporate classroom instruction as part of their design.[3] Thus, it is generally believed that the generative framework has nothing valuable to offer to language teachers (but see Whong, Gil & Marsden in press). In a break with tradition, however, I argue that the Bottleneck Hypothesis has some pedagogical implications.

In language classrooms, teaching techniques that emphasize communicative competence (Canale & Swain 1980; Savignon 1983) become popular in the 80ies and are still quite prevalent (although see Kumaravadivelu 2006 for a critique). Such techniques encourage learners to use context, world knowledge, argument structure templates, and other pragmatic strategies to comprehend the message, capitalizing on the fact that learners almost certainly use their expectations of what is said to choose between alternative parses of a sentence. In fact, Clahsen and Felser's (2006) Shallow Structure Hypothesis proposes that context, pragmatic knowledge, and argument structure are the only processing strategies available to adult learners. However, many L2 researchers question the direct connection between comprehending the L2 message and figuring out how the L2 syntax works (Cook 1996: 76; Gass & Selinker 2001: 317). It is believed that some attention to, or focus on, *grammatical form* is beneficial and necessary for successful learning (Long 1996). In this respect, communicative competence approaches – with their

---

3.   The White and colleagues studies investigating the verb movement parameter are the notable exception (e.g. White 1991). Their general conclusion on the effect of targeted instruction was quite pessimistic.

exclusion of focus on form – may not be the best way to accomplish the ultimate goal of L2 learning: building a mental grammar of the target language.

The Bottleneck Hypothesis supports such a conclusion and endorses increased emphasis on practicing grammar in the classroom. The functional morphology in a language has some visible and some hidden characteristics. Firstly, it may have phonetic form, and if it does, its distribution is in evidence and learnable. Secondly, it carries syntactic features that are responsible for the behavior of other, possibly displaced elements and phrases in the sentence. Thirdly, it carries one or more universal units of meaning. While the first trait of functional morphology is observable from the linguistic input, the second and third characteristics may not be so easy to detect. It is suggested here that practicing the functional morphology in language classrooms should happen in meaningful, plausible sentences where the syntactic effects and the semantic import of the morphology is absolutely transparent and non-ambiguous. In a sense, drilling of the functional morphology is inevitable if the form has to move from the declarative to the procedural memory of the learner and then get sufficiently automatic for easy lexical access.[4] Practicing functional morphology in context should be very much like lexical learning (because it *is* lexical learning), and, as everybody who has tried to learn a second language as an adult (or even a teenager) knows, learning lexical items is painful. Although rooted in a different theoretical foundation, the Bottleneck Hypothesis is akin in its pedagogical implications to the Focus on Form approach (Doughty 2001; papers in Doughty & Williams 1998; Long 1996) – see Pica, this volume –, the Input Processing theory of VanPatten (1996, 2002a, 2002b, 2007) – see Benati, this volume – and the Skill Acquisition theory of DeKeyser (1997, 2001, 2007) – see Lyster & Sato, this volume).

Thus the bottom-line of the chapter is: Practice your functional morphology! In ample clear, unambiguous context! As in learning other lexical items, it may be painful, but – no pain, no gain!

References

Adger, D. 2003. *Core Syntax: A Minimalist Approach*. Oxford: OUP.
Adger, D. 2006. Combinatorial variability. *Journal of Linguistics* 42: 503–530.

---

4. My view in this respect is opposed to the position of linguists like Michel Paradis (e.g., Paradis 2004, 2009) and Bonnie D. Schwartz (e.g., Schwartz, 1993, going back to Krashen's 1982 Monitor Model) that declarative knowledge cannot 'be transformed' into procedural knowledge. I am grateful to an anonymous reviewer for suggesting this contrast.

Belletti, A., Bennati, E. & Sorace, A. 2007. Theoretical and developmental issues in the syntax of subjects: Evidence from near-native Italian. *Natural Language and Linguistic Theory* 25: 657–689.

Bennett, M. & Partee, B. 1972. *Toward the Logic of Tense and Aspect in English*. Santa Monica, CA: System Development Corporation. (Also distributed by Indiana University Linguistics Club).

Canale, M. & Swain, M. 1980. Theoretical bases of communicative approaches to second language teaching and testing. *Applied Linguistics* 1: 1–47.

Chipere, N. 2003. *Understanding Complex Sentences: Native Speaker Variation in Syntactic Competence*. London: Palgrave Macmillan.

Clahsen, H. & Felser, C. 2006. Grammatical processing in language learners. *Applied Psycholinguistics* 27: 3–42.

Clahsen, H., Penke, M. & Parodi, T. 1993/94. Functional categories in early child German. *Language Acquisition* 3: 395–429.

Clahsen, H., Felser, C., Neubauer, K., Sato, M. & Silva, R. 2010. Morphological structure in native and nonnative language processing, *Language Learning* 60(1): 21–43.

Cook, V. 1996. *Second Language Learning and Language Teaching*, 2nd edn. London: Edward Arnold

Dabrowska, E. 1997. The LAD goes to school: A cautionary tale for nativists. *Linguistics* 35: 735–766.

Dabrowska, E. & Street, J. 2006. Individual differences in language attainment: Comprehension of passive sentences by native and non-native English speakers. *Language Sciences* 28: 604–615.

DeKeyser, R. 1997. Beyond explicit rule learning: Automatizing second language morphosyntax. *Studies in Second Language Acquisition* 19: 195–221.

DeKeyser, R. 2001. Automaticity and automatization. In *Cognition and Second Language Instruction*, P. Robinson (ed.), 125–151. Cambridge: CUP.

DeKeyser, R. 2005. What makes learning second-language grammar difficult? A review of issues. *Language Learning* 55: 1–25.

DeKeyser, R. 2007. Skill Acquisition Theory. In *Theories in Second Language Acquisition*, B. VanPatten & J. Williams (eds), 97–113. Mahwah NJ: Lawrence Erlbaum Associates.

Dekydtspotter, L., Sprouse, R. & Thyre, R. 1999/2000. The interpretation of quantification at a distance in English-French interlanguage: Domain-specificity and second language acquisition. *Language Acquisition* 8: 265–320.

Doughty, C. 2001. Cognitive underpinnings of focus on form. In *Cognition and Second Language Acquisition*, P. Robinson (ed.), 206–257. Cambridge: CUP.

Doughty, C. & Williams, J. (eds). 1998. *Focus on Form in Classroom Second Language Acquisition*. Cambridge: CUP.

Ferreira, F., Bailey, K. & Ferraro, V. 2002. Good enough representations in language comprehension. *Current Directions in Psychological Science* 11: 11–15.

Gass, S. & Selinker, L. 2001. *Second Language Acquisition: An Introductory Course*. Mahwah NJ: Lawrence Erlbaum Associates.

Giorgi, A. & F. Pianesi. 1997. *Tense and Aspect: From Semantics to Morphosyntax*. Oxford: OUP.

Grice, P. 1989. *Studies in the Way of Words*. Cambridge MA: Harvard University Press.

Haznedar, B. 2001. The acquisition of the IP system in child L2 English. *Studies in Second Language Acquisition* 23: 1–39.

Haznedar, B. & Schwartz, B.D. 1997. Are there optional infinitives in child L2 acquisition? In *Proceedings of the 21st annual Boston University Conference on Language Development*, E. Hughes, M. Hughes & A. Greenhill (eds.), 257–68. Somerville MA: Cascadilla Press.

Ionin, T. & Wexler, K. 2002. Why is 'is' easier than '-s'?: Acquisition of tense/agreement morphology by child second language learners of English. *Second Language Research* 18: 95–136.

Ivanov, I. 2009. Topicality and clitic doubling in L2 Bulgarian: A test case for the Interface Hypothesis. In *Proceedings of the 10th Generative Approaches to Second Language Acquisition Conference (GASLA 2009)*, M. Bowles, R. Foote & S. Perpiñán (eds.), 17–24. Somerville MA: Cascadilla Proceedings Project.

Jeon, K. 2007. Interaction-driven L2 learning: Characterizing linguistic development. In *Conversation Interaction in Second Language Acquisition: A Collection of Empirical Studies*, A. Mackey (ed.), 379–403. Oxford: OUP.

Krashen, S. 1982. *Principles and Practice in Second Language Acquisition*. Oxford: Pergamon.

Kumaravadivelu, B. 2006. *Understanding Language Teaching: From Method to Postmethod*. Mahwah NJ: Lawrence Erlbaum Associates.

Lardiere, D. 1998a. Case and tense in the 'fossilized' steady state. *Second Language Research* 14: 1–26.

Lardiere, D. 1998b. Dissociating syntax from morphology in a divergent end-state grammar. *Second Language Research* 14: 359–375.

Lardiere, D. 2005. On morphological competence. In *Proceedings of the 7th Generative Approaches to Second Language Acquisition Conference (GASLA 2004)*, L. Dekydtspotter et al. (eds.), 178–192. Somerville MA: Cascadilla Proceedings Project.

Lardiere, D. 2009. Some thoughts on the contrastive analysis of features in second language acquisition. *Second Language Research* 25(2): 173–227.

Long, M. 1996. The role of the linguistic environment in second language acquisition. In *Handbook of Second Language Acquisition*, W.C. Ritchie & T.K. Bhatia, (eds.), 413–468. New York NY: Academic Press.

Long, M., Inagaki, S. & Ortega, L. 1998. The role of implicit negative feedback in SLA: Models and recasts in Japanese and Spanish. *The Modern Language Journal* 82: 357–371.

Mackey, A., Abduhl, R. & Gass, S. 2012. Interactionist approach. In *The Routledge Handbook of Second Language Acquisition*, S. Gass & A. Mackey (eds.), 7–23. Abingdon: Routledge.

McCarthy, C. 2008. Morphological variability in the comprehension of agreement: An argument for representation over computation. *Second Language Research* 24(4): 459–486.

McDonald, J.L. 2006. Beyond the critical period: Processing-based explanations for poor grammaticality judgment performance by late second language learners. *Journal of Memory and Language* 55: 381–401.

McDonald, J.L. 2008a. Grammaticality judgments in children: The role of age, working memory, and phonological ability. *Journal of Child Language* 35: 247–268.

McDonald, J.L. 2008b. Differences in the cognitive demands of word order, plurals, and subject-verb agreement constructions. *Psychonomic Bulletin & Review* 15: 980–984.

Papafragou, A. & Musolino, J. 2003. Scalar implicatures: Experiments at the semantics-pragmatics interface. *Cognition* 86: 253–282.

Paradis, M. 2004. *A Neurolinguistic Theory of Bilingualism* [Studies in Bilingualism 18]. Amsterdam: John Benjamins.

Paradis, M. 2009. *Declarative and Procedural Determinants of Second Languages* [Studies in Bilingualism 40]. Amsterdam: John Benjamins.

Radford, A. 1990. *Syntactic Theory and the Acquisition of English Syntax*. Oxford: Blackwell.

Reinhart, T. 2006. *Interface Strategies*. Cambridge MA: The MIT Press.

Rothman, J. 2009. Pragmatic deficits with syntactic consequences? L2 pronominal subjects and the syntax-pragmatic interface. *Journal of Pragmatics* 41: 951–973.

Savignon, S. 1983. *Communicative Competence: Theory and Classroom Practice*. Reading: Addison-Wesley.

Schwartz, B.D. 1993. On explicit and negative data effecting and affecting competence and linguistic behavior. *Studies in Second Language Acquisition* 15(2): 147–163.

Slabakova, R. 2003. Semantic evidence for functional categories in interlanguage grammars. *Second Language Research* 19(1): 42–75.

Slabakova, R. 2006. Is there a critical period for the acquisition of semantics. *Second Language Research* 22(3): 302–338.

Slabakova, R. 2008. *Meaning in the Second Language*. Berlin: Mouton de Gruyter.

Slabakova, R. 2009. How is inflectional morphology learned? *EUROSLA Yearbook* 9: 56–75.

Slabakova, R. 2010. Scalar implicatures in second language acquisition. *Lingua* 120: 2444–2462.

Slabakova, R. & Gajdos, J. 2008. The Combinatorial Variability Hypothesis in the second language. In *Selected Proceedings from the 2007 Second Language Research Forum*, M. Bowles, R. Foote, S. Perpiñán & R. Bhatt (eds), 35–43. Somerville MA: Cascadilla Proceedings Project.

Street, J. & Dabrowska, E. 2010. More individual differences in language attainment: How much do adult native speakers of English know about passives and quantifiers? *Lingua* 120: 2080–2094.

Townsend, D. J. & Bever, T. G. 2001. *Sentence Comprehension: The Integration of Habits and Rules*. Cambridge MA: The MIT Press.

Tsimpli, I. & Sorace, A. 2006. Differentiating interfaces: L2 performance in syntax-semantics and syntax-discourse phenomena. In *Proceedings of the 30th annual Boston University Conference on Language Development, BUCLD 30*, D. Bamman, T. Magnitskaia & C. Zaller (eds), pp. 653–664. Somerville MA: Cascadilla.

Valenzuela, E. 2006. L2 end state grammars and incomplete acquisition of Spanish CLLD constructions. In *Inquiries in Linguistic Development. In honor of Lydia White*, R. Slabakova, S. Montrul & P. Prevost (eds), 283–304. Amsterdam: John Benjamins.

VanPatten, B. 1996. *Input Processing and Grammar Instruction: Theory and Research*. Norwood NJ: Ablex.

VanPatten, B. 2002a. Processing instruction: An update. *Language Learning* 52: 755–803.

VanPatten, B. 2002b. Processing the content of input processing and processing instruction research: A response to DeKeyser, Salaberry, Robinson and Harrington. *Language Learning* 52: 825–831.

VanPatten, B. 2007. Input processing in adult second language acquisition. In *Theories in Second Language Acquisition*, B. VanPatten & J. Williams (eds), 115–135. Mahwah NJ: Lawrence Erlbaum Associates.

White, L. 1991. Adverb placement in second language acquisition: Some effects of positive and negative evidence in the classroom. *Second Language Research* 7: 133–161.

White, L. 2003. *Second Language Acquisition and Universal Grammar*. Cambridge: CUP.

White, L. 2009. Grammatical theory: Interfaces and L2 knowledge. In *The New Handbook of Second Language Acquisition*, W.C. Ritchie & T.K. Bhatia (eds), 49–68. Bingley: Emerald.

Whong, M., Gil, K.H. & Marsden, H. (eds). In press. *Universal Grammar and the Second Language Classroom*. Berlin: Springer.

CHAPTER 2

Systemic Functional approaches to second language acquisition in school settings*

Ana Llinares
Universidad Autónoma de Madrid

The Systemic-functional Linguistic model (SFL) (Halliday 2004), with its main focus on the explanation of language use in context, has been widely applied in educational settings around the world, both from research and pedagogical perspectives. However, the applications of SFL to foreign language acquisition at lower educational levels are still very scarce. This chapter provides an overview of SFL inspired foreign language classroom research at pre-primary, primary and secondary levels, with the application of two SFL models: Halliday's (1975) functional model of child language development and genre and register theory. The chapter shows the advantages of SFL for the understanding of foreign language students' use of lexico-grammatical features to convey different meanings and functions, as well as to participate in the registers and genres of academic disciplines. It also illustrates the role of SFL in SLA research and the interest of combining SFL and other compatible approaches in the study of SLA in educational contexts.

The role of Systemic Functional linguistics (SFL) in second/foreign language acquisition

Second language acquisition (SLA) is a field that aims at addressing one main question: How do people learn languages after they have full command of their mother tongue? SLA research is not a discipline with a single theory. Early studies were surface-level linguistic approaches in which the target language was compared with the mother tongue (contrastive analysis; Lado 1957), the learner's language was compared to the target language (error analysis; Corder 1967) or was examined as a developing system in its own right (interlanguage; Selinker 1972). Subsequently, SLA was approached from three main disciplinary perspectives: generative

* I am very grateful to Tom Morton and Rachel Whittaker for their valuable comments on this chapter. My thanks also go to the anonymous reviewers for their insightful recommendations.

linguistics (with a focus on the learner's underlying linguistic competence; Chomsky 1957), psycholinguistic/cognitive models (with an interest in the learning process and individual factors; Pienemann 2003) and, more recently, contextual or social approaches to second language learning, such as Sociocultural Theory (Lantolf 2000). According to Mitchell and Myles (2004: 259), in the future, SLA will be investigated by different theoretical approaches (linguistic, processing, etc.), each focusing on different aspects, but attempts to establish connections among them will grow. An example of such a connection is the one between SFL (linguistic theory) and Vygotskian general learning theories – see Gánem-Gutérrez, this volume -. Both highlight the social nature of learning, the role of language as a semiotic tool and the relationship between the individual and culture. However, while Vygotskian approaches to SLA (Sociocultural Theory in particular) are acknowledged in the SLA literature, the role of SFL is hardly mentioned, or not mentioned at all, even in recent publications on social approaches to SLA. For example, Block's (2003) single reference to SFL in his book on *the social turn* in SLA consists in a brief account of Halliday's three metafunctions (see Block 2003: 72–73).

The contributions of SFL to language use and language learning are mainly centred on the role of language in the production and negotiation of social meanings. Halliday's Systemic Functional model (2004) was initially developed to explain the use of language in social contexts, focusing on the linguistic features characterising different texts and identifying their roles in the situations in which these texts are used. This model establishes, then, a direct relationship between the context in which the language is used and the linguistic choices made by the speakers. In SFL language is explained as an interrelated system of choices that are available for expressing meaning. A key feature of this approach is that language forms cannot be studied without taking into account the circumstances of their use and, therefore, an SFL description interprets simultaneously what language is and what people do with it. The language of the adult conveys three main metafunctions (ideational, interpersonal and textual). The ideational metafunction refers to the use of language to represent reality (realized through transitivity and lexis), the interpersonal metafunction is defined as the use of language to establish relations (realized through mood, modality, person, etc.) and the textual metafunction refers to the use of language to relate ideas in a text (by means of cohesion, theme, etc.). According to the SFL model, language is acquired in a social context, by interacting with other people. This is linked to the Vygotsky's (1962) view that language can only work as a characteristic of individual cognition when it happens in communication with others (see Gánem-Gutíerrez, this volume). As in Sociocultural Theory, verbal meaning is viewed as the product of the speakers' activities in a cultural and situational context (not as the content of a linguistic form excised from this context).

Halliday first applied his Systemic Functional model to the understanding of language development back in the 1970s. In contrast with a view of language as a system of rules, SFL considers that language is learnt because human beings need to do things with it, in other words, because language has functions and meaning potential (Halliday 1975). In SFL there is no sharp distinction between the system and the use of language. In fact, it is the context of language use and spontaneous interaction that make it possible for changes to happen in the child's linguistic system (Painter 2000).

In the analysis of the protolanguage of his own child, Halliday (1975) described the evolution of child language in terms of a number of communicative functions which can be grouped into two types: mathetic and pragmatic (later developed into ideational and interpersonal in the language of the adult). The mathetic functions refer to the use of language to learn about the world while the pragmatic functions are those used to interact with others. According to Halliday, linguistic structures are developed in relation to the functions they convey. His model, which was designed and developed to explain child language development, has recently been applied to the analysis of young learners' foreign language performance in instructional contexts (see Llinares 2006; Llinares & Romero-Trillo 2007). This work will be described in Section 2 below.

The circumstances in which foreign and second languages are learnt and developed are varied in terms of starting age, degree of exposure and purpose. Some SFL applications to educational contexts have studied language use and development in school settings in which a second language is used as a vehicle for learning academic content. In most of these studies, the target language was a second or additional language (not a foreign language) and, thus, present in the learners' environment outside the classroom (e.g. Mohan & Beckett 2003; Schleppegrell 2004). Recently, there has been very solid SFL research in foreign language settings, mainly focusing on writing development at higher education (Byrnes 2009, 2012; Neff et al. 2004). However, very little research has been done on the application of SFL to foreign language use and development at lower educational levels (but see Huang & Mohan 2009; Mohan & Huang 2002) or in contexts in which the foreign language is both object and vehicle of instruction, commonly known in Europe as content-and-language integrated (CLIL) programs.

This chapter offers an overview of SFL research in foreign language and CLIL contexts. While Byrnes's (2009) overview of SFL applications to foreign language acquisition mainly includes studies at higher educational contexts, the present chapter presents research carried out at lower educational levels (pre-primary, primary and secondary), addressing both students' spoken and written performance and development in the L2.

Applications of SFL to the study of foreign language acquisition and development in school contexts

SFL has contributed to two main areas of language development: (i) it has provided a solid functional view of first language development, mainly through the work carried out by Halliday (1975) and continued by Painter (2000); and (ii) it has very important research studies, within genre and register theory, on subject literacies and academic language use, which have been translated into practical pedagogical applications and recommendations for teachers (see, for example, Martin 1993). However, in comparison with the amount of research on these areas, SFL has been less influential in SLA research. According to Perrett (2000: 89), "...we need studies of learners in the process of actually using language, engaged in learning to use language, and of how their language use changes over time and their learning progresses". This section offers an overview of recent research that has applied the two SFL areas mentioned above (child functional language development and genre and register theory) to foreign language learning in school contexts, classified into three main groups of studies:

i.   Applications of Halliday's protolanguage functions to the analysis of pre-primary/primary EFL learners' language use.
ii. Applications of genre and register theory to EFL writing development in secondary schools.
iii. Applications of genre and register theory to CLIL secondary school contexts.

These studies will help illustrate the contribution of SFL to the understanding of SLA in the social context of the classroom, particularly in two recent areas of interest in SLA research: young learners' language development and content and language integrated learning.

Applying Halliday's protolanguage taxonomy to second language learners' functional language at an early age

Some of the reasons offered by Perrett (2000) to explain the scarcity of applications of SFL to second language learning, in contrast with the vast amount of research on first language development, is the uncertainty of planning an adult language study: "Will the learners drop out? Will they fossilize?" (Perrett 2000: 92). Applications of SFL to young learners' L2 use and development are equally scarce. One exception is the work carried out by Mohan and Huang (Huang & Mohan 2009; Mohan & Huang 2002), in which SFL is used to analyze form-function relations in students' discourse in a Mandarin Chinese as a foreign language classroom at primary level. Another exception is the application of Halliday's (1975) functional description of child language to the analysis of young learners' language use and development, which resulted in a number of studies that will be discussed in this section (Llinares 2006, 2007a, 2007b; Llinares & Romero-Trillo 2007).

It has often been claimed that the acquisition of a second language in childhood seems to be more successful in natural contexts. The classroom has been considered an artificial learning context that might be appropriate for adults but not for children (Foster-Cohen 1999). However, in their analysis of young children's language use in L1 instructional contexts, Geekie and Raban (1994) identify patterns in the interactions of children with their teachers in the classroom which map onto those found in the interaction between mothers and children. This study suggests that at least some classrooms may provide a 'natural' context for language use.

According to Wong-Fillmore (1991), one of the main requirements for SLA is that the learners feel the need to learn the L2. The learners' interest in using the L2 can be enhanced by responding to the children's intentions to communicate in that language and promoting different activities to achieve this purpose (Tabbors & Snow 1994). These two factors were analyzed in a number of studies belonging to the same project (*UAMLESC*), in which Halliday's (1975) functional categories of child language development were applied to young learners' L2 production across pre-primary school contexts with various degrees of immersion in the L2.

In this research project, one of the research questions regarding L2 learners' functional production was related to the frequency of different communicative or speech functions (Llinares 2007a; Llinares & Romero-Trillo 2007) across pre-primary contexts. A comparative analysis of EFL learners' functional production in a high-immersion context (where the learners were taught in the L2 for almost the whole school day) with that of native speakers of English of the same age (5/6 year-olds), working on the same tasks, revealed that both groups of learners' most frequent function was the personal function of language (Llinares & Romero-Trillo 2007), a mathetic function defined by Halliday (1975) as the use of language to express opinions, feelings and individual identity. This function seemed to arise naturally in high immersion contexts, especially in sessions of the type *show and tell*, where the learners had to describe a personal object or experience. In low-immersion contexts (where the children were taught in the L2 for one hour per day) this was also one of the most frequent functions. However, in these contexts, more than 80% of the instances of the personal function were performed in the L1 (Llinares, 2007a).

In order to see whether the learners with *low* exposure to the L2 increased their use of the personal function and other functions in the second language, a *quasi* experimental study was carried out, based on pedagogical intervention in one group. This consisted in the teacher's development of activities aiming at encouraging the students' realization of different functions in the L2. Four sessions were recorded and analyzed in one academic year in two groups from the same school and the same year. In the experimental group, in the first session, the teacher carried out her daily planned activities while in the last three she organized activities to specifically trigger the learners' performance of different functions in the foreign language. The control group followed daily classroom activities normally. The results showed that the students in the experimental group used a higher percentage of the functions in the L2 (90% in contrast with 75% in the control group). Although the difference between the control and the experimental groups in terms of frequency of the personal function was very small (65% in the experimental group and 52% in the control group), there was considerable difference in the language chosen to convey this function (more than 50% of the instances of this function were used in the L2 in the experimental group, in contrast with 15% in the control group).

A second research question was related to the opportunities that the learners were given to initiate their own interactional exchanges in the L2 (Llinares 2007a). After the pedagogical intervention described above, the activities designed to trigger different functions also seemed to promote a higher frequency of initiating turns by the learners. This was observed in the comparison between their performance before and after the treatment, which showed a significant difference between the experimental and the control group ($p = 0.01$).

A third research question had to do with the effect of different types of activities on the learners' *natural* oral production in the L2, measured again in the use of the L2 to convey different functions and the use of the learners' own *discourse initiations* (Llinares 2007b). In this study, the effect of task work and show and tell sessions was compared in two groups in a high-immersion school. The study showed that different activities triggered different functions. Task work sessions enhanced the learners' use of the heuristic function (a mathetic function of language to enquire about the world), whereas show and tell sessions encouraged the learners to use a high frequency of the personal and informative functions. Show and tell sessions were also found to trigger more initiating turns by all the students participating in the activity (those who were involved in the showing and telling and those who participated as audience).

All these studies show that young learners used similar functions when performing the same tasks or activities regardless of the degree of immersion in the L2, and that young learners' use of the L2 to convey these functions can be enhanced by implementing specific activities adapted to each context. These studies, then, seem to support Tabbors and Snow's (1994) claim that it is necessary to encourage the learners' attempts to communicate in the L2 by means of activities designed to do so. The role of the type of activity is highlighted in sociocultural approaches to language learning, which defend the relevance of the activity for what is learnt and how it is learnt. The studies reported here suggest that SFL, in line with other theories, provides a research tool to study these features of learner language, moving beyond the desk of the researcher into practical applications for L2 language teaching.

The findings reported on above focus on SLA in pre/primary contexts from a functional perspective. Obviously, different languages construct reality and establish relationships in different ways. In order to succeed in the functional use of the L2, learners have to learn the language necessary to convey these functions. Therefore, it is important to carry out studies that apply SFL to the analysis of young learners' L2 lexico-grammar. Long-term longitudinal studies, following the Systemic Functional concept of delicacy (moving from broader categories to subtypes), are essential in order to identify the learners' lexico-grammatical and functional/semantic progression.

SFL approaches to EFL writing development in secondary schools

Another interesting area of research is the application of SFL theory to foreign language writing in school contexts. Although there is very relevant research using SFL genre theory in the study of students' writing development in a foreign language in different parts of the world (see, for example, Byrnes 2012; Neff et al. 2004 and Yasuda 2011), the empirical work reported on in this chapter is pioneer as it focuses on pre-university levels. The research carried out by Martín-Úriz and colleagues was based on the analysis of Spanish pre-university students' writing in English by looking at linguistic and rhetorical features of texts as indicators of development in writing. This research team has studied different genres written by secondary school students (part of the *UAM Corpus of Written Interlanguage*), since they considered that studies that approach discourse competence from a genre and register perspective were necessary to make it possible to evaluate students' linguistic abilities at all levels (Martín-Úriz & Whittaker 2006). This is especially important now, given the role of the Common European Framework (Council of Europe 2001) in European foreign language teaching.

The studies on the *UAM Corpus of Written Interlanguage* examined the state of Spanish students' *generic competence* in English at the end of their period of schooling. These studies also aimed to find out if the presence of generic features – stages in the generic structure and realisation of register- correlated with quality: whether texts rated higher did, in fact, have more features of the required genre. Three genres were collected from secondary school classes. The genres were recount, argument and report or exposition. The students' general linguistic competence was measured by a cloze test. Different analyses of the compositions using SF genre and register theory were carried out, some results of which are summarized below.

In a comparative study of EFL students' compositions with texts written by native speakers or by highly proficient non-natives, analyses of the recount genre showed that EFL writers structured their texts in a way typical of spoken rather than written recounts, with long orientations (Martín-Úriz et al. 2008). Also non-native writers were less likely to produce a reorientation stage to close their texts. The study of the argument (in SF terms the hortatory exposition) used analysis of participants in the clause as social actors and process types, as well as SF Appraisal Theory (Martin & White 2005) to show how FL writers expressed ideology in their texts (Martín-Úriz et al. 2005). The expository text, or report genre in SF terms, was found to be the least successful of the three (Martín-Úriz et al. 2007). Here, genre analysis showed first that only 20% of the texts collected had the features expected for that specific genre. A study of Theme (use of first position in the clause-complex) showed statistically significant differences between the higher-rated compositions and the lower-rated ones.

All these studies using SF analyses of different kinds revealed where writing in a foreign language is similar to or differs from the expectations of the discourse community and make explicit statements in linguistic terms, which can be used to plan pedagogical interventions.

SFL and CLIL classrooms

Most teachers, educators and researchers involved in content-based instruction (immersion, CLIL, EAL, etc...) agree that some kind of language support is basic for the students' academic success. It is also commonly agreed that these educational contexts provide L2 learners with the opportunity, usually missing in traditional foreign language classrooms, of using and learning the second/foreign language in a natural way (Dalton-Puffer & Smit 2007). This second aspect is particularly important in foreign language contexts, where the learners' encounters with the L2 are confined to the classroom.

Following Cummins' (1979) seminal distinction between Cognitive Academic Language Proficiency (CALP) and Basic Interpersonal Communication Skills (BICS), language support in content-based instruction has to focus on two main aspects: the kind of language that students need to be successful in the different academic disciplines as well as the type of teacher-student or student-student interaction that facilitates learning (see Coffin 2010). SFL theory, with its view of language as a resource for making meaning, and where grammar and meaning/function go inextricably together, can provide answers to both types of research objectives. Although a number of studies have applied SFL to the role of interaction in content based-instruction (see for example, Gibbons 2006; Hammond & Gibbons 2005; Llinares & Morton 2010; Morton 2010), the next section will mainly address the first aspect mentioned by Coffin (2010): the application of SF register and genre theory to learners' use and development of the L2 when writing and speaking about academic content.

From the very beginning, Halliday had the objective of creating a grammar that was useful for language teaching (Halliday, McIntosh & Strevens 1966), a model which was successfully developed in collaboration with practising teachers. Both SF grammar and register and genre theory (first developed in studies such as Halliday & Hasan 1989 and Martin 1993) have been applied for years and in many different parts of the world in tackling linguistic problems in the school context (see, for example, Whittaker, O'Donnell & McCabe 2006). This work, inspired in Bernstein's (1975) theories of language and socialisation, began back in the 1970s in the United Kingdom and has been developed and applied in Australia (for example, Christie 2002; Christie & Martin 1997). A common feature of these studies is to highlight the important roles that language use and the transition from oral into written modes play in students' academic success.

Most of the applications of SF genre and register theory to educational contexts have focused on students that have English as a first or as an additional language (EAL) in an English-speaking community (Christie & Derewianka 2008; Coffin 2006; Schleppegrell 2004, among others). One particular novelty of the studies reported below is that they are based on CLIL contexts, in which the language of instruction is a foreign and not a second language (see Lasagabaster & Sierra's (2010) distinction between immersion and CLIL contexts in this regard). CLIL provides foreign language learners with the opportunity to participate in settings where language is used for authentic communicative purposes. Therefore, in order to study language use and learning in these contexts, it is necessary to apply theories like SFL or Sociocultural Theory, which understand learning as participation in situated activities.

The SF model applied in the studies reported below is both rhetorical and linguistic. This means that the analysis of the characteristics of CLIL learners' use of the L2 is based on the application of genre and register theory to educational contexts, paying attention to the linguistic resources required by these genres. The studies focus on the disciplines of social science (geography and history) which have been found difficult also for native speakers due to the complexity of representing time and the transition from historical recounts focusing on individual actors into the analysis of historical facts and sources (Coffin 2006; Groom 2004; Veel & Coffin 1996).

The three metafunctions distinguished by Halliday (2004) – ideational, interpersonal and textual – are key for the analysis of students' foreign language development in CLIL contexts. First, the ideational function (the use of language to represent reality) offers an instrument for the analysis of the language that students need to represent content, by focusing on the types of participants, processes and circumstances used in specific genres. Secondly, in CLIL contexts, students are not only expected to show knowledge of academic content, they also have to be able to use the foreign language to manage social relationships in the classroom, following the conventions of this social and academic context (Dalton-Puffer 2007a), in other words, they have to be able to use the interpersonal function of language (the use of language to establish social relationships with the others). This function is not only important in the regulative register (Christie 2002), allowing for the distribution of roles in classroom interaction, but it also plays a key role in the instructional register (the content that is being studied). When working with academic content, CLIL students need to be aware of the linguistic resources they can use to express evaluation and attitude to the content they are studying. The interpersonal function of language, then, represents a challenge for these students if they are expected to move beyond the mere delivery of facts (Dalton-Puffer 2007b). Finally, in CLIL classes it is important for students to develop coherent texts. The textual metafunction (the use of language to link ideas in texts) is especially important when working on students' writing development in the L2. The following sections include examples of recent research on the ideational and textual functions in CLIL classrooms.

Learning the language of content subjects (ideational metafunction). Researchers and practitioners using SFL are aware of the key role of language in education, and of the linguistic differences found in the different disciplines. In a research project based on the application of SF register and genre analysis of the language of history (Coffin 2006; Veel & Coffin 1996) in CLIL classrooms, a number of studies focused on the linguistic features that the students needed for the realization of the *ideational metafunction* (expression of content), including the types of processes used (semantic classes of verbs), the types of circumstances selected by the students to elaborate on that content and the types of logical relations used between clauses, and their linguistic expression (Llinares & Whittaker 2007, 2009, 2010; Whittaker & Llinares 2009).

In their analyses of the students' language performance in a first year secondary corpus (students aged 12–13) in two subjects of social science, the distributions of the process types and circumstances used by the students were found to be different for geography and history, with a higher frequency of action processes (verbs of doing) used in geography and a proportionally higher frequency of relational processes (verbs of being) used in history (Whittaker & Llinares 2009). These results show that different disciplines require different meanings and the students were able to display these different meanings in the L2. Interestingly, there was a similarity between the way the learners used process types and circumstances and those found in the texts they studied. This finding reveals that the students seemed to be learning to represent the knowledge required by each discipline by using subject-specific terminology and the lexico-grammatical expression of meaning typical of the genres they had come into contact with.

A different study compared CLIL students' production with that of their peers studying the same subjects in Spanish, with the purpose of discovering the language that was particularly difficult for CLIL students (Llinares & Whittaker 2010). The results of the analysis revealed an interesting difference regarding the register of the subject. The L1 students were found to be more proficient than the CLIL students in developing certain features of academic language. The former used more prepositional phrases to express circumstances (time, place, cause) while the CLIL students mainly used clause complexes, creating a more oral and less academic register. Academic language was also evident in the L1 students' use of abstractions, while CLIL students often had to resort to more everyday lexis. The results obtained in these two studies indicate that some features of the language of the disciplines seem to be learnt more incidentally while others, as reported in the second study, would require special attention and some kind of implicit or explicit teaching.

Creating coherent texts (textual metafunction). The ability to produce coherent texts to create disciplinary registers is a basic skill for academic writing. In a recent longitudinal study, Whittaker, Llinares and McCabe (2011) analyzed textual coherence and the structure of the nominal group in a number of texts written by CLIL secondary school students of history. The aim of the study was twofold: identify the degree of coherence in students' texts as shown by the extent of their use of L2 linguistic resources for the identification of participants (either new or already introduced) and their success in creating academic register as observed in the structure of the nominal group. The students' progression was measured throughout four years of secondary schooling, with results revealing improvement in the management of textual resources, as well as some development in the complexity of the nominal group over the four years. This progression seems to indicate that, provided the students are given opportunities to create texts in their academic discipline, they increasingly choose the appropriate linguistic resources in the foreign language to create cohesive and coherent texts. The study also shows that CLIL contexts seem to facilitate students' development of the textual function in writing, provided that the writing task is scaffolded with a previous oral discussion. This longitudinal analysis reveals the potentiality of applying SFL to developmental studies of learner language, as has been done in other educational contexts (see, for example, Byrnes 2012).

Combining SFL and other approaches to SLA

The studies reported in the previous section have illustrated the valuable contributions of SFL in the understanding of foreign language learning in various contexts. However, more and more studies have recently referred to the interest of combining different theoretical approaches when carrying out research in applied linguistics. Romero-Trillo (2008), for instance, uses the term from ecology *mutualistic entente* to refer to the combination of two independent linguistic disciplines to the benefit of both. In particular, he argues for the benefits of combining the empirical/quantitative focus of corpus linguistics with the qualitative approach to data interpretation as provided in pragmatic models, in order to obtain clearer and more robust results. A quantitative approach provides frequencies that would require a closer look at the data in order to interpret those frequencies in context.

SLA research has traditionally had both a descriptive and an explanatory purpose (Ellis 1994). Some approaches have aimed at describing the kind of language produced by learners, trying to identify regularities and changes, including comparative cross-sectional and longitudinal studies. Other approaches, in turn, have been more interested in explaining why learners make errors, why their language presents regularities or changes and what are the internal and external factors that account for them. SFL work in second language contexts has often been more interested in the description of learner language than in explaining the learning process. However, as this chapter has shown, SFL can also contribute to the explanation of the language used by learners, in terms of the external factors that explain why learners learn the way they do. In any case, a more comprehensive picture of how SLA functions in different contexts could be obtained if descriptive and explanatory models were combined. For example, SFL applications to SLA could be combined with other approaches also interested in the effect of the social context on second language learners' use and development of the L2. The SFL framework has an undeniably descriptive power with respect to language in context. This makes it possible for this model to combine nicely with approaches to SLA in which the context has a key role, such as Sociocultural Theory and Situated Learning (Lave & Wenger 1991). This section will review some of these interdisciplinary approaches, which I believe are key for a better understanding of SLA.

One interdisciplinary approach that has social context as the common denominator is the combination of SFL, sociolinguistics, Sociocultural Theory and conversation analysis (CA), as proposed by Young (2009). This combination of theories expands the SLA landscape as language learning is seen from linguistic, ethnographic and sociological perspectives. The 'mutualistic entente' between CA and SFL is highlighted by Young (2009: 7):

> A Systemic Functional analysis reveals the relationship between language form and language function, but a different approach is needed to show how participants create social meanings and identities in interaction. Conversation Analysis (CA) is the approach used to describe how participants use interactional resources in a practice [...]

Together with the interest in focusing on learner language as both product and process, another assumption shared by SFL and other current approaches to SLA is the importance of obtaining complete instances of learner language in use. The studies reported in the previous section are based on different spoken and written learner corpora, which comprise classroom sessions at pre-primary and primary levels across EFL contexts (*UAMLESC, UAM Learner English Spoken Corpus*), secondary school students' spoken and written productions in the L2 across different subjects (*UAM-CLIL*) and secondary school students' writing in EFL classes (*UAM Corpus of Written Interlanguage*). These corpora are examples of the type of data needed to carry out valid analyses of learner language. As argued by Perrett (2000: 93), "We can find out what learners actually do by collecting samples of learner language [...]. These samples need to be complete texts, complete instances of language and social use". The applications of SFL to foreign language learning, reported in this chapter, have been carried out on contextualised and complete instances of learners' spoken and written texts.

Llinares and Morton's (2010) analysis of students' oral explanations in CLIL classrooms combines SFL, CA, Goffman's (1981) participation framework and corpus linguistics, thus following Young's (2009) multidisciplinary proposal. While SFL provided this study with a lexico-grammatical model for the analysis of students' management of the explanatory genre in history classes, corpus linguistics allowed for a quantitative analysis of these lexico-grammatical resources. Therefore, the study combined a quantitative with a qualitative analysis of students' use of the L2, focusing on language as product. However, these authors were interested in the *how* as well as the *what* of these CLIL students' performance and went on to observe how students used explanations in different contexts, comparing class discussions and individual interviews on the same topic. The specific findings obtained using corpus linguistics and SFL were then analyzed in the interactional context in which they occurred. The SFL analysis of CLIL students' use of explanations revealed a more frequent and richer use of this function in interviews than in class discussions. In turn, the focus on learning as situated practice, using a CA approach to the analysis of the data, helped understand the reasons for such a difference: in the interviews the students participated more as principals (Goffman 1981), standing behind what they were saying. In sum, the study showed the importance of combining approaches as "[...] specific findings can lead us to explore phenomena in a more qualitative, dynamic way" (Llinares & Morton 2010: 50).

As indicated above, the view that learner language can only be understood within the context of use is shared by SFL and other social approaches to SLA. There are other approaches to SLA that are also interested in language use and interaction but fail to take into account the purpose (genre) and social context in which language is used. This is the case of SLA research on negotiation of meaning (Long 1983). Perrett (1990), in her study of native-speaker/non-native speaker interactions, draws on SLA research on negotiation of meaning – see Pica, this volume- using the SFL model. This allows her to incorporate two main variables that are missing in traditional research on negotiation of meaning: the effect of the genre of particular interactional contexts and the relation between grammar and speech functions.

Formal and SFL approaches to classroom interaction can also be combined in the study of the effect of corrective feedback in learners' L2 performance in instructional contexts. For example, Llinares, Morton and Whittaker (2012) suggest combining Lyster's (2007) model of corrective feedback focusing on form, with Mohan and Becket's (2003) proposal of *functional recasts*. This second type of recast aims at upgrading the students' output with more appropriate language to convey specific meanings conventionally adequate for academic registers and genres. The role of functional recasts is particularly important in CLIL contexts, where the students learn academic subject knowledge in a foreign language. The extract below, from Llinares et al. (2012), shows a CLIL history teacher's use of a functional recast in response to the student's explanation of the rebirth of the cities:

(1) S1: Eh, yes because there was a lot of people in the countryside working and they have no place for everybody so they went to the cities and they went there.
     T: ... so that is the, em, the reason of the rebirth of cities.

By providing this type of recasts the teacher is helping the student to use and learn the foreign language to express academic content.

To sum up this section, and following Painter (2000: 65), the SFL model does not only offer new insights regarding foreign language use and learning, but also allows for interdisciplinary studies, in combination with other SLA theories, as it conceives language development as both social and cognitive.

Conclusion: Implications for research and pedagogy

The studies presented in this chapter represent a variety of applications of two main important areas within Systemic Functional Theory: Halliday's functional language development in the language of the child and genre and register theory in education. The former was originally applied by Halliday (1975) and Painter (2000) to the study of the development of the first language of the child. The latter has been widely applied to the study of language learning in various L1 and L2 educational contexts. The studies summarized above provide new insights as they apply these SF theories to instructional contexts (both EFL and CLIL) in which the target language is a foreign language and, thus, mostly confined to the context of the classroom.

Different educational levels and learning contexts could benefit from different SF approaches to learners' second language learning and development. At lower levels (pre-primary and primary) learners are usually ready to participate in contextualized learning. It is, then, necessary to identify what purposes learners' attempts to communicate have (communicative functions), which activities enhance these functions and the lexico-grammar used by the learners to convey these meanings. In order to identify these features, one useful model is the application of Halliday's work on child language development. On the other hand, in contexts in which the L2 is not only an object of study but also a vehicle for learning academic content, genre and register theory can offer insightful descriptions of the lexico-grammar that students need in order to respond successfully to the genre and register conventions of specific subjects or disciplines.

The studies presented in this paper highlight the potential of applying SFL to both descriptive and quasi-experimental studies (Llinares 2007a) and have shown that SFL is a model that can be applied not only to cross-sectional studies but also to developmental studies of learner language development (see Whittaker et al. 2011). This chapter has also argued in favour of combining different theories and methodological approaches to SLA. In my view, in order for SFL to combine with other approaches to the study of SLA, these models need to share a view of language as both process and product and make use of complete sets of data of learner language used in context. In this sense, this chapter has shown the interest of combining SFL with corpus linguistics, CA and Sociocultural Theory, all of which have a view of language learning as situated practice (following Lave & Wenger 1991). The chapter has also suggested the research potential of combining SFL with other models that could be considered more distant, such as focus on form approaches to corrective feedback.

Finally, this chapter has illustrated the interest of applying SFL to SLA in two new types of instructional contexts: EFL learning at an early age and CLIL. In SFL, language form and content/meaning are integrated as learning content involves learning the language to express that content. Both in EFL at an early age and CLIL the content being spoken about becomes the context for language learning. In preschool/early primary classrooms, school content knowledge matches *home content* knowledge. In CLIL classes, in turn, it is the academic content that becomes the context for language learning. More studies should be developed in the future that apply SFL, also in combination with other approaches, to the study of learner language in these and other contexts, with a view of language that cannot be separated from the meanings it conveys and the context in which it is used.

References

Bernstein, B. 1975. *Class, Codes and Control 3: Towards a Theory of Educational Transmissions.* London: Routledge & Kegan Paul.

Block, D. 2003. *The Social Turn in Second Language Acquisition.* Edinburgh: Edinburgh University Press.

Byrnes, H. 2009. Systemic-functional reflections on instructed foreign language acquisition as meaning-making: An introduction. *Linguistics and Education* 20(1): 1–9.

Byrnes, H. 2012. Conceptualizing FL writing development in collegiate settings: A systemic functional linguistics approach. In L2 writing development: *Multiple Perspectives*, R. Manchón (ed.), 191–218. Berlin: Mouton de Gruyter

Christie, F. 2002. *Classroom Discourse Analysis.* London: Continuum.

Christie F. & Martin, J.R. (eds). 1997. *Genre and Institutions. Social Processes in the Workplace and School.* London: Cassell.

Christie, F. & Derewianka, B. 2008. *School Discourse: Learning to Write across the Years of Schooling.* London: Continuum.

Chomsky, N. 1957. *Syntactic Structures.* The Hague: Mouton.

Coffin, C. 2006. *Historical Discourse: The Language of Time, Cause and Evaluation.* London: Continuum.

Coffin, C. 2010. *Language support in EAL Contexts. Why Systemic Functional Linguistics?* 2–5. Reading: Naldic. (Special Issue of NALDIC Quarterly).

Corder, S.P. 1967. The significance of learners' errors. *International Review of Applied Linguistics* 5(4): 161–70.

Council of Europe. 2001. *Common European Framework of Reference.* Strasbourg: Council of Europe.

Cummins, J. 1979. Cognitive/academic language proficiency, linguistic interdependence, the optimum age question and some other matters. *Working Papers on Bilingualism* 19: 121–129.

Dalton-Puffer, C. 2007a. *Discourse in Content and Language Integrated Learning (CLIL) Classrooms* [Language Learning & Language Teaching 20]. Amsterdam: John Benjamin.

Dalton-Puffer, C. 2007b. Academic language functions in a CLIL environment. In *Diverse Contexts- Converging Goals*, D. Marsh & D. Wolff (eds), 201–210. Frankfurt: Peter Lang.

Dalton-Puffer, C. & Smit, U. 2007. Introduction. In *Empirical Perspectives on CLIL Classroom Discourse*, C. Dalton-Puffer & U. Smit (eds), 7–24. Frankfurt: Peter Lang.

Ellis, R. 1994. *The Study of Second Language Acquisition.* Oxford: OUP.

Foster-Cohen, S.H. 1999. *An Introduction to Child Language Development.* London: Longman.

Geekie, P. & Raban, B. 1994. Language learning at home and school. In *Input and Interaction in Language Acquisition*, C. Gallaway & B. Richards (eds), 153–180. Cambridge: CUP.

Gibbons, P. 2006. *Bridging Discourses in the ESL Classroom: Students, Teachers and Researchers.* London: Continuum.

Goffman, E. 1981. *Forms of Talk*. Oxford: Blackwell.

Groom, B. 2004. An analysis of a children's history text. In *Language, Education and Discourse*. J. Foley (ed.), 120–142. London: Continuum.

Halliday, M.A.K. 1975. *Learning How to Mean: Explorations in the Development of Language*. London: Arnold.

Halliday, M.A.K. 2004. *An Introduction to Functional Grammar*, 3d edn. Revised by C. M.I.M. Matthiessen. London: Hodder Arnold.

Halliday, M.A.K. & Hasan, R. 1989. *Language Context and Text: Aspects of Language in a Social-Semiotic Perspective*. Oxford: OUP.

Halliday, M.A.K., McIntosh, A. & Strevens, P. 1966. *The Linguistic Sciences and Language Teaching*. London: Longman.

Hammond, J. & Gibbons, P. 2005. Putting scaffolding to work: The contribution of scaffolding in articulating ESL education. *Prospect* 20(1): 6–30.

Huang, J. & Mohan, B. 2009. A functional approach to integrated assessment of teacher support and student discourse development in an elementary Chinese program. *Linguistics and Education* 20: 22–38.

Lado, R. 1957. *Linguistics across Cultures*. Ann Arbor MI: University of Michigan Press.

Lantolf, J.P. 2000. *Sociocultural Theory and Second Language Learning*. Oxford: OUP.

Lasagabaster, D. & Sierra, J.M. 2010. Immersion and CLIL in English: More differences than similarities. *ELT Journal* 64: 376–395.

Lave, J. & Wenger, E. 1991. Situated Learning: *Legitimate Peripheral Participation*. Cambridge: CUP.

Llinares, A. 2006. A pragmatic analysis of children's interlanguage in EFL preschool contexts. *Intercultural Pragmatics* 3: 171–193.

Llinares, A. 2007a. Young learners' functional use of the L2 in a low-immersion EFL context. *ELT Journal* 61: 39–45.

Llinares, A. 2007b. Classroom bilingualism at an early age: Towards a more natural EFL context. In *A Portrait of the Young in Multilingual Spain*, C. Pérez Vidal, M. Juan-Garau & A. Bel (eds), 185–199. Bristol: Multilingual Matters.

Llinares, A. & Morton, T. 2010. Historical explanations as situated practice in content and language integrated learning. *Classroom Discourse* 1(1): 46–65.

Llinares, A. & Romero-Trillo, J. 2007. Getting personal: Native speaker and EFL pre-school children's use of the personal function. *International Journal of Applied Linguistics* 17(2): 198–213.

Llinares, A. & Whittaker, R. 2007. Talking and writing in the social sciences in a foreign language: A linguistic analysis of secondary school learners of geography and history. *RESLA* (Special Issue): 83–94.

Llinares, A. & Whittaker, R. 2009. Teaching and learning history in secondary CLIL classrooms: From speaking to writing. In *CLIL across Educational Levels: Experiences from Primary, Secondary and Tertiary Contexts*, E. Dafouz & M. Guerrini (eds), 73–89. Madrid: Richmond-Santillana.

Llinares, A. & Whittaker, R. 2010. Writing and speaking in the history class: Data from CLIL and first language contexts. In *Language Use and Language Learning in CLIL Classrooms* [AILA Applied Linguistics Series 7], C. Dalton-Puffer, T. Nikula & U. Smit (eds.), 125–144. Amsterdam: John Benjamins.

Llinares, A., Morton, T. & Whittaker, R. 2012. *The Roles of Language in CLIL*. Cambridge: CUP

Long, M.H. 1983. Native speaker/non-native speaker conversation and the negotiation of comprehensible input. *Applied Linguistics* 4(2): 126–41.

Lyster, R. 2007. *Learning and Teaching Languages through Content: A Counterbalanced Approach* [Language Learning and Language Teaching 18]. Amsterdam: John Benjamins.

Martin, J.R. 1993. A contextual theory of language. In *The Powers of Literacy- A Genre Approach to Teaching Writing*, B. Cope & M. Kalantzis (eds), 116–136. Pittsburgh PA: University of Pittsburgh Press.

Martin, J.R. & White, P.R.R. 2005. *The Language of Evaluation, Appraisal in English*. London: Palgrave Macmillan.

Martín-Úriz, A. & Whittaker, R. 2006. Writing in English in Spanish schools: Register and genre. In *A Pleasure of Life in Words: A Festschrift for Angela Downing*, Vol. II, M. Carretero et al. (eds), 177–198. Madrid: Servicio de Publicaciones UCM.

Martín-Úriz, A., Barrio, M., Murcia, S, Ordóñez, L., Whittaker, R. & Vidal, K. 2005. Do foreign language learners express ideology through their texts? An analysis of secondary school writing. Paper presented at the XX International Systemic-Functional Linguistics Conference. Sydney: University of Sydney.

Martín-Úriz, A.,Whittaker, R., Barrio, M. & Murcia, S. 2007. Reports in EFL writing: Generic structure and Theme in relation to text quality. Paper presented at the 34th International Systemic Functional Linguistics Conference. Odense: University of Southern Denmark.

Martín-Úriz- A., Whittaker, R., Murcia, S. & Vidal, K. 2008. The expression of experiential meaning in EFL students' texts: an analysis of secondary school recounts. In *From Language to Multimodality: New Developments in the Study of Ideational Meaning*, C. Jones & E. Ventola (eds), 209–227. London: Equinox.

Mitchell, R. & Myles, F.2004. *Second Language Acquisition Theories*. London: Edward Arnold.

Mohan, B. & Beckett, G. H. 2003. A functional approach to research on content-based language learning: Recasts in causal explanations. *The Modern Language Journal* 87(3): 421–432.

Mohan, B. & Huang, J. 2002. Assessing the integration of language and content in a Mandarin as a foreign language classroom. *Linguistics and Education* 13: 405–433.

Morton, T. 2010. Using a genre-based approach to integrating content and language in CLIL: The example of secondary history. In *Language Use and Language Learning in CLIL Classrooms* [AILA Applied Linguistics Series 7], C. Dalton-Puffer, T. Nikula & U. Smit (eds), 81–104. Amsterdam: John Benjamins.

Neff, J. Ballesteros, F., Dafouz, E., Díez, M., Martínez, F., Rica, J. P.& Prieto, R. 2004. Formulating writer stance: A contrastive study of EFL learner corpora. In *Applied Corpus Linguistics: A Multidisciplinary Perspective*, U. Connor & T. Upton (eds), 73–90. Amsterdam: Rodopi.

Painter, C. 2000 Researching first language development in children. In *Researching Languages in Schools and Communities*, L. Unsworth (ed.), 65–86. London: Cassell.

Perrett, G. 1990. How do Learners Answer Questions? Discourse and the Development of Interlanguage. PhD dissertation, University of Sydney.

Perrett, G. 2000. Second and foreign language development. In *Researching Languages in Schools and Communities*, L. Unsworth (ed.), 87–110. London: Cassell.

Pienemann, M. 2003. Language processing capacity. In *The Handbook of Second Language Acquisition*, C.J. Doughty & M.H. Long (eds), 679–714. Oxford: Blackwell

Romero-Trillo, J. 2008. Introduction. In *Pragmatics and Corpus Linguistics: A Mutualistic Entente*, J. Romero-Trillo (ed.), Berlin: Mouton de Gruyter.

Schleppegrell, M. 2004. *The Language of Schooling: A Functional Linguistics Perspective*. Mahwah NJ: Lawrence Erlbaum Associates.

Selinker, L. 1972. Interlanguage. *International Review of Applied Linguistics* 10: 209–231.

Tabbors, P.O. & Snow, C.E. 1994. English as a second language in pre-school programs. In *Educating Second Language Children*, F. Genesee (ed.), 103–126. Cambridge: CUP.

Veel, R. & Coffin, C. 1996. Learning to think like an historian: The language of secondary school history. In *Literacy in Society*, R. Hasan & G. Williams (eds), 191–231. Longman: London.

Vygotsky, L.S. 1962. *Thought and Language*. Cambridge MA: The MIT Press.

Whittaker, R. & Llinares, A. 2009. CLIL in social science classrooms: Analysis of spoken and written productions. In *Content and Language Integrated Learning. Evidence from Research in Europe*, Ruiz de Zarobe, Y. & R. M. Jiménez Catalán (eds), 215–234. Bristol: Multilingual Matters.

Whittaker, R., O'Donnell, M. & McCabe, A. (eds). 2006. *Language and Literacy. Functional Approaches*. London: Continuum.

Whittaker R., Llinares. A. & McCabe, A. 2011. Written discourse development in CLIL at secondary school. *Language Teaching Research* 15(3): 343–362.

Wong-Fillmore, L. 1991. Second language learning in children: A model of language learning in social context. In *Language Processing in Bilingual Children*, E. Bialystok (ed.), 49–69. Cambridge: CUP.

Yasuda, S. 2011. Genre-based tasks in foreign language writing: Developing writers' genre awareness, linguistic knowledge, and writing competence. *Journal of Second Language Writing* 20(2): 111–133.

Young, R. 2009. *Discursive Practice in Language Learning and Teaching*. London: Blackwell.

CHAPTER 3

From input, output and comprehension to negotiation, evidence, and attention

An overview of theory and research on learner interaction and SLA*

Teresa Pica
The University of Pennsylvania

This chapter begins with an historical overview of theory and research on the role of learner interaction in the processes and sequences of second language acquisition (SLA). The overview highlights the foundational constructs of input, output, interaction, and comprehension, and current constructs of negotiation, attention, and evidence for SLA. The chapter also addresses the ways in which these constructs have illuminated the processes of SLA, shed light on the needs of the learner, and led to instructional approaches that facilitate effective second language (L2) outcomes. Examples of interaction-based approaches are provided. These include research validated strategies and tasks that provide opportunities for learners to interact in the L2 as they negotiate its meaning, attend to its linguistic forms and constructions, and access positive and negative evidence for their SLA

Introduction: Learner interaction: Theoretical perspectives, distinctions and relevance

When we look back at the 1960's and 1970's, those of us in the fields of TESOL, Applied Linguistics, and SLA, can recall a time when a great deal of foundational work on *input* was getting under way. Corder (1967) advanced this term as a label for the *universe of data* available to learners, and distinguished it from the *intake* that was internalized for integration with their interlanguage system. Building on

*   Due to Teresa Pica's untimely death on November 15, 2011, this chapter was finalized, in her memory, by Alison Mackey and Jenefer Philp who, with the assistance and suggestions of one of the editors, María del Pilar García Mayo, made minor changes and updates based on reviewers' feedback, following a path we jointly believe Tere would have approved.

Corder's important foundation, Krashen introduced the construct of *comprehensible input* (Krashen 1981). Throughout this period, Long (e.g., Long 1981), emphasized the importance of input that was made comprehensible through modified interaction, which he advanced with other scholars (e.g., Gass & Varonis 1985). Despite the attribution researchers gave to comprehensible input as necessary for SLA, they warned that it might not be sufficient for the achievement of a target-like L2 grammar. Their work since that time has revealed important findings on input, modified interaction, and on linguistic and interaction features that appear necessary as well. These findings will be described throughout this chapter.

Additional arguments on the insufficiency of comprehensible input were advanced by Swain (1985), who noted that learners needed to be able to process language for both its meaning and its grammatical form. She argued that the learner's output might be crucial to this achievement, and speculated that when learners were asked to modify the initially incomprehensible or inaccurate output they had produced, they might draw on their emergent grammatical resources to process language syntactically. Swain, too, went on to uncover additional SLA constructs and processes related to output production. These included the ability to notice needed new forms and features, to test hypotheses about interlanguage structures, and to analyze these processes through reflection and *metatalk*, i.e. talking about linguistic aspects of their own interactions (e.g., Swain 1998).

For the past several decades, researchers have turned to this important foundation as they introduced new constructs such as attention, noticing, and positive and negative evidence, and looked toward negotiation as a kind of interaction that could serve as a resource to learners in the acquisition process. Their many studies are described and analyzed next.

Learner interaction: Empirical perspectives, questions, and findings

One of the most comprehensive discussions of the role of input in SLA appears in Long (1996). According to Long, learners need access to input that provides positive evidence or data on L2 form as it encodes message meaning. Sources of positive evidence include spoken and written texts in their authentic state, as well as those that have been modified for comprehensibility through simplification, repetition, and elaboration of their linguistic features. Long argued, however, that positive evidence, although an excellent resource, was nonetheless insufficient for mastery of many L2 forms and constructions. Among them are linguistic elements with low perceptual saliency due to their encoding as bound, grammatical morphemes or occurrence in reduced, final syllables of nouns and verbs. Such linguistic elements often go unnoticed. Also difficult for learners to master through positive evidence alone are noun phrase articles, determiners, or gender markings that carry low semantic weight. Learners might notice the perceptual characteristics of such items, but are likely to overlook their grammatical or functional roles.

Even input that has been linguistically enhanced or enriched often defies learners' grasp as a source of evidence. As revealed in J. White (1998), enhancements of italics, bolding, enlargement, and underlining to possessive determiners did not make a significant difference in their acquisition of these forms. Similarly, as shown in Izumi (2002), forms that had been enhanced in texts provided to learners had little impact on their ability to use the forms in text reconstruction. Furthermore, as described in Trahey and L. White (1993), forms made more abundant to learners through *flooding* and repeated use in written and spoken texts (Trahey & L. White 1993) had minimal impact on their interlanguage grammar. Even when enhanced input was accompanied by instruction on its application to messages, it failed to influence learners' productive use (e.g., Doughty & Williams 1998: 239–240).

When learners have difficulty in noticing L2 forms and constructions or their grammatical or functional roles, there is a tendency for them to develop incomplete or incorrect representations. They might substitute incorrect versions for correct ones, or omit the forms altogether. As Long explained, this tendency reveals why learners are believed to need additional evidence about what is *not* in the L2. Such *negative* evidence can be accessed in a variety of ways, including formal instruction on L2 rules, explicit correction of L2 forms and constructions, and implicit feedback encoded as requests for message clarification (e.g., *what did you say?*), as confirmation (e.g., did you say *a book*?), and clarification requests, as prompts (e.g., *you said that was a.........?*), or as interlocutor responses that paraphrase or recast learner utterances.

Learners' need for evidence can be accommodated by cognitive processes that help them to *notice the gap* or difference between features of their interlanguage and the target L2 forms they wish to acquire (Schmidt & Frota 1986). This need arises as learners produce output and are given feedback. They then attempt to modify their output accordingly. Learners also need to *notice the hole* in their interlanguage for L2 items they still need to acquire (Doughty & Williams 1998). This type of need is a result of learners attempting to communicate a message, but realizing that they lack a grammatical form or lexical item that would allow them to do so with accuracy and appropriateness. This can occur during self-initiated messages as well as during their repair of messages that were not successful. They then search for positive evidence in their interlocutors' messages.

As Swain further argued, the positive and negative evidence that comes from input and feedback can be enhanced during interaction, when learners are asked to modify their message production toward greater comprehensibility or accuracy.

Such interaction provides them with opportunities to move from their rudimentary interlanguage grammar, with its pragmatic tendency to juxtapose constituent features to a grammar that is closer to that of the L2 they are learning. In so doing, they might modify syntactically what was originally a meaningful message, but whose form was wanting in scope, complexity, and target-like standards of acceptability (Linnell 1995; Swain 1985).

A further source of evidence is believed to come from the learner's own awareness of L2 forms and the ways in which they encode function and meaning. Awareness often arises during the learner's involvement in an interaction (e.g., Hulstijn 2001; Laufer & Hulstijn 2001) as they need to understand messages, search for ways to respond to questions, formulate responses, and evaluate their compliance with a target. To complete their involvement they need to apply their response to a new context.

Empirical studies have shown that a good deal of positive and negative evidence can be accessed during the course of informal conversation, open-ended communication, and the exchange of message meaning. Experientially oriented classrooms often make this assumption when they engage learners in role plays, opinion exchanges, and other types of communicative activities (Pica & Doughty 1985a, 1985b). However, these kinds of meaning-based interactions can lend themselves to an even flow of communication, with little need for learners to require complex positive evidence or gain access to crucial negative evidence that might move them beyond their current level of L2 development. As will be discussed below, interactions that are modified by learners' negotiation of meaning and form-focused intervention and instruction can address such challenges.

Modified interaction: Distinctions and contributions to SLA

Negotiation of meaning

Interaction can be modified by the negotiation of meaning, use of recasts, form focused intervention and instruction. When interaction is modified by the negotiation of meaning, teachers, classmates, and other interlocutors request clarification or confirmation from the learner through utterances that attempt to understand the learner's intended meaning. These brief, but frequent interludes help the learner to *focus on form* (Long & Robinson 1998; Doughty & Williams 1998) by shifting the learner's attention to the form of the message and to possible problems with its encoding. Simple signals such as *What did you say?* or *Please repeat* are often used as well as linguistically elaborated responses. When an interlocutor seeks to confirm the learner's message, and thereby reformulates it, this helps the learner to notice the gap between the interlanguage encoding of its meaning and the encoding of that meaning in the interlocutor's request. This is shown in the following brief exchange:

(1) Learner: My grass broken
    Interlocutor: Your glasses? Are your glasses broken?

The importance of interlocutors' mutual comprehension and the comprehensibility of their messages becomes especially acute when interaction is goal oriented and requires learners and interlocutors to exchange and integrate distinct pieces of information they each hold in order to solve a problem or complete a task. (Pica 2002; Pica & Washburn 2003; Pica, Lincoln-Porter, Paninos & Linnell 1996, and the sections on task-based interaction, below). Such a focus on message form is incidental, however, as learners' attention is necessarily devoted to repairing and resolving impasses in message communication. In many cases, the attention paid to a message is not directed at the accuracy of its grammatical form, but rather the preciseness of its content.

Below is an example of what frequently occurs when an interlocutor is asked to reproduce a picture based on directions from a learner:

(2) Learner: Two book. Draw two book.
    Interlocutor: Two? Did you say two?
    Learner: Yes

The learner answers *Yes* as a validation of his intention. The response is appropriate in the context of information sharing and discourse roles, but its formulation as a simple *yes*, rather than a phrase or sentence does not require the learner to draw on his interlanguage resources to produce. A syntactic response, in keeping with Swain's position on the contributions of modified output, would have been more contributive to the learner's interlanguage development.

Thus, one of the concerns about negotiation is that its inexactness for drawing attention to form and meaning limits its sufficiency as a source of positive and negative evidence for L2 learning. Nevertheless its frequency of occurrence during goal-oriented interaction makes negotiation of meaning a useful, if inexact resource to the learner.

Negotiation of form

When comprehensibility is not at issue, as often happens when teachers are familiar with their students' interlanguage errors and are engaged with them in classroom routines and lessons, the teachers may use negotiation signals to promote accuracy, through what has been referred to by Lyster (1998) and Lyster and Ranta

(1997) as the negotiation of form. This signaling technique was shown to be effective for learners as they attempted to correct their lexical errors and many of their syntactic errors as well. To modify their phonological errors, however, learners appeared to benefit from another kind of intervention, known as recasts (see, again, Lyster & Ranta 1997). These responses, known to be abundant in classroom and caregiver settings, have been the subject of numerous studies. Results of the studies have not been uniform, but detailed analyses have shed light on the conditions of proximity and setting in which recasts work best.

Recasts

When interlocutors respond to a learner by recasting the learner's message they restate what they believe to be the meaning of the message, but recode its errors into an accurate form. This recoded message provides positive evidence as input for learning. Its temporal proximity to the learner's error also provides negative evidence that helps the learner to notice the gap in form between the original message and the recast one. Recasts have been shown to be effective vehicles for negative evidence in experimental contexts (Long, Inagaki, & Ortega 1998; Mackey & Philp 1998; McDonough & Mackey 2006), including those that are carried out in quasi-experimental content-based (Doughty & Varela 1998) and language-based classrooms (Loewen & Philp, 2006). However, they pose potential ambiguity to learners in classrooms that emphasize communication of content and the exchange of message meaning. As Lyster (1998) has shown, recasts are similar in form and occurrence to teachers' follow-up utterances intended to express acceptance and approval of the students' responses to their questions. Often, students have no obvious way to distinguish the function of a recast based on its form.

Many studies support the effectiveness of the recast in drawing the learner's attention to form and meaning, but their results give rise to questions as to whether it is the positive, negative, or combined evidence that makes the recast an effective response to the learner. Other researchers point to studies in which recasts were not effective, presumably because their preservation of the message meaning had made their minor corrective properties difficult for learners to notice. In attempting to resolve this theoretical debate, individual studies (Ammar 2008; Ayoun 2001; Dilans 2010; Doughty & Varela 1998; Ellis & Sheen 2006; Erlam & Loewen 2010; Leeman 2003; Loewen & Philp 2006; McDonough 2007; Yang & Lyster 2010), compilations of studies (Doughty 2001; Nicholas, Lightbown & Spada 2001), as well as meta-analyses (Goo & Mackey 2013; Keck, Iberri-Shea, have shed considerable light on the ways in which recasts can best help the learner. These works reveal that both the positive and the negative evidence in a recast can be useful for SLA. Because recasts are encoded as immediate, semantically contingent response moves, their formal and functional properties are made more salient to the learner, so that they can be noticed and applied to the developing grammar. Thus, it is the immediacy in timing and saliency in the positioning of recasts that make them useful for SLA.

Beyond settling a theoretical debate, the analysis of recasts has revitalized the role of positive evidence in the L2 learning process. Meaningful, comprehensible input works best when given in responses, rather than initiation moves. Lending further support to this perspective is a study by Long et al. (1998) and a review by R. Ellis (1999). Together, they emphasize that when positive evidence is supplied in the form of enhanced texts that have been pre-modified on the basis of interlocutor judgments about the learner's abilities and needs, this evidence does not make a difference for the learner. However, when the evidence comes from immediate interlocutor responses that incorporate or reformulate the learner's very own message, it is shown to be beneficial to the learner. This form of adjusted input is far more direct and individualized than its pre-modified counterpart.

Form-focused intervention

Form-focused intervention occurs when conversational interaction becomes modified to achieve message comprehensibility, and does so in ways that draw the learner's attention to relationships of L2 form and meaning, through a *focus on form* (Doughty & Williams 1998; Long & Robinson 1998). *Focus on form*, as defined by Long and Robinson (1998: 23), is viewed as "an occasional shift in attention to linguistic code features – ... triggered by perceived problems with comprehension or production". A focus on form need not be triggered by communication problems, but might anticipate them through learner directed models, in which the learner's attention is directed towards a potentially problematic feature (Doughty & Williams 1998). In this instance, the modification toward comprehensibility and the form on which to focus supply positive evidence to the learner.

Form-focused intervention can occur within negotiation, as the need to repair conversational breakdowns brings interlocutors to shift attention from a sole emphasis on the exchange of message meaning to the perceptual or structural shape that encodes the meaning. This shift of attention is in keeping with the meaning of Long and Robinson's *focus on form* (1998). Not all negotiation shifts the learner's attention to form, however. For example, one interlocutor might fail to interpret the meaning another interlocutor intended due to differences in message content expectations or culturally-grounded world views. Such misinterpretation might lead to a negotiation of message meaning, even though the linguistic form of the message is acceptable, appropriate, and not the focus of the conversational repair. Such instances of focus on form serve as a source of positive evidence for SLA. Form-focused intervention can also occur as interlocutor recasts of learner utterances, as well as models, feedback, and other attention-focusing devices that reveal differences between learners' interlanguage and the requirements of their L2 target (Long 1996). In these instances, it is negative evidence to which learners gain access.

Form-focused instruction

Form-focused instruction has been defined as transmission of information about language code, and use of corrective feedback within the context of communicative activities (Lightbown & Spada 1990). Its features can include teacher use of display or evaluation questions, metalinguistic statements, and explicit corrective feedback. When the instruction refers to problems with form, especially the ways in which such problems can interfere with the communication of meaning, it serves as a source of negative evidence. When there is no immediate communication problem, as there is during negotiation, it supplies positive evidence of L2 forms and rules.

Form-focused instruction can supply information on ways in which learners might process input for its form and meaning. Such processing instruction serves as a source of positive evidence for L2 forms and rules. Processing instruction has been successful in helping learners to identify sentence constituents and understand message meaning (e.g. VanPatten & Cadierno 1993). Learners are given explicit instruction on how to process L2 input whose word order is different from that of their first language or is a marked alternative in the L2.

Processing instruction appears to be especially effective for assisting learners' comprehension of sentences with marked constituent order. As several studies have revealed, however, not all rules, forms, and structures are amenable to this approach. As was illustrated by Allen's work on French causative verbs (Allen 2000) and DeKeyser and Sokalski's studies on Spanish morphosyntax (DeKeyser & Sokalski 2001), rule-focused and practice-oriented instruction can be just as effective for aiding learners' sentence comprehension and interpretation and more effective in facilitating production of most grammatical forms and constructions.

Output production and modification

Along with interaction modified by negotiation, use of recasts, and form focused intervention and instruction, output can serve as a resource for evidence, as well as a mechanism for important learning processes. Some of the most compelling arguments about the role of output have come from Swain (1985, 1998), and originated with her review of test data on long-term French immersion learners. Her analysis revealed scores that were considerably lower in production accuracy than in the receptive areas of reading and listening, despite the learners' access to positive evidence encoded as input that was meaningful, copious, and comprehensible. To explain the data, Swain analyzed the discourse of the immersion classroom. Its emphasis on content transmission necessarily reduced students' opportunities to produce spontaneous L2 output and to adjust what might be a comprehensible, but grammatically inaccurate message into a syntactically more successful one. She proposed that if all learners, not just those in classroom settings, were given opportunities to modify their message production toward greater comprehensibility or accuracy, they might be able to move from an interlanguage characterized by semantic processing and juxtaposition of constituent features, to one distinguished by syntactic processing and message organization.

From her initial argument about *comprehensible output* as a necessary mechanism in SLA (Swain 1985: 252), Swain went on to propose that learners' production, especially their modified production of their responses during negotiation and collaborative undertakings, would be a source of positive and negative evidence, and a basis for learners' hypothesis testing. It could also help learners notice the insufficiencies of their own grammatical and lexical repertoires, and motivate them to listen more carefully for needed structures and words in new contexts in which such features might be found. Over the years, many of Swain's proposals have been confirmed through studies in authentic and controlled classroom settings (He & Ellis 1999; Izumi 2002; Linnell 1995; McDonough 2005; Paninos 2005; Pica, Holliday, Lewis & Morgenthaler 1989; Shehadeh 1999, 2001; Swain 1993; Swain & Lapkin 1998).

Some of the research has shown that output production prior to opportunities to hear input and notice its features is more effective for SLA than input noticing activities alone (Izumi 2002; Paninos 2005). Other studies have shown that interlocutor feedback can affect the learner's ability to produce syntactically complex and accurate structures (Linnell 1995) and to advance through the stages of question formation (McDonough 2005). These and other studies have revealed ways in which the impact of output on the learning process is heightened when it is produced in response to feedback. While feedback has long been viewed as a means whereby learners can seek additional input (see, again, Krashen 1976), and more recently as a source of negative evidence, it appears equally important as a trigger for learners to modify their production of output and thereby advance their interlanguage development.

Learner interaction and readiness

The importance of readiness for learners to process and internalize input for their L2 development has been a theme with considerable resonance across several decades of research on SLA. Early on, in advancing his *input hypothesis*, Krashen (1981) looked to the importance of the learner's readiness for what he considered optimal and sufficient input. As such, the input would need to be meaningful, comprehensible, and encoded slightly beyond students' current level of language development. Because these features were difficult to operationalize for empirical study, the construct remained acknowledged, but untested, until Manfred Pienemann's studies on developmental stages in German L2 and his *teachability hypothesis* on the role of instructional intervention in speeding up the learner's rate of passage through them. (Pienemann 1985, 1989). His findings revealed that learners could not skip any stages in their sequence of L2 development, but that appropriately timed instruction in features that were teachable, i.e., at the stage just beyond their current stage, could help them go through intermediate steps more quickly than they would have if left on their own.

Learners' readiness can also be seen within the scope of their readiness to use positive and negative evidence in their SLA. Thus, Pienemann (1989) and R. Ellis (1989) were able to show that learners at the *particle* stage in their German L2 development, benefited from instruction on the next, *inversion*, stage when given instruction on particle movement. This enabled them to extend their ability for separating particles from other constituents within phrases and for moving them to sentence final position, to the ability to separate and move particles internally, within a sentence as well. Learners at stages below *particle*, who could not yet separate particles from other constituents in phrases, were not yet ready and able to benefit from *inversion* instruction. Pienemann has advanced his Processability Theory, through which he has been able to predict cross-linguistically the syntactic structures that learners are ready to process at particular stages in their development. His studies of English, Japanese, and Swedish have provided empirical support to his claims (Pienemann 1998). Other studies on a variety of languages have since added further evidence for the validity of Processability Theory (Di Biase & Kawaguchi 2002 on Italian and Japanese, or Al Shatter 2011on Arabic).

Task-based interaction: Theoretical and empirical perspectives

Tasks that engage learners in meaningful, goal-oriented interaction in order to solve problems, complete projects, and reach decisions have been used for a broad range of purposes for SLA. In so doing, they play a unique and important role in responding to theoretical and methodological needs and practical issues in SLA (García Mayo 2007). Since their inception with Prabhu (Prabhu 1987), tasks have brought forth instructional design features that have made them suitable as course syllabus units (Willis 1996), classroom materials (Nunan 1989), and enhancements to the language curriculum (Crookes & Gass 1993). Unlike language exercises, which focus solely on linguistic accuracy for its own sake, tasks require learners to use language accurately and appropriately to address needs and objectives similar to those they face in the world outside the language classroom.

The most successful tasks are those that require learners to fill in an information gap in order to reach a pre-specified goal. To do that, they must transfer information from one to the other or exchange information among each other. As they do this, the learners are helped to solve problems, reach decisions, replicate pictures, and reconstruct stories. Information gap tasks promote opportunities for modified interaction as learners request clarification from each other. Among the most widely used information gap tasks are those that require learners to locate differences in texts and graphics held individually as they describe them to each other, to reconstruct passages and graphics, and to make decisions about phrases and sentences in texts, with justification for their choices. These are known as *Spot the Difference*, *Jigsaw*, and *Grammar Decision Making*.

Tasks have also come to serve as instructional tools that facilitate classroom SLA. As learners engage in goal-oriented task based interaction, they exchange messages and signal and respond to each other's difficulties with message comprehensibility. These moves enable them to provide each other with modified, comprehensible input and corrective feedback, and to respond to each other with their own modified output. In so doing, they are drawn to linguistic forms and their grammatical and semantic functions. In recent years, the roles of information gap tasks have broadened, as researchers have turned to them in order to address questions about the connections between comprehensible input and output and the learners' acquisition of L2 form. The linguistic modifications the learners produce shed light on cognitive processes such as attention, noticing, and awareness. Together, the modifications and processes serve as a source of data for researchers as they study developmental sequences and outcomes.

Many studies have employed classroom tasks to draw learners' attention to forms of limited communicative transparency and low salience, as well as for sequential features with considerable operational complexity. These linguistic and communicative properties made forms and features difficult to master despite learners' readiness to do so. In Doughty and Varela (1998), for example, students' reports of their science experiments provided contexts for them to produce past time morphology. When they made errors of suppliance, the researchers repeated and recast their utterances, and then tracked the results of this intervention over time. This commonly used classroom task, which was part of the everyday curriculum, thus turned into an effective learning tool for the students, as well as a helpful means of data collection for the researchers.

Information gap tasks involving *persuasion* and *description* were used by Newton and Kennedy (1996) to address questions about split and shared distribution of input in learners' use of conjunctions and prepositions. These researchers found that information bearing input was task related. Participants used more conjunctions on tasks in which they were asked to share the same information to persuade or describe, but used more prepositions on tasks in which they were each given different information to meet these aims.

With respect to output, many studies have used *information gap* tasks of *description* and *story construction* to address questions on pushed output in vocabulary learning and retention (de la Fuente 2002), relative clause formation (Izumi 2002), question development (Mackey & McDonough 2000), past tense formation (Takashima & Ellis 1999), and self correction (Swain & Lapkin 2001). The tasks have been useful in guiding learners to manipulate the target forms, negotiate and act on feedback in the process of carrying out the task. Results also suggest benefits for acquisition of certain forms.

Many studies have used information gap tasks to examine learners' production of modified output in response to corrective feedback. Their results have been positive and promising with respect to L2 form access and retention over time. For example, Iwashita (2003) used jigsaw and information gap tasks to generate corrective feedback for Japanese locative-initial constructions and verb morphology and the findings of the studies showed that there was a significant effect for task participation. Implicit negative feedback, and in particular recasts, were found to have overall positive effects on short-term development. In contrast, positive evidence alone – while more frequent than corrective feedback – only proved beneficial for learners with a more advanced command of the target structures.

Pica, Kang and Sauro (2006) and Pica, Sauro, and Lee (2007) have developed a method for devising *Spot the Difference, Jigsaw,* and *Grammar Decision Making* tasks that help students in content-based language courses to notice low salience forms and features that are difficult to master from course content alone. The tasks have been effective in drawing students' attention to low salience articles and verb endings in their course reading passages, and retaining them for subsequent use. Positive results were also found in studies by Muranoi (2000), who used problem solving role play tasks to generate feedback on English articles, by Leeman (2003), who used information gap tasks to promote feedback for noun-adjective agreement, and by Mackey and McDonough (2000), who used *Spot the Difference,* picture description and drawing, and collaborative story sequencing tasks to promote noticing for noun classifiers and questions. Subsequent studies by Mackey and

Oliver (2002) and McDonough (2005), which used similar tasks and feedback treatments, also found a positive impact on question formation.

However, task methodology has been employed largely in short-term research. Even when durations of several weeks' time were reported, these durations included delayed post-testing, carried out after the actual treatment was over (Doughty & Varela 1998; de la Fuente 2002; Iwashita 2003; Izumi 2002; Smith 2005; Takashima & Ellis 1999). Just as extending the period of time for post-testing is important for addressing questions on L2 retention, so too is extending the period of treatment time important for questions on learning processes and L2 outcomes, especially for those areas of SLA that defy short-term intervention. Ideally, a controlled environment would allow for the isolated study of key factors of input, interaction, feedback, and output in SLA. The use of tasks would surely provide a good deal of relevant data in these areas.

Realistically, though, finding learners willing to participate in a controlled study, over an extended time, is not an easy enterprise for SLA researchers. Opportunities to compensate through funding or through tutoring or teaching services, though possibly effective, are usually not feasible, due to cost and time constraints. This is where intact classrooms might play an important role. Although they do not allow for random selection and assignment, they can provide large cohorts of learners, who are likely to be available for weeks or months of treatment time. Most learners and their teachers would be familiar with the kinds of information exchange tasks that have originated from, and can be accommodated to, their current, familiar classroom curriculum. The combination of tasks and classroom settings can play a role in the methodology needed to address questions on SLA within and beyond the scope of interaction.

Task-based interaction in the classroom

L2 classrooms are first and foremost environments for teaching and learning. Although they also serve as environments for research, much of the research in classrooms to date has been aimed at describing instructional practices rather than testing the effects of instructional interventions on SLA. Studies that expanded the role of the classroom as an SLA research environment (e.g., Day & Shapson 1991; Doughty & Varela 1998; Harley 1989, 1993) are instructive in the design of future studies. All used activities and tasks that were consistent with the curriculum, schedule, and format of the classrooms where they carried out their studies, and were therefore not intrusive to the work of teachers and students.

Information gap tasks add an additional component to research in the classroom, however, due to their dual role as tools for data collection and instructional interventions. As learners work together to reach task goals, their L2 exchanges provide interaction-based data that can address questions on evidence, its accessibility through input, interaction, feedback, and output, and its relationship with cognitive processes such as noticing and attention. However, when designed with research concerns in mind, such tasks also carry the risk of appearing like tests to classroom participants, as indeed was found by Pica et al. (2006). Their attractiveness for communication can be offset by their inconsistency with the content of the classroom curriculum. Learners might be willing to carry them out over the short term, but are likely to lose interest in them over time.

To enhance their authenticity and ensure their long-term use, research tasks first need to be integrated into curriculum texts, topics and assignments, and have enough variety to warrant sustained participation. With this in mind, Pica et al. (2006) based their research tasks on the texts students were asked to read and discuss in their daily classroom life. In keeping with the course emphasis on academic English, task directions began with a purpose statement, i.e., that the task would help the students become *more accurate and precise* in their speaking and writing in areas such as reviewing, editing, organizing and reporting information. The tasks were simple to implement for long-term application by the teacher, as the researchers could not be on hand on a daily basis. Teacher, researcher, and student involvement was ongoing in task design, piloting, and revision. Directions were re-worded and revised frequently, based on numerous pilot runs. Such preparation, though labor intensive, was considered an investment by the researchers, affording both the opportunity to carry out more than one study, and to collaborate, present, and publish their work over time.

When discussing the value of interaction in the classroom, it is important to note that most studies to date have been conducted in English as a second language (ESL) contexts. We must keep in mind that a great deal of classroom learning goes on in English as a foreign language (EFL) and other foreign language contexts, which are equally deserving of researchers' attention. A few studies have examined this issue (e.g. Alcón Soler & García Mayo 2008, 2009; Alegría de la Colina & García Mayo 2009; Fujii & Mackey 2009; García Mayo 2002a, 2002b; García Mayo & Alcón Soler 2002), but there is still ample room for further research. In a concise overview of relevant findings, Philp and Tognini (2009) point out several key issues in foreign language interaction, such as the shared L1 which frequently leads to code switching, or the different amounts and types of corrective feedback that have been observed in FL contexts as opposed to SL contexts.

Conclusion and implications

The chapter has highlighted theoretical and empirical perspectives on L2 interaction. It has introduced theoretical constructs and reviewed claims about input, interaction, feedback, and output processes. It has described ways in which task-based interaction has contributed to this research and ended with a brief discussion of the ways in which classroom interaction can provide an environment in which instruction and research can thrive. As an added bonus, the classroom, as a consistent context in which learning through interaction occurs over an extended time, also gives researchers the opportunity to address current questions on SLA. This partnership between researchers and practitioners encourages the application of principles of interaction-driven learning and the use of tasks to the classroom, and the everyday needs and requirements of teachers, learners and curriculum.

As this chapter argues and illustrates, over the years, interaction has taken on a much broader role in the field of SLA, contributing research that has informed SLA theory about *noticing the gap* (Schmidt & Frota 1986), *focus on form* (Long 1996), and *modified, comprehensible output* (Swain 1985), and validated theoretical claims about the role of negative evidence (White 1991), the importance of recasts in meaning focused contexts (Doughty & Varela 1998), and *readiness for learning* (Pienemann 1989). Studies carried out across a range of interaction contexts and activities have informed the field about the role of interaction in meeting learners' needs to obtain input and evidence found in the texts they read and hear, and in the responses they receive to their questions and comments.

The findings regarding the role of interaction in SLA have also suggested new directions for the field, e.g. to lengthen the treatment and research time for both individual studies and multi-study comparisons.

From its introduction of theoretical constructs such as *evidence, noticing the gap, focus on form* and *readiness,* to its contributions of task-based activities and classrooms sites, the study of L2 interaction has made many contributions to SLA theory. As research has revealed, L2 interaction provides a rich resource for SLA. Through interaction, learners can access samples of L2 text and discourse. These can serve as evidence or information that learners can apply to their developing interlanguage system and use to modify and reconfigure its linguistic and communicative features. Understanding, describing, and predicting what makes the L2 accessible and the learner successful is central to the numerous studies described in this chapter. Findings from these studies have informed the broader field of SLA at empirical and theoretical levels.

Nonetheless, there is still much to explore in interaction research. Apart from the issues regarding classroom compatibility, treatment durations, and longer post test periods mentioned earlier in this chapter – all of which are in need of further study – a note regarding participant selection is also in order. The over-whelming majority of interaction studies draw their participants from university programs and/or affiliated language schools. While this is frequently the most feasible option for recruiting a large number of L2 learners, it is imperative to acknowledge that the research is extremely biased towards a 'prime-of-life' adult, academic population (Bigelow & Tarone 2004). While children are also fairly well represented in the research, non-academic contexts or groups with low literacy levels are hardly ever considered though they are certainly not exempt from learn-ing a second language. One exception is a study among low literacy learners by Bigelow, Delmas, Hansen and Tarone (2006), who found differences in percep-tion and recall of oral recasts according to literacy levels. Another example of work among nontraditional learners is a small-scale study by Mackey and Sachs (2012), which focused on older learners of English as a second language who were recruited from a Latino community center for senior citizens and a public charter school for adult education. Learners participated in interactional tasks with na-tive speakers and received corrective feedback. Results indicated a connection between L2 development and working memory capacity. While more challenging in their design, studies that look beyond the readily available college student par-ticipants will go a long way towards broadening the field of SLA and interaction research, thus further advancing our knowledge of how interaction helps push L2 development.

Lastly, more research is needed on the emerging field of computer-assisted language learning (CALL) or computer-mediated communication (CMC). More and more learners these days make use of chatrooms and similar internet fea-tures to interact with one another, and research on such online interaction has slowly been emerging alongside this development. While feedback appears to be provided in chatroom contexts (see Loewen & Reissner 2009), there are many crucial differences between computer-mediated interaction and face-to-face in-teraction. For one thing, responses frequently overlap, thus sometimes removing the feedback from its referent (Lai, Fei & Roots 2008). The text-based mode of communication also allows for more planning time (Smith 2010) as well as in-creased review of one's own utterances, which has been shown to lead to more self-corrections (Lai & Zhao 2006). Given the dramatically increasing use of technology in many language learning contexts, further research in this field is greatly needed.

As with previous innovations in the history of research in this area, these, among other new avenues for exploration, are likely to further expand our under-standing of the potential and limitations of interaction for second language learn-ing in different contexts, and lead to applications for language pedagogy.

References

Al Shatter, G. 2011. Processability approach to Arabic L2 teaching and syllabus design. *Australian Review of Applied Linguistics* 34: 127–147.

Alcón Soler, E. & García Mayo, M.P. 2008. Focus on form and learning outcomes with young learners in the foreign language classroom. In *Second Language Acquisition and the Younger Learner, Child's Play?* [Language Learning & Language Teaching 23], J. Philp, R. Oliver & A. Mackey (eds), 173–192. Amsterdam: John Benjamins.

Alcón Soler, E. & García Mayo, M.P. 2009. Interaction and language learning in foreign language contexts: Introduction. *International Review of Applied Linguistics* 47: 239–243.

Alegría de la Colina, A. & García Mayo, M.P. 2009. Oral interaction in task-based EFL learning: The use of the L1 as a cognitive tool. International Review of Applied Linguistics 47: 325–345.

Allen, L. 2000. Form-meaning connections and the French causative: An experiment in processing instruction. *Studies in Second Language Acquisition* 22: 69–84.

Ammar, A. 2008. Prompts and recasts: Differential effects on second language morphosyntax. *Language Teaching Research* 12: 183–210.

Ayoun, D. 2001. The role of negative and positive feedback in the second language acquisition of the passé composé and imparfait. *The Modern Language Journal* 85: 226–243.

Bigelow, M. & Tarone, E. 2004. The role of literacy level in SLA: Doesn't who we study determine what we know? *TESOL Quarterly* 38: 689–700.

Bigelow, M., Delmas, R., Hansen, K., & Tarone, E. 2006. Literacy and the processing of oral recasts in SLA. *TESOL Quarterly* 40: 1–25.

Corder, S.P. 1967. The significance of learners' errors. *International Review of Applied Linguistics* 5: 161–169.

Crookes, G. & Gass, S. (eds). 1993. *Tasks and Language Learning: Integrating Theory and Practice.*Clevedon: Multilingual Matters.

Day, E. & Shapson, S. 1991. Integrating formal and functional approaches in language teaching in French immersion: An experimental study. *Language Learning* 41: 21–58.

DeKeyser, R.M. & Sokalski, K.J. 2001. The differential role of comprehension and production practice. *Language Learning* 51(1): 81–112.

De la Fuente, M.J. 2002. Negotiation and oral acquisition of L2 vocabulary: The roles of input and output in the receptive and productive acquisition of words. *Studies in Second Language Acquisition* 24: 81–112.

Di Biase, B. & Kawaguchi, S. 2002. Exploring the typological plausibility of processability theory: Language development in Italian second language and Japanese second language. *Second Language Research* 18: 274–302.

Dilans, G. 2010. Corrective feedback and L2 vocabulary development: Prompts and recasts in the adult ESL classroom. *The Canadian Modern Language Review* 66: 787–815.

Doughty, C. 2001. Cognitive underpinnings of focus on form. In *Cognition and Second Language Instruction*, P. Robinson (ed.), 206–257. Cambridge: CUP.

Doughty, C. & Varela, E. 1998. Communicative focus on form, In *Focus on Form in Classroom Second Language Acquisition*, C. Doughty & J. Williams (eds), 114–138. Cambridge: CUP.

Doughty, C. & Williams, J. 1998. Pedagogical choices in focus on form. In *Focus on Form in Classroom Second Language Acquisition*, C. Doughty & J. Williams (eds), 197–261. Cambridge: CUP.

Ellis, R. 1989. Are classroom and naturalistic second language acquisition the same?' A study of the classroom acquisition of German word order rules. *Studies in Second Language Acquisition* 23: 305–328.

Ellis, R. 1999. Making the classroom acquisition-rich. In *Learning a Second Language through Interaction* [Language Learning & Language Teaching 11], R. Ellis (ed.), 211–229. Amsterdam: John Benjamins.

Ellis, R. & Sheen, Y. 2006. Reexamining the role of recasts in second language acquisition. *Studies in Second Language Acquisition* 28: 575–600.

Erlam, R. & Loewen, S. 2010. Implicit and explicit recasts in L2 oral French interaction. *The Canadian Modern Language Review* 66: 877–905.

Fujii, A. & Mackey, A. 2009. Interactional feedback in learner-learner interactions in a task-based EFL classroom. *International Review of Applied Linguistics* 47: 267–301.

García Mayo, M.P. 2002a. The effectiveness of two form-focused tasks in advanced EFL pedagogy. *International Review of Applied Linguistics* 12: 156–175.

García Mayo, M.P. 2002b.Interaction in advanced EFL grammar pedagogy: A comparison of form-focused tasks. *International Journal of Educational Research* 37(3–4): 323–341

García Mayo, M.P. (ed.). 2007. *Investigating Tasks in Formal Language Learning*. Clevedon: Multilingual Mattters.

García Mayo, M.P. & Alcón Soler, E. 2002. The role of interaction in instructed language learning. Introduction. *International Journal of Educational Research* 37: 233–236.

Gass, S.M. & Varonis, E. 1985. Task variation and nonnative/nonnative negotiation of meaning. In *Input in Second Language Acquisition*, S.M. Gass & C. Madden (eds), 41–161. Rowley MA: Newbury House.

Goo, J. & Mackey, A. 2013. The case against the case against recasts. *Studies in Second Language Acquisition* 35(1). In press.

Harley, B. 1989. Functional grammar in French immersion: A classroom experiment. *Applied Linguistics* 10: 331–359.

Harley, B. 1993. Instructional strategies and SLA in early French immersion. *Studies in Second Language in Acquisition* 15: 245–260.

He, X. & Ellis, R. 1999. Modified output and the acquisition of word meanings. In *Learning a Second Language through Interaction*, R. Ellis (ed.), 115–132. Amsterdam: John Benjamins.

Hulstijn, J. H. 2001. Intentional and incidental second-language vocabulary learning: A reappraisal of elaboration, rehearsal and automaticity. In *Cognition and Second Language Instruction*, P. Robinson (ed.), 258–286. Cambridge: CUP.

Iwashita, N. 2003. Negative feedback and positive evidence in task-based interaction: differential effects on L2 development. *Studies in Second Language Acquisition* 25: 1–36.

Izumi, S. 2002. Output, input enhancement, and the noticing hypothesis. *Studies in Second Language Acquisition* 24: 541–577.

Keck, C. M., Iberri-Shea, G., Tracy-Ventura, N. & Wa-Mbaleka, S. 2006. Investigating the empirical link between task-based interaction and acquisition: A meta-analysis. In *Synthesizing Research on Language Learning and Teaching* [Language Learning & Language Teaching 13], J. M. Norris & L. Ortega (eds.), 91–131. Amsterdam: John Benjamins.

Krashen, S. 1976. Formal and informal environments in language acquisition and language learning. *TESOL Quarterly* 10: 157–168.

Krashen, S. 1981. *Second Language Acquisition and Second Language Learning*. Pergamon: Oxford.

Lai, Ch. & Zhao, Y. 2006. Noticing and text-based chat. *Language Learning and Technology* 10: 102–120.

Lai, C., Fei, F. & Roots.R. 2008. The contingency of recasts and noticing. *CALICO Journal* 26: 70–90.

Laufer, B. & Hulstijn, J. 2001. Incidental vocabulary acquisition in a second language: The construct of task-induced involvement. *Applied Linguistics* 22: 1–26.

Leeman, J. 2003. Recasts and second language development: Beyond negative evidence. *Studies in Second Language Acquisition* 25(1): 37–63.

Lightbown, P. & Spada, N. 1990. Focus on form and corrective feedback in communicative language teaching: effects on second language learning. *Studies in Second Language Acquisition* 12: 429–448.

Linnell, J. 1995. Negotiation as a Context for Learning Syntax in a Second Language. PhD dissertation, University of Pennsylvania.

Loewen, S. & Philp, J. 2006. Recasts in the adult L2 classroom: Characteristics, explicitness and effectiveness. *The Modern Language Journal* 90: 536–556.

Loewen, S. & Reissner, S. 2009. A comparison of incidental focus on form in the second language classroom and chatroom. *Computer Assisted Language Learning* 22: 101–114.

Long, M. 1981. Input, interaction, and second language acquisition. In *Native and Foreign Language Acquisition, Annals of the New York Academy of Sciences* [Vol. 379], H. Winitz (ed.), 259–278.

Long, M. 1996. The role of the linguistic environment in second language acquisition. In *Handbook of Language Acquisition: Second language Acquisition* [Vol. 2], W.C. Ritchie & T.K. Bhatia (eds), 413–458. New York NY: Academic Press.

Long, M., Inagaki, S. & Ortega, L. 1998. The role of implicit negative feedback in SLA. *The Modern Language Journal* 82: 357–371.

Long, M. & Robinson, P. 1998. Focus on form: Theory, research, and practice. In *Focus on Form in Classroom Second Language Acquisition*, C. Doughty & J. Williams (eds), 15–41. Cambridge: CUP.

Lyster, R. 1998. Negotiation of form, recasts, and explicit correction in relation to error types and learner repair in immersion classrooms. *Language Learning* 48: 183–218.

Lyster, R. & Ranta, L. 1997. Corrective feedback and learner uptake: Negotiation of form in communicative classrooms. *Studies in Second Language Acquisition* 19: 37–66.

Lyster, R. & Saito, K. 2010. Oral feedback in classroom SLA: A meta-analysis. *Studies in Second Language Acquisition* 32: 265–302.

Mackey, A. & Goo, J. 2007. Interaction research in SLA: A meta-analysis and research synthesis. In *Conversational Interaction in Second Language Acquisition: A Collection of Empirical Studies*, A. Mackey (ed.), 407–452. Oxford: OUP.

Mackey, A. & McDonough, K. 2000. Communicative tasks, conversational interaction and linguistic form: An empirical study of Thai. *Foreign Language Annals* 33: 82–91.

Mackey, A. & Oliver, R. 2002. Interactional feedback and children's L2 development. *System* 30: 459–477.

Mackey, A. & Philp, J. 1998. Conversational interaction and second language development: Recasts, responses, and red herrings? *The Modern Language Journal* 82: 338–356.

Mackey, A. & Sachs, R. 2012. Older learners in SLA research: A first look at working memory, feedback, and L2 development. *Language Learning* 62(3): 704–740.

McDonough, K. 2005. Identifying the impact of negative feedback and learners' responses on ESL question development. *Studies in Second Language Acquisition* 27: 79–103.

McDonough, K. 2007. Interactional feedback and the emergence of simple past activity verbs in L2 English. In *Conversational Interaction in Second Language Acquisition: A Collection of Empirical Studies*, A. Mackey (ed.), 323–338. Oxford: OUP.

McDonough, K., & Mackey, A. 2006. Responses to recasts: Repetitions, primed production, and linguistic development. *Language Learning* 56: 693–720.

Muranoi, H. 2000. Focus on form through interaction enhancement: Integrating formal instruction into a communicative task in EFL classrooms. *Language Learning* 50: 617–673.

Newton, J. & Kennedy, G. 1996. Effects of communication tasks on the grammatical relations marked by second language learners. *System* 24: 309–322.

Nicholas, H., Lightbown, P. & Spada, N. 2001. Recasts as feedback to language learners. *Language Learning* 51: 719–758.

Nunan, D. 1989. *Designing Tasks for the Communicative Classroom*. Cambridge: CUP.

Paninos, D. 2005. The Role of Output in Noticing of Input for Second Language Acquisition. PhD dissertation, University of Pennsylvania.

Philp, J. & Tonigni, R. 2009. Language acquisition in foreign language contexts and the differential benefits of interaction. *International Review of Applied Linguistics* 47: 245–266.

Pica, T. 2002. Subject matter content: How does it assist the interactional and linguistic needs of classroom language learners? *The Modern Language Journal* 86: 1–19.

Pica, T. & Doughty, C. 1985a. Input and interaction in the communicative language classroom: A comparison of teacher-fronted and group activities. In *Input in Second Language Acquisition*, S. Gass & C. Madden (eds), 115–132. Rowley MA: Newbury House,

Pica, T. & Doughty, C. 1985b. The role of group work in classroom second language acquisition. *Studies in Second Language Acquisition* 7: 233–248.

Pica, T. & Washburn, G. 2003. Negative evidence in language classroom activities: A study of its availability and accessibility to language learners. *ITL Journal of Applied Linguistics* 141: 301–344

Pica, T., Holliday, L., Lewis, N. & Morgenthaler, L. 1989. Comprehensible output as an outcome of linguistic demands on the learner. *Studies in Second Language Acquisition* 11: 63–90.

Pica, T., Kang, H. & Sauro, S. 2006. Information gap tasks: Their multiple roles and contributions to interaction research methodology. *Studies in Second Language Acquisition* 28: 301–338.

Pica, T., Sauro, S. & Lee, J. 2007. *Three Approaches to Focus on Form: A Comparison Study of their Role in SLA Processes and Outcomes*. Champaign-Urbana IL: Second Language Research Forum.

Pica, T., Lincoln-Porter, F., Paninos, D. & Linnell, J. 1996. Language learner interaction: How does it address the input, output, and feedback needs of second language learners? *TESOL Quarterly* 30: 59–84.

Pienemann, M. 1985. Learnability and syllabus construction. In *Modeling and Assessing Second Language Acquisition*, K. Hyltenstam & M. Pienemann (eds.), 23–75. Clevedon: Multilingual Matters.

Pienemann, M. 1989. Is language teachable? Psycholinguistic experiments and hypotheses. *Applied Linguistics* 10: 52–79.

Pienemann, M. 1998. *Language Processing and Second Language Development: Processibility Theory* [Studies in Bilingualism 15]. Amsterdam: John Benjamins.

Prabhu. 1987. *Second Language Pedagogy*. Oxford: OUP.

Schmidt, R. & Frota, S. 1986. Developing basic conversational ability in a second language: A case study of an adult learner of Portuguese. In *Talking to Learn: Conversation in Second Language Acquisition*, R. Day (ed.), 237–336. Rowley MA: Newbury House.

Shehadeh, A. 1999. Non-native speakers' production of modified comprehensible output and second language learning. *Language Learning* 49: 627–675.

Shehadeh, A. 2001. Self- and other-initiated modified output during task-based interaction. *TESOL Quarterly* 35: 433–457.

Smith, B. 2005. The relationship between negotiated interaction, learner uptake, and lexical acquisition in task-based computer-mediated communication. *TESOL Quarterly* 39: 33–58.

Smith, B. 2010. Employing eye-tracking techniques in researching the effectiveness of recasts in CMC. In *Directions and Prospects for Educational Linguistics*, F.M. Hult (ed.), 79–98. New York NY: Springer.

Swain, M. 1985. Communicative competence: Some roles of comprehensible input and comprehensible output in its development. In *Input in Second Language Acquisition*, S. M. Gass & C.G. Madden (eds), 235–253. Rowley MA: Newbury House.

Swain, M. 1993. The output hypothesis: Just speaking and writing aren't enough. *The Canadian Modern Language Review* 50: 158–164.

Swain, M. 1998. Focus on form through conscious reflection. In *Focus on Form in Classroom Second Language Acquisition*, C. Doughty & J. Williams (eds.), 64–81. Cambridge: CUP.

Swain, M. & Lapkin, S. 1998. Interaction and second language learning: Two adolescent French immersion students working together. *The Modern Language Journal* 82: 320–337.

Swain, M. & Lapkin, S. 2001. Focus on form through collaborative dialogue: Exploring task effects. In *Researching Pedagogic Tasks: Second Language Learning, Teaching and Testing*, M. Bygate, P. Skehan & M. Swain (eds.), 99–118. New York NY: Longman.

Takashima, H. & Ellis, R. 1999. Output enhancement and the acquisition of the past tense. In *Learning a Second Language through Interaction* [Studies in Bilingualism 17], R. Ellis (ed.), 173–188. Amsterdam: John Benjamins.

Trahey, M. & White, L. 1993. Positive evidence and preemption in the second language classroom. *Studies in Second Language Acquisition* 15: 181–204.

VanPatten, B. & Cadierno, T. 1993. Explicit instruction and input processing. *Studies in Second Language Acquisition* 15: 225–243.

White, L. 1991. Adverb placement in second language acquisition: Some effects of positive and negative evidence in the classroom. *Second Language Research* 7: 133–161.

White, J. 1998. Getting the learner's attention: a typographical input enhancement study In *Focus on Form in Classroom Second Language Acquisition*, C. Doughty & J. Williams (eds), 85–113. Cambridge: CUP.

Willis, J.1996. *A Framework for Task-Based Learning*. Harlow: Longman.

Yang, Y. & Lyster, R. 2010. Effects of form-focused practice and feedback on Chinese EFL learners' acquisition of regular and irregular past tense forms. *Studies in Second Language Acquisition* 32: 235–263.

CHAPTER 4

Skill Acquisition Theory and the role of practice in L2 development

Roy Lyster and Masatoshi Sato
McGill University and Universidad Andrés Bello

This chapter presents an overview of research in support of Skill Acquisition Theory and the claim that contextualized oral practice in conjunction with feedback promotes continued second language growth. Skill acquisition is explained as a gradual transition from effortful use to more automatic use of the target language, with the ultimate goal of achieving faster and more accurate processing. By reviewing different yet compatible theoretical orientations of knowledge representations (e.g., implicit/explicit knowledge, exemplar-based/rule-based representations), the interplay between declarative and procedural knowledge is explained as bidirectional and relative to the context of instruction. The differential effects of guided practice and communicative practice are addressed and their benefits in conjunction with feedback are highlighted through reference to classroom-based second language acquisition (SLA) research. Finally, future directions regarding research on practice effects and types of practice are suggested.

Introduction

Proponents of Skill Acquisition Theory propose that second language (L2) learning entails a gradual transition from effortful use to more automatic use of the target language, brought about through practice and feedback in meaningful contexts. This chapter will review research that provides support for Skill Acquisition Theory and the corollary claim that, in order to promote continued L2 growth in classroom settings, opportunities for contextualized practice are needed to complement input-driven approaches designed to trigger noticing and awareness of target language features. We begin first by explaining the basic tenets of Skill Acquisition Theory, including proceduralization and automaticity, and their relevance to L2 acquisition. Because the goal of L2 learning is to achieve faster and more accurate processing during both comprehension and production, we underscore the similarities between procedural knowledge and implicit knowledge, while acknowledging different interpretations of the dynamic interplay between knowledge representations and processing. Specifically, we argue that, depending on instructional goals, contextualized practice can strategically serve not only to proceduralize declarative knowledge but also to help learners reassess and restructure inaccurate knowledge representations already stored in long-term memory. Finally, we illustrate, through reference to classroom-based second language acquisition (SLA) research, the benefits of providing L2 classroom learners with opportunities for contextualized practice in conjunction with feedback as a means to restructure and proceduralize their developing knowledge of the target language.

Proceduralization, automaticity, and L2 acquisition

Skill Acquisition Theory posits two interrelated representational systems comprising declarative knowledge and procedural knowledge. Declarative knowledge is static information such as historical or geographical facts encoded in memory. Procedural knowledge entails knowing how to do things, including the ability to apply rule-based knowledge to cognitive as well as motor operations. Common examples of skill acquisition in our daily lives are, for instance, how we learn to drive a stick-shift car or to play the piano. With respect to language, declarative knowledge refers to explicit mental representations of language items that may include word definitions or grammar rules, whereas procedural knowledge refers to knowledge about how to perform cognitive operations, such as producing language with less or no effort by accessing items stored in long-term memory.

According to Skill Acquisition Theory, declarative knowledge can be transformed into procedural knowledge through meaningful practice over many trials (Anderson 1983, 2005; DeKeyser 2007b). That is, repeated practice with feedback at propitious moments promotes the acceleration of *meaningful learning* rather than the acquisition of *mechanical skill* (Anderson, Greeno, Kline & Neves 1981: 206) and thereby contributes to automatization. As Anderson and Schunn (2000: 2) emphasized, the theory places "a premium on the practice which is required to learn permanently the components of the desired competence". Anderson's Adaptive Control of Thought (ACT*) model posits that these skills start from a stage where rules are learned in an explicit manner; then, after practice, tasks can be completed rapidly and efficiently with a smaller error rate even without thinking about the components and subcomponents involved in executing the task. A stage can be reached where the rules are no longer accessible for explanation. The process of this knowledge transformation is called proceduralization.[1]

Automaticity theory too pertains to the idea of facilitating automatic processing with less reliance on controlled processing. Schneider and Fisk (1983) argued that automatic productions are modular and executed according to hierarchical relationships among different skills. Because there is an upper limit to human attention, the number of tasks requiring controlled processing that can be executed concurrently is limited. What is necessary is practice to automatize the required skills so that attention can be freed up for deploying other skills. During this stage of automatization, controlled and automatic processes constantly interact. In other words, on the one hand, automatic processing may initiate controlled processing (e.g., by attentional response); on the other hand, controlled processing "modifies memory and leads to the development of automatic processing" (Schneider, Dumais & Shiffrin 1984: 23; see also Whitaker 1983).

Changes in knowledge representations and retrieval have been shown in neurocognitive and neurolinguistic research as well where memory circuits have been extensively investigated through brain-imaging techniques such as functional magnetic resonance imaging (fMRI) and event-related potentials (ERPs) (see Sabourin, Brien & Tremblay, this volume). Although without reference to Skill Acquisition Theory, Ullman (2004) argued that declarative and procedural knowledge are stored in different areas in the brain and, respectively, are associated with item-based knowledge (e.g., lexicons, bound morphemes, irregular forms, idioms) and rule-based knowledge (i.e., grammatical structures that require computations). According to this model, instead of a shift in knowledge types (i.e., proceduralization), it is claimed that degrees of dependence on the two types of memory systems increasingly change. Ullman (2001a) argued that late L2 learning (i.e., after puberty) relies on the declarative system whereas first language acquisition is largely associated with the procedural system. Importantly, it is argued that practice increases performance in procedural memory, helping learners to become increasingly dependent on the procedural system (Poldrack, Prabhakaran, Seger & Gabrieli 1999). This argument supports practice effects in Skill Acquisition Theory (see also Chein & Schneider 2005; Paradis 2009; Ullman 2001b, 2005; Van der Lely & Ullman 2001).

1.　Anderson's ACT models have evolved with slight modifications (e.g., how he sees the relationships between working memory and declarative knowledge or directionality of the shift of knowledge) over 20 years starting from ACTE (Anderson 1976), to ACT* (Anderson 1983), and to ACT-R (Anderson 1993). However, the basic tenets (e.g., practice effects and necessity of feedback) are the same among the models.

Fluency, speed of retrieval, and implicit knowledge

Automaticity is closely related to speed of processing as well as utterance fluency (Segalowitz 2010). Following Newell and Rosenbloom (1981) and in line with other SLA researchers (e.g., Robinson 1997), DeKeyser (2001) explained automatization from the perspective of the *power law of practice*: acquisition of a cognitive skill is defined by a power function which is explained by the equation $RT = a + bN^{-c}$, in which RT stands for reaction time.[2] That is, reaction time (or rather, to be more precise, the logarithm of reaction time) for a particular task decreases linearly with the logarithm of the number of practice trials taken; this learning curve of performance speed has been tested in various contexts of acquisition of cognitive skills (see Langley, Laird & Rogers 2009). Invoking foreign language learning as an illustration of learners sometimes achieving fluency while remembering grammar rules, Anderson (2005) argued that declarative and procedural knowledge can coexist although "the procedural, not the declarative, knowledge governs the skilled performance [fluency]" (2005: 282). Segalowitz and Freed (2004) posited a connection between L2 lexical access and oral fluency, claiming that (a) being able to access meanings quickly and efficiently reduces factors such as slow speech rate, pauses, and hesitation, which otherwise give listeners the impression of dysfluent speech, and (b) reaction times give information regarding readiness for oral gains because if a learner cannot process the given input quickly, he or she is unlikely to be ready for developing oral production skills (see also Samuels & Flor 1997). More recently, de Jong and Perfetti (2011) examined the effectiveness of a fluency-focused oral activity (i.e., the 4/3/2 task) on the development of temporal aspects of spontaneous production (e.g., speech rates). The learners who repeated the same speech several times (but during an individual computerized activity) improved their speech by reducing the length of pauses, increasing syllables-per-minute, and lengthening stretches of speech. Importantly, this effect was maintained in the long-term and the acquired knowledge was transferred to a new context, suggesting that successful proceduralization had occurred.

It is too simplistic, however, to define automaticity solely in relation to speed. The construct of automaticity, which can be considered as "the end result of a process of automatization...rather than of automatization as the process leading up to automaticity (which has proven hard to define)" (DeKeyser 2001: 130), has more specific criteria. Segalowitz (2000) explained that automaticity entails characteristics such as fast processing, ballistic processing, load independent processing, effortless processing, unconscious processing, and shift to instance processing

---

2. *N*: block number; a: the asymptote of learning; b: the difference between initial and asymptotic performance; c: learning rate (see details in Newell & Rosenbloom 1981).

(see also Schmidt 1992, though he is skeptical of applying Skill Acquisition Theory to fluency development). Hulstijn and de Graaff (1994) also argued that rapid execution of explicit knowledge (or declarative knowledge) should not alone be directly considered as successful proceduralization. This is because another important criterion of automatization is parallel processing and, thus, "merely observing that performance was fast does not necessarily indicate it was automatic" (Segalowitz 2003: 385; see Segalowtiz & Segalowitz 1993 for a distinction between speed-up and automatization). That is, speed is an absolute evaluation of performance but not tantamount to cognitive processing and thus may be an *epiphenomenon of automaticity* (Hulstijn, Van Gelderen & Schoonen 2009: 580).

Speed of retrieval during oral production is associated not only with fluency but also with implicit as opposed to explicit knowledge. In this regard, Skill Acquisition Theory shares certain dimensions with research on implicit/explicit knowledge. R. Ellis (1993) originally distinguished implicit/explicit and procedural/declarative dimensions in terms of (a) consciousness and the degree of control for the former, and (b) knowledge and process for the latter. However, he recently stated that these two knowledge types are similar: "implicit knowledge is 'procedural' in the sense conferred on this term in the ACT-R cognitive architecture" (R. Ellis 2009: 11). In fact, Anderson has also used the terms implicit knowledge and procedural knowledge interchangeably (Anderson 2005; Anderson & Lebiere 1998). It can be said, therefore, that procedural knowledge is functionally equivalent to implicit knowledge (but see Hulstijn 2002 for criticisms). What distinguishes the discussion of implicit/explicit knowledge from that of proceduralization then is that Skill Acquisition Theory focuses on the shift in knowledge (i.e., developmental processes) and how practice can facilitate this process, rather than on the nature of the types of knowledge and how they do or do not coexist in cognitive structures.

Although the question of how these two types of knowledge are related (or unrelated) and how they differentially contribute to L2 performance is still under debate (Bialystok 1981, 1994b; N. Ellis 1994, 2002; Han & Ellis 1998; White & Ranta 2002), these knowledge types are generally distinguished in terms of degrees of consciousness (Schmidt 1994) and representational system (Bialystok 1991; Dienes & Perner 1999). That is, when humans deploy explicit knowledge, they have knowledge of the procedures involved (e.g., being able to explain grammatical structures of a language), whereas implicit knowledge is constantly being used yet we are not necessarily aware of the underlying processing (e.g., speaking in our first language). As Hulstijn (2005) explained, explicit and implicit knowledge differ "in the extent to which one has or has not (respectively) an awareness of the regularities underlying the information one has knowledge of, and to what extent one can or cannot (respectively) verbalize these regularities" (2005: 130).

Because implicit processes catalyze first language acquisition, which entails automatic processes from birth (N. Ellis 2005) and thus seems relatively effortless, developing implicit knowledge is arguably the ultimate goal of L2 learning, regardless of the underlying process: that is, whether it must begin as implicit knowledge or whether it can derive from explicit knowledge. The issue that arises in classroom settings, however, is not only the extent to which explicit knowledge can become part of a learner's implicit system, but also the extent to which a learner's implicit knowledge needs to become more explicit, especially when the knowledge representations require restructuring. This issue will be further pursued in the next section.

The interplay between declarative and procedural knowledge

Skill Acquisition Theory provides a helpful framework for understanding L2 development in classroom settings and especially the developmental plateaus that many classroom learners reportedly attain. Among others (e.g., Bange, Carol & Griggs 2005; de Bot 1996; de Jong & Perfetti 2011; Hulstijn 1990; Johnson 1996; Lyster 1994, 2004, 2007; McLaughlin 1987, 1990; McLaughlin & Heredia 1996; O'Malley & Chamot 1990; Ranta & Lyster 2007; Sato & Lyster 2012; Towell & Hawkins 1994), DeKeyser in particular has argued in his program of research that the development of L2 knowledge is similar to the acquisition of other cognitive skills, especially in foreign language classrooms (DeKeyser 1997, 1998b, 2001, 2007b). Learners in such contexts allegedly commence the L2 developmental process through explicit information provided to them about how grammar works and, in successful cases, proceduralization is attained as automatized knowledge through practice. As proceduralization progresses, learners are able to draw on automatized knowledge so that cognitive resources are freed up for "processing message content instead of language" (DeKeyser 2007a: 288). In addition, achieving automaticity in L2 learning may help learners to be independent of interferences, thereby motivating them to further improve their skills and seek more contact with the target language (Segalowitz 2000, 2003; see also N. Ellis 2005; Segalowitz & Gatbonton 1995).

Characteristic of Skill Acquisition Theory, therefore, is the view that procedural knowledge derives gradually from declarative knowledge through meaningful practice. However, as Segalowitz (2003) noted, empirical research has not yet yielded "a tidy picture whereby learning grammatical structure proceeds simply from knowledge of examples to automatized (proceduralized) rules [or] from the effortful application of rules to the retrieval of memorized instances" (2003: 400). In this regard, the interplay between declarative and procedural knowledge in the context of instructed SLA is best seen as bidirectional and influenced by the in-structional setting. This is in keeping with Lyster and Mori's (2006) Counterbal-ance Hypothesis, which predicts that interlanguage restructuring can be triggered by instructional interventions that orient learners in the direction opposite to that which their target language learning environment has accustomed them. In a sim-ilar vein, Skehan (1998) argued for pushing learners who are either form-oriented or meaning-oriented in the opposite direction in order to strike a balance between the two orientations (see also Lyster 2007; Sato 2011).

On the one hand, in traditional second or foreign language classrooms that provide more opportunities to analyze the target language than to actually use it for communication, Bange, Carol and Griggs (2005) noted a tendency for instruc-tion to be concerned primarily with developing declarative knowledge and called for more opportunities for contextualized practice to help students proceduralize their declarative knowledge. They also identified an obvious challenge in this re-gard: procedural knowledge is acquired through action, so learners are expected, paradoxically, to accomplish actions they have not yet acquired. They argued that the solution to the paradox lies in interaction and, more specifically, in Bruner's (1977) notion of scaffolding between expert and novice. That is, to help learners to begin proceduralizing their declarative knowledge, teachers need to provide op-portunities for contextualized practice replete with scaffolding that enables learn-ers to express what they would be unable to express on their own.

On the other hand, in the case of more communicatively oriented or content-based settings, practice opportunities are also crucial, although not necessarily for proceduralizing rules already encoded as declarative knowledge via explicit in-struction but rather for developing declarative knowledge from the procedural knowledge that they acquired in more or less naturalistic ways. As Johnson (1996) pointed out, *naturalistic* approaches to language teaching, such as immersion, are designed to bypass the initial development of declarative knowledge and serve instead to directly develop procedural encodings of the target language. He argued that encodings that come into the system in an already proceduralized form "quickly become highly automatized and impermeable to change" (1996: 99; see also McLaughlin 1987). An early emphasis on communication in many communi-cative and content-based programs pushes learners to deploy procedures that op-erate on linguistic knowledge that has not yet been acquired in the target language, thus encouraging recourse to other mental representations such as knowledge of first language structures. In such contexts, the challenge for teachers is to push students to develop more target-like representations that otherwise compete with more easily accessible interlanguage forms (Ranta & Lyster 2007). Also with re-spect to learners who develop target language knowledge in the initial stages that is largely implicit and composed of unanalyzed chunks, Bialystok (1994a) argued that instruction designed to increase the analysis of implicit knowledge helps to make such knowledge more readily accessible and thus supports the development of literacy skills.

Most theoretical accounts of L2 development point to the important role of unanalyzed chunks or formulaic expressions, which "are stored and retrieved whole from memory at the time of use, rather than being subject to generation or analysis by the language grammar" (Wray 2002: 9). While contributing substantially to a learner's oral fluency, formulaic expressions provide a foundation for developing more rule-based knowledge later on. Thus, in classroom settings where L2 learners rely on the use of formulaic language in their early production – whether in contexts of communicative language teaching (Gatbonton & Segalowitz 2005), immersion (Weber & Tardif 1991), or *submersion* (Wong Fillmore 1979) – teachers are encouraged to engage students, increasingly over time, in analyses of formulaic items as a means of developing a more generative rule-based system.

In this regard, whereas Myles, Hooper and Mitchell (1998) showed that some learners were able to slowly acquire the structures underlying their use of formulaic expressions without any guided instruction, other studies suggest that, without guided instruction, learners fail to acquire the rules underlying unanalyzed chunks (e.g., Tode 2003; see also Skehan 1998). This is where form-focused instruction (Spada 1997, 2011) can play a pivotal role by drawing on tenets of Skill Acquisition Theory. For example, Lyster (2007) operationalized form-focused interventions in the context of content-based instruction as (a) noticing and awareness tasks that enable learners to restructure interlanguage representations, and (b) practice activities that enable learners to proceduralize more target-like representations. In the context of communicative language teaching, Gatbonton and Segalowitz (2005) proposed an approach promoting fluency through *creative automatization* entailing genuinely communicative and inherently repetitive tasks that elicit formulaic language in contexts of contextualized practice: "To enhance the automatizing effects of these activities, specially designed form-focused activities are included, as needed" (2005: 345).

Types of practice

Form-focused instruction comprises both guided practice and communicative practice. Guided versus communicative practice parallels R. Ellis's (2003) distinction between focused production tasks, which elicit specific language features, and unfocused production tasks, which elicit general samples of learner language. At one end of the practice spectrum, guided practice activities are designed to engage learners' awareness of rule-based representations and are thus useful for circumventing their over-reliance on communication strategies (e.g., avoidance, circumlocution, recourse to L1) and effecting change in the interlanguage (Ranta & Lyster 2007). At the other end of the practice spectrum, communicative practice activities engage learners in more open-ended and meaning-focused communication with fewer constraints to ensure accuracy, thereby promoting confidence and motivation to use the L2 and providing a safe playing field for students to take risks and test hypotheses during oral production. However, because they encourage quick access to lexicalized exemplar-based representations that facilitate spontaneous production, open-ended communicative practice activities may not engage learners' language awareness to the same extent, thereby reducing the potential for changes to the interlanguage system (Skehan 1998). For this reason, in cases where the areas of linguistic difficulty are sources of persistent errors, guided practice activities may be more effective than communicative practice.

In this vein, Lyster (2007) compared the instructional treatments used in a set of studies conducted in French immersion classrooms (i.e., Day & Shapson 2001; Harley 1989, 1998; Lyster 1994, 2004; Wright 1996), which targeted L2 features that the student participants were known to find difficult (i.e., grammatical gender, verbs of motion, second-person pronouns, conditional mood, perfective and imperfective past tense distinctions). The comparison revealed that guided practice activities with role plays and language games, in tandem with noticing and awareness tasks, led to more robust changes than more open-ended communicative tasks involving negotiation for meaning (i.e., the creation of childhood albums and the design of futuristic space colonies). To reiterate, this finding pertains to immersion classrooms and not to traditional L2 instructional contexts where early studies (e.g., Montgomery & Eisenstein 1985; Savignon 1972; Spada, 1987) found positive results for integrating more opportunities for communicative practice into otherwise form-oriented language classes.

While the design of the immersion classroom intervention studies prevent firm conclusions concerning the effects of practice in isolation, their overall positive yet variable outcomes can nonetheless be explained through Skill Acquisition Theory. Day and Shapson (2001), for example, in their study of the effects of instruction on the acquisition of the conditional mood in French L2, attributed the smaller gains made by participants in speaking relative to larger gains in writing to a time-lag between internalization of rule-based declarative knowledge and automatization of that knowledge in speaking, caused by competition between newly acquired forms and more easily accessible interlanguage forms. Their analysis of the oral data revealed the use of interlanguage forms usually attributed to younger immersion students, leading the authors to conclude that the main oral communicative task was too open-ended to alter the use of automatized routines in speaking, whereas the more controlled written tasks allowed for editing and correction that contributed to greater improvement in writing. Similarly, Skill Acquisition Theory was invoked in Lyster's (1994) study of the effects of instruction on the acquisition of second-person pronouns by French L2 learners to explain that the 13–14-year old participants (who had been exposed to French for many years in their early immersion program) needed to *unlearn* their overuse of *tu* in formal contexts (1994: 281). The form-focused instruction entailed both awareness-raising and guided practice activities involving role plays and peer correction. The restructuring of knowledge representations and the more appropriate use of *vous* in formal contexts of oral and written production were claimed to have resulted more from the guided practice activities than from the awareness activities alone.

Other research as well supports the argument that to select appropriate types of practice one needs to consider that practice effects are skill-specific, task-specific, and context-specific (for specificity effects, see Healy & Bourne 1995). That is, if one engages in repeated practice in a writing task, he or she will transfer the skill only to writing tasks. For example, Martin-Chang and Levy (2005) compared two learning contexts for improvement in reading fluency. Participants were presented new words either in context or in isolation: In the context-training condition the children read words given in a story, whereas in the isolated-training condition they were presented words on a computer screen as a word-naming game. After the training phase, the participants completed a test in which they were asked to read passages. The analysis of reading accuracy and speed revealed that the participants retained the words that they learned in the context condition more than those in the isolated condition. At first glance, this study seems to provide support for communicative over decontextualized learning for L2 development, as one may presume that encoding words in context requires deeper processing than encoding decontextualized words. Importantly, however, in the follow-up experiment, Martin-Chang and Levy (2006) showed the opposite to be the case when the test was given in an isolated manner (i.e., reading words in lists). They argued that this is evidence in support of transfer-appropriate processing. That is, skills learned in a certain condition are best transferred to a similar condition (see Anderson 2005; De Ridder, Vangehuchten & Gómez 2007; Franks, Bilbrey, Lien & McNamara 2000; Morris, Bransford & Franks 1977; Segalowitz 2000). Accordingly, only when the goal of learning is to complete language drills can drilling exercises be the most effective (DeKeyser 1998a).

In this sense, not only types of practice should be carefully chosen to trigger a successful and desired proceduralization loop depending on the specific skills that L2 learners need, but also different types of practice should be provided to learners because acquiring an L2 involves a broad range of skills (e.g., grammatical knowledge, oral fluency, pronunciation, communicative ability, pragmatic skills, writing skills). Drawing on the construct of transfer-appropriate processing, Lightbown

(2008) recommended that contexts of practice be varied in order to promote "richer, more contextualized representations of the learned material" (2008: 39). Lightbown also identified pedagogical reasons for varying types of practice. By varying practice conditions, teachers can reach students with different learning styles and preferences and also stimulate learners' interests. DeKeyser (2010) as well stressed the need for teachers to adapt practice activities to their students both in terms of individual differences and school culture.

In the same vein, it may be a pedagogically effective option to provide learners with practice that is difficult. There is evidence in cognitive psychology suggesting that skills acquired in a more difficult condition can be retained longer with greater likelihood of being used in a different context. Schneider, Healy and Bourne (2002), for example, examined foreign language vocabulary learning with paired-associate tasks in more or less difficult conditions (e.g., cue words were either unfamiliar or familiar). Results showed that the learners were better at retaining and transferring words that they learned in more difficult conditions than in easier conditions (see also Battig 1979). Another component of successful practice may be spacing between practice sessions (i.e., the spacing effect: see Dempster 1989). Pavlik and Anderson (2005) tested the accumulative effects of practice on vocabulary retention. Participants in their experiment were presented sets of new vocabulary (Japanese words with English translations) with different interval lengths between presentations. Words presented at longer intervals were retained longer and this effect was more pronounced as the amount of practice increased, suggesting that practice distributed over a longer period of time is more effective than intensive practice in a short amount of time (see also Cepeda et al. 2009). However, the optimal level of difficulty or spacing between practice sessions has yet to be determined, especially because these theories have rarely been tested in educational settings (i.e., classrooms).

Practice and feedback

According to Anderson (2005), "*meaningful*, elaborative processing is effective because it is better at driving the brain processes that result in successful recall" (198; emphasis added). Specifically with respect to L2 development, Segalowitz (2000) argued as well that fluency develops as a result of practice that has not only been extensive and repetitive, but that has also been genuinely communicative in nature and therefore transfer-appropriate. From a classroom perspective, however, designing practice activities that are both communicative in purpose and guided – in the sense of requiring accurate use of specific target forms – is no small undertaking. This is where feedback can play a central role. Feedback can be provided "within the context of meaningful and sustained communicative interaction" (Spada & Lightbown 1993: 218) and thus creates contexts for practice under "real operating conditions" (Johnson 1996: 141). At the same time, feedback serves to draw attention to target language forms in ways that contribute to a restructuring of interlanguage representations, as confirmed by several meta-analyses (Li 2010; Lyster & Saito 2010; Mackey & Goo 2007; Russell & Spada 2006). Specifically targeting only classroom studies of corrective feedback, Lyster and Saito's (2010) meta-analysis revealed greater effects for oral feedback in free constructed-response measures involving spontaneous oral production than in metalinguistic judgment tasks. They invoked transfer-appropriate processing to interpret this finding, suggesting that feedback provided during actual target language use creates discourse contexts for contextualized practice that are more transfer appropriate than decontextualized grammar lessons or communicative language teaching without corrective feedback.

Two classroom studies comparing the effects of practice with and without feedback yielded results in line with Skill Acquisition Theory whereby the effects of contextualized practice proved greater with feedback than without. Doughty and Varela (1998) investigated the effects of *corrective recasts* (a repetition of the error followed by a recast if necessary) on simple and conditional past tense forms in two content-based English as a Second Language (ESL) classrooms. The class receiving feedback during science tasks that elicited the target forms showed significant improvement in comparison to a class engaged in the same production tasks but without feedback. Similarly, Saito and Lyster (2012) compared the effects of instruction with and without recasts targeting pronunciation errors in the use of English /ɹ/ by Japanese learners of English. All students participated in four hours of form-focused tasks designed to develop their argumentative skills in English while drawing their attention to the target forms through typographically enhanced input and providing opportunities for production practice. During these tasks, one group received recasts following their mispronunciation or unclear pronunciation of /ɹ/ while no corrective feedback was provided to the other. Learners receiving recasts made significantly more progress than those not receiving recasts, again revealing that practice in tandem with feedback provides more support for the restructuring of interlanguage forms than practice alone.

Three other classroom studies investigated the effects of practice activities in conjunction with awareness-raising tasks and two different types of corrective feedback: recasts, which provide learners with the correct form and thus considered an *input-providing* type of feedback, and prompts, considered an *output-pushing* type of feedback (R. Ellis 2006: 29). Lyster's (2004) study investigated the effects of instruction and feedback on immersion students' acquisition of grammatical gender in French while Ammar and Spada (2006) investigated the acquisition of possessive determiners by French-speaking ESL learners. Yang and Lyster (2010) investigated the effects of form-focused practice activities and different feedback treatments on the accurate use of regular and irregular past-tense forms in English as a Foreign Language (EFL) classrooms at the university level in China. In all three studies, students receiving prompts made significantly more gains overall and these results were interpreted to mean that retrieval and opportunities for contextualized practice are more effective catalysts for L2 development than merely noticing target forms during interaction. As with other types of practice, prompts aim to improve control over already-internalized forms by providing opportunities for "pushed" output, hypothesized by Swain (1985, 1988) to assist learners in restructuring their interlanguage. Because learners can be prompted only to retrieve knowledge that already exists in some form (e.g., declarative knowledge), Long (2007) questioned their purpose, arguing that "acquisition of new knowledge is the major goal, not 'automizing' the retrieval of existing knowledge" (2007: 102). However, the ultimate goal of instruction is not to continuously present only new knowledge to students, without sufficiently providing subsequent opportunities for assimilation and consolidation of that knowledge. In school-based learning, it is equally important that students engage in repeated opportunities to retrieve and restructure their knowledge of the target language.

The effectiveness of prompts in these studies, however, varied according to context, showing large effects in written but not oral tasks in Lyster's study, for low-proficiency but not high-proficiency learners in Ammar and Spada's study, and for regular but not irregular forms in Yang and Lyster's study. Results of the latter study indicated significant treatment effects for all groups engaged in the practice activities. The finding that regular past-tense forms were affected more by prompts than recasts, whereas irregular past-tense forms were influenced by both recasts and prompts, was interpreted in the light of Skehan's (1998) model of a dual-coding system comprising two inter-related representational systems: an analytic rule-based system and a memory-driven exemplar-based system. On the one hand, learners benefitted from the practice effects of a teacher's prompt to retrieve and apply the regular past-tense rule during online communication, because the generative and compact rule-based system is otherwise difficult for learners to access during online processing. On the other hand, learners improved their control over irregular past-tense forms already stored in the exemplar-based system simply by hearing them in the input, because items stored in the exemplar-based system can usually be retrieved quickly and with fewer processing constraints and no computation.

Finally, the effects of production practice in tandem with corrective feedback provided by peers trained to do so were examined in a study of peer interaction by Sato and Lyster (2012). Four university-level EFL classes were assigned either to corrective feedback training groups (prompts or recasts), a peer-interaction-only group, or a control group. During the 10-hour intervention delivered over one academic semester, learners in the feedback groups provided corrective feedback to each other during meaning-focused communicative activities, while learners in the peer-interaction-only group engaged in the communicative activities only. Importantly, these EFL learners had high levels of grammatical knowledge and the study was designed to assess the proceduralization of that knowledge via production practice. Analyses of both accuracy and fluency (i.e., speech rates) revealed that all three experimental groups showed significant improvement in fluency; however, significant accuracy development was observed only in the feedback groups where learners tended to modify their initial erroneous utterances following peer corrective feedback, regardless of feedback type – modified output followed 88% of the recasts and 86% of the prompts. While peer interaction provided learners with ample opportunities to engage in repeated practice that contributed to faster processing of their already-existing knowledge, peer corrective feedback pushed them to practice more target-like representations and thus to restructure their interlanguage representations and to practice more target-like representations (see also Sato & Ballinger 2012).

Concluding remarks

As DeKeyser (2010: 156) noted, "Practice may be a time-tested and commonsensical idea for most teachers and learners, but it has taken a beating in recent decades". He attributes arguments against practice to its *drill and kill* reputation associated with audiolingual methods. He makes a strong case for types of practice that go beyond "drill and kill" and that fit instead within a "broader definition of systematic practice and fulfill specific functions in the learning process that mere communicative input and interaction cannot" (2010: 159). This chapter has provided theoretical support for the role of contextualized practice in L2 development by drawing on Skill Acquisition Theory and has also drawn on empirical classroom research to show evidence of its effects. The research reviewed here supports DeKeyser's (2010) argument that systematic practice – in its various manifestations as outlined throughout this chapter – can contribute to L2 development in ways that input-based (see Benati, this volume) and interactional approaches (see Pica, this volume) cannot.

To go beyond the role of noticing in L2 development – and what learners do and do not notice in classroom settings – SLA research could investigate more specifically the effects of different types of practice that help learners to proceduralize their knowledge of what has been noticed and encoded as declarative representations. A caveat in such an endeavour, however, is the difficulty of isolating

practice effects from other components of the instructional sequence. This is because practice activities are arguably most effectively implemented in conjunction
with awareness tasks and opportunities for feedback, as outlined in Ranta and
Lyster's (2007) proposal for an Awareness-Practice-Feedback instructional sequence. The quasi-experimental classroom studies reviewed in this chapter indicate that instructional interventions interweaving various awareness tasks with
opportunities for practice and feedback can lead to enhanced learner performance
to varying degrees. At the same time, this line of research on the effects of form-
focused instruction supports the idea of the interplay between declarative and procedural knowledge as bidirectional and relative to the context of instruction. That
is, contextualized practice in conjunction with feedback may have positive effects
not only on the speed of deployment of declarative knowledge during spontaneous
production but also on the destabilization of interlanguage representations that are
ostensibly fossilized and already available for spontaneous production.

Given DeKeyser's (1998a: 50) broad definition of practice as "engaging in an
activity with the goal of becoming better at it", its relevance in L2 development is
undeniable. Skill Acquisition Theory provides a particularly useful way of understanding L2 development in contexts of instructed SLA because of the way it explains the role of practice and its inextricable link with feedback. Although often
applied to learners in traditional classrooms who are expected first to develop declarative knowledge that is then proceduralized through opportunities for practice
and feedback, we have brought a new perspective to Skill Acquisition Theory in
this chapter by positing that the relationship between declarative and procedural
knowledge is not necessarily unidirectional. That is, learners whose early exposure
to the target language may have triggered primarily implicit learning processes can
benefit from practice and feedback opportunities designed to develop declarative
knowledge from the procedural knowledge that they had acquired in relatively
naturalistic ways. Despite the aforementioned caveat of controlling practice effects
as an independent variable in classroom settings, we conclude with a call for future
research to address the issue of what types of practice are most effective for con-
solidating emergent L2 knowledge and skills in a range of educational settings.

References

Ammar, A. & Spada, N. 2006. One size fits all? Recasts, prompts and L2 learning. *Studies in Second Language Acquisition* 28(4): 543–574.
Anderson, J. 1976. *Language, Memory and Thought*. Hillsdale NJ: Lawrence Erlbaum Associates.
Anderson, J. 1983. *The Architecture of Cognition*. Cambridge MA: Harvard University Press.
Anderson, J. 1993. *Rules of the Mind*. Hillsdale NJ: Lawrence Erlbaum Associates.

Anderson, J. 2005. *Cognitive Psychology and its Implications*, 6th edn. New York NY: Worth Publishers.

Anderson, J. & Lebiere, C. 1998. *The Atomic Components of Thought*. Mahwah NJ: Lawrence Erlbaum Asssociates.

Anderson, J. & Schunn, C. 2000. Implications of the ACT-R learning theory: No magic bullets. In *Advances in Instructional Psychology*, R. Glaser (ed.), 1–33. Mahwah NJ: Lawrence Erlbaum Associates.

Anderson, J., Greeno, J. Kline, P. & Neves, D. 1981. Acquisition of problem-solving skill. In *Cognitive Skills and their Acquisition*, J. Anderson (ed.), 191–230. Hillsdale NJ: Lawrence Erlbaum Associates.

Bange, P., Carol, R. & Griggs, P. 2005. *L'apprentissage d'une langue étrangère: Cognition et interaction*. Paris: L'Harmattan.

Battig, W. 1979. The flexibility of human memory. In *Levels of Processing and Human Memory*, L. Cermak & F. Craik (eds.), 23–44. Mahwah NJ: Lawrence Erlbaum Associates.

Bialystok, E. 1981. The role of linguistic knowledge in second language use. *Studies in Second Language Acquisition* 4(1): 31–45.

Bialystok, E. 1991. Metalinguistic dimensions of bilingual language proficiency. In *Language Processing in Bilingual Children*, E. Bialystok (ed.), 113–140. Cambridge: CUP.

Bialystok, E. 1994a. Analysis and control in the development of second language proficiency. *Studies in Second Language Acquisition* 16(2): 157–168.

Bialystok, E. 1994b. Representation and ways of knowing: Three issues in second language acquisition. In *Implicit and Explicit Learning of Languages*, N. Ellis (ed.), 549–569. San Diego CA: Academic Press.

Bruner, J. 1977[1960]. *The process of Education*. Cambridge MA: Harvard University Press.

Cepeda, N., Coburn, N., Rohrer, D., Wixted, J., Mozer, M. & Pashler, H. 2009. Optimizing distributed practice. *Experimental Psychology* 56(4): 236–246.

Chein, J. & Schneider, W. 2005. Neuroimaging studies of practice-related change: fMRI and meta-analytic evidence of a domain-general control network for learning. *Cognitive Brain Research* 25(3): 607–623.

Day, E. & Shapson, S. 2001. Integrating formal and functional approaches to language teaching in French immersion: An experimental study. *Language Learning 51(Supplement 1)*: 47–80.

de Bot, K. 1996. The psycholinguistics of the output hypothesis. *Language Learning* 46(3): 529–555.

de Jong, N. & Perfetti, C. 2011. Fluency training in the ESL classroom: An experimental study of fluency development and proceduralization. *Language Learning* 61(2): 533–568.

DeKeyser, R. 1997. Beyond explicit rule learning: Automatizing second language morphosyntax. *Studies in Second Language Acquisition* 19(2): 195–221.

DeKeyser, R. 1998a. Beyond focus on form: Cognitive perspectives on learning and practicing second language grammar. In *Focus on Form in Classroom Second Language Acquisition*, C. Doughty & J. Williams (eds), 42–63. Cambridge: CUP.

DeKeyser, R. 1998b. Exploring automatization processes. *TESOL Quarterly* 30(2): 349–357.

DeKeyser, R. 2001. Automaticity and automatization. In *Cognition and Second Language Instruction*, P. Robinson (ed.), 125–151. Cambridge: CUP.

DeKeyser, R. (ed.) 2007a. *Practice in a Second Language: Perspectives from Applied Linguistics and Cognitive Psychology*. Cambridge: CUP.

DeKeyser, R. 2007b. Skill acquisition theory. In *Theories in Second Language Acquisition: An Introduction*, B. VanPatten & J. Williams (eds.), 97–113. Mahwah NJ: Lawrence Erlbaum Associates.

DeKeyser, R. 2010. Practice for second language learning: Don't throw out the baby with the bath water. *International Journal of English Studies* 10(1): 155–165.

Dempster, F. 1989. Spacing effects and their implications for theory and practice. *Educational Psychology Review* 1(4): 309–330.

De Ridder, I., Vangehuchten, L. & Gómez, M. 2007. Enhancing automaticity through task-based language learning. *Applied Linguistics* 28(2): 309–315.

Dienes, Z. & Perner, J. 1999. A theory of implicit and explicit knowledge. *Behavioral and Brain Sciences* 22(5): 735–808.

Doughty, C. & Varela, E. 1998. Communicative focus on form. In *Focus on Form in Classroom Second Language Acquisition*, C. Doughty & J. Williams (eds.), 114–138. Cambridge: CUP.

Ellis, N. 1994. Introduction: Implicit and explicit language learning-an overview. In *Implicit and Explicit Learning of Languages*, N. Ellis (ed.), 1–31. San Diego CA: Academic Press.

Ellis, N. 2002. Frequency effects in language processing: A review with implications for theories of implicit and explicit language acquisition. *Studies in Second Language Acquisition* 24(2): 143–188.

Ellis, N. 2005. At the interface: Dynamic interactions of explicit and implicit language knowledge. *Studies in Second Language Acquisition* 27(2): 305–352.

Ellis, R. 1993. The structural syllabus and second language acquisition. *TESOL Quarterly* 27(1): 91–113.

Ellis, R. 2003. *Task-based Language Learning and Teaching*. Oxford: OUP.

Ellis, R. 2006. Researching the effects of form-focussed instruction on L2 acquisition. *AILA Review* 19: 18–41.

Ellis, R. 2009. Implicit and explicit learning, knowledge and instruction. In *Implicit and Explicit Knowledge in Second Language Learning, Testing and Teaching*, R. Ellis, S. Loewen, C. Elder, R. Erlam, J. Philp & H. Reinders (eds.), 3–25. Clevedon: Multilingual Matters.

Franks, J., Bilbrey, C., Lien, K. & McNamara, T. 2000. Transfer-appropriate processing (TAP) and repetition priming. *Memory & Cognition* 28(7): 1140–1151.

Gatbonton, E. & Segalowitz, N. 2005. Rethinking communicative language teaching: A focus on access to fluency. *The Canadian Modern Language Review* 61(3): 325–353.

Han, Y. & Ellis, R. 1998. Implicit knowledge, explicit knowledge and general language proficiency. *Language Teaching Research* 2(1): 1–23.

Harley, B. 1989. Functional grammar in French immersion: A classroom experiment. *Applied Linguistics* 10(3): 331–359.

Harley, B. 1998. The role of form-focused tasks in promoting child L2 acquisition. In *Focus on Form in Classroom Second Language Acquisition*, C. Doughty & J. Williams (eds), 156–174. Cambridge: CUP.

Healy, A. & Bourne, L. (eds.). 1995. *Learning and Memory of Knowledge and Skills: Durability and Specificity*. Thousand Oaks CA: Sage.

Hulstijn, J. 1990. A comparison between the information-processing and the analysis/control approaches to language learning. *Applied Linguistics* 11(1): 30–45.

Hulstijn, J. 2002. Towards a unified account of the representation, processing and acquisition of second language knowledge. *Second Language Research* 18(3): 193–223.

Hulstijn, J. 2005. Theoretical and empirical issues in the study of implicit and explicit second-language learning. *Studies in Second Language Acquisition* 27(2): 129–140.

Hulstijn, J. & de Graaff, R. 1994. Under what conditions does explicit knowledge of a second language facilitate the acquisition of implicit knowledge? A research proposal. *AILA Review* 11: 97–113.

Hulstijn, J., van Gelderen, A. & Schoonen, R. 2009. Automatization in second language acquisition: What does the coefficient of variation tell us? *Applied Psycholinguistics* 30(4): 555–582.

Johnson, K. 1996. *Language Teaching and Skill Learning*. Oxford: Basil Blackwell.

Langley, P., Laird, J. & Rogers, S. 2009. Cognitive architectures: Research issues and challenges. *Cognitive Systems Research* 10(2): 141–160.

Li, S. 2010. The effectiveness of corrective feedback in SLA: A meta–analysis. *Language Learning* 60(2): 309–365.

Lightbown, P. 2008. Transfer appropriate processing as a model for class second language acquisition. In *Understanding Second Language Process*, Z. Han (ed.), 27–44. Clevedon: Multilingual Matters.

Long, M. 2007. *Problems in SLA*. Mahwah NJ: Lawrence Erlbaum Associates.

Lyster, R. 1994. The effect of functional-analytic teaching on aspects of French immersion students' sociolinguistic competence. *Applied Linguistics* 15(3): 263–287.

Lyster, R. 2004. Differential effects of prompts and recasts in form-focused instruction. *Studies in Second Language Acquisition* 26(3): 399–432.

Lyster, R. 2007. *Learning and Teaching Languages through Content: A Counterbalanced Approach* [Language Learning & Language Teaching 18]. Amsterdam: John Benjamins

Lyster, R. & Mori, H. 2006. Interactional feedback and instructional counterbalance. *Studies in Second Language Acquisition* 28(2): 269–300.

Lyster, R. & Saito, K. 2010. Oral feedback in classroom SLA: A meta-analysis. *Studies in Second Language Acquisition* 32(2): 265–302.

Mackey, A. & Goo, J. 2007. Interaction research in SLA: A meta–analysis and research synthesis. In *Conversational Interaction in Second Language Acquisition: A Collection of Empirical Studies*, A. Mackey (ed.), 407–452. Oxford: OUP.

Martin-Chang, S. & Levy, B. 2005. Fluency transfer: Differential gains in reading speed and accuracy following isolated word and context training. *Reading and Writing* 18(4): 343–376.

Martin-Chang, S. & Levy, B. 2006. Word reading fluency: A transfer appropriate processing account of fluency transfer. *Reading and Writing* 19(5): 517–542.

McLaughlin, B. 1987. *Theories of Second-Language Learning*. London: Edward Arnold.

McLaughlin, B. 1990. Restructuring. *Applied Linguistics* 11(2): 113–128.

McLaughlin, B. & Heredia, R. 1996. Information-processing approaches to research on second language acquisition and use. In *Handbook of Second Language Acquisition*, W. Ritchie & T. Bhatia (eds), 213–228. San Diego CA: Academic Press.

Montgomery, C. & Eisentein, M. 1985. Reality revisited: An experimental communicative course in ESL. *TESOL Quarterly* 19(2): 317–334

Morris, C., Bransford, J. & Franks, J. 1977. Levels of processing versus transfer appropriate processing. *Journal of Verbal Learning & Verbal Behavior* 16(5): 519–533.

Myles, F., Hooper, J. & Mitchell, R.1998. Rote or rule. Exploring the role of formulaic language in classroom foreign language learning. *Language Learning* 48(3): 323–363.

Newell, A. & Rosenbloom, P. 1981. Mechanisms of skill acquisition and the law of practice. In *Cognitive Skills and their Acquisition*, J. Anderson (ed.), 1–55. Hillsdale NJ: Lawrence Erlbaum Associates.

O'Malley, J. & Chamot, A. 1990. *Learning Strategies in Second Language Acquisition*. Cambridge: CUP.

Paradis, M. 2009. *Declarative and Procedural Determinants of Second Languages* [Studies in Bilingualism 40]. Amsterdam: John Benjamins.

Pavlik, P. & Anderson, J. 2005. Practice and forgetting effects on vocabulary memory: An activation-based model of the spacing effect. *Cognitive Science* 29(4): 559–586.

Poldrack, R., Prabhakaran, V., Seger, C. & Gabrieli, J. 1999. Striatal activation during acquisition of a cognitive skill. *Neuropsychology* 13(4): 564–574.

Ranta, L. & Lyster, R. 2007. A cognitive approach to improving immersion students' oral language abilities: The Awareness-Practice-Feedback sequence. In *Practice in a Second Language: Perspective from Applied Linguistics and Cognitive Psychology*, R. DeKeyser (ed.), 141–160. Cambridge: CUP.

Robinson, P. 1997. Generalizability and automaticity of second language learning under implicit, incidental, enhanced and instructed conditions. *Studies in Second Language Acquisition* 19(2): 223–247.

Russell, J., & Spada, N. 2006. The effectiveness of corrective feedback for the acquisition of L2 grammar. In *Synthesizing Research on Language Learning and Teaching* [Language Learning & Language Teaching 13], J. Norris & L. Ortega (eds), 133–162. Amsterdam: John Benjamins.

Saito, K. & Lyster, R. 2012. Effects of form-focused instruction and corrective feedback on L2 pronunciation development of /ɹ/ by Japanese learners of English. *Language Learning* 62: 595–633.

Samuels, S. & Flor, R. 1997. The importance of automaticity for developing expertise in reading. *Reading and Writing Quarterly* 13(2): 107–121.

Sato, M. 2011. Constitution of form-orientation: Contributions of context and explicit knowledge to learning from recasts. *Canadian Journal of Applied Linguistics* 14(1): 1–28.

Sato, M. & Ballinger, S. 2012. Raising language awareness in peer interaction: A cross-context, cross-method examination. *Language Awareness* 21(1–2): 157–179.

Sato, M. & Lyster, R. 2012. Peer interaction and corrective feedback for accuracy and fluency development: Monitoring, practice, and proceduralization. *Studies in Second Language Acquisition* 34(4): 591–626.

Savignon, S. 1972. *Communicative Competence: An Experiment in Foreign-language Teaching*. Philadelphia PA: Center for Curriculum Development.

Schmidt, R. 1992. Psychological mechanisms underlying second language fluency. *Studies in Second Language Acquisition* 14(4): 357–385.

Schmidt, R. 1994. Deconstructing consciousness in search of useful definitions for applied linguistics. *AILA Review* 11: 11–26.

Schneider, W., Dumais, S. & Shiffrin, R. 1984. Automatic and controlled processing and attention. In *Varieties of Attention*, R. Parasuraman & D. Davies (eds), 1–27. London: Academic Press.

Schneider, V., Healy, A. & Bourne, L. 2002. What is learned under difficult conditions is hard to forget: Contextual interference effects in foreign vocabulary acquisition, retention, and transfer. *Journal of Memory & Language* 46(2): 419–440.

Schneider, W. & Fisk, A. 1983. Attentional theory and mechanisms for skilled performance. In *Memory and Control of Action*, R. Magill (ed.), 119–143. Amsterdam: North-Holland.

Segalowitz, N. 2000. Automaticity and attentional skill in fluent performance. In *Perspectives on Fluency*, H. Riggenbach (ed.), 200–219. Ann Arbor MI: The University of Michigan Press.

Segalowitz, N. 2003. Automaticity and second languages. In *Handbook of Second Language Acquisition*, C. Doughty & M. Long (eds.), 382–408. Oxford: Blackell.

Segalowitz, N. 2010. *Cognitive Bases of Second Language Fluency*. London: Routledge.

Segalowitz, N. & Freed, B. 2004. Context, contact, and cognition in oral fluency acquisition: Learning Spanish in at home and study abroad contexts. *Studies in Second Language Acquisition* 26(2): 173–199.

Segalowitz, N. & Gatbonton, E. 1995. Automaticity and lexical skills in second language fluency: Implications for computer assisted language learning. *Computer Assisted Language Learning* 8(2): 129–149.

Segalowitz, N. & Segalowitz, S. 1993. Skilled performance, practice, and the differentiation of speed-up from automatization effects: Evidence from second language word recognition. *Applied Psycholinguistics* 14(3): 369–385.

Skehan, P. 1998. *A Cognitive Approach to Language Learning*. Oxford: OUP.

Spada, N. 1987. Relationships between instructional differences and learning outcomes: A process-product study of communicative language teaching. *Applied Linguistics* 8(2): 137–161.

Spada, N. 1997. Form-focused instruction and second language acquisition: A review of classroom and laboratory research. *Language Teaching* 30(2): 73–87.

Spada, N. 2011. Beyond form-focused instruction: Reflections on past, present and future research. *Language Teaching* 44(2): 225–236.

Spada, N. & Lightbown, P. 1993. Instruction and the development of questions in L2 classrooms. *Studies in Second Language Acquisition* 15(2): 205–224.

Swain, M. 1985. Communicative competence: Some roles of comprehensible input and comprehensible output in its development. In *Input in Second Language Acquisition*, S. Gass & C. Madden (eds), 235–253. Rowley MA: Newbury House.

Swain, M. 1988. Manipulating and complementing content teaching to maximize second language learning. *TESL Canada Journal* 6(1): 68–83.

Tode, T. 2003. From unanalyzed chunks to rules: The learning of the English copula be by beginning Japanese learners of English. *International Review of Applied Linguistics* 41(1): 23–53.

Towell, R. & Hawkins, R. 1994. *Approaches to Second Language Acquisition*. Clevedon: Multilingual Matters.

Ullman, M. 2001a. The neural basis of lexicon and grammar in first and second language: The declarative/procedural model. Bilingualism: *Language and Cognition* 4(2): 105–122.

Ullman, M. 2001b. A neurocognitive perspective on language: The declarative/procedural model. *Nature Reviews Neuroscience* 2(10): 717–726.

Ullman, M. 2004. Contributions of memory circuits to language: The declarative/procedural model. *Cognition* 92(1–2): 231–270.

Ullman, M. 2005. A cognitive neuroscience perspective on second language acquisition: The declarative/procedural model. In *Mind and Context in Adult Second Language Acquisition*, C. Sanz (ed.), 141–178. Washington DC: Georgetown University Press.

Van der Lely, H. & Ullman, M. 2001. Past tense morphology in specifically language impaired and normally developing children. *Language Cognitive Processes* 16(2): 177–217.

Weber, S. & Tardif, C. 1991. Culture and meaning in French immersion kindergarten. In *Language, Culture and Cognition*, L. Malavé & G. Duquette. (eds), 93–109. Clevedon: Multilingual Matters.

Whitaker, H. 1983. Towards a brain model of automatization: A short essay. In *Memory and Control of Action*, R. Magill (ed.), 199–214. Amsterdam: North-Holland.

White, J. & Ranta, L. 2002. Examining the interface between metalinguistic task performance and oral production in a second language. *Language Awareness* 11(4): 259–290.

Wong Fillmore, L. 1979. Individual differences in second language acquisition. In *Individual Differences in Language Ability and Language Behaviour*, C. Fillmore, D. Kempler & W. Wang (eds.), 203–228. New York NY: Academic Press.

Wray, A. 2002. *Formulaic Language and the Lexicon*. Cambridge: CUP.

Wright, R. 1996. A study of acquisition of verbs of motion by grade 4/5 early French immersion students. *The Canadian Modern Language Review* 53(1): 257–280.

Yang, Y. & Lyster, R. 2010. Effects of form-focused practice and feedback on Chinese EFL learners' acquisition of regular and irregular past tense forms. *Studies in Second Language Acquisition* 32(2): 235–263.

CHAPTER 5

The Input Processing Theory in second language acquisition

Alessandro Benati
University of Greenwich

The importance of input has always been recognised in the field of second language acquisition and hence one of the key questions addressed by researchers is how second language (L2) learners process input when listening or reading. The purpose of the present chapter is threefold. First, a synopsis of VanPatten's Input Processing Theory (VanPatten 1996, 2004, 2007) is provided. Input Processing Theory aims to offer an explanation as to how L2 learners process input, how they make form-meaning connections and how they map syntactic structures onto the utterance. Secondly, a review of empirical research supporting input processing principles will be provided. Finally, theoretical and pedagogical implications from research within the input processing framework will be drawn.

Introduction

Input Processing Theory is not a full theory which can account for all processes involved in the acquisition of a second language. VanPatten's Input Processing Theory seeks to identify specific processing constraints L2 learners encounter when they process language input. As VanPatten has indicated (2007: 127) Input Processing is not a full theory of acquisition but "[...] it is only concerned with how learners come to make form-meaning connections or parse sentences". The main scope of Input Processing Theory and research is limited to examine which psycholinguistic strategies and mechanisms learners use to derive intake from input.

VanPatten (1996, 2004, 2007) developed the Input Processing Theory in order to explore how L2 learners process linguistic data in the input. Considering that the input processing capacity of L2 learners is limited, he claimed that only certain grammatical features would receive attention during input processing. According to VanPatten (1996), when learners process input, they filter the input which is reduced and modified into a new entity called 'intake', which is a subset of the input. Only part of the input L2 learners receive is processed and becomes intake, which is a subset of the input. Due to processing limitations, only part of the input L2 learners receive is processed and becomes intake.

VanPatten's Input Processing Theory consists of two key principles, each of which is further explicated with a series of sub-principles to account for adult second language input processing. The first principle asserts that learners are driven to look for the message in the input before they look at how the message is encoded linguistically. In other words, when L2 learners are engaged in meaningful interchanges, they are more concerned with meaning than with grammatical items. In the second principle, VanPatten asserts that the order in which learners encounter sentence elements is a powerful factor in assigning syntactic roles at sentence-level. For instance, L2 learners tend to process the first element in a sentence as the subject or agent of that sentence. VanPatten's perspective on processing linguistic data from the input is directly related to how L2 learners perceive and process input data (for other perspectives and research on second language processing and parsing see VanPatten & Jegerski 2010).

In the following sections of this chapter, Input Processing Theory will be explained and its processing principles and sub-principles presented. Empirical studies supporting the predictions made by the theory will be briefly reviewed. Finally, research and pedagogical implications will be outlined.

The Input Processing Theory

The Input Processing Theory (henceforth, IP theory) consists of two sub-processes: making form-meaning connections, and parsing. Learners make form-meaning connections from the input they receive as they connect particular meanings to particular forms (grammatical or lexical). For example, they tend to connect a form with its meaning in the input they receive (the morpheme -*ed*- at the end of the verb in English refers to an event in the past). Parsing consists of the process of mapping syntactic structure in the sentence so that the learner can ascertain what is the subject and what is the object in a sentence (see Harrington 2004 for further discussion of VanPatten's definition of parsing). In the case of parsing, L2 learners must be able to determine, for example, which is the subject and which is the object in a sentence they hear or read. Learners must be able to appropriately map syntactic structure into the sentence.

VanPatten (1996) originally identified a series of processing strategies used by L2 learners when they process linguistics data at input level. Processing strategies were predicated on a limited capacity for processing. They allow learners to selectively attend to incoming stimuli without being overloaded with information.

Table 1. VanPatten's (1996) original theoretical framework

P1. Learners process input for meaning before they process it for form.

P1(a). Learners process content words in the input before anything else.

P1(b). Learners prefer processing lexical items to grammatical items (e.g., morphological markings) for semantic information.

P1 (c). Learners prefer processing "more meaningful" morphology before "less" or "non-meaningful morphology".

(VanPatten 1996: 14)

P2. For learners to process form that is not meaningful, they must be able to process informational or communicative content at no or little cost to attention.

(VanPatten 1996: 15)

P3. Learners process a default strategy that assigns the role of agent to the first noun (phrase) they encounter in a sentence.

P3 (a). The first noun strategy can be overridden by lexical semantics and event probabilities.

P3 (b). Learners will adopt other processing strategies for grammatical role assignment only after their developing system has incorporated other cues (e.g., case marking, acoustic stress).

(VanPatten 1996: 32)

Table 1 illustrates those strategies as conceived of in VanPatten's (1996) original theoretical framework:

By 2004, more evidence in support of the IP theory had emerged and VanPatten reworked his theoretical framework providing a more detailed and clearer explanation of the processing principles (VanPatten 2004, 2007). The two main processing principles in VanPatten's (2004) revised theory are:

1. Principle 1 (P1). The Primacy of Meaning Principle. Learners process input for meaning before they process it for form.
2. Principle 2 (P2). The First Noun Principle. Learners tend to process the first noun or pronoun they encounter in a sentence as the subject/agent.

In the first principle (P1), VanPatten (2004: 7) suggested that during input processing, L2 learners initially direct their attention towards the detection of content words to understand the meaning of an utterance. Learners tend to focus their attention on content words in order to understand the message of the input they are exposed to. In doing so, they tend not to process the grammatical form, and consequently fail to make form-meaning connections. The Primacy of Meaning Principle is further subdivided into six sub-principles (see Table 2) developed by VanPatten in order to examine the interplay between various linguistic and cognitive processes during language comprehension.

Table 2. Summary of Principle 1 sub-principles (VanPatten 2004)

P 1 The Primacy of Meaning Principle. Learners process input for meaning before they process it for form.

P 1a. The Primacy of Content Words Principle: Learners process content words in the input before anything else. (VanPatten 2007: 117)

P 1b. The Lexical Preference Principle: If grammatical forms express a meaning that can also be encoded lexically (i.e., that grammatical marker is redundant), then learners will not initially process those grammatical forms until they have lexical forms to which they can match them. (VanPatten 2007: 118)

P 1c. The Preference for Non-redundancy Principle: Learners are more likely to process non-redundant meaningful grammatical markers before they process redundant meaningful markers. (VanPatten 2007: 119)

P 1d. The Meaning-Before-Non-meaning Principle: learners are more likely to process meaningful grammatical markers before non-meaningful grammatical markers.

P 1e. The Availability of Resources Principle: For learners to process either redundant meaningful grammatical forms or non-meaningful forms, the processing of overall sentential meaning must not drain available processing resources. (VanPatten 2004: 14)

P 1f. The Sentence Location Principle: Learners tend to process items in sentence initial position before those in final position and those in medial position. (VanPatten 2007: 125)

In the second principle (P2), VanPatten (2004: 15) asserts that the order in which learners encounter sentence elements is a powerful factor in assigning grammatical relations amongst sentence elements. L2 learners tend to process the first noun or pronoun they encounter in a sentence as the subject or agent. In certain syntactic structures this can cause learners to misinterpret sentences and consequently a delay in acquisition of the target linguistic feature. Like in the case of the first principle, VanPatten has developed a set of sub-principles that have been formulated taking into consideration a series of factors which might attenuate learners' misassignment of the first noun (see Table 3).

Table 3. Summary of Principle 2 sub-principles (VanPatten 2004)

Principle 2. The First Noun Principle. Learners tend to process the first noun or pronoun they encounter in a sentence as the subject/agent.

P 2a. The Lexical Semantics Principle: Learners may rely on lexical semantics, where possible, instead of the First Noun Principle to interpret sentences. (VanPatten 2007: 124)

P 2b. The Event Probabilities Principle: Learners may rely on event probabilities, where possible, instead of the First Noun Principle to interpret sentences. (VanPatten 2007: 123)

P 2c. The Contextual Constraint Principle: Learners may rely less on the First Noun Principle (or L1 transfer) if preceding context constrains the possible interpretation of a clause or sentence. (VanPatten 2007: 124)

VanPatten's IP theory captures a series of processing principles which guide L2 learners in their attempt to comprehend input in a target language. In the next section, each of these principles and sub-principles will be explained and some of the empirical evidence that supports them will be presented.

Processing Principles and Sub-Principles

The Primacy of Meaning Principle (P1)

Research has provided evidence on the various ways in which learners process input for meaning. Lee (1987) found that L2 learners of Spanish can extract the lexical meaning of verbs morphologically marked as subjunctive without having received any previous exposure to these forms. Lee (2002, 2003) and subsequently Lee and Rossomondo (2004) have provided empirical evidence which showed that learners can process and comprehend the meaning of a passage containing future tense verb forms in Spanish without previous knowledge of the target grammatical form. In these studies, L2 learners seemed to be primarily concerned with processing the meaning and not the forms contained in the text. These research findings support VanPatten's Primacy of Meaning Principle and the view that meaningful elements in the input are processed before less meaningful elements.

The Primacy of Content Words Principle (P1a)

The Primacy of Content Words Principle remains unchanged in VanPatten's reworked theoretical model (VanPatten 2004). This processing sub-principle suggests that learners use content words to grasp the meaning of a sentence. To comprehend meaning L2 learners will process things in the input that carry the most meaning (content words) at first. Content words are the most helpful cue for extracting meaning from the input. For example, in the sentence *the car is parked in the garage*, learners will process concrete words such as *car* and *garage* in the first instance. VanPatten (1990) investigated the possible interplay of content words, function words, and verb morphology when L2 learners of Spanish attempt to comprehend input. Bernhardt (1992) carried out a study exploring the different text processing strategies employed by native and inexperienced non-native readers of German. Lee (1999) analysed the strategies used by L2 learners of Spanish in comprehending a text. The overall findings from these empirical studies demonstrate that L2 learners focus on content words to build up their comprehension.

Lexical Preference Principle (P1b)

The second sub-principle of the first principle (P1) of VanPatten's IP theory is the so-called Lexical Preference Principle. This sub-principle suggests that L2 learners prefer processing lexical items before grammatical forms if they both encode the same semantic information. According to VanPatten (1996) this is a processing strategy used by early stage learners who give precedence to adverbials of temporal reference over morphological markers when interpreting tenses. VanPatten (2004, 2007) has further revised this sub-principle and asserted that if a grammatical form expresses a particular meaning that can be also encoded lexically, L2 learners will not process those grammatical forms until they have lexical forms to which they can match them. If L2 learners hear the following sentence *Last night I talked to John on the phone*, *last night* tells us that the action took place in the past. Despite the fact that *-ed* is the morphological form that also expresses pastness, learners will most likely pay attention and process the content lexical item before the morphological form because the lexical item is a free-standing unit which carries more meaning. Musumeci (1989) conducted a cross-linguistic study (Italian, French and Spanish) in which she examined how successfully learners assigned tense at sentence level under different exposure conditions. Lee, Cadierno, Glass and VanPatten (1997) also investigated how L2 learners of Spanish assign tenses. The group of learners who were exposed to a passage containing adverbials correctly identified more of the temporal references than did the learners who listened to the passage with only verb morphology to mark tense. Rossomondo (2007) has also carried out a study in an attempt to explore how L2 learners of Spanish assign future tense references in the input. The main findings of these three studies indicated that L2 learners seem to rely heavily on lexical items to comprehend the future meaning of the target morphological forms. VanPatten and Keating (2007) found that L2 learners of Spanish rely on lexical items in the early stages of learning to determine temporal references. Overall, the findings from the studies briefly reviewed in this section support VanPatten's Lexical Preference Principle in showing that the main factor influencing correct tense assignment was the presence or absence of lexical items (temporal adverbials) in the input sentences and not the verbal morphology.

The Preference for Non-redundancy Principle (P1c)
and The Meaning-Before-Non-meaning Principle (P1d)

In his original framework, Van Patten (1996: 14) stated that L2 learners prefer processing more meaningful morphology rather than less or non-meaningful morphology. An important construct to understand this sub-processing principle is the notion of communicative value. Communicative value refers to the contribution made to the meaning of an utterance by a linguistic form. In order to establish whether a linguistic form has low or high communicative value, we need to follow two criteria: inherent referential meaning and semantic redundancy. For example, grammatical gender marking in Romance languages illustrates non-meaningful morphology. Inflections on adjectives (*o/a*) in Italian are low in communicative value because they are redundant and lacking inherent semantic value. In the sentence *la giacca bianca* (the white blazer), the adjective *bianca* ends in *-a* because it is feminine and does not carry any semantic meaning in this sentence. In addition *-a-* is spread across the three words in the noun phrase and this makes it highly redundant. The gender marking on *bianca* is the feminine marker in the string and therefore the information carried in the form is also expressed elsewhere in the utterance. Being non-meaningful as well as redundant contributes to the problems second language learners face in processing these forms. In relation to the concept of communicative value and in an attempt to revise his original theory, VanPatten (2004) reformulated the notion of meaningful and non-meaningful morphology under two new sub-principles: The Preference for Non-redundancy Principle and The Meaning-Before-Non-meaning Principle. According to these sub-principles, L2 learners tend to process non-redundant grammatical forms before redundant grammatical forms. Lee's (1987) study demonstrated how L2 learners skip items (Spanish subjunctive forms) of low communicative value during processing. Bransdorfer's (1989, 1991) study also investigated L2 learner's ability to process meaning and form simultaneously in the preposition *de* or the definite article *la* in Spanish. The main findings of these empirical studies support VanPatten's theory as they indicate that redundant grammatical forms and non-meaningful grammatical forms are processed later than non-redundant and meaningful grammatical forms. In Principle P1d, VanPatten (2004: 14) stated that learners are more likely to process meaningful grammatical markers before non-meaningful grammatical markers. As VanPatten originally (1996: 24) suggested "[..] it is the relative communicative value of a grammatical form that plays a major role in determining the learner's attention to it during input processing and the likelihood of its becoming detected and thus part of intake". Non-meaningful grammatical forms do not contribute to the conveying of meaning and therefore non-meaningful grammatical forms are the most problematic part of input processing as L2 learners do not establish a form-meaning connection.

The Availability of Resources Principle (P1e)

In the 2004 revised version of the IP theory, VanPatten (2004: 14) integrated the second strategy of his original framework (*For learners to process form that is not meaningful, they must be able to process informational or communicative content at no or little cost to attention* – see Table 1) as a sub-principle of the Primacy of Meaning Principle. The Availability of Resources Principle suggests that when processing resources are low, L2 learners will focus their attention on the part of the sentence that they consider key. Comprehension for learners is initially quite effortful in terms of cognitive processing and working memory. This has consequences for what the input processing mechanisms will pay attention to. At the same time, learners are limited capacity processors and cannot process and store the same amount of information as native speakers can during moment-by-moment processing (VanPatten 2007: 116). Getting overall sentential meaning cannot be overly effortful if learners are to process redundant meaningful grammatical forms or non-meaningful forms. Learners can only process forms of lower communicative value if they do not have to struggle with understanding the meaning of the input they receive. If they struggle to comprehend the message, L2 learners will not have any attentional resources left to pay attention to form. For instance, sentence level input (e.g. short sentences) is easier to process than connected discourse. Wong (2003) provided evidence that L2 learners of French receiving sentence-level input performed better than a comparable group receiving discourse-level input on an assessment task of the target structures.

The Sentence Location Principle (P1f)

A new sub-principle was proposed in the 2004 version of VanPatten's Input Processing theory. In The Sentence Location Principle (P1f), VanPatten (2004: 13) argues that "[..] elements that appear in certain positions of an utterance are more salient to learners than others, namely, sentence initial position is more salient than sentence final position that in turn is more salient than sentence internal or medial position". This processing principle deals with how the specific position of a target form has an impact on whether or not that form is likely to be processed. In the sentence *Je ne pense pas que David Beckham soit très elegant* ("I do not think that David Beckham is very elegant") L2 learners will find it difficult to process the form the subjunctive form *soit* because it is in the middle of the sentence. When L2 learners listen to an utterance, they sensitively encounter all the elements from first to last and then try to grab the meaning. The Sentence Location Principle lays out a specific hierarchy of difficulty with regard to L2 features. A number of empirical studies (Barcroft & VanPatten 1997; Rosa & O'Neill 1998) have supported the Sentence Location Principle. These studies provided clear evidence in support of the view that sentence initial position is more salient than either sentence final position or sentence medial position. The main findings from these studies show that L2 learners repeated target items most successfully when these were in initial position.

To conclude, the first principle and its sub-principles in IP theory (see Table 2), clearly indicate that L2 learners process input for meaning first and that they rely on words rather than forms to obtain that meaning. When both words and forms encode the same meaning, L2 learners would still rely on words and skip grammatical forms as they do not have enough attentional resources to process forms. According to this theoretical framework forms of low or no communicative value or redundant forms tend to be processed much later or not at all. The clear disadvantage to these learners' strategies is that they will hinder L2 learners for processing grammatical forms since they do not need to process them to comprehend the utterance. And finally, L2 learners would process elements at the beginning of sentences before elements that appear in the middle and the end. Research on sentence-level processing, reviewed in this section, clearly indicates that when learners need to process meaning and form it will be the form that is always the second choice. The consequence for second language acquisition (SLA) is that form-meaning connections are not made and this causes delay in the acquisition of the formal properties of a target language.

The First Noun Principle (P2)

A second question posited by VanPatten (1996) is: How do L2 learners assign grammatical-semantic roles to nouns? He suggested that learners possess a default strategy that assigns the role of agent to the first noun they encounter in a sentence. In the First Noun Principle, VanPatten (2004) further clarifies this processing strategy. He argues that when L2 learners process sentences containing a SVO order, they do not encounter any problem to make correct syntactic mapping. However, if the language is not strictly SVO, with OV and OVS being frequent word orders, this processing principle used by L2 learners can cause a problem. L2 learners who hear the following sentence (English passive construction): *Chris was hit by Maria*, might process Chris as the subject of the sentence. L2 learners might interpret this sentence as if it was Chris who hit Maria as L2 learners would process the first item in the utterance as the agent (subject) of the sentence. Relying on the First Noun Principle might therefore cause a processing problem for learners. It will lead to a misinterpretation of the meaning of the sentence and therefore a consequent delay in the ability of L2 learners to accurately map syntactic structure in the utterance. The problem with learners' use of this processing strategy goes beyond miscomprehension but to the heart of acquisition. VanPatten (2004: 16) states:

[...] this particular principle may have a variety of consequences in a variety of languages. It is not just that learners may get word order wrong, it is also that they may not process case markings for some time, will have difficulties with the pronoun system in some languages, and so on.

Research on this processing principle has shown that L2 learners have the tendency to misprocess the form and supply incorrect information to their internal system. González (1997) documented the acquisition of different word orders for learners of Spanish with SVO being the first acquired word order pattern and OSV and OVS being the last acquired. Strings in which the object precedes the subject are problematic for L2 learners with difficulties. VanPatten and Wong (2004) argued that learners of French use the first noun strategy to assign the semantic role of agent to the first noun in *faire-causatif* sentences. In the sentence *Jean-Paul fait lire le journal à Henri* (Jean-Paul makes to read the newspaper to Henri/Jean-Paul makes Henri read the newspaper), there are two verbs (*fait* and *lire*) and two subjects/agents (*Jean-Paul* and *Henri*). L2 learners tend to misinterpret this sentence as if it were Jean-Paul who reads the newspaper. The overall findings of this empirical study suggest that L2 learners assign the role of subject to the first noun they encounter in a sentence. If the syntactic structure of the sentence is OVS or OV, this will lead to the misinterpretation of the sentence.

In the original version of the IP theory VanPatten (1996) indicates that this processing strategy might be overridden by lexical semantics and event probabilities (see Table 1). In 2004, VanPatten reviewed the First Noun Principle and developed a new sub-principle (The Contextual Constraint Principle). VanPatten's First Noun Principle (2004) in its new version has three main associated sub-principles (see Table 3). These sub-principles attempt to identify other factors, which might influence the way L2 learners parse sentences correctly and attenuate their use of the First Noun Principle. The First Noun Principle is the main processing principle used by L2 learners in assigning grammatical relations among sentence elements. However, VanPatten (2004) indicates that L2 learners are sensitive to at least three factors, which might override the First Noun Principle. These principles are explained in the following sections.

The Lexical Semantics Principle (P2a)

The first factor attenuating learners' use of the First Noun Principle is lexical semantics. The Lexical Semantic Principle suggests that L2 learners may rely on lexical semantics where possible instead of word order to interpret sentences. In the following sentence: *The cake was eaten by Chris*, the first noun *cake* is inanimate and it cannot perform the action. The word *Chris* is an animate noun and thus is solely capable of performing the action. In this sentence, because a *cake* cannot perform the action it is unlikely that L2 learners will misinterpret the meaning of the sentence. Some empirical support for the influence of the concept of animacy as a cue in the interpretation of a target sentence was provided by Gass (1989). Her findings support the view that L2 learners might rely on lexical semantics cues in parsing and interpreting sentences. The lexical semantics of the verbs *bring* and *give* do not allow inanimate subjects. In short, when "[...] only one noun is capable of the action..." learners correctly identify that noun as the agent (VanPatten 2007: 124).

The Event Probabilities Principle (P2b)

The second factor which influences learners' interpretation of sentences is real life scenarios. In the following passive sentence: *The student was scolded by the teacher*, both nouns (*teacher* and *student*) are capable of performing the action. However, in real life scenarios, the student would be unlikely to scold a teacher. According to the Event Probabilities Principle (P2b), L2 learners might rely on event probabilities, where possible, instead of word order to interpret sentences. VanPatten and Wong (2004: 11) demonstrated that learners of French do not misinterpret the following sentence: *Le Professeur fait étudier le verb "être" a l'élève* ("The professor makes the student study the verb "être"). They rely on the Event Probabilities Principle to process the sentence correctly. Other empirical findings that provide direct support for the Event Probabilities Principle (P2b) come from a recent study by Jackson (2007) on the acquisition of German word order. The results from this study revealed that L2 learners relied on not only word order strategies but also on lexical semantics and event probabilities to interpret the sentence correctly. Learners may well use event probabilities to attenuate their use of the first noun strategy. That is, "[...] it is possible (though not necessary) that real-life scenarios might override the First Noun Principle [...]" (VanPatten 2007: 123).

The Contextual Constraint Principle (P2c)

The third factor attenuating the First Noun Principle is context. In the Contextual Constraint Principle (P2c), VanPatten (2004) states that learners may rely less on the First Noun Principle if the preceding context constrains the possible interpretation of a clause or sentence. Contextual information can prevent readers from misinterpreting the correct meaning of a target sentence. In other words, this might be an additional resource which helps readers to parse sentences correctly.

VanPatten and Houston (1998) examined the effects of context on sentence interpretation. The results from this study showed that learners of Spanish rely less on the First Noun Principle when the sentences carried contextual information (*Ricardo está enojado porque lo insultó Susana en la reunión*- "Ricardo is angry because Susana insulted him in the meeting"). Overall the results from this study revealed that contextual information provides L2 learners with an additional cue for processing the formal elements of a sentence. VanPatten and Houston (1998) found that sentence-internal context attenuated learners' use of the first noun strategy for assigning grammatical roles. Malovrh (2006) investigated whether the placement of contextual information prior to or after the targeted object pronoun would differentially affect learners' accurately assigning agent/subject functions. He found no difference in learners' performance based on the placement of the contextual information. It is the presence of the contextual information that helps learners not its placement. In other words, "...contextual information...would push [learners] away from interpreting the targeted clause the wrong way" (VanPatten 2004: 17).

In sum, the second principle of the IP theory indicates that L2 learners rely on the First Noun Principle when parsing syntactic structures such as word order. Between 1994 and 2004 VanPatten developed a set of associated principles that delineated various factors such as lexical semantics, event probabilities and context that might attenuate learners' misassignment of the first noun. Research on sentence-level processing reviewed in this section showed that learners assign the role of agent to the first noun or pronoun that they encounter in an utterance. The consequence for SLA is that learners might misinterpret the meaning of an utterance and this can cause delays in the acquisition of a variety of language features (e.g. passive constructions, case markers).

Implications

Implications for pedagogy

IP theory and the overall results of the research conducted to support the principles and sub-principles of this theoretical framework provide the foundation on which the pedagogical model called Processing Instruction (PI) has been built (Lee & VanPatten 1995, 2003; VanPatten 1993,1996). As seen above, PI is an approach to grammar instruction whose aim is to help L2 learners circumvent the use of ineffective processing principles when they process input and to instil appropriate processing strategies so that they deliver better intake from the input. The main purpose of this pedagogical model derived from the Input Processing theory is to ensure that L2 learners process forms/structures correctly and efficiently in the input they receive. PI research has consistently showed that it is an effective pedagogical intervention to alter processing principles and ensure that L2 learners establish form-meaning connections and syntactic mappings correctly.

As underscored by Wong (2004: 33) "[...] the goal of processing instruction is to help L2 learners derive richer intake from input by having them engage in structured input activities that push them away from the strategies they normally use...". PI is an instructional intervention that guides learners to focus on small parts/ features of the targeted language when they process the input. The characteristics of PI have been described in detail in previous literature (Benati & Lee 2008, 2010; Farley 2005; Lee & Benati 2007a, 2007b; Lee & Benati 2009; Lee & VanPatten 1995, 2003; VanPatten 1996; Wong 2004, 2005).

Research on the effects of PI has revealed that this new approach can affect the acquisition process and help L2 learners to deliver appropriate and accurate intake to the developing system. PI has been claimed to be an effective form of intervention in altering inappropriate processing strategies (e.g., Primacy of Meaning Principle; First Noun Principle; Lexical Preference Principle; Preference for Non-redundancy Principle and many other sub-principles) and instilling appropriate ones. PI has also been found to be an effective approach to grammar instruction as its main effects have been measured in different target languages (French, Italian, English, German, Japanese, Spanish), different grammatical forms (past tense, present tense, gender morphology) and structures (word order, passive constructions). It is an effective form of instruction for learners from different proficiency levels, background and native languages (e.g. Italian, Chinese, English, Korean, Japanese: see Lee 2004; Lee & Benati 2009 for a full review of PI studies). A more recent trend in research (Benati & Lee 2008) within the IP theory and the PI model has investigated possible secondary effects of this approach on grammar instruction. This new line of research has explored whether L2 learners receiving PI on a particular processing principle were able to transfer their training to a similar form or structure affected by a similar processing problem. The results on secondary effects indicated that L2 learners receiving PI were able to transfer the training received for one form (past tense with imperfective aspect) to another form (subjunctive) affected by similar processing principles (Sentence Location Principle). The findings also showed that the L2 learners' processing group was able to transfer the processing instruction training received for one form (past tense with imperfective aspect) to another linguistic form (causative) affected by different processing principles (First Noun Principle).

Research on IP and PI has a number of implications for language pedagogy and in particularly grammar instruction. Firstly, it indicates that grammar instruction might be very effective when it is directed at manipulating input. Secondly, PI research has showed that traditional grammar teaching (paradigmatic explanations of rules which are followed by mechanical drills) is an inadequate approach to grammar instruction. Grammar instruction should be more meaning-based and tied to input and communication.

Implications for theory and research

VanPatten's IP theory (1996, 2004, 2007) has gained increased visibility and has made a series of contributions to theory building in SLA. First of all, VanPatten's IP theory has reaffirmed the important and vital role of input in the acquisition of a second language. Input is one of the most important elements in the acquisition of a second language and one of the key issues addressed by VanPatten in his theoretical framework is how input is processed during SLA. Learners process language data while they are trying to comprehend language. In doing so they try to extract meaning from the input. The amount and quality of the input they process (intake) is a crucial factor in the SLA process.

Secondly, this theoretical model provides support for the view in SLA theory that L2 learners acquire linguistic features depending on certain factors. In IP theory this is partly due to factors such as redundancy and meaningfulness. For example, forms that have high communicative value such as English -*ing* would be processed before other forms such as third person -s- which are always redundant.

Thirdly, IP theory makes a contribution to the argument that instruction has limited effects. In order for instruction to be beneficial it must take into consideration how things are processed in the input. PI aims at altering the processing principles (see Table 2 and Table 3) L2 learners take to the task of comprehension and helping them to make better form-meaning connections.

With this approach, VanPatten and his collaborators seek to help L2 learners to divert from their default processing strategies to attend to the specific form which requires acquisition. However, IP theory has raised a series of issues which are still to be fully addressed. The first issue concerns the role of first language (L1) transfer. In the First Noun Principle, VanPatten argues that L2 learners assign the grammatical role of agent to the first noun encountered in an utterance. VanPatten had originally considered and labelled this principle as a universal principle. However, he has recently acknowledged (VanPatten, 2007: 122) that L2 learners might transfer L1 parsing procedures to the L2 processing context (The L1 Transfer Principle, VanPatten, 2004: 330). Empirical research investigating L1 influence in L2 processing (VanPatten & Keating, 2007) has also showed that specific conditions (e.g., target language, learners' first language) and specific types of linguistic features might impact on whether or not L1 influences L2 processing. More empirical research is needed to tease out these conditions.

A second issue in VanPatten's theory is related to the scope of the IP theory. VanPatten (1996) asserts that input processing is mainly responsible for processing input and enriching learners' intake, which is subsequently used to confirm or reject hypotheses generated by Universal Grammar (Chomsky, 1965) or the learner's L1. Carroll (2004: 297) stated that "[..] the input processing model does not seek to be a model of input perception, parsing or sentence interpretation". VanPatten has confirmed that his theoretical model is not a model of parsing algorithms but a model of constraints. He argued (2004: 327) that second language input processing "[...] is concerned more with how learners *get words and grammatical forms to begin with* so that a grammar can be built". Learners encounter processing constraints (e.g. input load) which have an effect on how they parse input.

Despite a series of clarifications provided by VanPatten about the input processing framework, Carroll asserts that this model needs a theory of perception in reference to processing forms. In order for the model to account for processing problems (e.g., First Noun Principle; Sentence Location Principle), Carroll (2004: 296) has also argued that it needs a theory of parsing. If IP theory is about processing constraints, this theoretical model needs to fully define these constraining processes.

Harrington (2004) levels several charges at IP theory. For Harrington, the notion of *meaning* used in VanPatten's theory is difficult to operationalize and test. VanPatten's theory claims that L2 learners find it difficult to pay attention to certain forms at the initial encoding of the form-meaning connection. Harrington refers instead to the earlier perceptual stage or the later storage and retrieval stages. He is also critical of the notion of redundancy. He states that the redundancy of the third person -s as in *He eats the apple* becomes apparent to the learner only when they understand that both *he* and -s share the feature "a person talked about but not face-to-face" (Harrington 2004: 88–89). According to Harrington, at the initial stages of learning when the learner does not know the form, the -s would not be considered as redundant. These issues are still to be addressed.

A further issue for IP theory, as asserted by Carroll (2004), is to provide a more detailed analysis of how forms might emerge from stimuli which have been noticed. Carroll (2004: 297) argued that "[...] processing is not just the analysis of (some undefined) representations for meaning, it is also those operations involved in encoding novel grammatical information". According to Carroll, there is no processing of input for meaning before there are forms onto which those meanings can be mapped.

VanPatten (2004) has attempted to address some of these concerns by reformulating and re-explaining some of the input processing principles (e.g. Lexical Preference Principle, Early Constraint Principle). He has recognised that his theory is not 'a finished product but merely a starting point' (2004: 325). On one hand, he has succeeded to formulate a series of processing principles and to provide empirical support for those principles; on the other, more work is needed on the actual theoretical framework in terms of further defining the nature and scope of processing.

Conclusion

VanPatten's theoretical framework has evolved over the last twenty years from his original formulation of the theory (1996) to the refocused model (2004, 2007). The theory has provided an important contribution to SLA theorizing, particularly to the role of input and grammar instruction. As the theory will further evolve it will need to address and respond to remaining theoretical and empirical issues on the scope and nature of processing in SLA and new challenges in terms of open research questions ahead.

In this chapter, VanPatten's theory of IP was presented through its set of principles and sub-principles designed and formulated to explain how learners work with input, and make a connection between a form in the input and its meaning. This theory provides an understanding of how learners initially perceive and process linguistic data in the language they hear or read. IP deals with the processing problems L2 learners might encounter in dealing with the properties of the new language.

Mitchell and Myles (2004: 187–188) describe VanPatten's theory as explaining "[..] the apparent failure of second language learners to process completely the linguistic forms encountered in second language input, and hence to explain their impoverished intake which in turn restricts the development of grammatical form."

IP theory offers an input-based and input-processing perspective of SLA in the sense that it asserts that acquisition is dependent on the interpretation of the input learners are exposed to. Although research within this theoretical framework focuses only on one aspect of the SLA process, it is a rather important one as research on IP provides valuable information on what L2 learners do with input, what they process, what they do not process, and why. From theory and research in IP, an instructional approach has been derived: PI provides specific guidelines on how to develop instructional materials that intervene at the time learners are working with input to make form-meaning connections.

References

Barcroft, J. & VanPatten, B. 1997. Acoustic salience of grammatical forms: The effect of location stress, and boundedness on Spanish L2 input processing. In *Contemporary Perspectives on the Acquisition of Spanish: Production, Processing, and Comprehension*, W.R. Glass & A.T. Pérez-Leroux (eds), 109–121. Sommerville MA: Cascadilla Press.

Bernhardt, E. B. 1992. *Reading Development in a Second Language*. Norwood NJ: Ablex.

Benati, A. & Lee, J.F. 2008. *Transfer of Training Effects for Processing Instruction: Research and Practice*. Clevedon: Multilingual Matters.

Benati, A. & Lee, J.F. 2010. *Processing Instruction and Discourse*. London: Continuum.

Bransdorfer, R. 1989. Processing function words in input: Does meaning make a difference? Paper presented at the annual meeting of the American Association of Teachers of Spanish and Portuguese, San Antonio.

Bransdorfer, R. 1991. Communicative Value and Linguistic Knowledge in Second Language Oral Input Processing. PhD dissertation, University of Illinois at Urbana-Champaign.

Carroll, S. 2004. Commentary: Some general and specific comments on input processing and processing instruction. In *Processing Instruction: Theory, Research, and Commentary*, B. VanPatten, (ed.), 293–309.Mahwah NJ: Lawrence Erlbaum Associates.

Chomsky, N. 1965. *Aspects of the Theory of Syntax*. Cambridge MA: The MIT Press

Farley A. 2005. *Structured Input: Grammar Instruction for the Acquisition-Oriented Classroom.* New York NY: McGraw-Hill.

Gass, S. 1989. How do learners resolve linguistic conflicts? In *Linguistic Perspectives on Second Language Acquisition*, S. Gass. & J. Schachter (eds.), 183–199. Cambridge: CUP.

González, N. 1997. A parametric study of L2 acquisition: interpretation of Spanish word order. In *Contemporary Perspectives on The Acquisition of Spanish*, Vol. 1: *Developing Grammars*, A.T. Pérez-Leroux & W. R. Glass (eds.), 133–148. Somerville MA: Cascadilla Press.

Harrington, M. 2004. Commentary: Input processing as a theory of processing input. In *Processing Instruction: Theory, Research, and Commentary*, B. VanPatten (ed.), 79–92. Mahwah NJ: Lawrence Erlbaum Associates.

Jackson, C. 2007. The use and non-use of semantic information, word order, and case markings during comprehension by L2 learners of German. *The Modern Language Journal* 91: 418–432.

Lee, J.F. 1987. Comprehending the Spanish subjunctive: An information processing perspective. *The Modern Language Journal* 71: 50–57.

Lee, J.F. 1999. On levels of processing and levels of comprehension. In *Advances in Hispanic Linguistics*, J. Gutiérrez-Rexach & F. Martínez-Gil (eds.), 42–59. Somerville MA: Cascadilla Press.

Lee, J.F. 2002. The incidental acquisition of Spanish future tense morphology through reading in a second language. *Studies in Second Language Acquisition* 24: 55–80.

Lee, J.F. 2003. Cognitive and linguistic perspectives on the acquisition of object pronouns in Spanish. In *Spanish Second Language Acquisition: State of the Science*, B. Lafford & R. Salaberry (eds), 98–129. Washington DC: Georgetown University Press.

Lee, J. F. 2004. Commentary: On the generalizability, limits, and potential future directions of processing instruction research'. In *Processing Instruction: Theory, Research, and Commentary*, B. VanPatten (ed.), 311–323. Mahwah NJ: Lawrence Erlbaum Associates.

Lee, J.F. & Benati, A. 2007a. *Delivering Processing Instruction in Classrooms and Virtual Contexts: Research and Practice*. London: Equinox.

Lee, J.F. & Benati, A. 2007b. *Second Language Processing: An Analysis of Theory, Problems and Solutions*. London: Continuum.

Lee, J.F. & Benati, A. 2009. *Research and Perspectives on Processing Instruction*. Berlin: Mouton de Gruyter.

Lee, J. F. & Rossomondo, A. 2004. Cross experimental evidence for the incidental acquisition of Spanish future tense morphology. Paper presented at the Annual Symposium on Hispanic Linguistics, Minneapolis MN.

Lee, J.F. & VanPatten, B. 1995. *Making Communicative Language Teaching Happen*. New York NY: McGraw-Hill.

Lee, J.F. & VanPatten, B. 2003. *Making Communicative Language Teaching Happen*, 2nd edn. New York NY: McGraw-Hill.

Lee J.F., Cadierno,T., Glass, W. & VanPatten, B. 1997. The effects of lexical and grammatical cues on processing past temporal reference in second language input. *Applied Language Learning* 8: 1–27.

Malovrh, P.A. 2006. L2 sentence processing of Spanish OVS word order and direct object pronouns: an analysis of contextual constraints'. In *Selected Proceedings of the 9th Hispanic Linguistics Symposium*, N. Sagarra & A.J. Toribio (eds), 169–179. Somerville MA: Cascadilla.

Mitchell, R., & Miles, F. 2004. *Second Language Learning Theories*. London: Edward Arnold.

Musumeci, D. 1989. The Ability of Second Language Learners to Assign Tense at the Sentence Level: A Cross-linguistic Study. PhD dissertation, University of Illinois at Urbana-Champaign.

Rosa, E. & O' Neill, M. 1998. Effects of stress and location on acoustic salience at the initial stages of Spanish L2 input processing. *Spanish Applied Linguistics* 2: 24–52.

Rossomondo, A. E. 2007. The role of lexical temporal indicators and text interaction format on the incidental acquisition of Spanish future tense morphology. *Studies in Second Language Acquisition* 29: 39–66.

VanPatten, B. 1990. Attending to content and form in the input: An experiment in consciousness. *Studies in Second Language Acquisition* 12: 287–301.

VanPatten, B. 1993. Grammar instruction for the acquisition rich classroom. *Foreign Language Annals* 26: 433–450.

VanPatten, B. 1996. *Input Processing and Grammar Instruction: Theory and Research*. Norwood NJ: Ablex.

VanPatten, B. 2004. Input processing in second language acquisition. In *Processing Instruction: Theory, Research, and Commentary*, B. VanPatten (ed.), 5–31. Mahwah NJ: Lawrence Erlbaum Associates.

VanPatten, B. 2007. Input processing in adult second language acquisition. In *Theories in Second Language Acquisition*, B. VanPatten & J. Williams (eds), 115–135. Mahwah NJ: Lawrence Erlbaum Associates.

VanPatten, B. & Houston, T. 1998. Contextual effects in processing L2 input sentences. *Spanish Applied Linguistics* 2: 53–70.

VanPatten, B. & Jegerski, J. (eds). 2010. *Research in Second Language Processing and Parsing* [Language Acquisition and Language Disorders 53]. Amsterdam: John Benjamins.

VanPatten, B. & Keating, G. 2007. Getting tense: Lexical preference, L1 transfer, and native and non-native processing of temporal reference. Ms.

VanPatten, B. & Wong, W. 2004. Processing instruction and the French causative: Another replication. In *Processing Instruction: Theory, Research, and Commentary*, B. VanPatten (ed.), 97–118. Mahwah NJ: Lawrence Erlbaum Associates.

Wong, W. 2003. Textual enhancement and simplified input: effects on L2comprehension and acquisition of non-meaningful grammatical form. *Applied Language Learning* 13: 17–47.

Wong, W. 2004. The nature of processing instruction. In *Processing Instruction: Theory, Research, and Commentary*, B. VanPatten (ed.), 33–63. Mahwah NJ: Lawrence Erlbaum Associates.

Wong, W. 2005. *Input Enhancement: From Theory and Research to the Classroom*. New York NY: McGraw-Hill.

CHAPTER 6

Processability Theory

Explaining developmental sequences

Gisela Håkansson
Lund University

This chapter presents a psycholinguistic account of the developmental sequences found in second language acquisition (SLA). Building on Levelt's (1989) model of speech production, Processability Theory (PT: Pienemann 1998, 2005) proposes that the order in which morpho-syntactic structures are acquired will be controlled by the processing requirements of those structures. The cross-linguistic validity of PT will be illustrated by the analysis of learner data in some typologically diverse languages. The findings show that the hierarchical sequence of processing procedures is similar across languages, if the emergence criterion is used, and also that the influence of any previously acquired language is constrained by the processability of the structures. The implications of these findings for SLA research and profiling will be discussed.

Introduction

It is a well-known fact that some linguistic phenomena are acquired before others in the development of a target language. When it concerns morpho-syntactic development, there is a large body of observations from the early morpheme studies (Dulay & Burt 1973, 1974; Bailey, Madden & Krashen 1974), to the studies on negation (Ravem 1968; Wode 1978), and the word order analyses in the Multidimensional Model (Meisel, Clahsen & Pienemann 1981). The idea of stages in second language development is in accordance with the interlanguage view of Corder (1967), Nemser (1971) and Selinker (1972), who suggested that L2 development should be seen from the perspective of the learner and not in relation to a standard language norm. The assumption was that L2 learners create their own versions of the target language, and that they approach the target in a series of stages in the interlanguage continuum. Therefore, progress in the target language should be evaluated from the second language learner's own achievement – similarly to the view on language development in young L1 children.

The early studies were heavily criticised, mainly for methodological reasons, for example the restricted choice of morphemes and the use of accuracy orders and mean scores to show development. The study by Meisel et al. (1981) marked a shift of perspective in this regard. They suggested an emergence criterion instead of a mastery criterion. This means that the focus changed to how the individual learner proceeds from one stage to another, instead of measuring group scores of correctness. The claim was that, using this method, it could be demonstrated how certain given structures emerge before others.

A further issue concerns the explanation of the developmental patterns. The stages were described as instances of *a built-in-syllabus* (Corder 1967) and as representing "natural sequences" (Dulay & Burt 1974; Krashen 1977) but despite numerous observations of developmental sequences there were very few attempts to explain them.

The purpose of this chapter is to present the explanations for the developmental stages given by Processability Theory and how the stages are operationalized in a way to make detailed predictions that can be tested on different target languages.

Processability Theory

The aim of Processability Theory (henceforth, PT) is to explain the order in which morpho-syntactic phenomena emerge in the learner's production. The explanation lies in the architecture of the human language processor and the central assumption is that this processor works as a guide to and a constraint on language learning. The learner can only acquire what he/she can process, and the processing procedures are acquired in an implicational order. The hierarchy of processability is universal and can be applied to all languages. PT relates to Levelt's (1989) model of language production, in particular the part of the model that deals with the grammatical encoding of a message. The learner's route to the target language is interpreted as a development of processing procedures needed to handle grammatical structures. In Levelt's (1989) model, detailed processing procedures are suggested to explain speech production in adult native speakers. The procedures are automatized and make it possible for the speaker to handle communicative situations in real time: to interpret what others say, and planning and producing utterances at the same time. For adult native speakers these procedures operate automatically, but language learners have to develop them step-by-step.

According to the predictions of PT, first of all a new lexicon must be annotated, not only with forms and meanings, but also with syntactic categories and functional roles. When the L2 lexicon is annotated, the phrase procedure – with agreement between items – can operate. In many languages this is realized in overt noun phrase and verb phrase agreement. When the phrase procedure is automatized, the S(entence)-procedure becomes available to the learner, and noun phrase and verb phrase are joined together, in some languages resulting in subject-verb agreement. The PT assumption is that the procedures are accessible in this order, from the smaller units of the lexicon to the full sentence. The stages are acquired in implicational order, and each stage in the hierarchy serves as a necessary prerequisite for the next higher stage.

> [...] the task of acquiring a language includes the acquisition of the procedural skills needed for the processing of the language. It follows from this that the sequence in which the target language (TL) unfolds in the learner is determined by the developmental sequence of processing routines that are needed to handle the TL's components. (Pienemann & Håkansson 1999: 385)

For the grammatical description of the grammatical phenomena involved, PT uses Lexical-Functional Grammar (LFG) (Bresnan 2001; Kaplan & Bresnan 1982). The use of LFG makes it possible to extend the processing hierarchies to different languages. One of the key points is the *unification of features*; another key point is the *mapping of arguments*. In this chapter the procedures and their relation to feature unification will first be illustrated by examples from English. Table 1, which should be read bottom-up, depicts the hierarchy of processing procedures, the scope of feature unification and the outcome in English grammar for each stage. In the first stages there is no grammatical exchange between elements and the learner has to rely on bare words alone, but as the grammar develops there are more and more unification points. The different stages are acquired in an implicational order, i.e. the processability of one stage implies that also the preceding stages are processable.

In the initial phases of the acquisition process the learners do not use unification of features between words. The first stage only involves invariant forms of words or memorized chunks (lemmas or invariant forms of words or chunks, without the learner always being aware of the word boundaries). In the next stage (Stage 2), the category procedure is accessible to the learner and the words may be inflected after having been assigned word categories. The first inflections to appear

Table 1. Hierarchy of stages (based on Pienemann 1998)

Processing procedures	Feature unification	Outcome: English grammar
Stage 5: Subordinate clause procedure	Across clauses	Cancel inversion
Stage 4: S-procedure	Across phrases	SV agreement
Stage 3: Phrasal procedure	Within phrases	NP agreement
Stage 2: Category procedure	No	Lexical morphemes
Stage 1: Lemma access	No	invariant forms

are the lexical morphemes, for example, the English tense suffix (*play-ed*) or plural suffix *(car-s)*. The first example of unification of features between words emerges at Stage 3, when the phrasal procedure becomes available. At this stage, the learner is able to process the unification of features between words in a phrase, for example "many dog-s". At the next stage (stage 4), the inter-phrasal procedure is processable, and the learner is able to unify features between noun phrase and verb phrase and use inter-phrasal morphemes. In other words, sentence functions are available. This means that the learner is able to match a third-person-subject with an -s on the verb (e.g. *She play-s the piano*). Stage 5, finally, involves unification across clauses and gives access to the subordinate clause procedure. For English (and many other languages) this entails different demands on main and subordinate clauses. A direct question has subject-verb inversion (*What time is it?*) whereas the inversion has to be cancelled in an indirect question, the subordinate clause (*I wonder what time it is*). In this way, the scope of which features can be unified is gradually extended, so that the learner is first able to process words with local markings, then unify features within phrases, across phrases and finally across clauses.

The second key point of LFG that is utilized by PT is the mapping of arguments (see Pienemann & Keßler 2011; Pienemann, Di Biase & Kawaguchi 2005). The mapping of arguments proceeds from an early stage where learners are predicted not to distinguish the subject from the topic, to a later stage when discourse functions will be processable and passives and topicalizations will emerge in the learners' production. By linking the unification of features and mapping of arguments to the processing procedures it is possible to translate the developmental hierarchy into different languages as target languages.

Data and the emergence criterion

The scope of PT is the procedural knowledge and the very onset of the grammatical skills. This makes the emergence criterion, first used in Meisel et al. (1981), a useful tool to assess developmental stages. When the processing prerequisites for a given stage are in place, the linguistic structure is expected to emerge in the learners' production – if there are contexts for the structure in question. This implies, firstly, that it is important to use elicitation instruments to ensure that there will be linguistic contexts, and, secondly, that the researcher has to pay close attention to the first occurrence of a structure. The emergence of the structure is the point when the processing operations can be carried out, and not when they are always used. The emergence is an important marker in the acquisition process:

> From a descriptive viewpoint one can say that this is the beginning of an acquisi-
> tion process, and focusing on the start of this process will allow the researcher to
> reveal more about the rest of the process. (Pienemann 1998: 138).

This means that, unlike in many other theoretical frameworks, studies undertaken within PT do not look at the final state, or a state of mastery, with percentage of correctness. The use of an emergence criterion instead of a mastery criterion with percentage of correctness marks a perspective in language acquisition research where the focus is on how the individual learner proceeds from one stage to another, instead of a target language perspective, where the distance to the native speaker norm is measured, often with group means instead of individual learners. The emergence criterion is better suited to capture the dynamics of development by stating that a structure is processable.

The emergence criterion is not without problems, however. It is important to note that the first emergence criterion does not only mean that the learner produces a particular structure once – it has to be the first *systematic* occurrence. This is necessary in order to prove that the structure is processable. In order to rule out memorized chunks, or formulas, a distributional analysis has to be carried out to find where the structures are used. The aim is to state morphological and lexical variation. Morphological variation implies that for a morpheme to be counted as productive, and not a memorized chunk, there has to be a functional distinction, for example that the same word occurs in both singular form (*car*) in a singular context and plural form (*cars*) in a plural context. If the learner uses *cars* in all contexts, this is not counted as plural morphology. The selection of an appropriate suffix is not crucial, what is important is whether the learner has the ability to make a distinction between singular and plural. This means that both correct (*child-ren*) and incorrect (*child-s*) inflections will count as evidence of processing of plural, as long as there is a functional distinction. Overgeneralizations are good indicators of processability since the learner is not merely repeating what has been heard from others, but actively creating his/her own version. Overgeneralizations are expected to occur until the target structure is acquired. Lexical variation implies that a particular affix must be used with different lexical items. For example, the plural suffix must be added to different nouns (*dogs, cars, friends*). The exact number of lexical items necessary to determine productiveness (two, three or four) depends on how many contexts for a structure can be found in the data. The optimal corpus of data is one where there is a high data density, i.e. many obligatory contexts (for a discussion of how the emergence criterion is used in different studies, see Pallotti 2007).

Since PT deals with the processing procedures needed for language production, and since it is inspired by Levelt's (1989) model for speech production, it could be expected that the predictions only worked for on-line speech production, and that there are different constraints on different production modes. However, the study by Schönström (2010) on the acquisition of written Swedish shows that PT can be applied also to written data. This study explores the L2 acquisition of written Swedish by deaf learners, having Swedish Sign Language as their first language. The study comprised written narratives from pupils at a school for the deaf and hearing-impaired. Both written and signed narratives were collected. The elicitation methods were designed in a way to cover the structures predicted by PT, for example lexical, phrasal and inter-phrasal structures. For comparison, signed data was collected by free stories. The analysis of the written material shows that the development of written Swedish by deaf learners follows the stages predicted by the PT hierarchy. It is the same development that was found in the studies of spoken data (e.g. Glahn, Håkansson, Hammarberg, Holmen & Lund 2001). Similarly, Håkansson and Norrby (2007) found that the structures predicted by PT were at comparable levels in the oral and written production of L2 learners of Swedish and the implicational order of structures was found to be the same. The differences that were found concerned lexical choices and complexity measures such as degree of subordination. This means that the impact of planning time when learners write, in comparison to when they express themselves in spontaneous speech, does not change the requirements for structures to be processable in a hierarchical order. Learners are not able to "stretch" their interlanguage to include more levels in writing than in speech. The planning time can, however, influence other phenomena, not accounted for within PT.

Cross-linguistic validity and empirical evidence

The fact that the underlying processing procedures are universal makes it possible to apply the processability hierarchy to any language. Languages that have been studied are for example Arabic (Mansouri 2000, 2005), Chinese (Zhang 2004), English (Charters, Dao & Jansen 2011; Pienemann 1998), German (Baten 2011; Jansen 2008; Pienemann 1998), Italian (Di Biase & Kawaguchi 2002), and Japanese (Kawaguchi 2005; Di Biase & Kawaguchi 2002). The PT hierarchy suggested for Swedish was first tested in a meta-study with data from 14 empirical studies of the acquisition of Swedish morphology and syntax, involving over 1700 learners (Pienemann & Håkansson 1999). Since this first presentation of the Swedish PT hierarchy a number of studies with new data on Swedish L2 have been published, for example Eklund Heinonen (2009), Håkansson (2001), Håkansson and Norrby (2007, 2010), Philipsson (2007), Rahkonen and Håkansson (2008) and Schönström

(2010). In Glahn et al. (2001) the Swedish hierarchy was used as the basis to test the PT predictions on spoken data from L2 Swedish, Danish and Norwegian.

For each of the above mentioned languages, grammatical structures have been interpreted through LFG, and hierarchies of processing procedures have been established. Table 2 below illustrates the processing procedures and gives some examples of the grammatical outcome in English, Italian, Japanese and Swedish.

As shown in Table 2, there are similarities and differences between the four languages in terms of the grammatical outcome from the same underlying processing procedures. The starting point for all learners is stage 1, lemma access, and learners only use uninflected, invariant forms at first. At the stage of category procedure (stage 2) lexical morphemes emerge. To simplify the picture, only one example is given for each language (noun suffixes for plural in English, Italian and Swedish; verb suffixes for past in Japanese). At stage 3, the phrasal procedure, there are overt phrasal markings (morphemes for NP agreement and VP agreement). Major differences between the four languages are found at stage 4, of the S-procedure (Sentence procedure, with grammatical feature unification across phrases). For English, evidence for the emergence of S-structure is found in subject-verb agreement. Italian, however, is a pro-drop language, and the clitic object is regarded as better evidence for S-procedure than subject-verb agreement. In Japanese, the agreement between noun marking and marking on the predicate in the production of passives, causatives or benefactives is predicted to emerge at this level. For Swedish, finally, subject-verb inversion is the indicator of the processing of S-structure. At the stage of subordinate clause procedure, examples are given only for English and Swedish, and the suggested structure is the difference in word

Table 2. Processing procedures and outcome of English, Italian, Japanese and Swedish (after Di Biase & Kawaguchi 2002; Pienemann 1998; Pienemann & Håkansson 1999)

Processing procedures	Outcome: English grammar	Outcome: Italian grammar	Outcome: Japanese grammar	Outcome: Swedish grammar
5. Subclause procedure	Cancel inversion			Subclause word order
4. S-procedure	SV agreement	Topic-obj agreement	Noun – predicate marking	Subject-verb inversion
3. Phrasal procedure	NP agreement	NP agreement	VP agreement	NP agreement
2. Category procedure	Noun suffix	Noun suffix	Verb suffix	Noun suffix
1. Lemma access	Invariant forms	Invariant forms	Invariant forms	Invariant forms

order between main and subordinate clauses. Empirical data from learners of these languages have given support to the developmental hierarchy. The results demonstrate that it is possible to predict the order of emergence of morphological and syntactic structures in typologically different languages.

On the whole, data from L2 learners acquiring different languages have shown that morphological and syntactic phenomena are acquired in the predicted order and thus they give support to PT, both when it concerns spoken and written production data. However, there is a limitation in that these studies in that they often focus on structures from just a few stages, and not the whole hierarchy.

The support for PT is strongest in studies using the emergence criterion. The structures emerge in the order that is predicted by PT. Studies using accuracy percentages give a variable picture, which shows that the relationship between order of emergence and degree of accuracy is not clear. Some of the structures that are predicted to emerge early are not produced more accurately than structures later in the hierarchy. For example, analyses of L2 French (Bartning 2000; Dewaele & Veronique 2001) have demonstrated that accuracy is not higher for the phrasal level than for the inter-phrasal level, which could be expected if accuracy and development were the same. A similar example is the study by Klein Gunnewiek (2000) on the L2 acquisition of German word order by Dutch speakers. The results from this study show that the accuracy percentage was actually higher for one of the late word order patterns than for the early one. Studies such as these show that development and mastery are not related, and that language development does not proceed in a steady course towards more and more accuracy. "On the contrary, it is quite likely and well attested in empirical studies that accuracy rates develop with highly variable gradients in relation to grammatical items and individual learners" (Pienemann 1998: 137). Some structures are used in all obligatory contexts almost immediately as soon as they have emerged, whereas other structures display a slower development.

Another group of studies that have found contradictory evidence are investigations based on grammaticality judgment data. In order to decide on the grammaticality of a sentence, learners tap on their declarative knowledge, and not their procedural knowledge. Empirical studies show that for the same learner the results from declarative knowledge and procedural knowledge may differ. For example, when comparing written learner production to grammaticality judgement tasks, Philipsson (2007) found that the data from the learners' written production of L2 Swedish were compatible with the predictions from PT, while the results from the grammaticality judgements from the same learners were less uniform and often conflicted with the results from production data. In a similar approach Ellis (2008) compared the results from declarative and procedural knowledge of L2 English. He used two tests of implicit/procedural knowledge (oral imitation and oral narrative), which both resulted in the implicational order of structures predicted by PT, and two tests on explicit/declarative knowledge (grammaticality judgements), which yielded other results. For example, the category procedure (stage 2) was easiest in both conditions, but in the explicit tasks the structure from stage 5 scored second. When confronted with sentences to judge, learners seem to use another source of knowledge (declarative) and not the procedural skill that is used when producing language – even if the production is based on an elicited imitation task.

The role of transfer in developmental sequences

Transfer – or the influence of previously learned languages – is a much-discussed topic in SLA. It can affect all levels of language: phonology, lexicon, grammar, discourse and gesture. It is rarely, however, discussed in connection with development. PT offers a perspective on transfer of morpho-syntactic structures, which allows it to be integrated with developmental sequences. The basic idea is that learners cannot transfer what they cannot process. In other words, transfer from other languages cannot take precedence over the processability hierarchy. Morpho-syntactic structures are predicted to emerge in the same implicational order irrespective of the languages previously known by the learners. For example, the lexicon has to be annotated before morpho-syntactic processes can take place. Nevertheless, transfer is still an option, since it may facilitate the acquisition once the structure is processable.

This hypothesis, formulated as the Developmentally Moderated Transfer Hypothesis (DMTH) (Håkansson, Pienemann & Sayehli 2002; Pienemann, Di Biase, Kawaguchi & Håkansson 2005) stands in contrast to many suggestions in the literature, where transfer is claimed to be *the* most influential factor in L2 acquisition. For example, the Full Access/Full Transfer Hypothesis (Schwartz & Sprouse 1996) claims that the initial state of L2 acquisition is the full L1 grammar. This implies that the learner is expected to start with the assumption that the word order is the same in the L2 as in the L1.

The DMTH was first tested in a study of Swedish learners of L2 German (Håkansson, Pienemann & Sayehli 2002). This combination of source and target is interesting, since both languages are V2 languages, with obligatory subject-verb inversion after a preposed element in declarative sentences. According to the Full Access/Full Transfer Hypothesis the learners are expected to transfer this structure from the initial stage, since it is part of their first language. The DMTH, on the other hand, predicts that learners will not transfer subject-verb inversion until the earlier stages have emerged. The reason is that subject-verb inversion is placed at a high stage in the PT hierarchy (stage 4) and learners are expected to be able to process both the lexical (stage 2) and phrasal (stage 3) procedures before they are able to produce subject-verb inversion in the L2.

The study by Håkansson et al. (2002) involved 20 beginning 13–14 year old learners of L2 German, in their first and second year, respectively. The data was collected in an interview with a native speaker of German with only limited knowledge of Swedish, which made it natural for the learners to use their incomplete German skills in a conversation. The results gave full support to the DMTH and rejected the Full Transfer/Full Access hypothesis. As was hypothesized by the DMTH, the first year learners did not produce subject-verb inversion, despite the fact that they had access to the same structure in their L1 Swedish. Instead, they used the verb in third position, which is a structure that is ungrammatical both in Swedish and in German. This structure is common in the interlanguage of L2 learners with other first language, for example Romance languages (Meisel et al. 1981) and English (Jansen 2008). This shows that Swedish learners acquire subject-verb inversion in German just like any other learner. Another piece of evidence showing that the learners did not transfer the sentence patterns from Swedish is that they used very short sentences (mean value 2.91 words/sentence). If they had used transfer from the L1 Swedish they would have used both subject-verb inversion and longer sentences. A complicating factor in this data is that the Swedish learners had studied English in school before they took German. This means that transfer from English could also have been an option for them. However, this does not explain the short utterances, or the absence of preposed adverbs in some of the learners. If there were a direct transfer from their L2 English to L3 German, preposed adverbs would have been expected to occur. The dearth of adverb-fronted clauses in the learners' production is in agreement with the predictions of PT, since adverb fronting emerges later than subject-initial clauses. In other words, structures from stages 2 and 3 were expected to occur in the production of these early beginners, and this was also what was found.

The asymmetry that has been found in some studies on word order transfer gives additional support to the DMTH. As mentioned above, subject-verb inversion is hypothesized to emerge at Stage 4, after the category and phrasal procedures are already processable, and it is not expected to be transferred until it is processable. The SVO word order, on the other hand, belongs to Stage 2 and it can be transferred earlier. This is exactly what has been found in studies comparing pairs of languages. For example, French-Swedish bilinguals were found to transfer the French (SVO) word order into Swedish but not the Swedish subject-verb inversion into the production of French (Schlyter 1998). Færch (1994) found that English speakers transferred their SVO word order into L2 Danish, but Danish speakers did not transfer subject-verb inversion (the V2 word order) into L2

English to the same extent. Similarly, Rahkonen (1993) found more transfer by Finnish speakers learning Swedish, than by Swedish speakers learning Finnish. These examples show that the word order of the lower stages of the hierarchy is more often involved in transfer.

Support for the DMTH comes not only from word order studies. Other studies supporting developmentally moderated transfer are for example Cabrera's (2010) study on the acquisition of Spanish inchoative *se* (as in *La ventana se rompió* 'the window broke') by English-speaking learners, and the study by Charters et al. (2011) on the acquisition of English plural morphology in Vietnamese-speaking learners. In the study on inchoative structures, Cabrera came to the conclusion that "[...] transfer requires a certain level of competence in the L2" (Cabrera 2010: 168) since only advanced learners, but not beginning learners, transferred the distinction between alternating and non-alternating verbs from English to Spanish in an acceptability task. Beginning learners showed no preference for verb types. In a study on noun morphology, Charters et al. (2011) found that Vietnamese learners of English seemed to use a Stage 3 structure (phrasal agreement) before a Stage 2 structure (lexical morphology) and therefore contradicting the PT hierarchy. However, a closer analysis came to the interpretation that the two items were activated as independent concepts at the lexical level (numeral and noun) and reminiscent features of their Vietnamese processor. These two studies, each in their own way, demonstrate that different aspects of the L1 are transferred at different levels of proficiency.

Measuring language development by profiling

The idea of linking developmental stages to language assessment has been discussed for decades. For first language acquisition the mean length of utterance (MLU) is used to measure the developmental level, but there is no similar measure for SLA. In 1978, Larsen-Freeman made a call for an index in L2 development:

> What we need is a yardstick which will allow us to give numerical value to different points along a second language developmental continuum – numerical values that would be correlates of the developmental process and would increase uniformly and linearly as learners proceed towards full acquisition of a target language. (Larsen-Freeman 1978: 440)

The use of developmental stages as basis for measuring language is known as a profiling (Clahsen 1985; Crystal & Fletcher 1979). The idea is "[...] to analyse a corpus of one learner's spontaneous speech in order to reconstruct the linguistic rules of his/her interlanguage and in order to assess the developmental stage he/

she has already reached" (Clahsen 1985: 299). Profiling as a test method differs from traditional tests in using developmental data (instead of deviations from a norm) being research-based (instead of using more or less arbitrary structures) and looking for examples of contrasts instead of counting right or wrong. A construction-based assessment along these lines was proposed in Pienemann, Johnston and Brindley (1988). They selected morpho-syntactic structures for L2 English and had assessors rate the development of L2 learners on observation forms. This idea was later implemented in the computer program Rapid Profile (Keßler & Liebner 2011; Pienemann 1998). Rapid Profile is a tool for linguistic profiling directly based on PT. It provides a computer-assister screening procedure for the assessment of English as L2, and it builds on what is known about the L2 learners' development from empirical studies. The analyst listens to speech data from specifically designed communicative tasks and the information of the morpho-syntactic features is then entered in the computer. This is done as the analyst ticks the boxes with the particular structures. The program keeps track of the morphological and lexical variation needed to assess whether a structure can be considered productive, and evidence for the learner having reached a specific developmental level. If there are too few examples from a specific structure the program provides examples of more communicative tasks to ensure data density. Finally the feedback from the program gives information of the developmental level of the learner. The teacher can use the information given by this procedure in order to decide which structures the teaching should be focussing on.

Rapid Profile has been designed to give fast profiles, but there are some drawbacks such as the need to have trained observers to carry out the analyses. Also, there have to be communicative tasks to ensure that there are a sufficient number of obligatory contexts. In order to simplify the procedure, Ellis (2008) suggests that an Oral Imitation Test can be an easier way to find spontaneous "authentic" language production. Ellis tried out some of the PT structures in implicit (oral imitation) and explicit (grammaticality judgment) tasks and found that the predicted order emerged in the results from the oral imitation task. Ellis concludes that, "This test appears capable of producing data with the same essential characteristics as the free constructed response data which Processability research has utilized" (Ellis 2008: 17). Another attempt to make the analyses easier was made by Spinner (2011). Spinner examined short data samples from spontaneous production of L2 learners of English and found that the PT predictions were supported despite the limited length of each learner' data (45–194 words) and despite the fact that some structures did not appear.

Profiling bilingual development

Since PT is non-language specific and can be applied to different languages, it can also be used to profile development of more than one language. The developmental sequences may be realized in different morpho-syntactic structures, but they are based on the same underlying processing procedures. This gives rise to research questions concerning the issue of whether simultaneously bilingual children develop one linguistic system from start (Volterra & Taeschner 1978) or whether they establish a difference between the systems (De Houwer 1990). It also raises the question of how the languages interact. In a study of the simultaneous development of Japanese and English, Itani-Adams (2011) investigated the development of both languages, following the PT predictions. The child was a simultaneous bilingual child, with exposure to both Japanese (the mother) and English (the father) in the home environment. The analyses built on the hierarchies of Japanese and English that have been established by Kawaguchi (2005) and Pienemann (1998). The results demonstrated that both languages developed according to the PT hierarchy but they had different timing, so that a particular level in one language did not imply the same level in the other language. This supports the PT predictions and also the hypothesis of separate development.

Håkansson, Salameh and Nettelbladt (2003) and Salameh, Håkansson and Nettelbladt (2004) also investigated the bilingual development of children growing up with Arabic and Swedish. Arabic was the language spoken at home, and Swedish the language used in preschool. The age of onset of Swedish was about two, which is below the age that most researchers state is the onset of L2 acquisition. PT was used as a yardstick to measure the bilingual development and the analyses made use of the hierarchies for Arabic and Swedish that were suggested by Mansouri (2000, 2005) and Pienemann and Håkansson (1999).

The aim of the Swedish study was to examine whether children diagnosed with language impairment based on tests in Swedish could be identified as having language problems in both languages, using profiling based on the PT hierarchy. Of the twenty children participating in the study, ten children had typical development, and ten children had been diagnosed with language impairment. Data was collected three times over a period of 12 months. The hypothesis was that if the children had language impairment they would show low levels of development in both languages. If they had typical development, they might have lower level of Swedish because of less exposure (in preschool, in contrast to Arabic that was used in the homes). The results demonstrated implicational orders for both the Arabic and Swedish structures for both groups of children. When it came to the progress of the individual children the hypothesis was confirmed: The typically developing children used higher-stage structures in at least one language, whereas the children diagnosed with language impairment stayed at balanced low levels (two of the children even regressed in one or both of their languages) This shows that it is important to measure both languages when diagnosing children with language impairment. In children with typical development the two languages can have different timings, but in children with language impairment neither of the languages develops at the same speed as in typical development.

The profiling of language development in bilingual children is an unexpected outcome of PT. The fact that the underlying procedures are non-language specific makes it possible to follow the developmental route of typologically different languages like Japanese and English and Arabic and Swedish. However, using developmental stages established for L2 development raises many questions about similarities and differences between different types of learners: adult second language learners, child second language learners, and simultaneous bilinguals.

Concluding remarks

This overview of PT has demonstrated that it has the potential to predict and explain developmental stages for a wide range of typologically different languages. This is due to the fact that the underlying processing procedures are universal, and only the surface morpho-syntactic features are language-specific. The empirical studies reported on in this chapter have given support to the developmental sequences predicted by PT, both in spoken and written data. It is important to note, however, that many studies only account for a restricted number of structures. The whole picture of how processing procedures develop is not known yet, nor what drives development forward.

The findings reported here give rise to new questions in SLA research, such as the difference between procedural and declarative knowledge in L2 acquisition. Studies using data from grammaticality judgments, tapping declarative knowledge, do not lend support to PT predictions, but sometimes result in other orders of development (see Ellis 2008). The DMTH can shed light on some of the confounding results found in transfer studies. According to PT, the learner is assumed not to transfer structures until they are processable, and structures high on the hierarchy will therefore not be accessible for transfer at the initial stage. This means that some structures, such as the SVO word order, seem to be highly transferable already at the beginning stage, whereas other word orders, such as V2, are less prone to be transferred until the learner has reached a certain developmental stage.

PT has also proved to be useful in assessing language development, for example as a profiling instrument as in Rapid Profile. The possibility to measure development of both languages in bilinguals is a unique feature of PT, and makes it a powerful tool when it comes to diagnosing language impairment in bilingual children. It may be a coincidence that the structures selected in the PT hierarchies are the same for first and second language acquisition. But, when profiling both languages in children, we leave the field of SLA, and enter an arena where the borders between L1 and L2 acquisition are blurred. The major differences between L1 and L2 learners are found in studies from adult L2 learners and monolingual child learners. If the L1 – L2 differences are only found in these populations, we need to open up the field to new learner categories such as heritage learners, early child L2, late child L2, 2L1 children, L3 learners ... etc. These new learner categories are challenging theories of L1 and L2 acquisition.

References

Bailey, N., Madden, C. & Krashen, S. 1974. Is there a 'natural sequence' in adult second language learning? *Language Learning* 21: 235–243.

Baten, K 2011. Processability Theory and German case acquisition. *Language Learning* 61: 455– 505.

Bartning, I. 2000. Gender agreement in L2 French: Pre-advanced vs. advanced learners. *Studia Linguistica* 54: 225–237.

Bresnan, J. 2001. *Lexical-functional Syntax*. Malden MA: Blackwell.

Cabrera, M. 2010. Intransitive/inchoative structures in L2 Spanish. In *Selected Proceedings of the 12th Hispanic Linguistics Symposium*, C. Borgonovo, M. Español-Echevarría & P. Prévost (eds), 160–170. Somerville MA: Cascadilla Proceedings Project.

Charters, H., Dao, L. & Jansen, L. 2011. Reassessing the applicability of Processability Theory: The case of nominal plural. *Second Language Research* 27: 509–533.

Clahsen, H. 1985. Profiling second language development: A procedure for assessing L2 proficiency. In *Modelling and Assessing Second Language Acquisition*, K. Hyltenstam & M. Pienemann (eds), 283–331 Clevedon: Multilingual Matters.

Corder P. 1967. The significance of learners' errors. *International Review of Applied Linguistics* 5: 161 – 169.

Crystal, D. & Fletcher, P. 1979. Profile analysis of language disability. In *Individual Differences in Language Ability and Language Behaviour*, C. Fillmore, J. Kempler & W. Wang (eds), 167–188. New York NY: Academic Press.

De Houwer, A. 1990. *The Acquisition of Two Languages from Birth*: A Case Study. Cambridge: CUP.

Dewaele, J-M. & Veronique, D. 2001. Gender assignment and gender agreement in advanced French interlanguage: a cross-sectional study. Bilingualism: *Language and Cognition* 4: 275–297.

Di Biase, B. & Kawaguchi, S. 2002. Exploring the typological plausibility of Processability Theory: language development in Italian second language and Japanese second language. *Second Language Research* 18: 274–302.

Dulay, H & Burt, M. 1973. Should we teach children syntax? *Language Learning* 23: 245–258.

Dulay, H & Burt M. 1974. Natural sequences in child second language acquisition. *Language Learning* 24: 37–53.

Eklund Heinonen, M. 2009. Processbarhet på prov. Bedömning av muntlig språkfärdighet hos vuxna andraspråksinlärare. PhD dissertation, Uppsala University.

Ellis, R. 2008. Investigating grammatical difficulty in second language learning: Implications for second language acquisition research and language testing. *International Journal of Applied Linguistics* 18: 4–22.

Færch, C. 1994. Giving transfer a boost describing transfer variation in learners' interlanguage performance. *Scandinavian Working Papers on Bilingualism* 2: 1–22.

Glahn, E., Håkansson, G., Hammarberg, B., Holmen, A., Hvenekilde, A. & Lund, K. 2001. Processability in Scandinavian second language acquisition. *Studies in Second Language Acquisition* 23: 389–416.

Håkansson, G. 2001. Tense morphology and verb-second in Swedish L1 children, L2 children and children with SLI. Bilingualism: *Language and Cognition* 4: 85–99.

Håkansson, G. & Norrby, C. 2007. Processability theory applied to written and oral L2 Swedish. In *Second Language Acquisition Research: Theory-construction and Testing*, F. Mansouri (ed.), 81–94. Newcastle upon Tyne: Cambridge Scholars.

Håkansson, G. & Norrby, C. 2010. Environmental influence on language acquisition: Comparing second and foreign language acquisition of Swedish. *Language Learning* 60: 628–650.

Håkansson G., Pienemann M. & Sayehli S. 2002. Transfer and typological proximity in the context of second language processing. *Second Language Research* 18: 250–73.

Håkansson, G., Salameh, E.-K. & Nettelbladt, U. 2003. Measuring language development in bilingual children: Swedish-Arabic children with and without language impairment *Linguistics* 41: 255–288.

Itani-Adams, Y. 2011. *Bilingual first language acquisition*. In Pienemann & Keßler (eds), 121–130.

Jansen, L. 2008. Acquisition of German word order in tutored learners: A cross-sectional study in a wider theoretical context. *Language Learning* 58: 185–231.

Kaplan R. & Bresnan J. 1982. Lexical-Functional Grammar: A formal system for grammatical representation. In *The Mental Representation of Grammatical Relations*, J. Bresnan (ed.), 173–281. Cambridge MA: The MIT Press.

Kawaguchi, S. 2005. Agreement structure and syntactic development in Japanese as a second language. In Pienemann (ed.), 253–298.

Keßler, J.-U. & Liebner, M. 2011. Diagnosing L2 development. Rapid Profile. In Pienemann & Keßler (eds), 133–148.

Klein Gunnewiek, L 2000. *Sequenzen und Konsequenzen: Zur Entwicklung niederlandischer Lerner im Deutschen als Fremdsprache*. Amsterdam: Rodopi.

Krashen, S. 1977. Some issues relating to the Monitor Model. In *On TESOL '77*, H.C. Brown, D. C. Yorio & R. Crymes (eds). Washington DC: TESOL.

Larsen-Freeman, D. 1978. An ESL index of development. *TESOL Quartlerly* 12: 439–448.

Levelt, W.J.M. 1989. *Speaking: From Intention to Articulation*. Cambridge MA: The MIT Press.

Mansouri, F. 2000. *Grammatical Markedness and Information Processing in the Acquisition of Arabic as a Second Language* [Lincom Studies in Language Acquisition 2]. Munich: Lincom.

Mansouri, F. 2005. Agreement morphology in Arabic as a second language. In Pienemann (ed.), 117– 153.

Meisel, J. Clahsen, H. & Pienemann, M. 1981. On determining developmental sequences in natural second language acquisition. *Studies in Second Language Acquisition* 3: 109–135.

Nemser, W. 1971. Approximative systems of foreign language learners. *International Review of Applied Linguistics* 9: 115–123.

Pallotti, G. 2007. An operational definition of the emergence criterion. *Applied Linguistics* 28: 361–382.

Philipsson, A. 2007. Interrogative Clauses and Verb Morphology in L2 Swedish: Theoretical Interpretations of Grammatical Development and Effects of Different Elicitation Techniques. PhD dissertation, Stockholm University.

Pienemann, M. 1998. *Language Processing and Second Language Development: Processability Theory* [Studies in Bilingualism 15]. Amsterdam: John Benjamins.

Pienemann, M. (ed). 2005. *Cross-linguistic Aspects of Processability Theory* [Studies in Bilingualism 30]. Amsterdam: John Benjamins.

Pienemann, M. & Håkansson, G. 1999. A unified approach toward the development of Swedish as L2: A processability account. *Studies in Second Language Acquisition* 21: 383–420.

Pienemann, M. & Keßler, J.-U. (eds). 2011. *Studying Processability Theory* [Processability Approaches to Language Acquisition Research & Teaching 1]. Amsterdam: John Benjamins.

Pienemann, M., Johnston, M. & Brindley, G. 1988. Constructing an acquisition-based procedure for second language assessment. *Studies in Second Language Acquisition* 10: 217–243.

Pienemann, M., Di Biase, B. & Kawaguchi, S. 2005. Extending Processability Theory. Pienemann (ed.), 199–251.

Pienemann, M. Di Biase, B., Kawaguchi, S., & Håkansson, G. 2005. Processability, typological distance and L1 transfer. In Pienemann (ed.), 85–116.

Rahkonen, M. 1993. Huvudsatsfundamentet hos finska inlärare av svenska och svenska inlärare av finska (The main clause foundation among Finnish learners of Swedish and Swedish learners of Finnish). In *Svenskan i Finland 2*, V. Muittari & M. Rahkonen (eds), 199–225.

Rahkonen, M. & Håkansson, G. 2008. Production of written L2-Swedish – processability or input frequencies? In *Processability Approaches to Second Language Development and Second Language Learning*. J-U. Keßler (ed.), 135–161. Newcastle upon Tyne: Cambridge Scholars.

Ravem R. 1968. Two Norwegian children's acquisition of English syntax. In *Second Language Acquisition. A Book of Readings*, E. Hatch (ed.), 148–154. Rowley MA: Newbury House.

Salameh, E.-K., Håkansson, G. & Nettelbladt, U. 2004. Developmental perspectives on bilingual Swedish-Arabic children with and without language impairment: A longitudinal study. *International Journal of Language & Communication Disorders* 1: 65–71

Schlyter, S. 1998. Directionality in transfer? *Bilingualism: Language and Cognition* 1(3): 183–184.

Schönström, K. 2010. Tvåspråkighet hos döva skolelever. Processbarhet och narrativ struktur i svenska och svenskt teckenspråk. PhD dissertation, Stockholm University.

Schwartz, B.D. & Sprouse, R.A. 1996. Cognitive states and the Full Transfer/Full Access model. *Second Language Research* 12: 40–72.

Selinker, L. 1972. Interlanguage. *International Review of Applied Linguistics* 10: 209–231

Spinner, P. 2011. Second language assessment and morphosyntactic development. *Studies in Second Language Acquisition* 33: 529–561

Volterra, V. & Taeschner T. 1978. The acquisition and development of language by bilingual children. *Journal of Child Language* 5: 311–326.

Wode, H. 1978. The L1 vs. L2 acquisition of English negation. *Working Papers on Bilingualism* 15: 37–57.

Zhang, Y. 2004. Processing constraints, categorial analysis, and the second language acquisition of Chinese adjective suffix -de (ADJ). *Language Learning* 54: 437–468.

CHAPTER 7

Sociocultural Theory and second language development

Theoretical foundations and insights from research

Gabriela Adela Gánem-Gutiérrez
University of Essex

This chapter provides an overview of the theoretical foundations of Sociocultural Theory and an up-to-date account of current research stemming from this perspective. At the core of this theory is mediation, which refers to the process that enables humans to deploy physical and psychological tools to gain control over social and mental activity. Development is seen as the ability to internalise or make use of culturally created means of mediation, e.g., language, to gain such control. Language development is therefore seen as the ability to increasingly take part in social activity. In turn, this ability is implicated in linguistic change in a recurring and interdependent developmental cycle. The chapter discusses how crucial questions have been addressed by key Sociocultural Theory scholars and explores how future empirical investigation can further contribute to our understanding of second language acquisition (SLA).

Introduction

Sociocultural Theory (SCT) has its roots in the work of the Russian psychologist Lev Vygotsky. The essence of Vygotsky's theory of mind is captured in "the notion that human mental functioning results from participation in, and appropriation of, the forms of cultural mediation integrated into social activities" (Lantolf & Beckett 2009: 459). This, in turn, leads to Vygotsky's methodological argument that in order to understand an individual, it is necessary to study that individual in the context of his/her history, as a socio-cultural being. From a SCT perspective, learning a foreign/second (L2) language is, therefore, seen as the increasing ability to use the new language as a mediational tool, both socially and cognitively.

Unlike most authoritative sources available on SCT and L2 learning (e.g., Lantolf 2000; 2011; Lantolf & Thorne 2006, 2007; Swain, Kinnear & Steinman 2011), this chapter is not organised in relation to the various key concepts which form the foundations of Vygotsky's theory of mind. Instead, following a brief scene-setting description of the main tenets of SCT, I have organised this selective overview in three parts which, together, address major aspects concerning second language learning theorising: Views on the nature of L2 knowledge; views on the nature of L2 learning and development; and views on the L2 learner and the linguistic environment. Furthermore, each of the three sections is subdivided into *Theoretical foundations* and *Insights from research* in order to explore links between theoretical assumptions, empirical studies, and pedagogical practice, which is very much at the core of SCT. In the concluding section I explore some of the contributions that SCT has made to the general field of second language acquisition (SLA) and reflect on issues for future research.

SCT: Main tenets

Mediation and *praxis* are the two core concepts underlying current conceptualisation and application of Vygotskian theory to L2 learning. Mediation is defined by Lantolf and Thorne as "the process through which humans deploy culturally constructed artifacts, concepts, and activities to *regulate* (i.e. gain voluntary control over and transform) the material world or their own and each other's social and mental activity" (2006: 79). Since language is an essential regulatory means in this developmental process, L2 development is seen as the ability to use the L2 to mediate both communicative and mental activity. This ability is measured in terms of the extent and nature of the mediational mechanisms needed for *regulation* described in terms of three stages: object-regulation, the stage where human activity is supported and even determined by objects in the environment; other-regulation, when development is supported by other people; and finally, self-regulation, the capacity for independent strategic functioning (Lantolf & Thorne 2007: 202–207).

Praxis defined as "the dialectical [bidirectional] unity of theory and practical activity as an instrument of change" (Lantolf & Beckett 2009: 459) represents the backbone of pedagogy. For Vygotsky, theory provides the foundations for practice, which in turn helps refine and redefine theory. In the context of L2 learning and teaching, praxis embodies pedagogical activity aiming at mediating L2 development by guiding the interaction between theoretical conceptual knowledge, e.g., scientific concepts such as grammar concepts, and knowledge derived from our everyday experience, i.e., spontaneous concepts, which are empirically and implicitly learned (see Brooks, Swain, Lapkin & Knouzi 2010; Daniels 2007). This stance on pedagogical intervention ultimately permeates the various approaches to mediated activity discussed in the section on L2 learning and development below, e.g., work in the zone of proximal development, Concept-Based Instruction, and Dynamic Assessment.

The force behind the *social* formation of mind, as envisaged by Vygotsky, is dialectical change (Lantolf & Thorne 2006; Wertsch 1985). From this perspective, social activity does not just influence cognition, "[it] is the process through which human cognition is formed" (Lantolf & Johnson 2007: 878). Both concepts, the mediated nature of human activity and praxis as conceived by Vygotsky ultimately reflect a fundamental argument of SCT: the power of mediated activity relies on the recursive cycle which guides development. In other words, the use of tools, both physical and psychological, mediates change and, in turn, the transformed capacities resulting from that process become the basis for further construction of increasingly sophisticated tools, e.g., language (Lantolf & Thorne 2007).

On the nature of L2 knowledge

Theoretical foundations

I would like to begin this section by highlighting two general, but key issues in relation to knowledge underpinned by Vygotskian thought before focusing more specifically on the nature of L2 knowledge from a SCT perspective. First, SCT does not see knowledge, of any kind, as an entity or object that can be exchanged as a finished product between individual minds or "that exists outside particular situations of knowing; [knowledge] does not pre-exist the activity but is what is recreated, modified, and extended in and through collaborative knowledge building and individual understanding" (Wells 1999: 89). Second, Vygotsky put forward the notion of *concept*, particularly *scientific concepts*, as an ideal unit for instruction. According to Vygotsky, we acquire scientific knowledge at school in an abstract, but coherent, logical, way; scientific concepts can be important mediational mechanisms based on generalisation and abstraction. Importantly, this type of knowledge is suitable for explicit, i.e., conscious, examination (Lantolf 2011: 306). Scientific concepts contrast, but interact with, 'spontaneous concepts', those which are acquired "outside of the contexts in which explicit instruction [is] in place", that is through everyday experience (Daniels 2007: 311). Following this line of thought, we can – and do – construct scientific concepts as units to explicitly examine and further understand language, be it our L1 or an additional/foreign language.

Regarding L2 knowledge more specifically, SCT has been criticised for not locating "itself more explicitly with respect to linguistic theory" (Mitchell & Myles 2004: 220). Such reasoned observation has given rise to interesting responses by leading SCT scholars such as James Lantolf and Steven Thorne. On the one hand, they have emphasised key views on the nature of L2 knowledge and cognition which have always informed SCT research, albeit implicitly. On the other hand, and perhaps more importantly, they have now explicitly identified Cognitive linguistics (Langacker 2008) as a compatible theory which can provide a specific linguistic framework to SCT given their shared understanding of linguistic form as subservient to meaning (see Lantolf 2011: 304). Grammar is seen as a set of linguistic conventions appropriated from and through social interaction. Conventions about form are, however, shaped by the meanings that speakers want to convey and those meanings are rooted in each individual's history and specific communicative goals. Language is then the communicative -and cognitive- tool for individuals to fulfil "their own meaning-making needs" (Lantolf & Thorne 2006: 17) and therefore evolves as a constant, creative force, which is situated in activity and "unfolds in different ways under different circumstances" (Donato 2000: 47).

Based on this conceptualisation of language, it follows that from a SCT perspective, the conceptual meanings internalised from the social plane during our ontological development are an essential component of who we are. During our lives we learn to map, as well as shape, meanings and form, which leads to "the interesting question of whether learning additional languages in adulthood results in conceptual shifts in how a person talks and, therefore, thinks about events in the world" (Choi & Lantolf 2008: 191–192). Lantolf and colleagues propose that such an issue can be investigated by exploring relationships and co-occurrences between gesture, speech, and thought, – the latter two being particularly important for Vygotsky. Work in this area has been further informed by both, Slobin's (1996) thinking for-speaking (TFS) framework and McNeill's (2005) growth point (GP) hypothesis.

Following a weak version of the Sapir-Whorf linguistic relativity hypothesis, Slobin (1996: 91) contends that "as we gain experience using our language, our minds are trained in taking particular points of view for the purposes of speaking and that it seems to become exceptionally difficult for us to be retrained" (cited in Choi & Lantolf 2008: 192). As Choi and Lantolf (2008: 192) further explain, Slobin's TFS hypothesis suggests that: (a) "in the activity of speaking, thinking is filtered through language as speakers undertake to verbalize events and states in the world" and, importantly, TFS may influence both how we grammatically encode (talk) about events and how we attend to and experience those events; (b) linguistic categories are more or less supported by sensory experience; those categories which are more supported, e.g., plural markers, might present less difficulty for L2 learners, while those categories such as aspect, voice, definiteness, motion, represent a bigger challenge. Based on the Vygotskian concept of inner speech,[1] McNeill (2005) argues that gesture, as an intrinsic part of language, also needs to be considered to fully understand TFS. Gestures are material carriers of thinking which form a dialectical unity of imagistic depiction and a verbal representation (McNeill 2005: 98) or what he calls, a growth point (GP).

Insights from research

Choi and Lantolf (2008) and Negueruela, Lantolf, Jordan and Gelabert (2004) are two of the very few studies framed within the theoretical position outlined above which have begun to address the issue of whether or not L2 speakers are able to adopt the L2 TFS pattern for encoding motion events. Both of these studies used Talmy's (2000) motion event typology which categorises languages according to the way in which they encode 'path' of motion, that is the trajectory or site occupied by a figure and includes, among other categories, 'manner', i.e., the particular way the motion is performed: "languages pattern either like English, which most often encodes path in a satellite phrase (e.g., The cat ran *out of* the room) [and is therefore considered a satellite or S-framed language], or like Spanish, which [is considered a verb, V-framed, language since it] conflates path in the verb (e.g., El gato salió corriendo de la sala "The cat left running from the room")" (Choi & Lantolf 2008: 193). The argument is that the investigation of L2 speakers' ability (or lack of) to shift encoding patterns can be informed by analysing gesture while they narrate events since speakers' synchronisation of gesture-speech differs between the two language types when individuals describe motion events.

Both studies are similar in research design and address the same issue although the language combinations differ: English and Spanish in Negueruela et al. (2004) as opposed to English and Korean in Choi and Lantolf (2008). The participants in the studies were highly proficient in their L2 and had lived in a L2 speaking community between one and four years. As noted above, the general question addressed was: "Do advanced L2 speakers shift toward an L2 TFS pattern or do they rely on their L1 pattern as evidenced in the gesture/speech interface?" (Negueruela et al. 2004: 124).

The overall answer to the question based on the findings of these studies is negative. It appears that L2 speakers rely on their L1 thinking patterns when describing motion events; in other words, their preferences to express motion differ from those of L1 speakers. Negueruela et al. (2004: 134) and Lantolf and Thorne (2006: 105–108) provide a series of examples to illustrate this argument, but for

---

1.   Self-regulatory mental speech whose origins lie in social speech (Lantolf & Thorne 2006:72).

reasons of space I only focus on two instances relating to the fact that none of the L1 Spanish speakers used any of the fine-grained manner verbs of English in their description of *motion events* when narrating a story:

(1)   the [frog appears] . . . from inside the salad (L2 English)
      (path: both hands coming up toward the speaker's face)
      she goes to take a bite from the salad and out jumps the frog (L1 English)
      (no gesture)

In this example, the L2 speaker uses the English cognate of the Spanish verb *aparecer*, a common way of depicting the motion in Spanish, and conveys through gesture, the frog's path rather than the manner of its motion, thus producing what McNeill (2005) calls a manner fog, i.e. encoding manner exclusively in a gesture, instead of through semantic and syntactic structures.

   A second example comes from an L1 English speaker as she attempts to describe in L2 Spanish the motion of some salad (caused by a frog's movements) while it is being carried on a waiter's tray:

(2)   la ensalada [está ... como en medio aire] (L2 Spanish)
      'the salad [is like in mid-air]'
      (manner: hand shaking palm down)

The authors' interpretation of this example is that the speaker begins to produce what appears to be a progressive construction comprised of the auxiliary *estar* 'to be' and a verb in the progressive form. At this point, she pauses, which probably indicates that a lexical search is under way for a verb which conflates motion and manner.

   As mentioned above, the authors concluded that their participants sustained their L1 TFS pattern as reflected in their gesture-speech interface. However, there were suggestions that a shift for path might occur more easily than a shift for manner, albeit for highly proficient speakers of the L2; as the authors point out, much more research in this area is needed before any firmer conclusion can be reached. This brief review does not do justice to this, and other, complex and nuanced topics, nor to the two studies considered here, but I hope it captures the line of argumentation put forward by the authors. A further aspect regarding the study of gesture in the context of L2 learning is discussed in the section on learning and development below. I now turn to SCT's views on the nature of L2 learning and development.

On the nature of L2 learning and development

Theoretical foundations

In SCT, development refers to the increasing and transformative ability to exercise control over higher-order mental processes and functions[2] such as voluntary attention, and conscious control or awareness; in other words, development is seen as the ability of individuals (and groups) to make use of the culturally created means of mediation – originally made available by others through assisted performance– to increasingly control physical and mental activity (Lantolf 2005: 336). The transformative, dialectical process which accounts for the developmental connection between the social plane and mental activity is referred to as *internalisation* where imitation, play, and private speech (self-directed speech)[3] are examples of key mechanisms which enable the eventual achievement of self-regulation (Lantolf & Thorne 2006: 152–157).

Driving development is instruction which takes account of the *zone of proximal development* (ZPD). Vygotsky (1978: 86) defines this concept in terms of actual and potential development. The essence of actual development is self-regulation, i.e., what the individual is able to do independently. Potential development is what is beyond the independent understanding or problem solving abilities of that individual. Within one's potential development, the ZPD refers to the distance between what we can do independently and what we can do with assistance, en route to independence. As emphasised by Lantolf and Poehner (2011) and Poehner and Lantolf (2005), the ZPD is not statically defined by an outside task or piece of knowledge, such as a grammatical form, but is part of a larger process that defines learning in terms of the ever-shifting needs of the individual and the amount and quality of assistance required (see also Aljaafreh & Lantolf 1994). Given that the driving force of learning from this perspective is collaboration between novices and more experienced others, the ZPD is at the crux of pedagogical and methodological considerations regarding learning and development and how they are investigated and measured empirically.

Turning to the L2 context, learning and development entail the ability to appropriate, and re-shape, the L2 meaning-making tools: "Learning an additional language is about enhancing one's repertoire of fragments and patterns that enables participation in a wider array of communicative activities" (Lantolf 2005: 349)

---

2.   In contrast to lower/elementary-mental processes/functions, such as involuntary memory, involuntary attention, reflexes, spatial cognition, quantification ... etc (Vygotsky 1978).

3.   *Private speech* is considered a precursor of *inner speech*, i.e., socially rooted speech internalised by the individual and which serves a psychological, self-regulatory function (De Guerrero 2005; Lantolf &Thorne 2006).

and can eventually serve as a mediational mechanism to regulate mental functioning (Donato 2000: 45). Language ability can therefore be measured in terms of the
learner's use of the L2 and the level of accuracy of his/her performance which is, of
course, a view shared by other perspectives to L2 learning. However, through the
notion of the ZPD, SCT brings to the fore another essential aspect in determining
a learner's ability; that is, the *amount* and *type* of assistance required during task
performance. So, language development is ultimately determined by both the increasing ability to control our linguistic resources for communication and the increasing ability to make use of those resources for self and other regulation.

To investigate development Vygotsky proposed the genetic, or historical,
method which is considered one of his most important contributions to the study
of mind (Lantolf & Thorne 2006: 225). Vygotsky advocated a focus on the process
rather than the product of development, "analysis that returns to the source and
reconstructs all the points in the development of a given structure" (Vygotsky
1978: 65). The genetic method relates to four domains: The *phylogenetic* domain is
concerned with how the human mind evolved differently from other life forms by
means of culturally mediated tools; the *sociocultural* domain concerns mediation
and the different kinds of mediational tools adopted and valued by society; the
ontogenetic domain studies the appropriation of these mediational tools and how
they are integrated into cognitive activity during the individual's development. Finally, the *microgenetic* domain focuses on the overt, in-formation, instance of
learning as it happens during interpsychological activity "over a relatively short
span of time (for example... learning a word, sound, or grammatical feature of a
language" (Lantolf 2000: 3).

Insights from research

Based on the Vygotskian views and constructs outlined above, SCT scholars have
set out to investigate issues pertaining to the contextual factors enabling, or otherwise, development. If, as argued by Vygotsky, development originates in the social
plane and knowledge is co-constructed inter-psychologically to be subsequently
internalised by the individual, evidence for the social formation of mind must be
sought in social activity itself. This overarching premise has resulted in the empirical investigation of social interaction generally, and speech specifically
(although not exclusively), as the key mediational mechanisms in the process of
internalisation. This section provides an overview of current research pertaining
to these and interrelated issues.

Verbalisation

A key construct in the study of semiotic tools as mediational mechanisms for L2 learning is verbalisation. Verbalisation or 'languaging' refers to the act of *producing* language to mediate cognitive activity; the argument is that producing language, using language as a mediational tool for understanding, can aid internalisation of language and language concepts (Swain 2010: 115). Verbalisation can take place on an individual basis, e.g., self-explanation, or through collaborative activity, e.g., pair work. The latter has been a major area of empirical work among SCT researchers for the last three decades.

Swain and colleagues (Kowal & Swain 1997; Swain & Lapkin 2001) have identified *collaborative dialogue* as the type of dialogue "where language use and language learning can co-occur. Collaborative dialogue is language use mediating language learning. It is cognitive activity and social activity" (Swain 2000: 97). The work of these and other scholars (e.g., Donato 1994; Gánem-Gutiérrez 2004) has demonstrated how *collaborative dialogue* emerging from learners' interactions when engaged in problem-solving activity can lead to the co-construction and internalisation of L2 knowledge.

Verbalisation in the form of self-explanation has also been found to play an important role, for example in the learning of grammatical concepts. Based on the Vygotskian construct of Concept Based Instruction (CBI) (Gal'perin 1969; Vygotsky 1978, 1987), Negueruela (2008) and Negueruela and Lantolf (2006) proposed an instructional approach for enhancing L2 learning which respects the following principles:

–   Concepts are seen as the minimal pedagogical unit;
–   Those concepts have to be materialized, for example by means of diagrams, charts, models, which serve as didactic mediational tools for learners;
–   As part of this pedagogical model, concepts must be verbalised as the act of (self) explanation becomes a psychological tool for gaining regulation.

Based on pioneering work on CBI (Knouzi, Swain, Lapkin, & Brooks 2010; Lapkin, Swain & Knouzi 2008; Swain, Lapkin, Knouzi, Suzuki & Brooks 2009), Gánem-Gutiérrez and Harun (2011) investigated the potential of CBI, and in particular of verbalisation (individual and dyadic), as a mediational tool for supporting the understanding of tense-aspect marking in L2 English. The participants were six postgraduate volunteers at a British University. They were all advanced L2 English speakers (five L1 Arabic and one L1 Thai). The study relied on a pre/post-test design to investigate the level of improvement in the participants' understanding of the concept in question as a result of the CBI treatment. This consisted of looking at slides, which included diagrams and animation; the slides explained tense-aspect marking in English and were based on Radden and Dirven's (2007) cognitive linguistics model to facilitate a semantically grounded understanding of the concept. Participants were asked to either self-explain, for those working individually, or discuss, if working in pairs, the content of the slides. All verbalisations were audiorecorded and subsequently transcribed for analysis. The day after the CBI treatment, participants completed the tense-aspect post test.

Quantitative findings demonstrated that five of the six participants improved their understanding of tense-aspect marking in English. The second aim of the study was to investigate, through microgenetic analysis (Vygotsky 1978; see also Gánem-Gutiérrez 2008), the specific role of verbalisation during the CBI procedure. The authors reported that verbalisation played an important role for participants to manage the task and for helping them to gain regulation in relation to their understanding of the concept. In particular, some semiotic tools, for example reading aloud, repetition, and use of discourse markers, supported individual and collaborative reasoning through functions such as focusing, questioning, explaining, and inferencing (see also Knouzi et al. 2010).

The use of socially rooted semiotic tools as reasoning aids has also been documented in other studies; for example, repetition, i.e., verbatim replication of either what others say or self-repetition, has been shown to help sustain interaction and act as a tool for problem-solving (McCafferty 1994; Roebuck & Wagner 2004). Repetition can aid reasoning (Buckwalter 2001); and it can act as a regulatory tool for the appropriation of language as well as for achieving intersubjectivity; that is, for co-creating a shared perspective on the task, which is essential for successful collaborative activity, e.g., for the co-construction and maintenance of scaffolding[4] (see DiCamilla & Antón 1997). The use of the L1 has received increasing attention both in studies investigating interaction in general (Alegría de la Colina & García Mayo 2009; Brooks & Donato 1994; Buckwalter 2001; De Guerrero and Villamil 2000; Lee 2008) and also in its own right (Antón & DiCamilla 1998; Ohta 2001; Swain & Lapkin 2000).

More recently, Gánem-Gutiérrez (2009) and Gánem-Gutiérrez and Roehr (2011) have demonstrated how discourse markers such as *and, but, or, oh, now, then, y'know, I mean* (Schiffrin 1987) act as verbal aids which support and enable task handling and reasoning. For instance, interjections and similar particles can act as transitional tools which help students move the task along. Markers of cause and result relationships such as *so, because,* and coordinate conjunctions such as

---

4.   The neo-Vygotskian metaphor of scaffolding refers to those facilitating actions that the tutor or more expert peer brings into the interaction in order to help the novice through their process of internalisation (Mitchell & Myles 2004).

and, tend to support reasoning and are, therefore, important regulatory mechanisms during verbalisation.

Gesture

The study of gesture is increasingly gaining the attention of L2 learning researchers in general and SCT scholars in particular. The latter have focused on two aspects of gesture, i.e., the appropriation of gesture specific to the L2 culture and, to a greater extent, the use of gesture as a mediational tool for regulation – inter and intra-psychologically– by L2 learners (Gullberg & McCafferty 2008; Lantolf & Thorne 2006). Gesture is understood here as face, hand, and body movements which co-occur with speech and carry both communicative and psychological meaning. It is because of this dual property that gesture is considered "an enhanced window into mental processes" (McNeill & Duncan 2000 cited in Lantolf 2010: 133).

In an early study on the use of gesture as a tool for L2 regulation by learners of L2 Spanish and L2 Japanese, McCafferty (1998) found similarities between gesture and private speech at semantic and functional levels during narrative tasks. Both gesture and private speech were found to have similar regulatory functions; for example the results showed that beats were primarily used as a form-focused device to help produce an appropriate verb form, while iconic (representing objects or actions) and metaphoric gestures (representing abstract ideas) aided speakers to both, convey meaning, but also cognitively to retrieve lexical items (see also McCafferty 2006; Lee 2008). Furthermore, semantic elements ascribed to private speech were also found in gesture, e.g., a link between its use and the psychological predicate[5] of an utterance.

In a more recent study, Lantolf (2010) discusses a case study of an advanced L2 learner of French and her use of gesture as a mediational mechanism for linguistic problem-solving. This descriptive study shows how a learner makes use of gesture as a mediational tool for thinking while she tries to decide on the appropriate aspectual form (*passé composé* vs. *imparfait*) she needs for narrating an event. In this paper, Lantolf puts forward the thought provoking idea that it might be possible to teach L2 learners to use gesture as a strategic device for enhancing cognitive activity although this needs to be explored in the future.

---

5.   This Vygotskyan concept refers to a statement of an event or state, which can only be understood with reference to the context, i.e., "the psychological predicate and its context are mutually referring" (McNeill 2005: 106).

Internalisation

Private speech is considered a key mechanism for internalisation, the process through which language, originally available in the social environment, becomes a tool or resource for cognitive activity. In relation to L2 learning, internalisation is the process through which the learner appropriates the L2 for cognitive, self-regulatory activity as well as for communication. Private speech is characterised by reduced phonology; elliptical or abbreviated morphosyntactic features; and reduction of form which tends to be compensated by semantic richness (Lantolf & Thorne 2007; see also De Guerrero 2005). Private speech has been studied in relation to (a) its role as an aid to internalisation of the L2 (Ohta 2001); and (b) its regulatory role when L2 learners encounter either cognitive or language problems; that is, as an aid to gaining self-regulation and exercising control over the task at hand (Donato 1994; Frawley & Lantolf 1985; McCafferty 1994, 1998).

Centeno-Cortés and Jiménez Jiménez (2004) represents an example of a study investigating the use of L2 for cognitive regulation. They compared the use of private speech by native speakers of Spanish and L1 English speakers of L2 Spanish at two different levels of proficiency (intermediate vs. advanced) during individual cognitive problem-solving activities. While the advanced L2 speakers used a combination of Spanish and English private speech in the preliminary stages of problem-solving activity, most switched to the L1 when reasoning became more intense. Moreover, when participants maintained the reasoning process in the L2, they either responded incorrectly to the problem or gave up. Intermediate L2 speakers consistently used private speech in their L1 to tackle the task.

Evidence of the role of private speech as an aid to internalisation of the L2 has most notably been presented by Ohta (2001) in her longitudinal case study of seven adult students of Japanese throughout an academic year. Analysis of 34 classroom hours of transcribed data including peer-interactions, as well as teacher-fronted sessions, demonstrates the role of private speech as a means to tackle pronunciation or grammatical problems and to test hypotheses, for example. Three main types of private speech were identified: *repetition*, for instance of the tutor or classmates' utterances; *manipulation*, for example through language play when sounding words, breaking down words or constructing their own utterances in a private manner; and *vicarious responses*, i.e., a learner covertly answering a question addressed to another student or completing or correcting somebody else's utterance (p. 40).

Assessing development

A most contended issue in the field of second language learning is that of defining what counts as evidence of learning and here Vygotskian theory has proved to be invaluable. Key to this is the concept of the zone of proximal development (see above). This construct has been extensively used as a tool for assessing, understanding, documenting, and indeed promoting development. Aljaafreh and Lantolf's (1994)[6] is a seminal study rooted in the ZPD which explored the role of other-regulation during the provision of feedback. This study has been influential among SCT scholars and practitioners alike because apart from demonstrating the importance of taking into account quality and amount of mediation required as well as performance to assess development, it has also been a blueprint for operationalising the construct for practical purposes. The study's well known regulatory scale has, directly or indirectly, informed a substantial body of research into regulation, feedback, and assessment.

Some of the main contributions of research based on the ZPD have been: (1) Identifying strategies and recommendations for the effective provision of feedback; for instance, the co-creation of collaborative frameworks through dialogue and intersubjectivity, and the importance of receiving gradual, contingent, and situated help; in other words, help attuned to the learner during (pedagogical) interaction (Aljaafreh & Lantolf 1994); (2) providing evidence of the ways in which L2 learners use and provide assistance, and of some of the benefits that collaborative activity brings to L2 learning in the classroom (De Guerrero & Villamil 2000; Donato 1994; Ohta 2001); and (3) providing evidence about the differential effect that sensitivity, or lack of, to the ZPD for the provision of feedback might have on L2 learning (Nassaji & Swain 2000).

For some years now scholars, primarily led by Matthew Poehner, have been urging for more active and systematic exploitation of the potential of the ZPD as Vygotsky originally intended; that is, as a tool to understand poor performance with the aim to promote change, i.e., to use it to diagnose learners' abilities as well as to orient practitioners in supporting developmental processes simultaneously (Lantolf & Poehner 2011: 12–13). Dynamic Assessment (DA) represents such pedagogical application of this concept and it is characterised by seeing instruction and assessment as two aspects of one and the same educational activity. Assessing performance within the framework of DA involves gauging individual ability as a point of departure for providing assistance while taking into consideration the amount and quality of that assistance for assessment purposes. Another important element is the extent to which the individual is able to subsequently transfer the mediated performance to tasks similar to those where DA was implemented (Lantolf & Poehner 2011; Poehner 2008, 2009). This is an emerging area of L2 learning research and there are only a handful of published empirical studies to

---

6.   This study is not described in any detail here because it is widely cited and reviewed in work on the ZPD.

date. Furthermore, a main concern of those studies has been to describe how practitioners have interpreted DA and implemented it in their own teaching context,
indeed a crucial matter (see Antón 2009; Poehner 2009), but only a preliminary
step into full investigation of the effects of DA for L2 development.

A robust study on the implementation of DA in an L2 context has been reported by Poehner (2008). The focus of his study was L2 French morphology with
specific reference to the use of perfective and imperfective aspect by six advanced
L2 French university students. Poehner's design followed four stages: 1. pre-tests,
dynamic and non-dynamic; 2. intervention, on a one-to-one tutoring basis for
eight weeks; 3. post-tests, dynamic and non-dynamic; and 4. two transfer sessions.
Analysis of the data involved tracking the participants' development both within
as well as across mediation sessions. Microgenetic analysis, provides evidence of
participants' changing abilities as they gradually required less explicit assistance
and began to respond to mediation more autonomously or, as Poehner describes
it, "they began to reciprocate in more agentive ways" (p. 138). A main pedagogical
objective of the study was to outline ways in which practitioners can implement
DA effectively by taking advantage of 'mediator-learner dialoguing' (p. 116) in
order to estimate learners' abilities accurately, identify precise sources of difficulty,
and promote and document changes in learners' performance. A challenge for
pedagogues interested in implementing this instructional approach is how to make
it work with groups of students, e.g., in L2 classrooms rather than on a one-to-one
basis as most studies to date have done. Ongoing projects exploring group implementation are reported in Ableeva (2008); Erben, Ban, and Summers (2008); and
Kozulin and Garb (2002).

As evident in the amount and scope of research mentioned in this section,
documenting some of the processes and mechanisms involved in L2 learning has
been a particular strength of SCT. The following section focuses on another key
aspect of L2 learning, the role of the learner which, from this perspective, involves
engagement with the learning environment.

On the L2 learner and the linguistic environment

Theoretical foundations

The learner brings to the task of L2 learning his/her biological capacities, life experiences educational history, goals, motivation, beliefs, perceptions, values, and
so on. This ontological baggage, necessarily and continuously, influences the active (re)creation of the linguistic signs originally afforded by others, and which are

eventually manipulated and appropriated by the self in order to communicate as well as to share and regulate mental capabilities. This understanding of the learner is what the concept of *agency* embodies: the power to act (Donato 2000; Kramsch 2000), and what renders cognition a socially rooted and a socially shared capacity whose origins and development can, therefore, be tracked back to social interaction.

An L2 environment rich in developmental affordances is, from this perspective, an environment where both, physical and psychological mediational tools are available for the co-construction of zones of proximal development. This conceptualisation goes beyond what the notion of 'linguistic environment' conveys and is captured in van Lier's term 'semiotic budget' which, as he puts it, "does not refer to the amount of 'input' available, nor the amount of input that is enhanced for comprehension, but to the opportunities for meaningful action that the situation *affords*" (my italics) (van Lier 2000: 252). To adequately understand the multilayered complexity of L2 learning as situated activity where learners and environment form a dialectical unit, it is necessary to examine the various components without losing sight of the whole. Activity Theory (AT) can be an invaluable lens to achieve such a task. *Activity Theory* (see Engeström 2001; Lantolf & Thorne 2006) is then a theoretical and methodological framework based on Vygotskian thought for the analysis of complex relationships and developmental processes. For Vygotsky, intentionality, motives, and goals are what drives higher forms of human activity, e.g., the type of mental activity required for learning an L2; it follows that to reveal those motives and goals, it is necessary to study activity as a whole, contextualised, dynamic process. Therefore, not only do we need to focus on the L2 learner as an active agent, but we also need to understand other dimensions of mental behaviour:

> *how* the person is acting (i.e., in consort with artifacts or other individuals), *where* the person is acting (e.g., the experimental laboratory, the classroom, the public domain, etc.), *why* the person is acting (i.e., the motives and goals underlying the activity, and *when* the activity occurs since the same person can carry out the same task in a different way at two different points in time (Lantolf & Pavlenko 2001: 114).

AT provides the foundations to capture the various factors which can play a role in L2 learning as situated activity. This demands that the learner's actions are understood in relation to the mediational tools available, the rules of the social context or community where learning and teaching take place, and the actions of the other participants within the community (Engeström 2001) as Engeström's (2001: 135) 'activity triangle' illustrates:

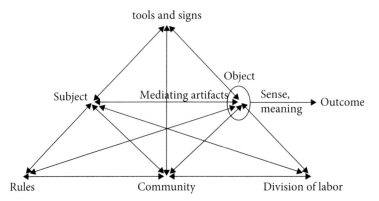

Figure 1. The activity triangle (Journal of Education and Work http://www.tandfonline.com)

In sum, AT is an approach to the study of dialectical relationships and, therefore, is the essence of Vygotskian thought. In the words of Roth and Lee (2007: 196):

> saying that a relation is dialectical is equivalent to saying that any part that one might heuristically isolate within a unit presupposes all other parts; a unit can be analyzed in terms of component parts, but none of these parts can be understood or theorized apart from the others that contribute to defining it.

To understand an individual, one needs to examine that individual as a social being, as a socio-culturally formed mind.

Insights from research

Research informed by AT therefore takes 'activity' as the minimal unit of analysis in order to adopt a holistic, non-reductionist, approach to the object of study; AT is a lens that allows us to zoom in and out the various transformative processes, factors, and relationships that can afford or constrain development. In this section, I present an overview of current research informed by this approach to understanding the L2 learner and the (linguistic/semiotic) environment (for an in-depth account of Activity Theory and L2 learning see Lantolf & Thorne 2006).

Focus on the learner: Our goal-oriented actions are facilitated or constrained by the dynamic interplay between tensions resulting from who we are and the particular contexts and relationships in which activity is instantiated as current, and previous, research clearly demonstrates. Studies by Coughlan and Duff (1994) and van Lier (2008), among others, have argued for making a distinction between *task* and *activity*. These studies present evidence of how L2 learners' orientation towards tasks has important repercussions on activity; i.e., what individuals or groups actually do while performing a task and which differs between different learners doing the same task and even when a particular individual performs a task in two different occasions. Importantly, some of these studies also demonstrate the evolving nature of motivation and the L2 self as identity(ies) are negotiated and re-negotiated with further engagement and investment in the new culture.

In a recent study on L2 motivation based on a six-week study abroad programme experience, Allen (2010) set out to investigate (a) the motives which informed students' engagement in L2 learning and how study abroad participation related to these motives; and (b) the goals the learners' had for the study abroad period and which elements afforded or constrained the realisation of those goals. Allen reported that enhanced L2 motivation and persistence in using the L2 emerged for the students whose motive for L2 learning was primarily linguistic, e.g., desire to achieve fluency or proficiency for academic, professional, and/or personal enhancement; but not for those whose motive was primarily pragmatic, e.g., to enhance a future career or enjoy travelling. These results were closely linked to the ability -also higher for linguistically oriented students- of participants to articulate specific goals and manage conflicting goals, and the ability to negotiate relationships with study abroad peers and the host family. In sum, participants whose L2 motivation benefitted from the study abroad period were those who "posited themselves as active agents of language learning, making sustained efforts to pursue linguistic goals" (Allen 2010: 47). The author advocates an interventionist approach to study abroad where goal-mediated action is facilitated for example by supporting students in the self-centred planning and execution of specific tasks which require structured interaction within the community.

Focus on tool: In the area of Computer-Assisted Language Learning (CALL), AT has informed the investigation of computer mediated interaction as a mechanism to promote L2 development. For instance, Thorne (2003) and Basharina (2007) have studied intercultural communication and L2 development in telecollaborative projects while Hémard (2006) combined Human-Computer Interaction (HCI) and AT to theorise about CALL evaluation with specific reference to task design and learner-computer interaction on the one hand; and to apply AT to the development of a sound, and much needed, hypermedia evaluation framework, on the other. An important and valid argument in her work is the need for improving the quality of online pedagogies which, in her view, have been at the mercy of "business models built on the need for fast and efficient delivery" (2006: 262). Based on a very rich data set including user walkthroughs, observations, and transcripts of recorded comments made by individual students and dyads working together, Hemard demonstrates the value of AT for enabling a much deeper level of analysis than other CALL evaluation frameworks.

Focus on skill: In the context of teaching Japanese as a foreign language (JFL) in Canada, Haneda (2007) used AT to examine the strategic behaviour of nine university students from various ethnolinguistic backgrounds including Taiwan, Canada, Japan, and Korea when writing in the foreign language. The participants' L2 proficiency ranged from intermediate to advanced. The main aim of the study was to use AT to better understand "the [participants'] differential modes of engagement in writing in an FL" (Haneda 2007: 302) as the foundations for improving pedagogical practice more closely tailored to students' needs. Three modes of engagement were identified: (a) writing as a language exercise and as a means of developing overall FL skills; (b) writing as a means to creating a coherent argument; (c) writing as a communicative activity. In the first instance, the author argues that if writing is perceived as a language exercise, little attention is paid to a potential reader (other than the teacher) or to the cultural activity system in which the writing is embedded. The second mode of engagement is considered an extension of the first in that there is awareness of a potential readership beyond the teacher, but the writer still fails to consider the linguistic and cultural tools appropriate to the target community. Finally, in the third mode, writing is seen as a true communicative act where a perceived audience guides the choice of "register, expression, and overall rhetorical structure" of the task at hand (Haneda 2007: 322). Haneda therefore argues for a re-conceptualisation of teaching writing in the L2 classroom where literacy in general is at the heart of the curriculum.

Conclusion

This chapter has outlined the theoretical principles which underpin SCT and provided a selective overview of current research informed by this approach to L2 learning and teaching. As a whole, the work of SCT scholars evolves from the three central tenets in Vygotsky's theory of mind:

– the mediated nature of human activity;
– the dialectic relationship between theory and practice, i.e., praxis;
– the genetic method as key to understanding development.

Vygotsky's radical views on the origins of (cognitive) development have had a profound influence on various scientific disciplines, including SLA. As this account has demonstrated, the contributions of SCT to SLA theory building and research are significant. At a theoretical level SCT has challenged prevalent views on the nature of L2 knowledge as well as on the importance of the social plane and the semiotic environment for L2 learning. SCT research has contributed to a deeper understanding of developmental mechanisms, in particular the role of speech, both private and social. This body of research has provided a significant account of specific mediational tools, and their socio-cognitive functions, deployed by learners when engaged in collaborative activity and verbalisation. Furthermore, Vygotsky's conceptualisation of development as being socially derived has important methodological repercussions as it is apparent in the theory's research methodology, i.e., the genetic method, particularly through the domain of microgenesis: "Microgenesis, refers simultaneously to both the *method* and the *object* of study. *Microgenetic* or historical analysis allows us to investigate and understand a particular event (learning as an *object* of study)" (Gánem-Gutiérrez 2008: 121). At a practical level SCT is committed to actively promoting development in the L2 classroom. As emphasised by Lantolf (2011: 42), SCT's "commitment to educational praxis" is driven by its views on the dialectic and, therefore, interdependent relationship between theory and practice. This, and its approach to empirical investigation, set it apart from other SLA theories, including socially oriented ones.

The theory's views on the essence of research as well as on how this has to be conducted have been an essential contribution to the SLA field; not least for their driving force in theory building debate between sympathising and sceptic scholars. Nonetheless, the very nature of its methodological approach is at the centre of what can be considered the shortcomings of SCT research. For instance, most of the studies discussed in this chapter are small scale investigations, and necessarily so given that it is precisely the intricacy and complexity of the localised, situated nature of activity that historic analysis aims to unravel. At a practical level, carrying out microgenetic analysis is time-consuming, which does not facilitate the study of large groups. Another contentious issue is the question of demonstrating the transferability and endurance of those instances of learning attested in the mediated activity which normally constitutes both the treatment and the data gathering in SCT research. The key to this issue is in the very nature of *activity* as discussed earlier in the chapter. Further research is therefore still needed regarding important issues such as the extent to which the kind of interventions outlined in some of the studies reviewed in this chapter can speed up L2 developmental processes; the extent to which co-constructed knowledge and collaborative activity enable individuals to increasingly fulfil their meaning-making needs (see Lantolf & Thorne 2006: 17) and effectively participate in communicative activities as members of L2 communities. It is also necessary to carry out further empirical investigations into the various mechanisms activated and deployed in dialogical activity to gain a more nuanced understanding of their potential as tools for individual and collective development. I believe that future SCT research will have to strike the right balance between safeguarding the study of the unique and seeking the patterns if it is to consolidate and enhance its already influential contribution to SLA theory building. SCT is by no means alone in the field's struggle to develop 'causal explanations' for learning as Mitchell and Myles (2004: 219) remind us, but for SCT this is even more pressing given its intrinsic and explicit commitment to lead L2 development through pedagogical intervention.

Acknowledgements

I wish to thank Roger Hawkins, the book editors, and the anonymous reviewers for their valuable comments on earlier versions of this chapter.

References

Ableeva, R. 2008. The effects of Dynamic Assessment on L2 listening comprehension. In *Sociocultural Theory and the Teaching of Second Languages,* J.P. Lantolf & M.E. Poehner (eds), 57– 86. London: Equinox.

Alegría de la Colina, A. & García Mayo, M.P. 2009. Oral interaction in task-based EFL learning: The use of the L1 as a cognitive tool. *International Review of Applied Linguistics* 47: 325–345.

Aljaafreh, A. & Lantolf, J. P. 1994. Negative feedback as regulation and second language learning in the zone of proximal development. *The Modern Language Journal* 78: 465–483.

Allen, H.W. 2010. Language-learning motivation during short-term study abroad: An activity theory perspective. *Foreign Language Annals* 43(1): 27–49.

Antón, M. 2009. Dynamic assessment of advanced second language learners. *Foreign Language Annals* 42(3): 576–598.

Antón, M. & DiCamilla F. 1998. Socio-cognitive functions of L1 collaborative interaction in the L2 classroom. *The Canadian Modern Language Review* 54: 314–342.

Basharina, O.K. 2007. An Activity theory perspective on student-reported contradictions in international telecollaboration. *Language Learning & Technology* 11(2): 82–103.

Brooks, F. & Donato, R. 1994. Vygotskyan approaches to understanding foreign language learner discourse during communicative tasks. *Hispania* 77: 262–274.

Brooks, L. Swain, M. Lapkin, S. & Knouzi, I. 2010. Mediating between scientific and spontaneous concepts through languaging. *Language Awareness* 19(2): 89–110.

Buckwalter, P. 2001. Repair sequences in Spanish L2 dyadic discourse: A descriptive study. *The Modern Language Journal* 85(3): 380–397.

Centeno-Cortés, B. & Jiménez Jiménez A.F. 2004. Problem-solving tasks in a foreign language: The importance of the L1 in private verbal thinking. *International Journal of Applied Linguistics* 14(1): 7–35.

Choi, S. & Lantolf, J.P. 2008. Representation and embodiment of meaning in L2 communication: Motion events in the speech and gesture of advanced L2 Korean and L2 English speakers. *Studies in Second Language Acquisition* 30: 191–224.

Coughlan, P. & Duff, P.A. 1994. Same task, different activities: Analysis of SLA task from an Activity Theory perspective. In *Vygotskian Approaches to Second Language Research,* P. Lantolf & G. Appel (eds), 173–194. Norwood NJ: Ablex.

Daniels, H. 2007. Pedagogy. In *The Cambridge Companion to Vygotsky,* H. Daniels, M. Cole & J.V. Wertsch (eds), 307–331. Cambridge: CUP.

De Guerrero, M.C.M. 2005 *Inner Speech – L2: Thinking Words in a Second Language*. Berlin: Springer.

De Guerrero, M. C. M. & Villamil, O. 2000. Activating the ZPD: Mutual scaffolding in L2 peer revision. *The Modern Language Journal* 84: 51–68.

DiCamilla, F.J. & Antón, M. 1997. Repetition in the collaborative discourse of L2 learners: A Vygotskian perspective. *The Canadian Modern Language Review* 53: 609–33.

Donato, R. 1994. Collective scaffolding in second language learning. In *Vygotskian Approaches to Second Language Research*, P. Lantolf & G. Appel (eds), 33–56. Norwood NJ: Ablex.

Donato, R. 2000. Sociocultural contributions to understanding the foreign and second language classroom. In *Sociocultural Theory and Second Language Learning*, J. Lantolf (ed.), 27–50. Oxford: OUP.

Engeström, Y. 2001. Expansive learning at work: Toward an activity theoretical reconceptualization. *Journal of Education and Work* 14: 133–156.

Erben, T. Ban, R. & Summers, R. 2008. Changing examination structures within a College of Education: The application of dynamic assessment in pre-service ESOL Endorsement Courses in Florida. In *Sociocultural Theory and the Teaching of Second Languages*, J.P. Lantolf & M.E. Poehner (eds), 87–114. London: Equinox.

Frawley, W. & Lantolf, J.P. 1985. Second language discourse: A Vygostskyan perspective. *Applied Linguistics* 6: 19–44.

Gal'perin, P.I. 1969. Stages in the development of mental acts. In *A Handbook of Contemporary Soviet Psychology*, M. Cole & I. Maltzman (eds), 249–73. New York NY: Basic Books.

Gánem-Gutiérrez, G.A. 2004. The Processes of Collaborative Activity in Computer-Mediated Tasks: in Search of Microgenesis. PhD dissertation, University of Southampton.

Gánem-Gutiérrez, G.A. 2008. Microgenesis, method and object: A study of collaborative activity in a Spanish as a foreign language classroom. *Applied Linguistics* 29(1): 120–148.

Gánem-Gutiérrez, G.A. 2009. Repetition, use of L1, and reading aloud as mediational mechanisms during collaborative activity at the computer. *Computer Assisted Language Learning* 22(4): 323–348.

Gánem-Gutiérrez, G.A. & Harun, H. 2011. Verbalization as a mediational tool for understanding tense/aspect marking in English: An application of Concept-Based Instruction. *Language Awareness* 20(2): 99–119.

Gánem-Gutiérrez, G. A. & Roehr, K. 2011. Use of L1, metalanguage, and discourse markers: L2 learners' regulation during individual task performance. *International Journal of Applied Linguistics* 21(3): 297–318.

Gullberg, M. & McCafferty, S.G. 2008. Introduction to gesture and SLA: Toward an integrated approach. *Studies in Second Language Acquisition* 30(2): 133–146.

Haneda, M. 2007. Modes of engagement in foreign language writing: An activity theoretical perspective. *Canadian Modern Language Review* 64(2): 297–327.

Hémard, D. 2006. Design issues related to the evaluation of learner – Computer interaction in a web-based environment: Activities vs. tasks. *Computer Assisted Language Learning* 19(2–3): 261–76.

Knouzi, I. Swain, M. Lapkin, S. & Brooks, L. 2010. Self-scaffolding mediated by languaging: Microgenetic analysis of high and low performers. *International Journal of Applied Linguistics* 20(1): 23–49.

Kowal, M. & Swain, M. 1997. From semantic to syntactic processing. How can we promote it in the immersion classroom? In *Immersion Education: International Perspectives*, R.K. Johnson & M. Swain (eds), 284–309. Cambridge: CUP.

Kozulin, A. & Garb, E. 2002. Dynamic assessment of EFL text comprehension of at-risk students. *School Psychology International* 23: 112–27.

Kramsch, C. 2000. Social discursive constructions of self in L2 learning. In *Sociocultural Theory and Second Language Learning*, J.P. Lantolf (ed.), 133–154. Oxford: OUP.

Langacker, R.W. 2008. The relevance of Cognitive Grammar for language pedagogy. In *Cognitive Approaches to Pedagogical Grammar*, S. De Knop & T. De Rycker (eds.), 7–35. Berlin: Mouton de Gruyter.

Lantolf, J.P. 2000. Introducing sociocultural theory. In *Sociocultural Theory and Second Language Learning*, J.P. Lantolf (ed.), 1–26. Oxford: OUP.

Lantolf, J.P. 2005. Sociocultural and second language learning research: An exegesis. In *Handbook of Research in Second Language Teaching and Learning*, E. Hinkel (ed.), 335–353. Mahwah NJ: Lawrence Erlbaum Associates.

Lantolf, J.P. 2010. Mind your hands: The function of gesture in L2 learning. In *Sociocognitive Perspectives on Language Use and Language Learning*, R. Batstone (ed.), 131–147. Oxford: OUP.

Lantolf, J.P. 2011. The sociocultural approach to second language acquisition: Sociocultural theory, second language acquisition, and artificial L2 development. In *Alternative Approaches to Second Language Acquisition*, D. Atkinson (ed.), 24–47. New York NY: Routledge.

Lantolf, J.P. & Beckett, T.G. 2009. Research timeline: Sociocultural theory and second language acquisition. *Journal of Language Teaching* 42(4): 459–475.

Lantolf, J.P. & Johnson, K.E. 2007. Extending Firth and Wagner's (1997) ontological perspective to L2 classroom praxis and teacher education. *The Modern Language Journal* 91: 877–892.

Lantolf, J.P. & Pavlenko, A. 2001. (S)econd (L)anguage (A)ctivity: Understanding second language learners as people. In *Learner Contributions to Language Learning: New Directions in Research*, M. Breen (ed.), 141–158. London: Longman.

Lantolf, J.P. & Poehner, M.E. 2011. Dynamic assessment in the classroom: Vygotskian praxis for L2 development. *Language Teaching Research* 15: 1–23.

Lantolf, J.P. & Thorne, S.L. 2006. *Sociocultural Theory and the Genesis of Second Language Development*. Oxford: OUP.

Lantolf, J.P. & Thorne, S.L. 2007. Sociocultural theory and second language acquisition. In *Theories in Second Language Acquisition*, B. van Patten & J. Williams (eds), 201–224. Mahwah NJ: Lawrence Erlbaum Associates.

Lapkin, S. M. Swain & Knouzi I. 2008. Postsecondary French as a second language students learn the grammatical concept of voice: study design, materials development, and pilot data. In *Sociocultural Theory and the Teaching of Second Languages*, J.P. Lantolf & M. Poehner (eds), 228–55. London: Equinox.

Lee, J. 2008. Gesture and private speech in second language acquisition. *Studies in Second Language Acquisition* 30: 169–190.

McCafferty, S.G. 1994. The use of private speech by adult ESL learners at different levels of proficiency. In *Vygotskian Approaches to Second Language Research*, J.P. Lantolf & G. Appel (eds), 117–134. Norwood NJ: Ablex.

McCafferty, S.G. 1998. Nonverbal expression and L2 private speech. *Applied Linguistics* 19: 73–96.

McCafferty, S. G. 2006. Gesture and the materialization of second language prosody. *International Review of Applied Linguistics* 44: 195–207.

McNeill, D. 2005. *Gesture and Thought*. Chicago IL: Chicago University Press.

McNeill, D. & Duncan, S.D. 2000. Growth points in thinking-for-speaking. In *Language and Gesture*, D. McNeill (ed.), 141–161. Cambridge: CUP.

Mitchell, R. & Myles, F. 2004. *Second Language Learning Theories*, 2nd. edn. London: Arnold.

Nassaji, H. & Swain, M. 2000. A Vygotiskian perspective on corrective feedback in L2: The effect of random versus negotiated help on the learning of English articles. *Language Awareness* 9(1): 34–51.

Negueruela, E. 2008. Revolutionary pedagogies: Learning that leads (to) second language development. In *Sociocultural Theory and the Teaching of Second Languages*, J.P. Lantolf & M.E. Poehner (eds), 189–227. London: Equinox.

Negueruela, E. & Lantolf, J. 2006. Concept-based pedagogy and the acquisition of L2 Spanish. In *Spanish Second Language Acquisition: From Research to Application*, R. Salaberry & R. Lafford (eds). Washington DC: Georgetown University Press.

Negueruela, E. Lantolf, J.P. Jordan, S.R.& Gelabert, J. 2004. The private function of gesture in second language speaking activity: A study of motion verbs and gesturing in English and Spanish. *International Journal of Applied Linguistics* 14: 113–147.

Ohta, A. S. 2001. *Second Language Acquisition Processes in the Classroom: Learning Japanese*. Mahwah NJ: Lawrence Erlbaum Associates.

Poehner, M.E. 2008. *Dynamic Assessment: A Vygotskian Approach to Understanding and Promoting Second Language Development*. Berlin: Springer.

Poehner, M.E. 2009. Group dynamic assessment: Mediation for the L2 classroom. *TESOL Quarterly* 43: 471–91.

Poehner, M.E. & Lantolf, J. P. 2005. Dynamic assessment in the language classroom. *Language Teaching Research* 9: 1–33.

Radden, G. & Dirven, R. 2007. *Cognitive English Grammar*. Amsterdam: John Benjamins.

Roebuck, R. & Wagner, L.C. 2004. Teaching repetition as a communicative and cognitive tool: evidence from a Spanish conversation class. *International Journal of Applied Linguistics* 14(1): 70–89.

Roth, W.M. & Lee, Y.J. 2007. "Vygotsky's neglected legacy": Cultural-Historical Activity Theory. *Review of Educational Research* 77: 186–232.

Schiffrin, D. 1987. *Discourse Markers*. Cambridge: CUP.

Slobin, D. 1996. From 'thought and language' to 'thinking for speaking'. In *Rethinking Linguistic Relativity*, S. Gumperz & S. Levinson (eds), 70–96. Cambridge: CUP.

Swain, M. 2000. The output hypothesis and beyond: Mediating acquisition through collaborative dialogue. In *Sociocultural Theory and Second Language Learning*, J.P. Lantolf (ed.), 97–114. Oxford: OUP.

Swain, M. 2010. 'Talking-it-through': languaging as a source of learning. In *Sociocognitive Perspectives on Language Use and Language Learning*, R. Batstone (ed.), 112–130. Oxford: OUP.

Swain, M. & Lapkin, S. 2000. Task-based second language learning: The uses of the first language. *Language Teaching Research* 4(3): 251–274.

Swain, M. & Lapkin, S. 2001. Focus on form through collaborative dialogue: Exploring task effects. In *Researching Pedagogic Tasks: Second Language Learning, Teaching and Testing*, M. Bygate, P. Skehan & M. Swain (eds), 99–118. London: Longman.

Swain, M., Kinnear, P. & Steinman, L. 2011. *Sociocultural Theory in Second Language Education*. Bristol: Multilingual Matters.

Swain. M., S. Lapkin, I. Knouzi, W. Suzuki & L. Brooks 2009. Languaging: University students learn the grammatical concept of voice in French. *Modern Language Journal* 93: 6–30.

Talmy, L. 2000. *Toward a Cognitive Semantics*, Vol. II: *Typology and Process in Concept Structuring*. Cambridge MA: The MIT Press.

Thorne, S.L. 2003. Artifacts and cultures-of-use in intercultural communication. *Language Teaching & Technology* 7: 38–67.

Van Lier, L. 2000. From input to affordance: Social-interactive learning from an ecological perspective. In *Sociocultural Theory and Second Language Learning,* J. Lantolf (ed.), 245–260. Oxford: OUP.

Van Lier, L. 2008. Agency in the classroom. In *Sociocultural Theory and the Teaching of Second Languages,* J.P. Lantolf & M.E. Poehner (eds.), 163–188. London: Equinox.

Vygotsky, L.S. 1978. *Mind in Society.* Cambridge MA: Harvard University Press.

Vygotsky, L.S. 1987. *The collected Works of L. S. Vygotsky,* Vol. 1: *Problems of General Psychology. Including the Volume Thinking and Speech.* R.W. Reiber & A.S. Carton (eds). New York NY: Plenum.

Wells, G. 1999. *Dialogic Inquiry: Toward a Sociocultural Practice and Theory of Education.* Cambridge: CUP.

Wertsch, J.V. 1985. *Vygotsky and the Social Formation of Mind.* Cambridge MA: Harvard University Press.

CHAPTER 8

Investigating L2 spoken syntax

A Usage-based perspective

Regina Weinert[1], María Basterrechea[2] and María del
Pilar García Mayo[2]
Northumbria University[1] and Universidad del País Vasco (UPV-EHU)[2]

This chapter explores the implications and applications of research into
native spoken language in the context of second language learning and use.
Spoken language structures differ in fundamental ways from those of written
language and require to be analysed on their own terms. The chapter outlines
the principles underlying qualitative research into native spoken syntax,
including a discussion of methodological and analytic challenges, and suggests
that this research is aligned with usage-based and related cognitive language
models. Methodological and analytic issues are then illustrated in the area of
subordination and clause complexes in native speaker and English as a second
language (L2). The chapter concludes with a summary of core issues in the study
of L2 spoken syntax and grammar.

Introduction

Spoken language is learnt before written language and it constitutes the main
means of daily communication for most unimpaired children and adults. It seems
reasonable to suggest that it should be of principal concern to linguists, as stated
by Bloomfield (1935). While technical developments were needed to enable the
comprehensive analysis of spoken language, its case still needs to be made many
years later, due to what Linnell (2005) calls the *written language bias in linguistics*
in Western societies. Miller and Weinert (1998/2009) show that across several
languages, informal spoken and formal written language differ substantially in
their structures and they explore the implications of the nature of spoken language for linguistic theory, language descriptions, language acquisition and
language typology. In the context of second language (L2) study, the effect of medium is discussed, but the implications for syntactic analysis *per se* are rarely
treated as a core issue.

The aim of this chapter is to offer a perspective on how to do justice to spoken language grammar in its description and to illustrate the issues this raises for the analysis of L2 speech. The chapter therefore does not centrally consider L2 *development*, rather the focus is on demonstrating that research into native spoken language can and often needs to inform the study of spoken L2. This is seen as a prerequisite for researching developmental processes and their outcomes, including the assessment of language proficiency. The chapter takes account of readers who may not be familiar with spoken language analysis. Given the wide scope of relevant research, the discussion and references in this chapter are necessarily representative and highly streamlined.

This chapter first provides an illustrated overview of the structure of native spoken language. It then sets out approaches which place spoken language grammar at the centre of their concerns and considers their alignment with usage-based, cognitive models of language. This is followed by a discussion of the methodological and analytic challenges facing the spoken language researcher, including comments on the role of corpus data. Finally, the section considers general implications and applications of work on native spoken language for L2 learning and teaching, leading to a call for more investigations into L2 spoken language grammar, especially in advanced stages. A second section of the chapter demonstrates how research into native spoken language can underpin such investigations. A rich ground for exploration is the area of *subordination*, which continues to be used as a criterion for assessing L2 complexity and level of competence. The section provides an outline of some typical native spoken language adverbial constructions in English and then examines samples of native and L2 spoken *because/cos*-clauses and some *if*-clauses in their discourse and interactional context.

Spoken language: From data to analysis and model

Properties of spoken language

General lists are a hostage to fortune, but a brief overview of the main properties of spoken language is needed to set the scene. Spontaneous spoken language is subject to processing and production conditions which are very different for written language. Spoken language is produced in real time, unedited, fast and subject to working memory constraints. It involves prosodic, temporal and voice quality features and it is typically produced face-to-face, in a particular context or situation and accompanied by non-verbal communication. Speakers share background and situative knowledge to varying degrees, which is played out in interaction. These conditions are reflected in linguistic structure such as widespread unintegrated syntax, preference for main over subordinate clauses, use of units below clause size, simple noun phrases, structures adapted to informational and interactional purposes arising from the conditions of speaking, prominent use of deictics, pronouns and particles or discourse markers to signal relations between units, as well as hearer and hesitation signals. This is illustrated by the following short exchange. Our comments are suggestive of the many issues of syntactic analysis which are raised by spoken language and which a large amount of research wrestles with.

Extract 1: Academic supervision session

The extract comes from a ca. 60 000 word corpus of 13 British English academic supervision sessions (originally collected by Andrea Krengel at the universities of Leeds and Sheffield). Speaker B is a lecturer and Speaker A is a doctoral student (both female). We can assume that the speakers have a high level of education. The doctoral project involves examining the strategies of people who are trying to give up smoking and who are worried that they may eat too much as a consequence. A and B are talking about research methods. Transcription conventions can be found in the Appendix. Underlining in this extract indicates the full extent of overlapping speech.

⟨A1⟩   I didn't think keeping a diary of everything they ate was really a feasible
⟨B1⟩   they're not going <u>to do it</u>
⟨A2⟩   <u>no exactly</u>
⟨B2⟩   are they
⟨A3⟩   no
⟨B3⟩   but you they might have something you might have a question like (ehm) how much did you eat today ehm less than usual about the same as <u>usual</u>
⟨A4⟩   <u>yeah</u> something like that
⟨B4⟩   yeah
⟨A5⟩   something really simple which they can just pop it in
⟨B5⟩   yeah I really like this I think that cigarette diaries are really good I can see the results here you've got the three groups and you could have
⟨A6⟩   (mhm)
⟨B6⟩   eh total cigarette consumption in one week
⟨A7⟩   yeah
⟨B7⟩   and week two and week three
⟨A8⟩   yeah that's what I thought I thought it would be quite nice

In A1 the speaker probably intended to complete the noun phrase *a feasible* with *idea* or something similar. Speaker B anticipates A's meaning through context, indicated by her response in B1. B3 shows some dysfluency as the speaker changes her formulation: *but you/they might have something/you might have a question.* There are 10 declarative main clauses which start with a subject pronoun. There are 3 complement clauses (A1, B5, A8); all of the main clauses to which they relate are short and involve the verb *think* used epistemically rather than semantically, raising the question of the level of subordination and integration; two have no complementiser, one is introduced by *that* (Thompson & Mulac 1991). There is one contact relative clause – no relative pronoun is used (A1). In A5 there is a relative clause introduced by the relative pronoun *which*; the clause contains a re-sumptive pronoun (*which they can just pop it in*), raising the issue of complexity (Miller & Weinert 1998/2009). There is one typical spoken cleft in A8, *that's what I thought*, considered *formulaic* by e.g. O'Keeffe et al. (2007), i.e. such clefts are typically lexically restricted. There are some units which are not clauses (B3, A4, A5), e.g. B3 le*ss than usual/about the same as usual.* The proportion of pronouns is high, despite the academic topic. In A4 *something like that* looks formulaic. There are interactional features such as the use of *yeah, mhm* and the tag in B2. Intona-tion allows us to determine a boundary in B5 *I can see the results | here you've got the three groups* – *here* goes with the following clause. Content analysis might have led to the same assignment since there are no results yet of the doctoral project. B5 underlines B's attitude with *really*. There are not many hesitation markers (*eh, ehm*). The extract is relatively orderly and easy to understand, but we could con-tinue discussing the nature and status of various syntactic units and their relations for a good while. What needs to be resisted by anyone not familiar with spoken language analysis is the attempt to superimpose an order which is not there, im-ported from familiarity with written language conventions. To quote Sandra A. Thompson, "What are the categories and units of grammar? Which of the ones we've grown up on, and been trained to see, would we see if we looked at just in-teractional data?"[1] It is helpful to invoke a model of language which is consonant with finding answers to these questions.

Cognitive, construction and usage-based grammars

Spoken language research has by necessity been data-driven since intuitions about spoken language are notoriously unreliable (Labov 1975). Claims have to be based on recordings and transcripts of spontaneous speech. There are many different contexts of spoken language use, but studying native language data as produced and comprehended by speakers in interaction is not merely a type of genre or so-cio-linguistic investigation which establishes how language knowledge manifests in practice. Firstly, informal, unscripted and spontaneous spoken language is prior

---

1.   \<http://www.linguistics.ucsb.edu/people/thompson.html>

and primary, it is not just any variety. Secondly, the medium of speech is fundamentally different from the medium of writing and this applies to all types. Finally, the linguistic categories developed for written language often do not apply to spoken data. This is not to deny overlap between spoken and written forms or differences within types of spoken language and across speakers from different educational backgrounds, but to argue that spoken forms need to be analysed in their own right.

It is not such a big step for work on spoken language to become aligned with usage-based models of language. The attraction for the spoken language analyst is that usage-based grammar accommodates the surface realities of language, does not discard any linguistic phenomena as peripheral *a priori* and maintains that linguistic structures cannot be studied in isolation from meaning, function, context, use and users. There is a long continuing line of linguistic work which subscribes to this view, such as the Firthian tradition (Palmer 1968) and Systemic Functional approaches (Halliday 1985/1994; Llinares, this volume). The explicit and comprehensive formulation of cognitive, construction and usage-based grammars came as a response to Chomskyan generative grammar – the term *usage-based model* was coined by Langacker (1987, 1988). Rather interestingly, they did not spring from an (explicit) engagement with spoken language. However, usage-based models are valuable for all types of data-driven analysis. Due to space constraints, we cannot provide a detailed account of the various cognitive language models and their empirical verification, but refer the reader to the relevant literature, incuding work on L2 (see e.g. Barlow & Kemmer 2000; Croft & Cruse 2004; Dąbrowska 2004; Goldberg 2006; Robinson & Ellis 2008; Weinert 2010). We confine ourselves therefore to the main principles underlying a usage-based approach to grammar:

1. Innateness – whether of language specific or general cognitive mechanisms – is seen as an empirical issue.
2. Language is seen as symbolic, consisting of *form-function pairings*, i.e. *constructions*, which are shaped by usage, i.e. linguistic expressions and generalisations are the result of meaningful communicative acts. Constructions are seen as theoretical primitives.
3. The most parsimonious grammar is not necessarily considered the best one, rather the ultimate litmus test is psychological reality. A usage-based theory of language is potentially maximalist, accommodating the particular as well as the general and allowing for multiple levels of categorisation and representation.
4. There is no sharp divide between the grammar and the lexicon.

Such a view of language is dynamic, envisaging a close link between performance and competence.

Research on spoken language then seeks to establish how the grammar of talk can be characterised when seen as emerging from and reflecting the dynamics of spontaneous interaction. One strand has become known as *Interactional Linguistics*, while there has been much cognate research into spoken language which does not label itself as such.[2] Interactionally oriented linguists combine structural, functional, phonetic/prosodic and increasingly also non-verbal, multi-modal perspectives in analysis (e.g. Dahlmann & Adolphs 2009; Depperman, Fiehler & Sprang-Fogazy 2006; Ford 1993; Hakulinen & Selting 2005). Many of these researchers incorporate Conversation Analysis (CA) and recent work also explicitly invokes Construction Grammar (e.g. Günthner and Imo 2006). Seedhouse (2005: 165) sees a fundamental difference between the *CA mentality* with its emphasis on the *social act*, and the *linguistic mentality* which is primarily interested in *language*. Very broadly, CA focuses on the organisation of talk and interaction, its co-construction between participants, and the deployment of grammar and lexis for social purposes. In practice, most, if not all, spoken language researchers who are interested in the qualitative analysis of linguistic structure also perform an analysis of conversation, whether this is labelled CA or not. They interpret its content and the role of linguistic devices according to their understanding as (native) speakers of the language and invoke a range of theoretical concepts needed to account for phenomena above the level of syntax and their effect on grammatical/syntactic structure. These include discourse analytic notions such as information structure and rhetorical structure to characterise clausal relations, for instance, which are not only relevant to spoken language. By the same token, CA raises issues regarding the nature of grammatical structures when related to turn-taking and turn-construction (Ford, Fox & Thompson 2002). We cannot resolve here whether fundamental differences exist between these approaches, nor can we examine the varied practices in their name. However, they all place the study of language in context at the centre of their investigations and in principle allow us to approach spoken language structure on its own terms. Our main concern in this chapter is syntax and especially clauses or clausal relations and we will conclude this section with some comments on *constructions*. As noted above, constructions are considered as form-function pairings. Different syntactic constructions enable language users to perform different communicative acts and to organise information in connected discourse, e.g. make statements, ask questions, introduce entities, highlight information, indicate perspective and relate items of information,

---

2.   See Miller and Weinert (1998/2009) for references to the work of early and contemporary scholars on a number of languages, also Schlobinski (1997) and Weinert (2007).

among others. While some stable, recurring constructions can be identified, they are part of a network and within each category it is possible to find finer distinctions, depending on specific lexis and deixis (see e.g. Aarts 2007 on linguistic gradience).

Carving up language into constructions is not driven by a theoretical prerogative to be economical in description, rather it is subject to complex decisions on the basis of grammar and function. For instance, *there BE X* in English can be labelled existential or existential-presentative, indicating whether it is considered to have one or two general functions (see Miller 2010); further distinctions are possible, with concomitant restrictions on tense etc. (e.g. presentative *there's your money*, uttered while handing over the money, vs.*there's been your money*); and for spoken language we need to consider contracted *there's* with plural nouns, e.g. *there's biscuits in the tin*, which is a candidate for formulaic, i.e. unitary status. This approach contrasts with one which posits general rules, e.g. on number agreement or tense forms, and imposes constraints on their application.

Constructions are considered to have meaning and expressions which apparently only differ in syntactic form can give rise to subtle differences in truth-conditions, but more crucially, they signal different conceptualisations. For example, in *to play Monopoly is fun* vs. *Monopoly is fun to play*, *BE fun* can be seen as semantically distinct in each case, as a result of the construction it appears in. In terms of argument structure, *Monopoly is fun to play* is similar to *Monopoly is fun*, but *to play Monopoly is fun* is not (see Croft & Cruse 2004: 48–50 for possible analyses). Conversely, lexis can also contribute to the nature of constructions. For instance, spoken English makes use of single *if*-clauses to issue directives, e.g. *if you just sign your name there*. Such clauses have a conventionalised pragmatic function. When a consequent in the shape of a main clause is present and when a conditional reading is possible, the status and function of the *if*-clause may depend on individual lexical items. Stirling (1999) observes that expressions such as *if you'd like to* give prominence to a directive meaning, e.g. *if you pop your arm up there I'll check your blood pressure* vs. *if you'd like to just pop your arm up there I'll check your blood pressure*. Interaction itself shapes the nature of such constructions as the speaker may pause after the *if*-clause and wait for the patient to carry out the instruction, before explaining what she is going to do. This brings us to the issue of methodology and the challenges facing the analyst of spoken language syntax.

Researching spoken language: Corpus transcription and units of analysis

Corpus linguistics is regularly viewed as a methodology, not a theory (see McEnery & Gabrielatos 2006 for discussion), although it is in any case not a homogeneous discipline. Usage-based models fundamentally need corpus-based analysis

(Grondelaers, Geeraerts & Speelman 2007), as do spoken language researchers (whatever else they may need). Native and L2 spoken language research requires a judicious mix of larger and smaller, specialist corpora – larger ones in order to assess whether a particular linguistic phenomenon is available in a language (before dismissing it as non-native) and smaller ones which allow native/L2 comparison in comparable contexts and which draw out the contribution of genre to structure.[3] The range of existing spoken corpora and analytic tools is by now wide for a number of languages. This chapter focuses on some fundamental issues.

Two main methodological challenges are how to transcribe spoken data and how to segment it, closely linked to the issue of annotation and data searching. The answers depend on the purpose of the research and the theory behind it. Crucially, a given transcription is always interim and represents the perceptions and analyses of a given transcriber or team of transcribers. The more coding in a transcription, the further away users are from the original data and the more they are hemmed in by someone else's analysis (see also Kennedy 1998). Retaining raw data – audio/video-recordings and minimally coded word level transcriptions – is essential. Attempts to standardise transcription conventions are helpful up to a point, but there are limits to what can be considered theory-neutral and cross-linguistically universal, e.g. imposed by the role and nature of prosody, but also in terms of grammatical categories (see Haspelmath 2010). In addition, descriptions of specific linguistic phenomena always involve assumptions of some kind, hence they are theoretical (see Miller, 2010 for the notion of "theory"). Mechanised string searches can be very useful, but should not pre-empt analysis. The study of spoken language syntax continues to require manual analysis and depends on close familiarity with the data as running conversation.

In terms of syntax, the issue of unitisation has to be clarified. Miller and Weinert (1998/2009) argue in detail in their Chapter 2 that the sentence has to be abandoned as a syntactic unit of spoken language. The sentence is considered a low-level discourse unit relevant to written language, a cultural construct which has evolved and changed over time. The "clause", on the other hand, is a syntactic unit since it is the locus of the densest dependencies and distributional properties. The same applies to the smaller unit *phrase* (noun phrase, prepositional phrase, etc.), for the same reason. The core of syntactic units can normally be identified, whereas their boundaries and their combination are a challenge in the analysis of spoken language. Prosodic and temporal features such as pauses are often crucial

---

3.   While there is a necessary debate regarding the status of the native speaker as a model for language learners, working without the notion of a target would seem rather radical and impractical, especially in instructional settings. In the case of spoken language, there is at least the need to be aware of what native speakers do.

in assigning structure and can mark syntactic boundaries, but frequently they do not. Prosody is multi-functional, serving informational, interactional and affective purposes. It is therefore important to take these features into account but not to use them as a primary means of identifying syntactic units (the same applies to non-verbal signals).

There is no need to throw out all familiar basic syntactic categories and start devising a completely new set for spoken language from scratch before we even start – apart from abandoning the notion of the sentence. At the same time, analysis regularly involves re-examining, re-assigning and re-labelling *traditional* structures and devices and, crucially, assigning new structures and coining new labels for specifically spoken constructions. For instance, spoken sequences such as *my brother he's a brilliant cook*, are assigned an NP + CLAUSE structure, rather than being analysed in terms of movement such as left-dislocation. By the same token, spoken structures are not derived from re-constructed versions. A WH-clause in a sequence such as [*what you do* (speaker takes hold of the camera) *you twist it like this* (speaker has removed the camera lens)] is considered an unintegrated clause introduced by a deictic which focuses on the subsequent discourse. The speaker did not apparently intend to say *what you do is twist it like this* and the WH-clause therefore does not originally belong to an integrated two-part cleft with *is* omitted and *you* added (Weinert & Miller 1996). The relatedness of constructions in a language and in mental representation is another matter.

Implications and applications of spoken language research

Some grammars and applied linguistics publications have started to deal systematically with the grammar of spoken language (e.g. Biber et al. 1999; Carter & McCarthy 2006; Carter, McCarthy, Mark & O'Keeffe 2011; Fiehler 2006; O'Keeffe, McCarthy & Carter 2007) but even within the vast enterprise of English teaching, the gap between what is known about spoken English and course materials still appears to be wide (Cullen & Kuo 2007). Some learner grammars include useful information on typical spoken features and at the same time refer to spoken language as *rule-breaking* (e.g. Rug & Tomaszewski 2003). While there may be much evidence of native speaker *usage*, there is often uncertainty and controversy with regard to whether this usage is also standard, acceptable or desirable. Reference grammars, teachers and language users diverge in their judgments (Davies 2005; Goh 2009).

There is a need to critically evaluate pedagogical application as well as an urgent task to supply "the missing link" of L2 spoken language corpora in order to inform this endeavour (Aijmer 2009; Fernández-Villanueva & Strunk 2009; Gilquin, Granger & Maquot 2007). One such large-scale corpus is the expanding

Louvain International Database of Spoken English Interlanguage – LINDSEI, a project directed by Sylvian Granger and colleagues. LINDSEI includes data from learners with a variety of first languages, which can be compared to similar native speaker data, collected by Sylvie DeCock as LOCNEC (*The Louvain Corpus of Native English Conversation*). At present, studies into discourse-pragmatics predominate, with work on formulaic language also having received considerable attention.[4] Qualitative work on grammar is only slowly catching up.[5] There is also a body of spoken data collected within the second language acquisition tradition of input and interaction and task-based research (e.g. Alcón Soler & García Mayo 2009; Mackey 2007 – see Pica, this volume). The focus of this research is somewhat different, being concerned with establishing which tasks are conducive to learning, mostly using global measures such as accuracy, complexity or the extent of meta-linguistic reflection, yet it shares a methodology which involves native baseline data and various types of qualitative analysis and can benefit from being linked to work on native spoken language. We move on now to an illustration of how specific aspects of L2 spoken syntax can be studied in the light of research into native spoken language from a perspective which is usage-based, corpus-based, functional and interactional.

Investigating native and L2 spoken language

Subordination and clause complexes in native speaker usage

The label *subordination* covers a wide range of dependency phenomena in spoken and written language. Haiman and Thompson (1984) even suggest abandoning the concept of subordination for language in general, due to its varied manifestations.[6] At the very least, *subordination* is not an absolute but a graduated phenomenon which is as much discourse-pragmatic as syntactic. The notion of subordination comes up against serious challenges in the analysis of spoken language (Miller & Weinert 1998/2009). While typical spoken features manifest

---

4.   See also the work on L2 development from the perspective of usage-based linguistics, (eg. Eskildsen & Cadierno 2007).

5.   A list of references and links to LINDSEI can be found on the Centre for English Corpus Linguistics (CECL) website.
<http://www.uclouvain.be/en-cecl.html>
<http://www.uclouvain.be/en-cecl-lindsei.html>

6.   Clause combining has been a central concern of Sandra A. Thompson's work and of systemic functional linguistics (e.g. Halliday 1985/1994; Mann & Thompson 1987; Matthiessen 2002).

differently across constructions and languages, some broad principles have been observed for adverbial causal, conditional, concessive and temporal clauses (which combine), and even for relative and complement clauses (usually considered to be embedded). So-called subordinate clauses exhibit various levels of integration with main clauses, can carry main ideational weight, have semantic or pragmatic links with other clauses or discourse, and some types can function independently (e.g. Cheshire 2003; Günthner 1993; König & Van der Auwera 1988; Laury 2008; Matthiessen 2002; Miller & Weinert 1998/2009; Weinert 2007). This is illustrated schematically below. Longer extracts from conversations are provided later. In line with spoken language transcription, no capitals are used (except for the pronoun 'I'). All examples are authentic spoken British English taken mostly from informal everyday conversation, but they illustrate phenomena which have been found across a variety of speakers, regions and genres.

Integrated adverbial clauses: In examples such as (1–3) the main and adverbial clauses are uttered under one intonation contour and present an information unit. Syntactically, in each case we have two clauses which are related explicitly with an adverbial connector and a close semantic relation holds between the adverbial clause and the whole of the main clause. The adverbial clauses do not function independently.

(1) they only did that because they want to win the election
(2) we'll decide when you're here
(3) he helped out even though he was really busy

Loosely integrated adverbial clauses. In the following examples (4–8) the adverbial clauses and the main clauses or discourse to which they relate are separate information units and the adverbial clause is an elaboration or comment. In (7–8) the adverbial clause is uttered by a different speaker in response, not as a completion of the first speaker's utterance. ↘ ↗ indicates falling/rising intonation and (.) a pause.

(4) I take the train↘(.) cos you can do some work or just relax
(5) we'll go walking in the peaks↘ (.) unless it rains
(6) I'll go home now↘ (.) if we've finished
(7) ⟨A⟩   she never calls
     ⟨B⟩   cos she's too wrapped up in her own things
(8) ⟨A⟩   so he admitted it
     ⟨B⟩   yeah after I more or less forced it out of him

Examples (1–8) illustrate the point, but it is important to bear in mind that we are not always dealing with neat two-clause sequences. Adverbial clauses are regularly part of longer sections of discourse, involving intervening clauses and other units, speaker and hearer signals and changes of speaker.

Pragmatic clauses. Both in the integrated and loosely integrated examples (1–8) the adverbial connector creates a semantic link at the level of content, allowing a rephrasing as responses to information questions such as *why do you take the train* or *under what conditions will we not go walking.* The looser the arrangement, the looser the link may become. The adverbial clauses can then take on pragmatic functions and change the informational import, illustrated by (9–13), uttered by one speaker in each case.

(9)   there's a match on↘ cos they've closed off bramall lane
(10)   will you be finished soon↗ cos I could do with some food
(11)   before I forget (.) here are the tickets
(12)   if you're interested (.) there's some ice cream
(13)   let's open the chocolates↘ (.) although . we've given up for lent

Because/cos in examples such as (9) is referred to as "epistemic" *because/cos*, since the clause accounts for the speaker's knowledge, i.e. closure of Bramall Lane usually allows the conclusion that a football match is taking place. In (10) a reason is given for asking the question in the first place. Example (11) does not provide information about the time when the tickets will be handed over and (12) does not establish a condition-consequent relation for the presence of ice-cream, rather the adverbial clauses are used as alerters. In (13) *although* initiates a correction rather than a concessive relation, with important consequences, i.e. the speaker may decide not to open the chocolates after all. In these pragmatic cases the adverbial clause is illocutionary independent, but it relates to surrounding discourse. Some clauses are entirely independent.

Independent speech-act clauses

(14)   if you'd like to sign here
(15)   if I could just answer that phone
(16)   when you're ready

(14) is a directive, (15) is a performative and (16) an exhortative, asking the hearer to act sooner rather than later. Such clauses have conventionalised, independent pragmatic functions. The selection of loosely integrated and pragmatic clauses alerts us to the varied structures and functions of adverbial constructions in spoken language, which can be quite different from those found in writing.

Syntactic complexity in a second language

The above considerations have implications for assessing syntactic structures and complexity in the L2. Foster, Tonkyn and Wigglesworth (2000) have devised the *Analysis of Speech Unit,* which has been adopted in task-based research, in order to promote a more consistent segmentation of spoken language. Foster et al. (2000) acknowledge the use of independent adverbial clauses, arguing that they should not be analysed as subordinate. They count as subordinate only those adverbial clauses which are within the same tone unit as at least one of the other preceding clause elements of the AS-unit. Apart from the tone unit being a problematic concept, there is also a potential risk of misrepresenting spoken language with the approach. The central rationale behind the AS-unit is that it can serve as a basis for assessing language proficiency and for evaluating the complexity of non-native language, assuming that the ability to plan at the multi-clause level is a feature of native speech. Yet much of native language use is unplanned and the level of subordination is quite low, quite apart from the issue of subsuming diverse phenomena under its label. Furthermore, different activities call for different types of discourse and syntactic structures, which is in fact implied by the authors' discussion of highly interactional talk. How we view native spoken language therefore also affects the questions we ask of L2 data. This will now be illustrated with some examples of native and L2 uses of *because/cos* – the second most frequent adverbial connector in spoken English. Two examples of *if* – the most frequent connector – will also be given.

Native and L2 spoken adverbial clauses

This section presents *sample* qualitative analyses of native and L2 *because/cos-*clauses in their discourse and interactional context, with some examples of *if-*clauses. The analysis is drawn from a larger project based on the LINDSEI format. Some background to the research is provided below.

The data. The native speaker conversational extracts come from 20 LOCNEC dialogues, compiled by Sylvie De Cock in 1995–1997 (e.g. De Cock 2007), amounting to ca 55,000 words. Participants were British university students studying at the University of Lancaster, mostly undergraduate students of English and Linguistics, from Northern England and Wales, ten female and ten male students. The L2 data comes from the IkerSPEAK Corpus, compiled in 2009/2010 by Regina Weinert and María Basterrechea at the University of the Basque Country (UPV/

EHU) in Vitoria-Gasteiz, Spain.[7] It involves 22 participants, 17 third or fourth year students of English Studies and 5 postgraduate Master students in the Master's Programme in Language Acquisition in Multilingual Settings at UPV/EHU (15 females and 7 males). Participants had been exposed to both Basque and Spanish since birth or early childhood and their English proficiency level was between a B2 and a C1 level in the Common European framework of reference for languages (Council of Europe 2001). The conversation data was collected in the LOCNEC/LINDSEI format and amounts to ca 44,000 words of non-native talk. Each LOCNEC and IkerSPEAK participant carried out ca 13 minutes of conversation with the relevant project researcher, starting on a topic of the participants' choice from a list of three (an experience, country or film which had made an impression on them), followed by more general talk arising from the topic and participants' studies. Some additional native data will also be used for illustration. Transcription conventions can be found in the Appendix. Information on prosody and pausing is based on auditory judgments.

Structure: the independence of because/cos-clauses. Spoken *because/cos*-clauses mostly follow the clause or discourse to which they relate (Biber et al. 1999; 94% in LOCNEC and 99% in IkerSPEAK). They enjoy a great deal of syntactic and discourse freedom in this position (Chafe 1984; Weinert & Miller 1998/2009: 56–57). Research suggests that most *because/cos*-clauses and the preceding clause/unit are uttered as or function as related but separate units (e.g. Couper-Kuhlen 1996; Ford 1993; Schleppegrell 1991).[8] Structure is often reflected in prosody and pausing, although there are no perfect correlates.

There are various ways of assessing the independent status of *because/cos*-clauses. A dependent structure can be paraphrased as *the reason why X is the case is Y* as opposed to the looser *X is the case and the reason is Y*. In information structural terms, the first main clause often provides old information. Compare examples (17) and (18). Example (17) is our earlier example (1), which refers to the German government rescinding a decision to prolong the life of old nuclear power stations, which they did prior to local elections.

(17)   they only did that because they want to win the election

Example (17) can be rephrased as *the only reason why they did that is etc.*, but not with *they only did that and the reason is etc.* In addition, *because* cannot be omitted.

---

7.   The project was run by Regina Weinert while she was a visiting Ikerbasque Senior Research Fellow in 2009/2010. The research was hosted by the Language and Speech Laboratory (LASLAB), University of the Basque Country (Director: María del Pilar García Mayo).

8.   These aspects have received much attention in German, triggered by attempts to account for the use of two word orders with *weil* (because), e.g. Günthner (1993).

The sequence could be tagged with *don't they*, but the crucial criterion is that it allows to be tagged with *didn't they*, indicating the informational unity of the two clauses.

Example (18) is from LOCNEC. B has just observed that Chinese people are generally not used to seeing foreigners. In B1 she partially corrects herself, contrasting the case of Beijing with the city of Shinnying.

(18) ⟨B1⟩   it's it's not so much in beijing but in shinnying where I was which
               is north east china
      ⟨A⟩   (mhm)
      ⟨B2⟩   they ⟨X⟩ they don't get foreigners at all (.) cos it's not a tourist
               place

In B1/B2 new information is provided by *in shinnying* [...] *they don't get foreigners at all*. B2 could be paraphrased with *they don't get foreigners at all and the reason is that it's not a tourist place*. If this sequence were to be tagged, it would be *cos it's not a tourist place is it*. A causal relation could still obtain in the absence of *cos*. Note that the assignment of structure and the relationship between clauses in B1 is complex, e.g. *but in shinnying* could relate to the previous reduced cleft *it's not so much in beijing* or to *they don't get foreigners at all*, with two intervening elaborative WH-clauses. The status of the *cos*-clause itself remains largely unaffected, given the information structure of *they don't get foreigners at all*. However, even this small section of discourse illustrates the complex task of analysing spoken language in its own right and the attention to detail required in order to assess what is native or non-native-like in spoken learner language.

The *because/cos*-clauses can relate to larger sections of discourse, where the unit for which a reason is given may not necessarily be adjacent to the *because/cos* clause. In example (19), from a corpus of native academic consultations, A, a lecturer, advises B, a psychology student, on how to carry out a questionnaire (data collected by Andrea Krengel in 1997).

(19) ⟨A1⟩   right (..) but you need also to (.) in some way set that up before I
               don't know you've you've got to do this carefully haven't you
      ⟨B1⟩   yeah
      ⟨A2⟩   because you don't want to be giving too much away

The *because*-clause in A2 can be seen to provide a reason for the content of two clauses in A1, *but you need also to (.) in some way set that up* and *you've you've got to do this carefully*. It is not clear whether *before* is intended as an adverbial which links to the preceding clause, or as a temporal connector which introduces a clause but is then abandoned. *I don't know* is probably an uncertainty or mitigation marker. The *because*-clause is separated from the two clauses to which it can be seen to relate by a tag in A1 and a hearer signal in B1. A sign of its independent status is that if a tag were to be added, we would get *because you don't want to be giving too much away do you*, but *don't you* or *haven't you* are highly unlikely.

In (20) from IkerSPEAK the *because*-clause in B2/B3 relates semantically to B1, but providing a reason can be seen to be prompted by A2's *did you*, since *well because* is uttered after *did you* and the overlap with *(mhm)* starts on *well*.

(20) ⟨A1⟩   and did you have any preferences [out of these ⟨X⟩
      ⟨B1⟩   [yes I loved (eh) Munich
      ⟨A2⟩   did you [(mhm)
      ⟨B2⟩   [well because it's a small
      ⟨A3⟩   yeah
      ⟨B3⟩   you know it's a small city and it has old traditions
      ⟨A4⟩   [(mhm)
      ⟨B4⟩   [I don't know it [was ⟨X⟩
      ⟨A5⟩   [but it's not so small ⟨laughs⟩

The *because*-clause in (20) could also be tagged, i.e. *it's a small city isn't it and it has old traditions hasn't it*. More likely in this context, if A were to respond following B3, it would be with a question such as *is it* or *has it*, or even a comment such as *so you like small cities*, or *so you loved Munich because it's cosy and quaint*, but the response is unlikely to be *do you (love Munich because...)*. In fact, A does relate to the content of B4 in A5 with *but it's not so small*.

In example (21) from LOCNEC we have a case where the *because*-clause ushers in a series of clauses which are all part of the reason. Speaker B has been talking about a drama course she took when she was at school. The examination involved a group of pupils performing a play. She contrasts the mock exam with the real exam performance.

(21) ⟨B1⟩   and we performed it in front of our parents and everybody and it was quite good
      ⟨A1⟩   it must be quite difficult
      ⟨B2⟩   it was quite difficult actually because (.) for the mock of the exam we did a (erm) basically a day in a life
      ⟨A2⟩   oh yes
      ⟨B3⟩   which was (erm)
      ⟨A3⟩   (mhm)
      ⟨B4⟩   it wouldn't have got us any marks in the real thing I mean we we did okay in the mock
      ⟨A4⟩   [(mhm)
      ⟨B5⟩   [but it didn't have a point or a theme or anything

⟨A5⟩   (mhm)

⟨B6⟩   it was just us we all just did the characters we can do and just put them together basically but I think for the real thing we we we were under pressure to find an actual topic

In B2 *because*, which is followed by a micro-pause, introduces a series of clauses which explain why the real exam performance was difficult. Trying to assess whether the first of these clauses is integrated with the preceding clause or discourse would not only miss the point of the structuring. It would fail to capture the fact that the first clause following *because* only makes sense in conjunction with the following discourse. In other words, if we want to assess whether non-native speakers can operate at the multi-clause level, we should be interested at least as much in what follows *because/cos*. The L2 speaker in (22) demonstrates her ability to construct multiple reasons in a way which is similar to (21). B had a poorly paid job while living in England. In B1 she means that she was working ten *hours* a day, not ten *years*.

(22) ⟨B1⟩   but (.) I didn't have much much problems with the money because (.) I was ten years working

⟨A1⟩   [yeah yeah

⟨B2⟩   [every day and I had lunch and dinner [in the restaurant

⟨A2⟩   [(mhm) okay [well

⟨B3⟩   [so I just had to had breakfast at home

⟨A3⟩   yes

⟨B4⟩   you know I just bought milk (eh) (.) cookies and

⟨A4⟩   (mhm) [⟨laughs⟩

⟨B5⟩   [⟨laughs⟩ chocolates .

In (22) B1, B utters *because* at quick speed and then pauses briefly before launching into a series of reasons why she did not have problems with money when she lived in London, despite earning very little. Again, the first clause following *because* does not on its own provide the reason. Both native and L2 speakers stage complex circumstantial descriptions which eventually deliver the reason promised by *because/cos*.

Function: semantic vs pragmatic because/cos. The examples discussed so far in this section can all be interpreted semantically. Examples (23–24) illustrate pragmatic reasoning, where the *because/cos*-clauses are illocutionary independent.

(23)   it's nicer than Melbourne↘ cos I went there as well

The *cos*-clause in (23) cannot be interpreted as answering the questions *why is it* [Sydney] *nicer than Melbourne*, rather the native speaker uses it to justify her opinion that Sydney is nicer than Melbourne – she *knows/judges* that it is nicer on the basis of having been to both places. Example (24) belongs to a section in which the L2 speaker B states that she would prefer to go to an English-speaking country to learn English.

(24) ⟨B1⟩   and italians they don't have very high level of english [because
      ⟨A1⟩   [(mhm)
      ⟨B2⟩   I've been there and they say the my mum [because
      ⟨A2⟩   [(mhm)
      ⟨B3⟩   they say la mia mamma

In B1/B2 she provides evidence for her opinion that Italians do not have a high level of English by citing her own experience of having listened to incorrect English there. A semantic interpretation does not work (*why do Italians not have a high level of English? because I've been there* etc). In contrast, the second *because*-clause in B2/B3 is semantic, providing a reason for *they say the my mum*, i.e. they transfer this structure from their own language (*why do they say the my mum? because they say la mia mamma*). The distinction is not always so clear-cut, however, and can be affected by lexis. For instance, evaluations (*it's interesting because, it's no problem because*) can lend themselves to both a pragmatic and a semantic interpretation, depending on whether they are seen as based on opinion or fact and as serving interactional or transactional purposes. Pragmatic/epistemic reasoning is ripe for cross-linguistic L1 and L2 comparison.

Prosody and structure. Example (25) illustrates the problems in assigning structure on the basis of prosody. This issue arises in native usage and is exacerbated in L2 analysis, where it is not easy to establish what is *native-like*. Example (25) is from IkerSPEAK. The L2 speakers in this corpus utilise a range of narrative, affective and interactional modulations.

(25) ⟨B⟩   and PEOple were Open and they WANted to but I COULdn´t
              because I couldn´t exPLAIN [myself it was lack of of LANguage
              yeah↗ (.)
      ⟨A⟩   [yeah yeah yeah yeah

In (25) the speaker has a regular intonation contour, with very high pitch on the stressed syllables and the unstressed syllables all roughly on the same medium level. The patterns suggest that each clause is a separate information unit while at the same time all of them belong together; they are separated from the preceding discourse, which ends on a low falling tone, and from the following discourse by the tag *yeah*, which has a slight rise, and a brief pause. Despite being part of a larger discourse unit marked by intonational boundaries, it would not seem appropriate to consider the *because*-clause "subordinate", both on intonational and informational grounds.

Syntactic complexity: if-clauses. Both the LOCNEC and the IkerSPEAK participants prefer preposed *if*-clauses, using mostly quite short *condition – consequent* sequences as well as some more complex *if*-clause structures. Examples (26) and (27) are from IkerSPEAK. In (26), B explains that he is basically an optimist when it comes to finding work. He sets up a complex scenario in B1 and B2, starting with an *if*-clause in B1 and then provides a consequent in B3, which is also complex, consisting of four clauses.

(26) ⟨B1⟩   and if if a moment comes when when you well y = I don't know
                what the university has to (eh) cut (eh) personnel [or something
                like that
       ⟨A1⟩   [mhm mhm
       ⟨B2⟩   and and they say oh oh ⟨name of participant B⟩ we are sorry you
                go out [well is the
       ⟨A2⟩   [mhm
       ⟨B3⟩   it won't be days but I don't know I have the the sensation I I'll find
                something

In (27), B talks about working overtime in a restaurant. She omits a pronoun *(they told me)* in B1, *if I wanted to stay* refers to working on in the evenings, and *double* is stressed, with the speaker at the same time gesturing that she is talking about money. B is a very expressive speaker and uses units below clause-level to good effect in the conversation.

(27) ⟨B1⟩   there were people part time but but there was like me and told
                me if I wanted to stay
       ⟨A1⟩   mhm
       ⟨B2⟩   double you know

Example (26) demonstrates an impressive (discourse) complexity, (27) an equally impressive simplicity. Nothing would be gained and much lost by expecting the speaker in (28) to produce an integrated conditional with a full main clause in this context.

What the discussion and analysis above demonstrate is that researchers who examine L2 spoken syntax and clause combining need some background in spoken language analysis and that the native "target" cannot be taken for granted.

Conclusion

Oral proficiency and approximating native-like spoken language use do not necessarily equal syntactic complexity, rather it is the achievement of discourse-pragmatic aims through the appropriate, functionally, interactionally and socially relevant choice of structures in specific contexts. Going straight *from corpus to classroom* with our knowledge is no doubt helpful. Yet the application of research into native spoken language to teaching is also usefully mediated through research into L2 usage. This research benefits from an explicit recognition of the special nature of spoken language, which takes us to three programmatic questions:

Which empirically attested native spoken structures and features do L2 learners use/not use?

How do prosody, pausing and filled pauses interact with or obscure L2 learners' structures?

Is there any evidence that L2 learners, especially instructed ones, attempt to use typically written structures and features when speaking?

We suggest that it is essential to have an informed view of how the conditions of speaking shape spoken language structures in fundamental ways. In this sense, reflecting on usage serves as a prerequisite or orientation for the analysis of developmental processes and their outcomes. A usage-based perspective in principle combines a social, psycholinguistic, linguistic and developmental perspective and therefore has much to offer to spoken language researchers. The approaches mentioned in this chapter have a number of contact points, although much dedicated communication is necessary in order to identify where and how bringing them together can further our understanding of spoken language use and learning and the role of teaching. Research also needs to address sociolinguistic matters, such as attitudes towards spoken language features and judgments regarding acceptable usage among language users, learners, teachers and researchers. This is a substantial task without which our best efforts to raise the profile of the human capacity for spoken language and its nicely adapted devices may fail.

Acknowledgements

We wish to thank two anonymous reviewers for their useful comments. The first author would like to ackowledge funding from a Senior Research Fellowship in 2009/10 from Ikerbasque (Basque Foundation for Science) and to thank the University of the Bassque Country (UPV/EHU) and LASLAB (www.laslab.org) for hosting the research. The third author wishes to acknowledge funding from the following research grants: FFI2009-10264 and CSD2007-00012 (Spanish Ministry of Education), IT-311-10 (Basque Government) and UFI11/06 (University of the Basque Country).

References

Aarts, B. 2007. *Gradience. A Study of Grammatical Indeterminacy*. Oxford: OUP.

Aijmer, K. 2009. *Corpora and Language Teaching* [*Studies in Corpus Linguistics* 33]. Amsterdam: John Benjamins.

Alcón Soler, E. & García Mayo, M.P. (eds). 2009. Interaction and language learning in foreign language contexts: Introduction. *International Review of Applied Linguistics (IRAL)* 47(3–4): 239–243.

Barlow, M. & Kemmer, S. (eds). 2000. *Usage-Based Models of Language*. Stanford CA: Centre for the Study of Language and Information.

Biber, D., Johansson, S., Leech, G., Conrad, S. & Finegan., E. 1999. *Longman Grammar of Spoken and Written English*. Harlow: Longman.

Bloomfield, L. 1935. *Language*. London: Allen and Unwin.

Carter, R. & McCarthy, M. 2006. *The Cambridge Grammar of English: A Comprehenisve Guide to Spoken and Written English*. Cambridge: CUP.

Carter, R. M., McCarthy, M., Mark, G. & O'Keeffe, A. 2011. *English Grammar Today*. Cambridge: CUP.

Chafe, W. 1984. How people use adverbial clauses. In *Proceedings of the Tenth Annual Meeting of the Berkeley Linguistics Society*, C. Brugman & M. Macaulay (eds), 437–449. Berkeley CA: Berkeley Linguistics society.

Cheshire, J. 2003. Social dimensions of syntactic variation: the case of when clauses. In *Social Dialectology*, D. Britain & J. Cheshire (eds), 245–261. Amsterdam: John Benjamins.

Council of Europe. 2001. *Common European Framework of Reference for Languages: Learning, Teaching, Assessment*. Cambridge: CUP.

Couper-Kuhlen, E. 1996. Intonation and clause combining in discourse: The case of because. In Special Issue *Interaction-Based Studies of Language*, C.E. Ford & J. Wagner (eds). *Pragmatics* 6(3): 389–426.

Croft, W. & Cruse, D.A. 2004. *Cognitive Linguistics*. Cambridge: CUP.

Cullen, R. & Kuo, I-Chun, V. 2007. Spoken grammar and ELT course materials: A missing link? *TESOL Quarterly* 41 (2): 361–386.

Dąbrowska, E. 2004. *Language, Mind and Brain*. Edinburgh: EUP.

Dahlmann, I. & Adolphs, S. 2009. Spoken corpus analysis: Multi-modal approaches to language description. In *Contemporary Approaches to Corpus Linguistics*, P. Baker (ed.), 125–139. London: Continuum.

Davies, W. 2005. Deutschlehrer und Deutschlehrerinnen (in Deutschland) als Geber und Vermittler von sprachlichen Normen. In *Germanistentreffen: Deutschland – Großbritannien – Irland*. Proceedings of conference organised by DAAD, 323–338. Dresden, October 2004. Bonn.

De Cock, S. 2007. Routinized building blocks in native speaker and learner speech: Clausal sequences in the spotlight. In *Spoken Corpora in Applied Linguistics*, M.C. Campoy & M. J. Luzón (eds), 217–233. Bern: Peter Lang.

Depperman, A., Fiehler, R. & Sprang-Fogazy, T. (eds). 2006. *Grammatik und Interaktion.* Radolfzell: Verlag für Gesprächsforschung.

Eskildsen, S.W. & Cadierno, T. 2007. Are recurring multi-word expressions really syntactic freezes? Second Language Acquisition from the perspective of Usage-Based Linguistics. In *Collocations and idioms 1: Papers from the First Nordic Conference on Syntactic Freezes, Joensuu, Finland, May 19–20, 2006.* M. Nenonen & S. Niemi (eds), 86–99. Joensuu: Joensuu University Press.

Fernández-Villanueva, M. & Strunk, O. 2009. Das Korpus Varkom – Variation und Kommunikation in der gesprochenen Sprache. *Deutsch als Fremdsprache* (0011-9741) – 46(2): 67–73.

Fiehler, R. 2006. *Was gehört in eine Grammatik gesprochener Sprache? Erfahrungen beim Schreiben eines Kapitels der neuen Duden-Grammatik.* In A. Depperman, R. Fiehler & T. Sprang-Fogazy (eds), 21–41. Radolfzell: Verlag für Gesprächsforschung. <http://www.verlag-gespraechsforschung.de/2006/pdf/grammatik.pdf>

Ford, C. E. 1993. Grammar in Interaction. *Adverbial Clauses in American English Conversations.* Cambridge: CUP.

Ford, C., Fox, B. & Thompson, S. A. 2002. Constituency and turn increments. In *The Language of Turns and Sequences*, C. Ford, B. Fox & S. A. Thompson (eds), 14–38. London: OUP.

Foster, P., Tonkyn, A. & Wigglesworth, G. 2000. Measuring spoken language: A unit for all reasons. *Applied Linguistics* 21(3): 354–375.

Gilquin, G. Granger, S. & Paquot M. 2007. Learner corpora: the missing link in EAP pedagogy. *Journal of English for Academic Purposes* 6(4): 319–335

Goh, C. 2009. Perspectives on spoken grammar. *ELT Journal* 63(4): 303–312.

Goldberg, A. 2006. *Constructions at Work. The Nature of Generalizations in Language.* Oxford: OUP.

Grondelaers, S., Geeraerts, D. & Speelman, D. 2007. A case for a cognitive corpus linguistics. In *Methods in Cognitive Linguistics* [Human Cognitive Processing 18], M. González-Márquez, I. Mittelberg, S. Coulson & M. Spivey (eds), 149–169. Amsterdam: John Benjamins.

Günthner, S. 1993. weil – man kann es ja wissenschaftlich untersuchen" – Diskurspragmatische Aspekte der Wortstellung in WEIL-Sätzen' *Linguistische Berichte* 143: 37–59.

Günthner, S. & Imo, W. (eds). 2006. *Konstruktionen in der Interaktion.* Berlin: Mouton de Gruyter.

Haiman, J. & Thompson, S.A. 1984. 'Subordination' in Univeral Grammar. In *Proceedings of the Tenth Annual Meeting of the Berkeley Linguistics Society*, C. Brugman & M. Macaulay (eds), 510–523. Berkely CA: Berkeley Linguistics Society.

Hakulinen, A. & Selting M. (eds). 2005. *Syntax and Lexis in Conversation. Studies on the Use of Linguistic Resources in Talk-in-Interaction* [Studies in Discourse and Grammar 17]. Amsterdam: John Benjamins.

Halliday, M.A.K. 1985/1994. *Introduction to Functional Grammar,* 2nd edn. London: Edward Arnold.

Haspelmath, M. 2010. Framework-free grammatical theory. In *The Oxford Handbook of Grammatical Analysis,* B. Heine & H. Narrog (eds), 341–365. Oxford: OUP.

Kennedy, G. 1998. *An Introduction to Corpus Linguistics.* London: Longman.

König, E. & Van der Auwera, J. 1988. Clause integration in German and Dutch conditionals, concessive conditionals and concessives. In *Clause Combining in Grammar and Discourse* [Typological Studies in Language 18], J. Haiman & S.A. Thompson (eds), 101–133. Amsterdam: John Benjamins.

Labov, W. 1975. *What Is a Linguistic Fact?* Lisse: Peter de Ridder.

Langacker, R.W. 1987. *Foundations of Cognitive Grammar,* Vol. I: *Theoretical Prerequisites.* Stanford CA: Stanford University Press.

Langacker, R.W. 1988. A usage-based model. In *Topics in Cognitive Linguistics* [Current Issues in Linguistic Theory 50], B. Rudzka-Ostyn (ed.), 127–161. Amsterdam: John Benjamins.

Laury, R. (ed.). 2008. *Crosslinguistic Studies of Clause Combining: The Multifunctionality of Conjunctions* [Typological Studies in Language 80]. Amsterdam: John Benjamins.

Linnell, P. 2005. *The Written Language Bias in Linguistics: Its Nature, Origins and Transformations.* London: Routledge.

Mackey, A. (ed.). 2007. *Conversational Interaction in Second Language Acquisition.* Oxford: OUP.

Mann, W.C. & Thompson, S.A. 1987. *Rhetorical Structure Theory: A Theory of Text Organisation.* Marina del Rey CA: Information Sciences Institute.

Matthiessen, C.M.I.M. 2002. Combining clauses into clause-complexes. A multi-faceted view. In *Complex Sentences in Grammar and Discourse. Essays in Honor of Sandra Thompson.* J. Bybee & M. Noonan (eds), 235–319. Amsterdam: John Benjamins.

McEnery, T. & Gabrielatos, C. 2006. English corpus linguistics. In *The Handbook of English Linguistics*, B. Aarts & A. McMahon (eds), 33–71.Oxford: Blackwell.

Miller, J. 2010. *A Critical Introduction to Syntax.* London: Continuum.

Miller, J. & Weinert, R. 1998/2009. *Spontaneous Spoken Language. Syntax and Discourse.* Oxford: OUP.

O'Keeffe, A., McCarthy, M. & Carter, R. 2007. From Corpus to Classroom: *Language Use and Language Teaching.* Cambridge: CUP.

Palmer, F.R. (ed) 1968. *Selected Papers of J.R.Firth, 1952–59.* Bloomington IN: Indiana Press.

Robinson, P. & Ellis, N. (eds) 2008. *Handbook of Cognitive Linguistics and Second Language Acquisition.* New York NY: Routledge.

Rug, W. & Tomaszewski, A. 2003. *Grammatik mit Sinn und Verstand.* Stuttgart: Klett.

Schleppegrell, M. J. 1991. Paratactic because. *Journal of Pragmatics* 16: 323–337.

Schlobinski, P. 1997. *Syntax des gesprochenen Deutsch.* Opladen: Westdeutscher Verlag.

Seedhouse, P. 2005. Conversation Analysis and language learning. *Language Teaching* 38: 165–187.

Stirling, L. 1999. Isolated *if*-clauses in Australian English. In *The Clause in English* [Studies in Language Companion Series 45], P. Collins & D. Lee (eds), 273–294. Amsterdam: John Benjamins.

Thompson, S.A. & Mulac, A. 1991. The discourse conditions for the use of the complementizer *that* in conversational English. *Journal of Pragmatics* 15: 237–251.

Weinert, R. (ed.). 2007. *Spoken Language Pragmatics. Analysis of Form-Function Relations.* London: Continuum.

Weinert, R. 2010. Formulaicity and usage-based language: Linguistic, psycholinguistic and acquisitional manifestations. In *Perspectives on Formulaic Language. Acquisition and Communication*, D. Wood (ed.), 1–20. London: Continuum.

Weinert, R. & Miller, J. 1996. Cleft constructions in spoken language. *Journal of Pragmatics* 25: 173–206.

Appendix

Transcription markers

⟨A⟩ ⟨B⟩	speaker
(.) (..) (...)	pauses: short (<1 second), medium (1–3 seconds) and long (> 3 seconds)
[	the start of overlapping speech
=	truncated words
(eh) etc.	filled pauses are placed in brackets
(mhm) etc.	hearer signals are placed in brackets
↘ ↗	low falling/high rising intonation
⟨X⟩ ⟨XX⟩	unclear syllables and words
⟨laughs⟩	non-verbal signals

CHAPTER 9

Connectionist models of second language acquisition

Ping Li and Xiaowei Zhao
Pennsylvania State University and Emmanuel College

Connectionist models have had a profound impact on theories of language science, but researchers have only recently started to explore the implications of these models in second language acquisition. In this chapter we first provide a review of connectionism and second language acquisition. We then discuss models that focus on the complex interactive dynamics involved in learning a second language, with special reference to the effects of age of acquisition on lexical representation and the competition that is engaged during the learning and representation of two languages. We show that connectionist approaches provide significant insights into long-standing debates, including mechanisms of organization and plasticity in the development of two competing linguistic systems.

Introduction

As the world becomes more globalized, more people are learning a second or third language. As a result, research on second language acquisition, bilingualism, and multilingualism has become more important in formulating and testing mainstream theories of language and cognition. In addition to behavioral methods, researchers have also in recent years used neuroimaging and computational methods to tackle complex issues involving second language acquisition and bilingualism. In natural language learning situations, especially in the case of second language learning, it is often difficult to directly manipulate the learning environment in parametric ways (e.g., difficult to control input quantity or quality). Computational models offer particular advantages in dealing with such complex interactions between variables by systematically bringing target variables under experimental control while holding other variables constant (McClelland 2009). In this chapter we focus on computational modeling to second language acquisition with particular reference to connectionism.

Connectionism, also known as Parallel Distributed Processing (PDP) or artificial neural networks, is an important theoretical framework as well as a computational tool for the study of mind and behavior. Connectionism advocates that learning, representation, and processing are parallel, distributed, and interactive in nature. It argues for the emergence of human cognition as the outcome of large networks of interactive processing units operating simultaneously. Language as a hallmark of human behavior has received in-depth treatment since the beginning of connectionist research. However, researchers have only recently begun to explore the significance and implications of these models in second language acquisition and bilingualism. In this chapter, we aim at providing an integrative review of what has been done and what is in need of further investigation in this area. We will illustrate ways in which connectionist models can be used effectively to study second language acquisition.

The theory

Given that the audience of this book may not be very familiar with computational modeling or connectionist networks, it is necessary for us to first briefly introduce some basic concepts and terms to provide a context for discussion.

What is connectionism?

With the advent of computers and subsequent computational thinking, the 1950's witnessed the cognitive revolution, along with the birth of artificial intelligence, cognitive science, psycholinguistics, and related areas of study of the mind (see Gardner 1985, for a historical tour). A key idea that led to the cognitive revolution was that we could view the brain as a type of digital computer, and by studying how digital computers process information, we could make inferences about how the human mind (and the brain) works.

However, researchers have come to realize that there are fundamental differences between computers and the human mind/brain. One fundamental difference lies in the way in which computers versus brains process information. Digital computers operate on serial processes, carrying out instructional commands one after another at an extremely fast speed (the world's fastest computer, as of 2010, runs at 2566 teraflops; 1 teraflop = 1012 floating point operations per second). By contrast, the human brain relies on parallel processing, involving simultaneous activities in a massive network of billions of neurons and trillions of synaptic connections between neurons. The speed of individual neurons in transmitting signals in terms of rate of firing is many orders of magnitude slower than digital computers (milliseconds rather than nanoseconds), but parallel computation allows for fast and effective human information processing. Because of parallel computation, the brain represents external information as patterns of neural activity rather than random collections of neuronal firing. These patterns emerging from joint actions of multiple neurons are well coordinated both spatially (i.e., which neurons become active) and temporally (i.e., when neurons becomes active). Such patterns of neural activity, unlike coded computer programs, dynamically change in response to external stimuli and to the learning of specific experiences.

This view of how the brain works leads to the idea of *emergentism*, that is, that thoughts (e.g., percepts, concepts, semantics) emerge from parallel interactions among the computing neurons. Connectionism provides a theoretical framework for modeling the emergence of human thoughts in the brain. The basic idea of connectionism can be traced back to the 1940's, but it was popularized only in the mid-1980's as a powerful tool in the study of cognition and language. In 1986 McClelland, Rumelhart and the PDP (Parallel Distributed Processing) Research Group developed the PDP models, and published two volumes that contained descriptions of the PDP theories and models, new algorithmic designs, and applications of PDP to the study of language, memory, and learning. The two volumes quickly attracted widespread attention and brought PDP and connectionism under the spotlight. Given the relevance of connectionism to bilingual models, below we will discuss a few basics of the theory and methods first. Readers who are interested in the details of such models or looking for further references can consult Li and Zhao (2012).

Nodes and weights. Connectionism emphasizes *brain-style computation* (Rumelhart 1989), in that information processing in connectionist models is considered a process that simulates information processing in the real brain, albeit in a simplified form. With this emphasis, a connectionist model is built on two fundamental components: simple processing elements (*units*, *nodes*, or *artificial neurons*), and connections among these processing elements (hence the term 'connectionism'). Like real neurons, a node receives input from other nodes. The input signals are accumulated and further transformed via a mathematical function (e.g., a sigmoid function) to determine the activation value of the node. A given connectionist network can have varying numbers of nodes, many of which are connected so that activations can spread from node to node via the corresponding connections, either within the same level or across levels. Like real synapses, the connections can have different levels of strength (*weights*), which can be adjusted according to learning algorithms (see below) thereby modulating the amount of activation a source node can influence a target node. In this way, the network can develop unique combinations of weights and activation patterns of nodes in representing different input patterns from the learning environment.

Unlike computer programs that are dedicated to specific tasks and are fixed *a priori*, the weights and activation patterns in connectionist networks are continuously adapted during learning. It is these adaptive changes that make connectionist networks rather than computer programs interesting models of human behavior. The ability of the human brain to derive the 'optimal' set of synaptic connections for problem solving is the basis of neural information processing that has inspired connectionist theories of learning, memory, and language. Each individual neuron in the brain (or a node in the model) is not very powerful, but a simultaneously activated network of many neurons makes human cognition possible and makes connectionist models powerful in simulating human cognition.

Learning algorithm. Different connectionist networks use different algorithms to adjust weights to achieve learning. These algorithms can be classified roughly into two groups: *supervised* and *unsupervised* learning. A typical connectionist network with supervised learning consists of three layers of nodes: input layer, hidden layer, and output layer. The input layer receives information from input patterns (e.g., representations of alphabetic features), the output layer provides output patterns produced by the network (e.g., classifications of alphabets according to shapes), and the hidden layer forms the network's internal representations as a result of the network's learning to map from input to output (e.g., the visual similarities between 'O' and 'Q'). The most widely used supervised learning algorithm in psychological and cognitive studies is "backpropagation" (Rumelhart, Hinton & Williams 1986): each time the network learns an input-to-output mapping, the discrepancy (or error, δ) between the actual output (produced by the network based on the current connection weights) and the desired output (provided by the researcher) is calculated, and the error is propagated back to the network so that the relevant connection weights can be changed relative to the amount of error (represented as the so-called Delta rule: $\Delta\omega = \eta^*\delta$, where $\Delta\omega$ indicates change of weight, η the rate of learning, and δ the error). Continuous weight adjustments according to the Delta rule lead the network to fine-tune its connection weights in response to regularities in the input–output relationships. At the end of the learning process, the network derives a set of weight values that allows it to take on any pattern in the input and produce the desired pattern in the output.

An important connectionist model for language based on supervised learning is the *Simple Recurrent Network* (SRN; Elman 1990). The SRN combines the classic three-layer backpropagation learning with a recurrent layer of context units. During the training of a SRN, temporally extended sequences of input patterns (e.g. a sequence of words within a sentence) are sent to the network, and the goal/target of the network is to predict the upcoming items in the sequences (i.e. predicting the next word given the current word input in the sentence). Similar to the backpropagation learning, a SRN achieves this goal by modifying its weights. The context units, however, keep a copy of the hidden-unit activations at a prior point in time, which are then provided along with the new input to the current stage of learning (hence *recurrent* connections). This method enables connectionist networks to effectively capture the temporal order of information, since the context units serve as a dynamic memory buffer for the system. Given that language unfolds in time, the SRN therefore provides a simple but powerful mechanism to identify structural constraints in continuous streams of linguistic input (see Elman, 1990 for a detailed description of SRN and its application to language studies).

In contrast to supervised learning models, unsupervised learning models use no explicit error signal at the output level to adjust the weights. A popular unsupervised learning algorithm is the self-organizing map (or SOM; Kohonen 2001), which consists of a two-dimensional topographic map for the organization of input representations, where each node is a unit on the map that receives input via the input-to-map connections. At each training step of SOM, an input pattern (e.g., the phonological or semantic information of a word) is randomly picked out and presented to the network, which activates many units on the map, initially randomly. The SOM algorithm starts out by identifying all the incoming connection weights to each and every unit on the map, and for each unit, compares the combination of weights (called *the weight vector*) with the combination of values in the input pattern (*the input vector*). If the unit's weight vector and the input vector are similar or identical by chance, the unit will receive the highest activation and is declared the *winner* (the best matching unit, see Figure 1 for an example). Once a unit becomes highly active for a given input, its weight vector and that of its neighboring units are adjusted, such that they become more similar to the input and hence will respond to the same or similar inputs more strongly the next time. This process continues until all the input patterns elicit specific response units in the map. As a result of this self-organizing process, the statistical structure implicit in the input is captured by the topographic structure of the SOM and can be visualized on a 2-D map as meaningful clusters. Finally, although not an inherent property of SOM, different maps can be linked via adaptive connections trained on the Hebbian learning rule (Hebb 1949), a neurally inspired and biologically plausible mechanism of associative learning and memory. The Hebbian learning rule can be expressed simply as $\Delta w_{kl} = \beta \cdot \alpha_k \cdot \alpha_l$, where β is a constant learning rate, and Δw_{kl} refers to change of weights from input k to l, and α_k and α_l the associated activations of neurons k and l. The equation indicates that the connection strengths between neurons k and l will be increased as a function of their concurrent activities. The Hebbian rule essentially simulates the principle that "neurons that fire together wire together".

Representing linguistic features. Connectionist language researchers have been concerned with how to accurately represent various linguistic aspects in their models. Christiansen and Chater (2001) argued that "input representativeness" is

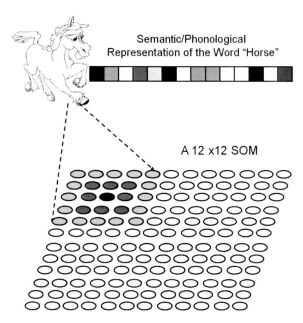

Figure 1. An illustration of the SOM training process. When an input vector representing the meaning or sound of a word (e.g., "horse") is presented to the network, a best matching unit (the black node) becomes highly active. Its weight vector and that of its neighboring units (the gray nodes) are adjusted proportionally, such that they become more similar to the input. The size of the neighborhood usually decreases as the training progresses, and eventually only the best matching unit itself is included in the neighborhood

crucial for computational modeling of language. This key issue becomes even more important for studies of second language acquisition since cross-language overlap or similarity of two languages have significant implications for patterns of bilingual processing, representation, and acquisition (see Chapters 7 and 10 of Grosjean & Li 2013 for more discussion of cross-language similarity and its neurocognitive consequences).

In connectionist models, a crude way to represent lexical entries is to use the so-called 'localist' representation, according to which each item corresponds to a single, unitary processing unit in the network; the value of the unit is often determined arbitrarily or randomly. An alternative way is to represent lexical entries as distributed representations, according to which a given lexical item is represented by multiple nodes and their weighted connections, in other words, as a distributed pattern of activation of relevant micro-features. For example, one can use either localist phonological representation of words (one word, one unit), or distributed representation based on articulatory features of phonemes for a word. The latter requires the assembly of multiple units corresponding to multiple phonetic features for representing a given phoneme in a word, but is more useful for simulating realistic language learning. Li and MacWhinney (2002) provided a method for automatically generating distributed phonological representations for English words, which can be extended to other languages such as Chinese (Zhao & Li 2009).

Methods for generating distributed semantic representations of words can be roughly classified into two groups. One is the feature-based representation, for which empirical data are often used to help generate the features describing the meaning of words, as in McRae, Cree, Seidenberg and McNorgan (2005). The other is the corpus-based representation that derives meanings of words through co-occurrence statistics from large-scale language or speech corpora. Zhao, Li and Kohonen (2011) recently developed the Contextual Self-Organizing Map, a software package that can derive corpus-based semantic representations based on word co-occurrences in multiple languages. The feature-based representation and corpus-based representation methods can also be integrated to enhance representational accuracy, as used in our recent work (see below 'Linguistic realism of the model'). Such efforts for developing methods to capture realistic linguistic features in phonology and semantics should help to build models that can more accurately simulate language acquisition in monolingual and bilingual contexts.

Connectionism and other interactive theories. Connectionism as a theoretical framework of language acquisition has also inspired a few influential theories in language science, such as the Optimality Theory (OT) and the Competition Model (CM). Optimality Theory (Prince & Smolensky 1993) was originally developed to account for the acquisition or processing of phonology in the monolingual context. It assumes that there is a set of constraints shared by language users, and these constraints can be ranked (and re-ranked) with regard to the hierarchy or level of importance values for processing or learning of each language. OT argues that the observed forms of language are the optimal outputs with the maximum *harmony* from the interaction of these conflicting constraints based on their importance levels. OT has been applied in both first and second language acquisition and it has its roots in connectionism. Indeed, the computation of the optimal outputs resembles the search for minimum error in connectionist models as discussed above.

The CM was first developed by Bates and MacWhinney (1982) to provide a mechanistic account of language acquisition. A basic concept of the CM is cue, an information resource that allows language users to successfully link linguistic form with meaning. The second key concept of the CM is that cues compete or converge in an utterance (hence the term *Competition Model*). The CM highlights the dynamic interaction of cues in response to the processing environment, in which the statistical characteristics of the input and the learning characteristics of the language user jointly determine the processing outcome. This view of cue and cue interaction is deeply rooted in the connectionist perspective to cognition. In terms of

L2 learning, CM emphasizes that 1) cues from the newly studied L2 and those from L1 dynamically interact to affect learning outcomes, and 2) the underlying learning mechanisms are similar across L1 and L2 acquisition (for CM studies of second language acquisition, see Li & MacWhinney 2012; Liu, Bates & Li 1992 and Tokowicz & MacWhinney 2005). A more recent version of the CM is the *Unified Competition Model* (MacWhinney 2012), according to which there is a set of risk factors associated with L2 learning including negative transfer from L1, and that the learner needs to utilize a set of protective factors such as immersion, active thinking in L2, and internalization of L2 speech. Those who can maximize the benefits of the protective factors will end up with better learning outcomes in the second language.

Connectionist models of multiple languages

Connectionist networks have been applied to account for a wide range of important empirical phenomena in linguistic behavior, such as speech perception, speech production, semantic representation, reading acquisition, and language acquisition (see for example, Westermann, Ruh & Plunkett 2009 for a recent review of connectionist language acquisition). However, there has been only a handful of connectionist models designed specifically to account for multiple language processing or acquisition, although this number is growing very rapidly. With regard to bilingual language processing, the best-known model is the Bilingual Interactive Activation (BIA) model (Dijkstra & van Heuven 1998) based on the original IA (interactive activation) model of McClelland and Rumelhart (1981) for visual word recognition in the monolingual context. The BIA model has been shown to be able to capture bilingual language processes in visual word recognition (for a review of BIA, see Chapter 4 of Grosjean & Li 2013). However, it does not incorporate learning mechanisms because it was designed to account for proficient bilingual speakers' mental representation and lexical processing. In what follows, we will focus on models that incorporate dynamic learning mechanisms in the bilingual or second language context.

Models of bilingual learning. Connectionist models of bilingual language learning have been developed by several researchers, for example, by Thomas (1997), French (1998), Li and Farkas (2002), and Zhao and Li (2010). One of the critical ideas of connectionism as discussed above is emergentism, the hypothesis that static linguistic representations (e.g., words, concepts, grammatical structures) are emergent properties, dynamically acquired from the learning environment (the input data). In an early attempt in this direction, Thomas (1997) used a Bilingual Single Network (BSN) model to learn the orthography to semantics mapping in word recognition. The BSN used a standard three-layer network with the back-propagation algorithm to transform a word's orthography (input) to a word's semantic representation (output) through the network's internal representation (hidden units). The model was trained on simplified artificial vocabulary from two languages (L1 and L2), and the network was exposed to both L1 and L2 material, either in a balanced condition (equal amount of training) or unbalanced condition (L1 trained three times as often as L2). The modeling results indicated that under both conditions, the network was able to develop distinct internal representations for L1 vs. L2, although in the unbalanced condition the L2 words were less clearly represented as compared with those in the balanced condition.

The BSN model, despite its simplification in representation, showed that connectionist models are able to account for both language independence and language interaction within a single network. Incorporating sentence-level input, French (1998) tested a Bilingual SRN (BSRN) model trained on artificially generated sentences of the N-V-N structure in English and French. The network was exposed to bilingual input as in Thomas (1997), with the two artificial languages intermixed at the sentence rather than the word level (with the input having a certain probability of switching from one to the other language). The model's task, as in Elman's (1990) SRN model, was to predict the next word given the current word input in the sentence. Learning in the SRN, as discussed earlier, leads to the emergence of distinct linguistic representations as a result of the network's analysis of the context in which the current word occurs among the continuously unfolding input. Simulations with the BSRN model showed that distinct patterns of the two languages emerged after training: words from the two languages became separated in the network's internal representations (the hidden-nodes activations). The model provided support to the hypothesis that the bilingual input environment itself (mixed bilingual sentences in this case) is sufficient for the development of a distinct mental representation of each language, without invoking separate processing or storage mechanisms for the different languages.

One significant issue with previous connectionist models is the use of highly simplified, artificially generated (and often *localist*) input representation as the proxy for linguistic material. Although such *synthetic* inputs are easy to construct and can greatly streamline the modeling process, it raises the question of whether results from the models reflect the actual statistical properties of natural linguistic input to which the learner or language user is exposed. Acknowledging this limitation, Li and Farkas (2002) proposed a self-organizing model of bilingual processing (SOMBIP), in which training data derived from actual linguistic corpora were used for the model. The SOMBIP was based on the SOM architecture discussed above. Through Hebbian learning, the model connects two SOM maps: one trained on phonological representations and the other on semantic representations. The phonological representations of words were based on articulatory features of phonemes (Li & MacWhinney 2002), whereas the semantic representations were derived from the extraction of co-occurrence statistics in child-directed, bilingual, parental speech. Both of these methods gave the SOMBIP more linguistic and developmental realism than the BSN or BSRN.

Simulation results from the SOMBIP model are highly consistent with the general patterns of BSN and BSRN, in that the simultaneous learning of Chinese and English leads to distinct lexical representations for the two languages, as well as structured semantic and phonological representations within each language. This pattern suggests that natural bilingual input contains necessary and sufficient information for the learner to differentiate the two languages. An interesting aspect is that SOMBIP provides a different way to assess proficiency. By having the network exposed to fewer sentences in the L2, the model simulates a novice learner having limited linguistic experience, compared to the BSN's balanced versus unbalanced training schedule (L1 trained three times as often as L2). This is a more natural way of modeling proficiency and, interestingly, it yielded comparable results to those from the unbalanced BSN: the *novice* network's representation of the L2 was more compressed and less clearly delineated, compared to the *proficient* network. The SOMBIP model later evolved into the DevLex (Developmental Lexicon) model in an attempt to provide a general mechanistic account for both monolingual and bilingual learning and processing (Li, Farkas & MacWhinney 2004; Li, Zhao & MacWhinney 2007; see further discussion below).

Models of bilingual forgetting. Most connectionist bilingual models have focused on language learning or representation, rather than on language attrition (forgetting). Language attrition refers to the situation that bilinguals lose the skills of one language (L1 or L2) due to the dominant usage/learning of another language. Most empirical studies of language attrition so far are descriptive in nature due largely to the lack of systematic control of a large amount of linguistic variables involved (see Bardovi-Harlig & Stringer 2010 for a review of these variables). Connectionist modeling may serve to turn language attrition research into an experimental science, due to its flexibility in parametric manipulation of the relevant variables and in testing relevant theoretical hypotheses.

Meara (2004) examined lexical attrition using a computational model. His model included binary lexical nodes that can be activated (remembered) or deactivated (forgotten) based on simple Boolean logic functions of the status of its two neighboring nodes. Meara attempted to simulate the effect of intra-lexical relationship on the time course of attrition and his results indicated that the lexicon in general follows a smooth curve of attrition. The model, however, is oversimplified and suffers from a lack of contact with realist language data.

Zinszer and Li (2010) introduced a more realistic model of bilingual lexical attrition. Like the SOMBIP model, their model included two self-organizing maps connected by Hebbian learning. The semantic representations and phonological representations of English and Chinese words were derived from actual linguistic corpora, as in SOMBIP. The researchers aimed to identify the effect of Age of Onset (AoO) of the L2 on bilingual L1 lexical attrition so as to chart the time course of attrition over a developmental trajectory. In their model, L1 (Chinese) was trained first, and then at varying AoO points, L1 input ceased and L2 (English) input began. Evaluation of the model's performance of production (from semantics to phonology) and comprehension (from phonology to semantics) of the L1 showed that first, like in Meara's work, the model was able to produce a gradual decline in the performance of L1 lexical comprehension following each AoO, suggesting a plausible time course of decay that is compatible with existing observations based on case studies (e.g., Hutz 2004). Second, the model demonstrated a discrepancy in the rate of attrition between comprehension and production (gradual decline vs. sudden drop), which highlighted potentially independent attrition effects for comprehension versus production within a single language user. Finally, the model revealed an inverse relationship in the rate of attrition between AoO and comprehension decay (the later the AoO, the more quickly attrition occurs). Such effects are important for understanding the dynamic changes in the competition of two languages during learning.

DevLex-II: A scalable connectionist model of bilingual language learning

In this section, we discuss the DevLex-II (Developmental Lexicon II) model as an example to illustrate how connectionist models can be used to study second language learning and bilingual representation and processing. We claim that the model is "scalable" because it can be used to simulate a large set of realistic linguistic lexicon, in single or multiple languages, and with various bilingual language pairs (e.g., Chinese-English, Spanish-English, etc.). We will not get into all the technical details of the model here,[1] as our goal is to provide the reader with a specific example of how connectionist models can be used effectively to address various issues central to second language acquisition. In particular, for a long time the literature has focused on the issue of L2 Age of Acquisition (AoA) in connection to the so-called critical period hypothesis or aged-related effects in language learning (Birdsong 1999; Hernandez & Li 2007). In our model we attempt to address the mechanisms underlying developmental changes in language learning so as to provide a better account of AoA effects (see also Chapter 7 in Grosjean & Li 2013).

---

1. Interested readers are referred to Li, Zhao and MacWhinney (2007) and Zhao and Li (2010).

A sketch of the model

DevLex-II is a multi-layer, unsupervised, SOM-based neural network model, as diagrammatically depicted in Figure 2. It includes three basic levels for the representation and organization of linguistic information: phonological content, semantic content, and the output sequence of the lexicon. The core of the model is a SOM that handles lexical-semantic representation. This SOM is connected to two other SOMs, one for input (auditory) phonology, and another for articulatory sequences of output phonology. Upon training of the network, the semantic representation, input phonology, and output phonemic sequence of a word are simultaneously presented to and processed by the network. This process can be analogous to a child's analysis of a word's semantic, phonological, and phonemic information upon hearing a word.

On the semantic and phonological levels, the network constructs the representational patterns for the corresponding linguistic information according to the standard SOM algorithm but with a minor modification. Particularly, a self-adjustable *neighborhood function*, which gradually shrinks depending on the network's error level, was introduced in the model to realistically simulate bilingual lexical development (especially L1 and L2 interaction). On the phonemic output level, DevLex-II

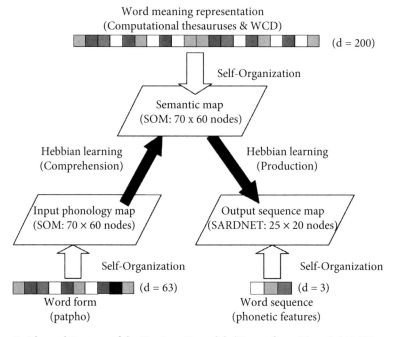

Figure 2. The architecture of the DevLex-II model. (Figure from Zhao & Li 2010 Reproduced with permission from Taylor and Francis)

uses an algorithm called SARDNET (James & Miikkulainen 1995), which is a type of temporal or sequential learning network based on SOM.[2] The addition of the SARDNET algorithm to the model is based on considerations that word production is a temporal sequence ordering problem, and that language learners, especially children and adult L2 learners, face the challenge to develop better articulatory control of the phonemic sequences of words.

As in SOMBIP, in the DevLex-II models the associative connections between maps are trained via Hebbian learning rule. The idea here is that, as training progresses, the weights of the associative connections between the frequently and concurrently activated nodes on two maps will become increasingly stronger with training. After the cross-map connections are stabilized, the activation of a word form can evoke the activation of a word meaning via form-to-meaning links (to model word comprehension). If the activated unit on the semantic map matches the correct word meaning, we claim that the network correctly comprehends this word; otherwise the network makes a comprehension error. Similarly, the activation of a word meaning can trigger the activation of an output sequence via meaning-to-sequence links (to model word production). If the activated units on the phonemic map match the phonemes making up the word in the correct order, we determine that our network correctly produces this word; otherwise the network makes an error in production.

Linguistic realism of the model

As discussed above, many previous connectionist models of language are based on the use of an artificially generated lexicon, often limited in size. To achieve linguistic and developmental realism in DevLex-II, we used as our simulation material the Chinese and English lexicons based on the MacArthur-Bates Communicative Development Inventories (the CDI; Bates et al. 1994; Dale & Fenson 1996). Each lexicon included 500 words chosen from the Toddler list of the corresponding CDI. The words were extracted roughly according to their order of acquisition by the toddlers, excluding words like homographs, word phrases and onomatopoeias. The words in the lexicons were classified as nouns, verbs, adjectives, and closed-class words. Thus, a total of 1000 real words based on CDI vocabularies are trained in our model, which demonstrates its scalability for realistic learning.

Input to the model was coded as vector representation of the phonemic, phonological, or semantic information of words. We used the PatPho software to generate the sound patterns of words based on articulatory features of English and

---

2.   See Li et al. (2007) for further technical details and the rationale for the neighborhood function and SARDNET.

Chinese (Li & MacWhinney 2002; Zhao & Li 2010). For semantic representations, we used two types of information: (1) the co-occurrence probabilities of words computed from the parental input in the CHILDES database (MacWhinney 2000); this was done by a word co-occurrence detecto (WCD), a special recurrent neural network that learns the lexical co-occurrence constraints of words by reading a stream of input sentences one word at a time and learning the adjacent transitional probabilities between words which it represents as a matrix of weights (see Li et al. 2004 for details); (2) the semantic features based on computational thesauruses available for each of the two languages, which were derived from the WordNet database (Miller 1990) for English and a computational database called HowNet for Chinese (http://www.keenage.com). The two types of information above were then combined to form each word's semantic vector.[3]

To model the impact of age of acquisition (AoA) on L1 and L2 representations, we simulated two learning scenarios in our model: early L2 learning, and late L2 learning. In early L2 learning, the onset time of L2 input to the model was slightly delayed relative to that of L1 input, and in late L2 learning the onset time of L2 input was significantly delayed relative to that of L1. These two learning scenarios can then be compared with modeling results from SOMBIP that learned the L2 input simultaneously with L1 input. By systematically manipulating the relative timing of L1 versus L2 input, the DevLex-II model should yield results to identify the impact that L1 has on L2 lexical representation and organization.

Performance of the model

One key finding from our simulations is illustrated in Figure 3, which shows how lexical items from the two languages are distributed differently across the two learning conditions described above. Black regions indicate those nodes that represent the L2 (English) words whereas white regions the L1 (Chinese) words learned by the model.

Overall, the figure shows that the relative onset time of L2 versus L1 plays an important role in modulating the overall representational structure of the L2. For the early L2 acquisition situation (Figure 3a), our network shows clear distinct lexical representations of the two languages at the semantic levels and within each language. The results imply that the early learning of two languages allows the system to easily separate the lexicons during learning. However, if the L2 was introduced late, the lexical organization patterns were significantly different from

---

3.   For the sake of computational simplicity, we kept the semantic vector of a word unchanged during the training. It may be possible to enrich the semantic vector over the time course of learning, as shown in Li et al. (2004).

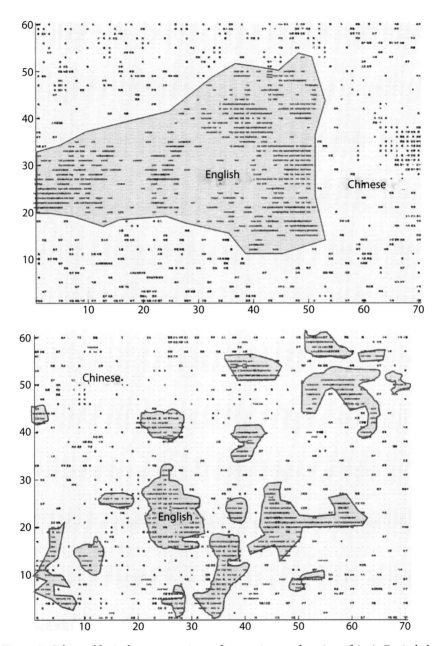

Figure 3. Bilingual lexical representations of semantics as a function of AoA. Encircled areas correspond to L2 (English) words. (a): early L2 learning; (b) late L2 learning

those found in early L2 learning, as shown in Figure 3b. This finding also contrasts with the results from the SOMBIP model discussed above. No large independent areas for L2 words appeared this time. In fact, we can say that the L2 representations were parasitic on or auxiliary to those of L1 words: compared with L1 words, the L2 words occupied only small and fragmented regions, and were dispersed throughout the map. There were small L2 compressed chunks that were isolated from each other, and interspersed within L1 regions. Interestingly, the parasitic nature of the L2 representation is reflected in the locations of the L2 words which depended on how similar they were to the L1 words in meaning (for semantic map) or in sound (for phonological map; not shown here).

Inspecting the bilingual representations on the semantic and phonological maps, we also found that the words were not evenly distributed in L1 and L2. Some areas were very dense while other areas very sparse. To explore differences in density across the three learning situations, we developed a method to calculate the density of words in their semantic and phonological neighborhoods (see page 517 on Zhao & Li 2010 for technical details). The result of this calculation shows that under the late L2 learning situation, the density of the L2 words reaches a very high level for both phonology and semantics, which differs sharply from the learning situation. A consequence of this density difference is that for language production in the L2, the retrieval of the phonological sequence or semantic content of a word could be much harder for late learners than for early L2 learners, because the competition between words is strong, leading to potentially higher rates of confusion. This hypothesis was supported by the simulation data in that the late L2 learning situation had more comprehension and production errors for L2 words than for L1 words. It is also consistent with recent empirical findings showing that bilinguals, as compared with monolinguals, often have more difficulties generating fast and accurate names in picture naming or word naming tasks (Gollan et al. 2005).

To further quantify the impact of L2 onset time on the lexical structure of L2 words, we used a k-nearest neighbor (k-NN) classifier, which is a method for classifying an object by assigning it to a class most common among its k closest neighbors in a feature space (Duda, Hart & Stork 2000). This measure allows us to see if each L2 word was clustered together with its peers belonging to the same category (see Li et al. 2004 for further details). Higher k-NN rates imply that the words belonging to a same category tend to group together. Figure 4 features the results of this analysis, which indicates clear differences between the two learning situations with regard to the network's ability to develop coherent lexical categories. One particularly interesting finding is that the scores did not change very much for nouns (near ceiling performance in both cases), while they dropped dramatically for closed-class words across the early to late learning spectrum. This could be due to the concrete nouns used in our training set, which mostly have high

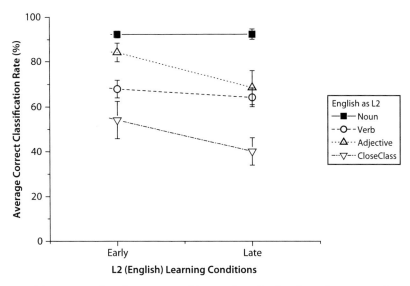

Figure 4. The correct classification rate of L2 words in the four lexical categories by a 5-NN classifier. The value changes as a function of the L2 learning history. Each data point was calculated based on five trials. The error bar stands for standard deviation

imageability and close translation equivalents in the other language, in contrast to the closed-class words that may be abstract and therefore harder to acquire by late second language learners.

Due to the influence of these different distribution and word density patterns, lexical development may also be impacted by different L2 learning history. In Figure 5, we present the number of L2 words that can be successfully produced by our network as a function of the L2 words available to the network at different stages. Not surprisingly, the vocabulary sizes of the L2 words increased over time under both learning situations. A regression analysis indicated more rapid learning for the early than the late learning situation (see the slope function of the fitting line).

Why is late L2 learning so different from early L2 learning situations? We believe that this 'age' effects in L2 learning may reflect the changing learning dynamics and neural plasticity of the learning system. In the late learning situation, the L2 is introduced at a time when the learning system has already dedicated its resources and representational structure to the L1, and the L1 representations have been consolidated. The L2 can only use existing structures and associative connections that are already established by the L1 lexicon. This is the sense in which we say that the L2 lexicon is parasitic on the L1 lexicon (Hernandez, Li & MacWhinney 2005). In terms of the network's plasticity, the decrement of the neighborhood sizes on each map at a later stage of learning also significantly constrains its plasticity for

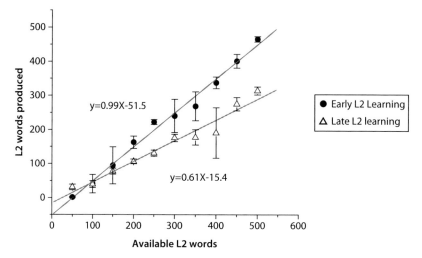

Figure 5. Correctly produced words as a function of available L2 words at different stages. Error bars indicate standard deviations, and the lines were fitted through linear regression analyses.

radical re-organization. In contrast, for early L2 learning, the network still has significant plasticity and can continually reorganize the lexical space for the L2. Rather than becoming parasitic on the L1 lexicon, early learning allows the L2 lexicon to present significant competition against the L1 lexicon. Thus, our findings suggest that the nature of bilingual representation is the result of a highly dynamic and competitive process in which early learning significantly constrains later development, shaping the time course and structure of later language systems.

Concluding remarks

Despite the many interesting studies reviewed in this chapter, development of computational models in bilingual language acquisition has been limited and slow, especially compared with the rapid progresses in connectionist modeling of monolingual representation and acquisition. Thus, much work needs to be done in this domain. At the same time, researchers have increasingly recognized the importance of computational models for identifying mechanisms underlying representation and processing (Dijkstra & van Heuven 2002; Thomas & van Heuven 2005) and for capturing developmental patterns across the lifespan of the bilingual learner (French & Jacquet 2004; Hernandez, Li & MacWhinney 2005; Li & Farkas 2002; Zhao & Li 2010). A significant challenge in future computational research will be the integration of models of bilingual language processing and second language learning; see some recent examples in Li (2013, ed.). Another challenge will be the incorporation of supervised mechanisms into models based on unsupervised learning (e.g. DevLex-II), given adult learners often learn their L2 in highly supervised contexts such as classrooms.

One distinct advantage of connectionist modeling is that it allows us to manipulate variables of interest more flexibly and to study their interactions in a more systematic way. In many cases it is difficult or impossible to directly manipulate these variables in empirical studies through parametric variations (e.g., to orthogonally cross all levels of one variable with all levels of another variable). In the case of second language, for example, one cannot easily manipulate the time and amount of L1-L2 learning, L2 input quantity and quality, and frequency of L1 and L2 lexical input in naturalist learning situations. In computational modeling, the relevant manipulation is not only possible, but necessary. Through modeling we can systematically identify the interactive effects of the two languages in terms of L2 onset time, L2 input frequency, amount of L1 versus L2 input, order of L1 versus L2 learning, and so on, on both the learning trajectory and the learning outcome. In addition, because modeling attempts to provide mechanistic accounts of empirical phenomena, it forces researchers to describe the phenomenon to be studied more precisely, and to specify the hypotheses and predictions more explicitly so that the phenomenon can be implemented in the model and the hypotheses be verified or tested. For example, in the DevLex-II model described above, the researchers need to consider how to define what successful word learning means, involving how word form and word meaning are associated, how they are organized with other words, and they compete among a larger pool of phonologically or semantically similar items, all of which also need to be quantified in the analyses (e.g., the use of methods to calculate word neighborhood density and categorization accuracy).

Finally, one important issue to bear in mind is that computational models need both to be informed by empirical data and to inform empirical studies. This means that researchers need to understand what empirical patterns and what hypotheses are available, but not be satisfied with the model's ability to simply fit the data or replicate the empirical patterns. Instead, they should make predictions as to what the data would look like under one hypothesis versus another, thereby effectively evaluating competing hypotheses and informing theories of language processing and bilingualism. In other words, a good model should be evaluated not only against empirical data (i.e., on how well it displays patterns observed in empirical studies), but also against its ability to generate new ideas and predict new patterns, thereby inspiring future research. To illustrate by way of example, the Devlex-II model has been applied to simulate cross-language priming, which refers to bilinguals' faster response to semantically related pairs than to unrelated word pairs across languages. When a spreading activation mechanism is added, our model predicts that, for late L2 learners, priming effects in the L1-L2 direction (from L1 primes to L2 targets) should be stronger than those in the L2-L1 direction. Moreover, such "priming asymmetry" should decrease as the bilingual's L2 proficiency increases. Such predictions are borne out in a recent study (see Zhao & Li 2013 for details, and the corresponding empirical data in Zhao, Li, Liu, Fang & Shu 2011). In short, computational models can help delineate the picture of the complex interactive dynamics involved in the acquisition and organization of not just one language, but multiple linguistic systems.

References

Bardovi-Harlig, K. & Stringer, D. 2010. Variables in second language attrition. *Studies in Second Language Acquisition* 32: 1–45.

Bates, E., & MacWhinney, B. 1982. Functionalist approaches to grammar. In *Language Acquisition: The State of the Art,* E. Wanner & L. Gleitman (eds.), 173–218. Cambridge: CUP.

Bates, E., Marchman, V., Thal, D., Fenson, L., Dale, P., Reznick, J. S., Reilly, J. & Hartung, J. 1994. Developmental and stylistic variation in the composition of early vocabulary. *Journal of Child Language* 21: 85–123.

Birdsong, D. (ed.). 1999. *Second Language Acquisition and Critical Period Hypothesis.* Mahwah NJ: Lawrence Erlbaum Associates.

Christiansen, M.H. & Chater, N. 2001. Connectionist psycholinguistics: Capturing the empirical data. *Trends in Cognitive Sciences* 5: 82–88.

Dale, P.S. & Fenson, L. 1996. Lexical development norms for young children. *Behavior Research Methods, Instruments, & Computers* 28: 125–127.

Dijkstra, T. & van Heuven, W.J.B. 1998. The BIA model and bilingual word recognition. In *Localist Connectionist Approaches to Human Cognition,* J. Grainger & A.M. Jacobs (eds), 189–225. Mahwah NJ: Lawrence Erlbaum Associates.

Dijkstra, T. & van Heuven, W.J.B. 2002. The architecture of the bilingual word recognition system: From identification to decision. Bilingualism: *Language and Cognition* 5: 175–197.

Duda, R., Hart, P.E., & Stork, D. 2000. *Pattern Classification,* 2nd ed. New York NY: John Wiley and Sons.

Elman, J. 1990. Finding structure in time. *Cognitive Science* 14: 179–211.

French, R.M. 1998. A simple recurrent network model of bilingual memory. In *Proceedings of the 20th Annual Conference of the Cognitive Science Society,* M.A. Gernsbacher & S.J. Derry (eds), 368–373. Mahwah NJ: Lawrence Erlbaum Associates.

French, R.M. & Jacquet, M. 2004. Understanding bilingual memory. *Trends in Cognitive Science* 8: 87–93.

Gardner, H. 1985. *The Mind's New Science: A History of the Cognitive Revolution.* New York NY: Basic Books.

Gollan, T.H., Montoya, R.I., Fennema-Notestine, C. & Morris, S.K. 2005. Bilingualism affects picture naming but not picture classification. *Memory & Cognition* 33: 1220–1234.

Grosjean, F. & Li, P. 2013. *The Psycholinguistics of Bilingualism*. New York NY: John Wiley & Sons.

Hernandez, A. & Li, P. 2007. Age of acquisition: Its neural and computational mechanisms. *Psychological Bulletin*,133: 638–650.

Hebb, D. 1949. *The Organization of Behavior: A Neuropsychological Theory*. NewYork NY: Wiley.

Hernandez, A., Li, P. & MacWhinney, B. 2005. The emergence of competing modules in bilingualism. *Trends in Cognitive Sciences* 9: 220–225.

Hutz, M. 2004. Is there a natural process of decay? A longitudinal study of language attrition. In *First Language Attrition: Interdisciplinary Perspectives on Methodological Issues* [Studies in Bilingualism 28], M.S. Schmid, B. Köpke, M. Keijzer & L. Weilemar (eds), 189–206. Amsterdam: John Benjamins.

James, D, & Miikkulainen, R. 1995. SARDNET: A self-organizing feature map for sequences. In *Advances in Neural Information Processing Systems*, G. Tesauro et al. (eds), 577–584. Cambridge MA: The MIT Press.

Kohonen, T. 2001. *Self-organizing Maps*, 3rd edn. Berlin: Springer.

Li, P. (ed.) 2013. Computational modeling of bilingualism: An introduction. *Bilingualism: Language and Cognition* 16(2): A Special Issue.

Li, P. & Farkas, I. 2002. A self-organizing connectionist model of bilingual processing. In *Bilingual Sentence Processing*, R. Heredia & J. Altarriba (eds), 59–85.: Oxford: Elsevier.

Li, P. & MacWhinney, B. 2002. PatPho: A phonological pattern generator for neural networks. Behavior Research Methods, *Instruments & Computers* 34: 408–415.

Li, P., & MacWhinney, B. 2012. Competition model. In *The Encyclopedia of Applied Linguistics*, C.A. Chapelle (ed.). Malden MA: John Wiley & Sons.

Li, P. & Zhao, X. 2012. Connectionism. In *Oxford Bibliographies Online: Linguistics*, M. Aronoff (ed.). Oxford: OUP.

Li, P., Farkas, I. & MacWhinney, B. 2004. Early lexical development in a self-organizing neural network. *Neural Networks* 17: 1345–1362.

Li, P, Zhao, X. & MacWhinney, B. 2007. Dynamic self-organization and early lexical development in children. *Cognitive Science: A Multidisciplinary Journal* 31: 581–612.

Liu, H., Bates, E. & Li, P. 1992. Sentence interpretation in bilingual speakers of English and Chinese. *Applied Psycholinguistics* 13: 451–84.

MacWhinney, B. 2000. *The CHILDES project: Tools for analyzing talk*. Hillsdale NJ: Lawrence Erlbaum Associates.

MacWhinney, B. 2012. The logic of the unified model. In *The Routledge Handbook of Second Language Acquisition*, S. Gass & A. Mackey (eds), 211–227. New York NY: Routledge.

McClelland, J.L. 2009. The place of modeling in cognitive science. *Topics in Cognitive Science* 1: 11–28.

McClelland, J. & Rumelhart, D. 1981. An interactive activation model of context effects in letter perception, Part 1: An account of basic findings. *Psychological Review* 88: 375–407.

McClelland, J., Rumelhart, D. & the PDP Research Group. 1986. *Parallel Distributed Processing: Explorations in the Microstructure of Cognition*, Vol. 2. Cambridge MA: The MIT Press.

McRae, K., Cree, G.S., Seidenberg, M.S. & McNorgan, C. 2005. Semantic feature production norms for a large set of living and nonliving things. *Behavior Research Methods* 37: 547–559.

Meara, P. 2004. Modelling vocabulary loss. *Applied linguistics* 25: 137–155.

Miller, G.A. 1990. WordNet: An on-line lexical database. *International Journal of Lexicography* 3: 235–312.

Prince, A. & Smolensky, P. 1993. Optimality Theory: Constraint interaction in generative grammar [Technical Report 2]. New Brunswick NJ: Rutgers University Center for Cognitive Science.

Rumelhart, D. 1989. The architecture of mind: A connectionist approach. In *Foundations of Cognitive Science*, M. Posner (ed.), 133–160. Cambridge MA: The MIT Press.

Rumelhart, D., Hinton, G. & Williams, R. 1986. Learning internal representations by error propagation. In *Parallel Distributed Processing: Explorations in the Microstructures of Cognition*, D. Rumelhart, J. McClelland & the PDP Research Group (eds), 318–362. Cambridge MA: The MIT Press.

Thomas, M.S.C. 1997. Connectionist Networks and Knowledge Representation: The Case of Bilingual Lexical Processing. PhD dissertation, Oxford University.

Thomas, M.S.C. & Van Heuven, W. 2005. Computational models of bilingual comprehension. In *Handbook of Bilingualism: Psycholinguistic Approaches*, J.F. Kroll & A.M.B. de Groot (eds), 202–225. Oxford: OUP.

Tokowicz, N. & MacWhinney, B. 2005. Implicit and explicit measures of sensitivity to violations in second language grammar: An event-related potential investigation. *Studies in Second Language Acquisition* 27: 173–204.

Westermann, G., Ruh, N. & Plunkett, K. 2009. *Connectionist approaches to language learning. Linguistics* 47: 413–452.

Zhao, X. & Li. P. 2009. An online database of phonological representations for Mandarin Chinese. *Behavior Research Methods* 41: 575–583.

Zhao, X., & Li, P. 2010. Bilingual lexical interactions in an unsupervised neural network model. *International Journal of Bilingual Education and Bilingualism* 13: 505–524.

Zhao, X., & Li, P. 2013. Simulating cross-language priming with a dynamic computational model of the lexicon. *Bilingualism: Language and Cognition*.

Zhao, X., Li, P. & Kohonen, T. 2011. Contextual self-organizing map: Software for constructing semantic representation. *Behavior Research Methods* 43: 77–88.

Zhao, X., Li, P., Liu, Y., Fang, X. & Shu, H. 2011. Cross-language priming in Chinese-English bilinguals with different second language proficiency levels. In *Proceedings of the 33rd Annual Conference of the Cognitive Science Society*, L. Carlson, C. Hölscher & T. Shipley (eds), 801–806. Austin TX: Cognitive Science Society.

Zinszer, B. & Li, P. 2010. A SOM model of first language lexical attrition. In *Proceedings of the 32nd Annual Conference of the Cognitive Science Society*, S. Ohlsson & R. Catrambone (eds), 2787–2792. Austin TX: Cognitive Science Society.

CHAPTER 10

Dynamic Systems Theory as a comprehensive theory of second language development

Kees de Bot[1],Wander Lowie[1], Steven L. Thorne[2]
and Marjolijn Verspoor[1]
University of Groningen and University of Free State[1], University of
Groningen and Portland State University[2]

In this contribution it is argued that Dynamic Systems Theory (DST) can be
seen as a comprehensive theory that can unify and make relevant a number of
different 'middle level' theories on Second Language Acquisition (SLA) which in
our view are theories that attend to different levels of granularity and different
time scales, provided of course that the middle level theories are commensurable
with DST principles. Such theories, such as ecological and cultural-historical/
sociocultural approaches to development, and cognitive, emergent, and
distributed theories of language, place language development in the wider
perspective of societal change and interaction with cultural and material aspects
of the environment.

Introduction

The aim of this chapter is to elucidate the contribution of Dynamic Systems Theory
(DST)[1] to the field of second language development. We use the term second language development (SLD) rather than second language acquisition (SLA) in ac-
knowledgement of two issues: the first is the bidirectionality of change in one's
language ability and performance (involving both growth and attrition), in contrast to the unidirectional vector associated with the term acquisition; the second
is to emphasize a shift from seeing language as a product or thing and rather to
emphasize linguistically relevant and enabled processes. Our use of the term SLD
is in alignment with Long's (1993) much quoted definition as it includes the two
directions of development:

---

1.   We use the term DST to refer to a group of theories including Complexity Theory that focus
on the development of complex adaptive systems over time

> SLA theory encompasses the simultaneous and sequential acquisition and loss of second, third, fourth, etc. languages and dialects by children and adults learning naturalistically or with the aid of instruction, as individuals or in groups, in second or foreign language settings. (Long 1993: 225)

We argue that DST is a useful theory in SLD in that it recognizes that a language (be it first, second or third), language learners (young or old), and language communities (in naturalistic or instructional settings) are each complex, dynamic systems. *Systems* are groups of entities or parts that function together. Any system is inclusive of embedded sub-systems, all of which dynamically interrelate with one another. The term *dynamic* as it is used in DST has a fairly straightforward meaning and refers to the changes that a system undergoes due to internal forces and to energy from outside itself. All complex (sub-) systems change continuously, at times subtly, at other times abruptly. A DST approach posits that similar principles hold at every level of the system, sub-system, sub-sub-system, and so on. Therefore, we feel that DST might be considered the long needed comprehensive theory that Littlewood (2004) found missing in the field.

In his discussion of theories of second language learning, Littlewood (2004) distinguishes theories that focus on cognitive processes and theories that start from the context of learning. He argued that a theory that integrates these two approaches was still missing:

> Such a theory is not yet available and (in view of the complexity of second language learning and the different forms that it takes) there is even some doubt as to whether it would be desirable or possible. What we have at present are therefore "middle-level" rather than comprehensive theories of second language learning. (Littlewood 2004: 514)

We argue that DST principles hold for aspects of the language user and language development at many different levels of granularity and therefore a DST perspective has the potential to connect *middle-level* theories that tend to focus on social, cognitive, or contextual issues in relative isolation. Thus we will argue in this chapter that DST can be considered a comprehensive theory in that its core principles can be seen to obtain at multiple temporal and spatial scales and in application to dynamics occurring along the brain-body-world continuum.

While the main characteristics of dynamic systems and their application in the study of SLD have been discussed extensively in various publications (de Bot, Lowie & Verspoor 2007; Dornyei 2009; Larsen-Freeman & Cameron 2008; Verspoor, de Bot & Lowie 2011), it may be useful to briefly mention the main characteristics of dynamic systems as far as relevant for SLD. DST is about change of systems over time. Systems change through interaction with their environment and internal reorganization. Developmental patterns are dependent on initial conditions and the availability of resources, both material and mental. Due to interaction of variables over time, development can be unpredictable. In human systems intentions will guide the developmental path and narrow down the range of options. Language and language development are typically dynamic in this sense.

In one of the first comprehensive publications on a dynamic approach to SLD, Herdina and Jessner (2002) have argued that a model of SLD should include components that can explain not only growth, but also decline and that the development of a second language should be placed in a larger framework of multi-competence. This takes into account the fact that the next language learned is not a totally new entity but an additional component in a multilingual system in which the new system interacts with components acquired earlier. They present their Dynamic Model of Multilingualism, which indeed does bring together sociolinguistic and psycholinguistic aspects of SLD, but without explicating the mechanisms of change in the language system.

DST principles at different levels of granularity across time

DST is a theory of change that takes time as a core issue. Dynamic systems are complex, adaptive systems in which variables affect each other over time. Systems are sets of interacting components. They are complex because they develop over time in a non-linear fashion and they "emerge spontaneously from the interaction of a large number of agents and/or a large number of items" (Lee et al. 2009: 4). They are adaptive because the interacting components react to each other over time. Because DST emphasizes change over time, research focuses not on the more or less static phases themselves, but on the transitions between phases. As Spivey (2007: 23) suggests, "The emphasis is on the journey, not the destinations." Because most research in applied linguistics, including the work on developmental stages, has been typically product oriented, the change of focus from product to process will have implications for the field.

In research on dynamic systems, recurrent patterns at different scales in space and time haven been studied extensively. The best known area is the study of fractals, defined by Mandelbrot, its founding father as: "a rough or fragmented geometric shape that can be split into parts, each of which is (at least approximately) a reduced-size copy of the whole" (Mandelbrot 1982: 34). A famous space example is the shape of the British coast, which is self-similar when viewed at different levels of relief. A well-known time example (which is not undisputed), is the recapitulation hypothesis which states that ontogeny is a recapitulation of phylogeny (Haeckel 1866), that is, the developmental pattern of the individual goes through the same stages as that of the species. In the same vein, Jakobson (1941) proposed the regression hypothesis, which states that language development in the individual child reflects the development of that language over time and the mirror image of development can be found with language disorders and attrition.

In an analogy to space fractals, we propose that DST provides an overarching framework through which to view commensurable SLD theories or approaches that range from global to more detailed levels of analysis. The global level can be found, for example, in the ecological approach as described by Kramsch (2002) and van Lier (2000), which is holistic in nature, uses mainly qualitative research techniques, and recognizes the complexities and multi-dimensional interactions of factors involved in SLD. For their part, cultural-historical/sociocultural approaches (to be discussed below) view an individual's cognitive and linguistic development as interdependent with and primarily informed by cultural milieu, processes and practices, and the contingencies of local social and material conditions. In both the ecological and cultural-historical schools of thought (see van Lier (2004) for a synthesis), communicative activity is always seen as contextualized, situated and embodied.

The more detailed level can be found in research by Van Geert (2009), whose work was inspired by the mathematical sciences and who uses the DST 'toolkit,' as it is generally described, to model and simulate language development. The main aim of this line of research is to develop models in which the interaction of relevant variables over time can be studied. The range of potentially interacting variables is wide, psycholinguistic factors like word retrieval may interact with social factors, such as amount and type of contact with the second language, and social psychological factors such as attitude and motivation may interact with success in learning. On the linguistic level, development of grammar may interact with the development of the lexicon. Empirical studies are used to get a first estimation of the impact of a limited set of relevant factors, and based on that information language development is simulated and ideally coupled with empirical studies to validate the models. Verspoor et al. (2011) explain this approach in great detail and also report on the only modeling study on SLD at this time, carried out by Caspi (2010), which looks at the interaction over time of different subsystems in the L2.

The more global and more detailed approaches have in common that they do not claim to explain or predict development and both also recognize that the systems at different levels of granularity will continually interact. One of the main tenets of DST is that simple causal relations do not exist; rather, there are always multiple interacting variables that make the process of development unpredictable to a greater or lesser degree.

Just as the self-similarity in the domain of space fractals can be found at different scales, so can self-similarity be found on different time scales. For example, we expect language development over a full lifespan, decades, or years to show similar developmental variability and patterns as at shorter periods such as months, weeks, days, hours, seconds and milliseconds.[2] For the study of language development, one of the issues to keep in mind is that timescales interact: a change in the retrievability of a lexical item at the millisecond scale may have an impact on the scale of seconds in language production, which in its turn may have an impact on storage on the scale of days, weeks, or even larger time scales. Similarly, changes at the life span scale, such as the discontinuation of the use of a certain language, may have an impact on micro-time scales since non-use typically leads to a slowing down of retrieval processes. We are aware of only a few studies that have attempted to gather related data on different time scales. De Bot and Lowie (2010) and Plat (2011), for instance, looked at the development of word naming latencies in a longitudinal case study over 3 years, comparing changes over the years and weeks but also on variation in latencies at the millisecond level during experimental sessions. They show that the context of language use at larger time scales affects language processing at the millisecond level.

Thus, a DST approach emphasizes the critical importance of both spatial and temporal dynamics, dimensions that have largely been ignored in the study of SLD. Therefore, we suggest that a DST based approach to SLD may be able to fill the gap between more holistic qualitative approaches and more detailed quantitative and experimental approaches to the study of SLD.

DST and social theories

SLD theories at the more global level are social theories that address how individuals change and transform through interaction with their social and material environments. A relatively comprehensive theory that offers a compelling, if also yet to be fully explored companion to DST, is that of cultural-historical/sociocultural approaches to human development that are associated with Vygotskian and post-Vygotskian theories (see Gánem-Gutiérrez, this volume).

Opinions regarding a liaison between DST and Vygotskian theories, however, have been mixed, with proponents forging considerable common ground for this move (Ellis 2011; Jörg 2009; Larsen-Freeman & Cameron 2008; van Geert 1994, 1998), some remaining ambivalent (Lantolf 2007) and others who argue that a union of DST and cultural-historical approaches to development is functionally untenable due to the incommensurability of their respective ontologies and concerns (Kirshner & Kellogg 2009).

---

2. Most studies on SLD have been done on the weeks and months scale, though some of the work on language attrition has focused on the change over decades (Schmid 2011).

This section will not offer a definitive statement on this issue nor try to forge a rapprochement between these frameworks, but will broadly outline cultural-historical aspects of developmental theory and constructively interface them with DST. After a general introduction to cultural historical theory, focus is placed on two issues: cognition and development (and its loci) and the role of time/change in these processes.

Cultural-historical approaches to human development, particularly those that are explicitly aligned with the early 20th century psychologist L. S. Vygotsky, describe development as foundationally informed by participation in culturally organized systems of activity. Illustrating the importance of social relations for developing mental functions, Vygotsky's (1981: 163) describes the following:

> Any function in the child's cultural development appears twice, or on two planes. First it appears on the social plane, and then on the psychological plane. First it appears between people as an interpsychological category, and then within the child as an intrapsychological category. This is equally true with regard to voluntary attention, logical memory, the formation of concepts, and the development of volition.

This view of development sharply contrasts with theories which presume the environment to be a mere trigger for genomic expression, or which posit linear stage development that is largely a function of biological maturation. Rather, Vygotskian lineage research, broadly construed, suggests that human mental development is dynamically and non-linearly constructed through engagement with the historical accumulation of *culture*, the latter understood as symbolic and material artifacts, patterns, and processes that are themselves embedded in and distributed across interacting systems of activity. In this way, cultural-historical approaches describe the development of individuals and collectives as emergent of the historically formed social and material conditions of everyday life, including those comprising formal instructional settings such as L2 classrooms (e.g., Luria 1976).

Over the years, Vygotsky's work has been usefully augmented by approaches such as ecological psychology (e.g, Bateson 1972; see also Engeström 1987), dialogism (Bakhtin 1986; Linell 2009), extended and embodied theories of cognition (Atkinson 2010; Barsalou 2008; Clark 2008), usage-based linguistics (Tomasello 2003), and views of language that emphasize meaning and activity (Thorne & Lantolf 2007; Volosinov 1973), its distributed qualities (Cowley 2009), and its characterization as a complex adaptive system (Ellis 2011; The Five Graces Group 2009). It is this syncretic and post-Vygotskian perspective that is taken here (see also Thorne & Tasker 2011).

To begin with a few preliminary observations, humans are open systems and development arises as a function of interaction within complex, historically formed, and dynamically changing social, symbolic, and material ecologies. When viewed this way, individual learning of whatever kind cannot be clearly separated from social dynamics and conditions. Rather, human activity and development form an *ensemble* process that plays out along a brain-body-world continuum (e.g., Spivey 2007). This open system principle includes a number of entailments, one of which is a focus on mediation – that objects and other people in the environment co-produce action and thinking in unison with individual human agents. Another is that cognition, action, and communication are processes that are inherently distributed across individuals, artifacts, environments, and through individual and collective memory, across time periods as well (e.g., Lemke 2000; Wertsch 2002).

In relation to cognition and also communication, it should be noted that the principle of distribution is not meant to suggest symmetry or equal division, but rather serves as a reminder that thinking is not *brain bound* (Clark 2008, p. xxvii, in Cowley and Steffensen 2010). Rather, the insight is that cognitive density can shift from brains to bodies and to a range of physical and representational media (texts, built structures, the face of a friend, landscapes, the smell of bread) in the flow of activity. The notion of distribution suggests a third entailment, that of units of analysis such as 'organism-environment systems' (e.g., Järvilehto 2009), which describe how change within an organism is accompanied by change to the environment and a reorganization of organism-environment relations. More simply put, Shotter (2003: 10) reminds us that "[...]we live in surroundings that are also living". In these ways, human development is seen as fundamentally contingent on specific temporal, social, and material conditions.

In one concrete convergence between DST and cultural-historical conceptions of development, Van Geert (1994) has argued that the Vygotsky's construct of the zone of proximal development (ZPD) can be seen as a dynamic process that enables the emergence of non-linear developmental patterns. The seeds for this DST-informed redefinition can be seen in Vygotsky's (1978: 86–87) own formulation of the ZPD:

> The [ZPD] defines those functions that have not yet matured but are in the process of maturation ... the [ZPD] permits us to delineate the child's immediate future and his dynamic developmental state, allowing not only for what already has been achieved developmentally but also for what is in the course of maturing.

In another direct connection to DST, Stetsenko and Arievitch (2004: 67) describe the dynamical nature of human development as follows:

> Human development, including ... self and society, knowledge and science – all appear as emergent properties of the same reality of collaborative human practices ... This conceptualization opens ways to address the dialectical manifold transitions

and mutual penetrations among all of these facets of a unified system of human social life, including transitions ... that take place in a constant, never-ending dynamical flow of collective practices. It also allows a clear role to be ascribed to the processes and products of human subjectivity, such as knowledge systems and theories, in the larger contexts of social practices.

Vygotsky acknowledged the critical issue of time and its role in development. In an attempt to overcome the nature-nurture dichotomies that dominated psychology and philosophy early in the 20th century (and still today), he proposed four mutually influencing temporal domains and applied them to the study of human development, which here we align with DST's fractal temporal approach described earlier. The most expansive of these temporal frames is the phylogenesis of humans as a species, which encompasses the approximately two million-year coevolution of human biology in relation to the emergence of language, material tools, and increasingly complex symbolic and cultural practices. Two examples of the co-evolutionary interplay of biology and culture include the evolution of the human hand and oppositional thumb (providing greater manual dexterity), which is isomorphic with the archaeological record showing an increasing complexity of material artifacts and implements. A second example involves the enlargement of the frontal cortex of the human brain that occurred in tandem with the emergence of language, communication, and complex cultural practices (see Cole 1996; Deacon 1997; Evans & Levinson 2009; Tomasello 1999).

The second time frame is the sociocultural domain, which describes the multigenerational development of human cultures, with the implication that humans are born into an existing environment that provides powerful conceptual and material resources for communication, problem solving, and acting on the world through the creation of symbolic tools and material implements. Tomasello (1999: 37) coined the phrase 'ratchet effect' to describe the preservation and creative modification of both material and symbolic forms of culture from generation to generation.

The third temporal domain focuses on the ontogenesis of individuals over the life span. Here, Vygotsky recognized two lines of development: biological maturation through chronological aging, and the creative internalization of cultural forms of cognition and action beginning in infancy and continuing across the life span. As mentioned earlier, ontogenesis can be described as the nexus of the phylogenetic and sociocultural domains as the individual develops as a function of the interaction between both biological and cultural inheritances (Lantolf & Thorne 2006: 45).

The fourth domain is microgenesis, which describes the particular mental functions, abilities, and processes that develop over shorter periods of time. As described by Valsiner (1997), microgenesis is embedded in ontogeny. In practice, this means that a "person's active relating with the immediate context can be viewed as centered upon the personal construction of sense, together with the culturally prestructured and purposive nature of the given setting" (1997: 241). This view articulates with the DST emphasis on the importance of 'initial conditions', the notion that each developmental iteration of a system (or mutually influencing sets of systems) is informed by immediately prior states (de Bot 2008). A version of this perspective is also espoused in contemporary usage-based linguistics, that "all linguistic knowledge ... derives in the first instance from the comprehension and production of specific utterances on specific occasions of use" (Tomasello 2000: 237–238), where each 'occasion of use' is situated in cultural-material contexts that are themselves products of collective historical accumulation.

Each of these four temporal domains mutually influence one another to a greater or lesser degree. The domains of ontogenesis and microgenesis are arguably the most relevant and utilized time frames for applied linguistics and second language (L2) research, though studies focusing on the phylogenetic domain (Tomasello 1999) and the sociocultural domain (Cole 1996; Scribner & Cole 1981) have been highly productive in illuminating the relationships between human cultures and the universal and heterogeneous qualities of higher order, which is to say, socioculturally informed, mental functions. This proposal for looking at human development through the lens of fractal and mutually influencing times scales has an additional function in that it elides the dualism of biology and culture by avoiding 'downward reductionism' – hypotheses of development that arguably overly emphasize biology, as well as 'upward reductionism,' which refers to theorizations that foreground social and environmental conditions as entirely formative of human consciousness and cognition (Valsiner & van der Veer 2000). In this system, biology, durative cultural dynamics, and the immediacy of particular times and spaces can be seen as interdependent and mutually contingent upon one another.

We suggest that the cultural-historical/sociocultural approach to time periods and developmental processes is both commensurable with, and usefully contributes specificity to, DST's fractal approach to time and change as outlined elsewhere in this chapter.

DST and language theories

Social theories focus mainly on the social interaction needed for language development. In order to focus on language development itself, we also need a theory of language that aligns with DST principles.

For many decades, a dominant view of language theory and language acquisition has been that language is modular, with separate and independent subsystems for sound, meaning and structure. These subsystems would interact with one another through interfaces. The main focus within this paradigm has been on the syntactic structure, which is regular and predictable: There is a universal grammar (UG) (all languages share basic principles) and humans are endowed with an innate language acquisition device, which enables humans to decode the language specific structural settings. The main arguments for this approach have been that language users are creative because they can produce sentences that they have never heard or used before, and that there are *constraints*, because there are limits to the structures and shapes sentences may have. The main focus within this paradigm has been to find universals: What do humans have in common while developing their L1 or L2?

This question has been addressed using the categorical differentiation of property theories from transition theories, where property theories are those that focus on the nature of a representational phenomena or condition while transition theories examine processes, change, use, and the like (see Cummins 1983). Within SLA, Gregg (2003) suggests that the property vs. transition distinction maps to key questions that have guided UG research, namely 'what is the nature of language?' and 'how is this knowledge acquired?' For the most part, however, UG research observes, and in-part constructs, a dichotomization of research into either static 'what' or process *how* questions, with a decided empirical emphasis on the former. We suggest, following Ellis and Larsen-Freeman (2006), that property theories should be conflated with, or subsumed by, transition theories, since fundamentally, structure (resource consolidation for future action) emerges from process, and not the other way around (Hopper 1998). While a conceptual distinction of property vs. transition theories may be relevant for some purposes, transition dynamics need to be acknowledged as the analytic primary. To what extent a UG approach to SLD is compatible with a DST perspective is a matter of debate (e.g., Gregg 2010). The present, more or less generally accepted position seems to be that innate knowledge about grammar may be part of the human cognitive system, but is not necessary to explain the emergence of even complex constructions (Herdina & Jessner, 2002, ch. 4; Larsen-Freeman & Cameron 2008; Plaza-Pust 2008)

Even though the UG view of language has by no means been accepted by all applied linguists and has often been explicitly rejected, ignored, or contested (see Tomasello 2004; Tomasello & Abbot-Smith 2002), it is only recently that a more coherent picture has emerged that posits a different theoretical point, which requires neither a specialized language faculty nor a universal grammar to account for creativity and constraints. There is no single theory that deals with all aspects of what language is, how it is organized, how it is processed, how it is used, how it changes, how it is acquired, and how it is learned as a second language, but there is a group of compatible theories that together could fall under the umbrella of *usage-based* or *emergentist* theories that are compatible with a dynamic systems theory (DST) approach: cognitive linguistics, emergentism, connectionist theories, grammaticalization theory, activation theory, and usage-based L1 acquisition. All of these theories highlight certain aspects of language, language change, language acquisition, or the developmental process, but none of these theories by themselves gives a coherent picture of all these aspects at the same time. However, as N. Ellis (1998) and a more recent publication by Robinson and Ellis (2008) have attempted to show, these theories complement each other and can be applied to a dynamic view of SLD. What follows is a brief description of these theories and a summary of the implications such a dynamic, usage-based approach may have for second language development (SLD).

Cognitive linguistic theory (CLT) (Langacker 2008) addresses what language is and how it relates to human cognition and conceptualization. The assumption is that language is primarily about making meaning. CLT strongly rejects the modular view of language that is independent of all other human cognition and conceptualization. It argues that language is directly influenced by human cognition and processing abilities and reflects therefore human categorization, conceptualization, imagination, and schematization. It further argues that a continuum of constructions at all levels (morpheme, word, collocation, phrase, formulaic sequence, clause, sentence and discourse level utterance) reflects the conceptualization and structural organization underlying human languages and their processing (Goldberg 2003; Langacker 2008). CLT is very much in line with a DST perspective, because of the complete interconnectedness of the subsystems both in the mind and in the linguistic system, and because of the assumed dependency on both internal and external resources, such as perception, cognition, conceptualization, and human interaction.

But how has such a completely interconnected linguistic system developed to begin with? Hopper (1998) argues that the regular patterns that we find in any language at all levels do not occur because of some preprogrammed language faculty, but because they have simply emerged. In emergent grammar there is no such thing as an abstract grammar in the mind, but a network of expressions and constructions as a result of an iterative process. The regular patterns found in language are therefore the result of language use and are actually nothing but conventions established through time (cf. Evans & Levinson 2009: 444ff.).

> The notion of Emergent Grammar is meant to suggest that structure, or regularity, comes out of discourse and is shaped by discourse in an ongoing process. Grammar is, in this view, simply the name for certain categories of observed repetitions in discourse. (Hopper 1998: 156)

Hopper's line of thinking is in line with DST in that it considers language and language change a result of interaction with the environment and internal reorganization. Implicit in this view is that the present level of change depends critically on the previous level of change. Grammaticalization studies (Bybee 2008; Hopper 1996) have shown how established patterns in languages may change through use, overuse and abuse, often starting with a small change in one part of the system, which then eventually will affect other parts of the system. This view is in line with DST thinking in that systems are constantly changing, that small changes in one place may have an effect on other parts of the system, and that these changes are not linear.

The idea that language is creative and that new constructions and complexities occur is also compatible with connectionist models (Elman 1995) that have shown that through simple iterations complex patterns may emerge. In other words, complex patterns do not have to be innate, because they can also emerge through small iterations. An additional point is that the UG argument that language must be innate because there are *constraints,* i.e. there are natural limits to what is possible in a language, can be countered from a DST perspective. Even though there are many approaches to complexity, chaos and dynamic systems, they share the common assumption that eventually all complex systems begin to self-organize, show regularities and will settle in so-called attractor states temporarily.

The idea that language learning is an iterative process is also in line with Activation Theory (Rumelhart & McClelland 1987): The more frequently one hears something, the more easily it is activated, the more frequently it is used and the faster it is learned, or as Hopper (1998: 161) has described it, "[e]mergent regularities are aggregations; they are the sediment of frequency." Within Activation Theory, most work has been done at the lexical level, but MacWhinney also developed a computational model with self-organizing maps (SOMs) at different linguistic levels (morphology, syllable structure, lexicon, syntax and so on). In line with other usage-based theories, MacWhinney's unified model (UM) (2008) takes input as the source for learning. It learns by comparing the input, searching for similarities and differences. However, MacWhinney's model emphasizes that in addition to pure frequency, the role of cue availability, validity and reliability helps determine the course of acquisition, which relates to the opacity of patterns. *Cue availability* refers to how often a cue is present in the input, and *cue reliability* refers to the degree to which a cue is used consistently. *Cue validity* is the product of cue availability and reliability. A fully valid cue is a cue that is always there when it needs to be for communication purposes (in other words, it is fully available) and that is used consistently (it is fully reliable). A good example of a valid cue would be the verb *is* after *he* or *she.* An example of cues that are not valid at all is in the English article system. We can be sure that *a* and *the* are probably the most frequent words in the language (cue availability), but their use is notoriously difficult to acquire for learners whose L1 does not have a similar system. The reason is that both *a* and *the* have many different uses and functions, so the cue reliability and therefore the cue validity are very low. In other words, in line with DST thinking, MacWhinney points out that there cannot be just one causal factor in acquisition, but a combination of factors that interact.

To summarize, even though cognitive linguistics focuses on the meaningful interrelationships within the language system in general, it recognizes that this system is complex and dynamic, that it has emerged through social interaction, and that it will keep on changing. Emergentist and connectionist approaches focus especially on how it is possible that complexities can emerge in language through simple iterations, and grammaticalization theory concentrates on the detailed processes that may occur in language change. Activation theory and MacWhinney's unified model focus especially on the factors, such as frequency of occurrence, that play a role in language acquisition and use. In line with DST, all these usage-based theories implicitly or explicitly agree that the patterns that may occur at the general system level (a language in general) will also occur at the more specific, individual level.

DST and SLD theories

Whereas social theories focus on the interactions needed for language development and linguistic theories focus on the parts of the language system that can develop, SLD research at finer levels of granularity may focus for example on the extent to which individuals can or cannot learn or acquire an L2 or on the way language may be processed. This section will discuss SLD approaches that would be compatible with DST principles, but which will challenge many of the commonly established dichotomies that exist in the literature.

End states versus steady states

From a DST perspective notions of growth and decline cannot be separated. A dynamic approach to SLD leads to a re-evaluation of some of the foundational assumptions regarding language acquisition (Weideman 2011), the most important being that the learner never reaches an endpoint or end state, because the language system is constantly changing due to interaction with the environment and internal reorganization. Research on language attrition has demonstrated that a language learned at one point in life is not well maintained after periods of non-use, though there is some evidence that some sub-systems such as syntactic ones are less vulnerable than others such as maintenance of the lexicon.

In different types of research on L2 development, it has been suggested that there is some sort of end point to L2 acquisition, both for adults and for children. This has been referred to as or the endstate of L2 development in terms such as fossilization or ultimate attainment. For example, in the literature on the role of UG, the term endstate has been used to refer to "L2 speakers whose interlanguage grammars can be deemed, on independent grounds, to have reached a steady state" (Goad & White 2004: 120).

Some authors suggest that there really is a final stage, while others view it more as a steady state. In a DST-based approach, there may be steady states in language development, but there is no endstate. Systems have no inherent telos, and they are dependent on interaction with their environment and change over time of their internal structures. It is the case that some changes caused by internal reorganization may not be externally visible and may appear to be stable but the underlying processes may have changed. There will always be some degree of variability within a system.

Some of the SLD literature accepts the possibility of mono-causal factors leading to stasis. In contrast, R. Ellis (1994) argued that learner internal factors such as age and motivation, and learner external factors such as communicative pressure, amount and opportunity for contact, and feedback on L2, form a nexus of factors that precludes the possibility that a single variable could explain fossilization, though he acknowledged that transfer from the mother tongue seems to be an important factor. In her discussion of this issue, Larsen-Freeman (2005) is critical with respect to several aspects of fossilization, stating that "despite its longevity, despite its theoretical and practical significance, and despite the fact that everyone can relate to it, there are problems with the concept of fossilization: It defies easy definition, description, and explanation." (2005: 189).

Views on fossilization more in line with DST principles would the ones proposed by Selinker and Perdue, because they recognize the interacting complexities, the fact that there is no end state (but rather steady states), and that variability remains. The term fossilization was originally coined by Selinker (1972). He mentioned five types of processes that lead to fossilization: language transfer, transfer of training, strategies of second language learning, communication strategies and overgeneralization of L1. The combination of the use of these processes "produce what we might term entirely fossilized interlanguage competence: (Selinker, Swain & Dumas 1975). In his earlier writings, he seemed to suggest that the whole interlanguage system would come to a standstill, but in later publications, he modified this position by moving to "an empirically more manageable concept of plateaus in L2 learning rather than cessation of learning ... [since] it is impossible to show that a given individual has stopped learning" (Selinker & Lakshmanan 1992: 212). Perdue (2000) discusses fossilization in the context of untutored SLA of the Basic

Variety. While in most studies on fossilization the focus is on specific aspects of interlanguage, Perdue (2000: 653) argues that "[t]he Basic Variety (Klein & Perdue 1997) can be seen as a first attempt at comprehensively describing a low level of potential fossilization". This means that it is not parts or subsystems that fossilize, but the language system as a whole. The Basic Variety is seen as the result of the interaction of three sets of factors that according to Klein (1986) determine the adult's development of a second language: the initial cognitive/linguistic disposition of the adult learner, exposure to the language, and the speaker's propensity to acquire (Perdue 2000: 651). Obviously, he considers the interaction between these factors over time a reason for the different stages of development. As N. Ellis and Larsen-Freeman (2006) argue, the Basic Variety can be seen as an attractor state of the developing language system, while the three sets of conditions are reminiscent of some of the characteristics of dynamic systems: sensitive dependence on initial conditions, interaction with the environment, and the internal state of the system. *Propensity to acquire* refers also to the learner's intentions and attitudes towards learning the language, and that is a part of our thinking about DST and SLD that still needs to be explored within this context. The Basic Variety can also be viewed as the result of the *carrying capacity* of the developmental system. Given the resources available, that is how far the system can develop.

Things versus processes

DST is essentially a theory of change. As we have discussed earlier, change takes place at all levels of cognition simultaneously, both in space and time. What we also know about dynamic systems is that they are complex and adaptive, which implies that all subsystems can affect one another over time. This will hold for all areas of cognition, each at its own time scale. It may be obvious that this crucial concept of continuity runs counter to the idea of any closed modules. From a DST point of view, the idea of modules will have to be replaced by a set of embedded interacting subsystems. Each of the subsystems can be seen as one dimension in a changing multidimensional landscape, which is referred to as State Space (see, for instance Spivey 2007). If we insist on drawing a parallel to traditional linguistics, we could regard phonology, syntax and the lexicon as changing subsystems (as proposed by Larsen-Freeman, 1997), and within each of these subsystems embedded subsystems for different languages (similar to what is proposed by Paradis (2004), provided that we acknowledge that the subsystems interact and have fuzzy borders (Lowie, Verspoor & Seton 2010). However, a crucial difference between modules and subsystems is that for subsystems no distinction can be made between declarative and procedural knowledge, as there is no subsystem that consists of a store of static information. Or, in Spivey's (2007: 139) words:

> Mental content does not consist of objects but of events. Individual representations are not temporarily static *things* in the mind (...). Representations are *processes* in and of themselves, sparsely distributed patterns of neural activation that change nonlinearly over the course of several hundreds of milliseconds, and then blend right into the next one.

This implies that even lexical information, which in linguistic theories has been referred to as most typically declarative (see Fodor 1983), and which has conveniently been equated to a dictionary-like store of information, will have to be redefined as (part of) a process. And if words are not *mental objects*, but are *operators on mental states* (Elman 2011: 16) then we lose ground for the deep-rooted distinction between lexicon and syntax. Instead, language processing from a DST point of view, must be seen as a probabilistic context dependent process. This stipulation follows logically from the consistent application of DST to our thinking about language processing. Moreover, the unstable basis for the traditional distinction between subsystems is supported by empirical work that has made use of connectionist models of language learning. Using Simple Recurrent Networks (SRNs, see Elman 1990) that learn patterns via probabilistic calculations, it has already been demonstrated that semantic and syntactic information can be integrated by grouping words that have similar distributional characteristics (Tabor & Tanenhaus 1999). In recent work, Elman (2011) has shown how network dynamics can generate sentences based on the distributional properties of words, as "the state of the network resulting from any given word is what encodes its expectancies of what will follow" (Elman 2011: 22). So it is the context in which a word is used that determines its meaning.

The lack of clear dividing lines and the implications of fuzzy subsystems have important consequences for the multilingual language user. Although it has already been convincingly demonstrated that different languages cannot be strictly separated (Dijkstra & van Heuven 2002), let alone "stored separately," the impact of context on multilingual language processing has not yet been thoroughly explored. Some recent reaction time experiments involving the application of cognitive dynamics to multilingual processing tentatively suggest that language processing is strongly dependent on the context of language use (Plat 2011). The intensive use of one language seems to affect the representational dynamics of both languages tested.

Several studies have looked at SLD from a DST perspective, focusing mainly on how different variables may interact over time. In other words, they assume that different sub-systems may grow at different rates and show non-linear development. Moreover, they will affect each other differently over time. For example, Verspoor, Lowie and Dijk (2008) showed that the developing language system of an advanced Dutch learner of English as produced in academic texts alternates in focus on lexicon or syntax. They found an asymmetrical competitive interaction between the development of the average sentence length in words (a sentence complexity measure) and the type-token ratio (or TTR, a lexical creativity measure). Thus, when academic writing proficiency increases, there seems to be a trade-off between more varied word use and longer sentences at different stages in the developmental process.

Spoelman and Verspoor (2010) examined the development of different complexity measures of a beginning Dutch learner acquiring Finnish, in particular the development of complexity at the word, noun phrase and sentence level. They found that as word complexity increases, both noun phrase and sentence complexity increase as well, so there might be a symmetrically supportive relation. However, noun phrase complexity and sentence complexity were shown to alternate in their development and therefore the relationship between noun phrase and sentence complexity illustrate both elements of competition as well as mutual enhancement over time.

In a longitudinal DST study on L2 writing development, Caspi (2010) traced four variables – lexical complexity, lexical accuracy, syntactic complexity, and syntactic accuracy – in four different advanced learners over a period of approximately 10 months. She found precursor relationships between these four variables in the order just given. In other words, learners first make their words more complex before they are used more accurately; after that the syntax becomes more complex and then more accurate.

In a cross-sectional study from a DST perspective, Verspoor, Schmid and Xu (2012) showed that five different proficiency levels (from beginner to high intermediate) could be distinguished from each other by looking at broad, frequently occurring measures known to distinguish between proficiency levels: sentence length, the Guiraud index, all dependent clauses combined, all chunks combined, all errors combined, and the use of present and past tense. However, almost all specific constructions showed non-linear development, variation and changing relationships among the variables as one would expect from a dynamic perspective. Between levels 1 and 2 mainly lexical changes took place, between levels 2 and 3 mainly syntactic changes occurred, and between levels 3 and 4 both lexical and syntactic changes appeared. The transition between levels 4 and 5 was characterized by lexical changes only: particles, compounds and fixed phrases.

In summary, these studies have shown that different sets of variables grow and decline over time, many times affecting each other differently over that time.

Conclusions

In this contribution we have argued that DST can be seen as a comprehensive theory that can unify and make relevant a number of different *middle level* SLD theories (Littlewood 2004), which in our view are theories that attend to different levels of granularity and different time scales, provided of course that the middle level theories are commensurable with DST principles. Such theories, such as eco-logical and cultural-historical/sociocultural approaches to development, and cognitive, emergent, and distributed theories of language, place language develop-ment in the wider perspective of societal change and interaction with cultural and material aspects of the environment.

As examples of such theories, we have given socio-cultural theories of devel-opment and dynamic usage based theories of language. We have also tried to show that some research lines in SLD have taken a dynamic stance implicitly. Finally we have argued that language development is a time course in which not only all as-pects of cognition interact but in which cognition is embedded in the sociocul-tural domain AND is an embodied process. This is not necessarily the choice for a convenient research paradigm. However, the alternative is to pretend that language *acquisition* is a product of linear development with a clear end state. We hope to have shown in this contribution that language development is not as simple as that. Much can be expected from the multiple DST/complexity perspectives that have been introduced and refined over the past decade, with the overarching goal of articulating a comprehensive understanding of language development as an emer-gent process that is fractally distributed in time and across sociocultural spaces.

References

Atkinson, D. 2010. Extended, embodied cognition and second language acquisition. *Applied Linguistics* 31(5): 599–622.

Bakhtin, M.M. 1986. *Speech Genres and Other Late Essays*. Austin TX: University of Texas Press.

Barsalou, L. 2008. Grounded cognition. *Annual Review of Psychology* 59: 617–645.

Bateson, G. 1972. *Steps to an Ecology of Mind: Collected Essays in Anthropology, Psychiatry, Evo-lution, and Epistemology*. Chicago IL: University of Chicago Press.

Bybee, J. 2008. Usage-based grammar and second language acquisition. In *Handbook of Cogni-tive Linguistics and Second Language Acquisition*, P. Robinson & N. Ellis (eds), 216–236. New York NY: Routledge.

Caspi, T. 2010. A Dynamic Perspective on Second Language Development. PhD dissertation, University of Groningen. <http://irs.ub.rug.nl/ppn/329338412>

Clark, A. 2008. *Supersizing the Mind: Embodiment, Action, and Cognitive Extension*. Oxford: OUP.

Cole, M. 1996. *Cultural Psychology. A Once and Future Discipline*, Cambridge MA: Belknapp Press.

Cowley, S. 2009. Distributed language and dynamics. *Pragmatics & Cognition* 17: 495–507.

Cowley, S. & Steffensen, S. 2010. Signifying bodies and health: a non-local aftermath. In *Signifying bodies: Biosemiosis, Interaction, and Health*, S. Cowley, J. Major, S. Steffensen & A. Dinis (eds), 331–355. Braga: Faculty of Philosophy of Braga, Portuguese Catholic University.

Cummins, R. 1983. *The Nature of Psychological Explanation*. Cambridge MA: The MIT Press.

Deacon, T. 1997. *The Symbolic Species: The Co-evolution of Language and the Brain*. New York NY: Norton.

de Bot, K. 2008. Introduction: Second language development as a dynamic process. *The Modern Language Journal* 92:166–178.

de Bot, K., & Lowie, W. M. 2010. On the stability of representations in the multilingual lexicon. In *Cognitive Processing in Second Language Acquisition* [Converging Evidence in Language and Communication Research 13], M. Pütz & L. Sicola (eds), 117–134. Amsterdam: John Benjamins.

de Bot, K., Lowie, W. & Verspoor, M. 2007. A dynamic systems theory approach to second language acquisition. Bilingualism: *Language and Cognition* 10: 7–21.

Dijkstra, T. & van Heuven, W.J.B. 2002. The architecture of the bilingual word recognition system: From identification to decision. Bilingualism: *Language and Cognition* 5(3): 175–197.

Dornyei, Z. 2009. *The Psychology of Second Language Acquisition*. Oxford: OUP.

Ellis, N. 1998. Emergentism, connectionism, and language learning. *Language Learning* 48: 631–664.

Ellis, N. 2011. The emergence of language as a complex adaptive system. In *Routledge Handbook of Applied Linguistics,* J. Simpson (ed.), 654–667. New York NY: Routledge.

Ellis, N., & Larsen-Freeman, D. 2006. Language emergence: Implications for applied linguistics. *Applied Linguistics* 27(4): 558–589.

Ellis, R. 1994. *The Study of Second Language Acquisition*. Oxford: OUP.

Elman, J. L. 1990. Finding structure in time. *Cognitive Science* 14: 179–211.

Elman, J. 1995. Language as a dynamical system. In *Mind as Motion*, R. Port & T. van Gelder (eds), 195–225. Cambridge MA: The MIT Press.

Elman, J.L. 2011. Lexical knowledge without a lexicon? *Mental Lexicon* 6(1): 1–33.

Engeström, Y. 1987. *Learning by Expanding: An Activity Theoretical Approach to Developmental Research*. Helsinki: Orienta-Konsultit.

Evans, N. & Levinson, S. C. 2009 The myth of language universals: Language diversity and its importance for cognitive science. *Behavioral and Brain Sciences* 32(5): 429–492.

Fodor, J. 1983. *The Modularity of Mind: An Essay on Faculty Psychology*. Cambridge MA: The MIT Press.

Goad, H. & White, L. 2004. Ultimate attainments of L2 inflection. *EUROSLA Yearbook* 4: 119–145.

Goldberg, A. 2003. Constructions: A new theoretical approach to language. *Trends in Cognitive Sciences* 7: 219–224.

Gregg, K.R. 2003. The stage of emergentism in second language acquisition. *Second Language Research* 19: 95–128.

Gregg, K.R. 2010. Review article: Shallow draughts: Larsen-Freeman and Cameron on complexity. *Second Language Research* 26(4): 549–560.

Haeckel, E. 1866. *Generelle Morphologie der Organismen*. Berlin: Georg Reimer.

Herdina, P. & Jessner, U. 2002. *A Dynamic Model of Multilingualism: Perspectives of Change in Psycholinguistics*. Clevedon: Multilingual Matters.

Hopper, P. 1996. Some recent trends in grammaticalization. *Annual Review of Anthropology* 25: 217–36.

Hopper, P. 1998. Emergent grammar. In *The New Psychology of Language: Cognitive and Functional Approaches to Language Structure*, M. Tomasello (ed.), 155–175). Mahwah NJ: Lawrence Erlbaum Associates.

Järvilehto, T. 2009. The theory of the organism-environment system as a basis of experimental work in psychology. *Ecological Psychology* 21: 112–120.

Jakobson, R. 1941. *Kindersprache, Aphasie und allgemeine Lautgesetze*. Uppsala: Universitets Aarskrift.

Jörg, T. 2009. Thinking in complexity about learning and education: A programmatic view. *Complicity: An International Journal of Complexity and Education* 6: 1–22.

Kirshner, D. & Kellogg, D. 2009. Lev Vygotsky as muse to complex learning/teaching: A response to Ton Jörg's programmatic view. *Complicity: An International Journal of Complexity and Education* 6: 45–55.

Klein, W. 1986. *Second Language Acquisition*. Cambridge: CUP.

Klein, W. & Perdue, C. 1997. The basic variety (or: Couldn't natural languages be much simpler?). *Second Language Research* 13(4): 301–347.

Kramsch, C. 2002. *Language Acquisition and Language Socialization*. London: Continuum.

Langacker, R.W. 2008. Cognitive grammar as a basis for language instruction. In *Handbook of Cognitive Linguistics and Second Language Acquisition*. P. Robinson & N. Ellis (eds), 66–88. New York NY: Routledge.

Lantolf, J. 2007. Sociocultural source of thinking and its relevance for second language acquisition. Bilingualism: *Language and Cognition* 10: 31–33.

Lantolf, J. & Thorne, S.L. 2006. *Sociocultural Theory and the Genesis of Second Language Development*. Oxford: OUP.

Larsen-Freeman, D. 1997. *Chaos/complexity science and second language acquisition. Applied Linguistics* 18(2): 140–165.

Larsen-Freeman, D. 2005. Second language acquisition and the issue of fossilization: There is no end and there is no state. In *Studies of Fossilization in Second Language Acquisition*, Z. Han & T. Odlin (eds), 189–200. Clevedon: Multilingual Matters.

Larsen-Freeman, D. & Cameron, L. 2008. *Complex Systems and Applied Linguistics*. Oxford: OUP.

Lee, N., Mikesell, L., Joaquin, A., Mates, A. & Schumann, J. 2009. *The Interactional Instinct. The Evolution and Acquisition of Language*. Oxford: OUP.

Lemke, J. 2000. Across the scales of time: Artifacts, activities, and meanings in ecosocial systems. *Mind, Culture, and Activity* 7: 273–290.

Linell, P. 2009. *Rethinking Language, Mind, and World Dialogically: Interactional and Contextual Theories of Human Sense-making*. Charlotte NC: Information Age Publishing.

Littlewood, W. 2004. Second language learning. In *The Handbook of Applied Linguistics*, C. Elder and A. Davies (eds), 501–524. Oxford: Blackwell.

Long, M. 1993. The assessment of SLA theories. *Applied Linguistics* 14(3): 225–249.

Lowie, W. M., Verspoor, M. & Seton, B. J. 2010. Conceptual representations in the multilingual mind: A study of advanced Dutch learners of English. In *Inside the Learner's Mind: Cognitive Processing and Second Language Acquisition* [Converging Evidence in Language and

Communication Research 13], M. Pütz & L. Sicola (eds), 135–148. Amsterdam: John Benjamins.

Luria, A. R. 1976. *Cognitive Development. Its Cultural and Social Foundations.* Cambridge MA: Harvard University Press.

MacWhinney, B. 2008. A unified model. In *Handbook of Cognitive Linguistics and Second Language Acquisition*, P. Robinson & N. Ellis (eds), 341–371. New York NY: Routledge.

Mandelbrot, B. 1982. *The Fractal Geometry of Nature.* New York NY: W.H. Freeman.

Paradis, M. 2004. *A Neurolinguistic Theory of Bilingualism* [Studies in Bilingualism 40]. Amsterdam: John Benjamins.

Perdue, C. 2000. Untutored language acquisition. In *Routledge Encyclopedia of Language Teaching and Learning*, M. Byram (ed.), 49–654. London: Routledge.

Plat, H. 2011. Language in Use: Variability in L1 and L2 Language Processing. MA thesis, University of Groningen.

Plaza-Pust, C. 2008. Dynamic systems theory and Universal Grammar: Holding a turbulent mirror to development in grammars. *The Modern Language Journal* 92(2): 250–269.

Robinson, P. & Ellis, N. 2008. *Handbook of Cognitive Linguistics and Second Language Acquisition.* New York NY: Routledge.

Rumelhart, D. & McClelland, J. 1987. Learning the past tense of English verbs: Implicit rules or parallel processing? In *Mechanisms of Language Acquisition*, B. MacWhinney (ed.), 195–248. Hillsdale NJ: Lawrence Erlbaum Associates.

Schmid, M. 2011. *Language Attrition.* Cambridge: CUP.

Scribner, S. & Cole, M. 1981. *The Psychology of Literacy.* Cambridge MA: Harvard University Press.

Selinker, L. 1972. Interlanguage. *International Review of Applied Linguistics* 10: 209–231.

Selinker, L. & Lakshmanan, U. 1992. Language transfer and fossilization. In *Language Transfer in Language Learning* [Language Acquisition and Language Disorders 5], S. Gass & L. Selinker (eds), 197–216. Amsterdam: John Benjamins.

Selinker, L., Swain, M. & Dumas, G. 1975. The interlanguage hypothesis extended to children. *Language Learning* 75: 139–152.

Shotter, J. 2003. Cartesian change, chiasmic change: The power of living expression. *Janus Head* 6(1): 6–29.

Spivey, M. 2007. *The Continuity of Mind.* Oxford: OUP.

Spoelman, M. & Verspoor, M. 2010. Dynamic patterns in development of accuracy and complexity: A longitudinal case study in the acquisition of Finnish. *Applied Linguistics* 31: 532–553.

Stetsenko, A., & Arievitch, I. 2004. Vygotskian collaborative project of social transformation: History, politics, and practice in knowledge construction. *Critical Psychology* 12: 58–80.

Tabor, W. & Tanenhaus, M. K. 1999. Dynamical models of sentence processing. *Cognitive Science* 23(4): 491–515.

'The Five Graces Group' (Beckner, C., Blythe, R., Bybee, J., Christiansen, M. H., Croft, W., Ellis, N. C., Holland, J., Ke, J., Larsen-Freeman, D., Schoenemann, T.). 2009. Language is a complex adaptive system. Position paper. *Language Learning* 59 (Supplement 1): 1–27.

Thorne, S.L. & Lantolf, J. P. 2007. A linguistics of communicative activity. In *Disinventing and Reconstituting Languages*, S. Makoni & A. Pennycook (eds), 170–195. Clevedon: Multilingual Matters.

Thorne, S.L. & Tasker, T. 2011. Sociocultural theories and applied linguistics. In *Routledge Handbook of Applied Linguistics*, J. Simpson (ed.), 487–500. New York NY: Routledge.

Tomasello, M. 1999. *The Cultural Origins of Human Cognition*. Cambridge MA: Harvard University Press.

Tomasello, M. 2000. Do young children have adult syntactic competence? *Cognition* 74: 209–253.

Tomasello, M. 2003. *Constructing Language: A Usage-Based Theory of Language Acquisition*. Cambridge MA: Harvard University Press.

Tomasello, M. 2004. What kind of evidence could refute the UG hypothesis? Commentary on Wunderlich. *Studies in Language* 28: 642–645.

Tomasello, M. & Abbot-Smith, K. 2002. A tale of two theories: Response to Fisher. *Cognition* 83: 207–214.

Valsiner, J. 1997. Magical phrases, human development, and psychological ontology. In *Sociogenetic Perspectives on Internalization*, C. Lightfoot & B. Cox (eds), 237–255. Mahwah NJ: Lawrence Erlbaum Associates.

Valsiner, J. & van der Veer, R. 2000. *The Social Mind. Construction of the Idea*, Cambridge: CUP.

van Geert, P. 1994. Vygotskian dynamics of development. *Human Development* 37: 346–365.

van Geert, P. 1998. A dynamic systems model of basic developmental mechanisms: Piaget, Vygotsky and beyond. *Psychological Review*, 105: 634–677.

van Geert, P. 2009. A comprehensive dynamic systems theory of language development. In *Language Development over the Lifespan*, K. de Bot & R. Schrauf (eds), 60–104. New York NY: Routledge.

Van Lier, L. 2000. From input to affordances. In *Sociocultural Theory and Second Language Learning*, J. Lantolf (ed.), 245–259. Oxford: OUP.

Van Lier, L. 2004. *The Ecology and Semiotics of Language Learning: A Sociocultural Perspective*. Dordrecht: Kluwer.

Verspoor, M., de Bot, K. & Lowie, W. (eds). 2011. *A Dynamic Systems Approach to Second Language Development: Methods and Techniques*. Amsterdam: John Benjamins.

Verspoor, M., Lowie, W. & van Dijk, M. 2008. Variability in second language development from a dynamic systems perspective. *The Modern Language Journal* 92: 214–231.

Verspoor, M., Schmid, M.S. & Xu, X. 2012. A dynamic usage based perspective on L2 writing development. *Journal of Second Language Writing*.

Volosinov, V. N. 1973. *Marxism and the Philosophy of Language*. New York NY: Seminar Press.

Vygotsky, L.S. 1978. *Mind in Society. The Development of Higher Psychological Processes*, M. Cole, V. John-Steiner, S. Scribner & E. Souberman (eds), Cambridge MA: Harvard University Press.

Vygotsky, L.S. 1981. The genesis of higher mental functions. In *The Concept of Activity in Soviet Psychology*, J.V. Wertsch (ed.), 144–188. New York NY: M.E. Sharpe.

Weideman, A. 2011. *A Framework for the Study of Linguistics*. Pretoria: Van Schaik.

Wertsch, J. 2002. *Voices of Collective Remembering*. Cambridge: CUP.

CHAPTER 11

Electrophysiology of second language processing

The past, present and future

Laura Sabourin, Christie Brien and Marie-Claude Tremblay
University of Ottawa

This chapter reviews past and current contributions from event-related brain potential (ERP) research to the field of L2 processing. ERPs are able to measure cognitive brain processes at a very fine-grained temporal resolution and allow for determining when linguistic processes are occurring. The technique allows for investigations of whether L1 and L2 processing differences are mainly due to the fact that L2 processing takes longer or whether different neural procedures (as evidenced by different components being present) occur in L1 and L2 processing. Findings from studies of monolingual, bilingual and (where available) multilingual participants are reviewed to determine the effects of proficiency, age of acquisition and similarity between languages on the processing of languages learned later in life.

Introduction

The field of linguistics has recently begun using brain-based measures to determine how language is processed. Current neuroimaging techniques allow researchers to determine not only where language is being processed (using, for example, functional Magnetic Resonance Imaging) but when and how these processes take place as well (using electrophysiological techniques such as Event-Related brain Potentials (ERPs)). Due to their excellent temporal resolution, ERPs are a great technique to study language processing, which is known to occur at the level of milliseconds. As such, ERPs have the potential to help determine the different processes that are occurring during the task of linguistic comprehension.[1]

---

1. Technically, the ERP technique could also inform researchers about the nature of linguistic production. However this is a much more difficult task due to the noise created in the signal from muscle movements. Production will not be discussed further.

ERPs have been used in language research to investigate processing in real time. Language processing is a complex task which involves the processing of phonetic, lexical, and grammatical information as well as more general sentential context. Further, there is evidence that comprehension processes are of a highly interactive, impressionable nature, which entails that any stage of contextual processing may be affected by another stage (i.e., Swaab, Brown & Hagoort 1997). Given this level of complexity, numerous studies have implemented the sensitive temporal resolution of ERPs to measure automatic sentence processing in real time in order to investigate the neurocognitive bases of linguistic processes (i.e., Friederici 2002). Such studies have investigated, among other issues: (a) the separability of the lexicon and grammar, and the underlying mechanisms involved, (b) whether or not language functions are domain specific or domain independent, (c) possible biological correlates involved, be they brain structures, neural circuits, or molecular systems, as well as the temporal order of their involvement and whether or not they interact, and (d) how might all of the issues above differ in second language (L2) learners, and whether or not age of acquisition (AoA) and proficiency are factors.

Although ERPs are a great tool that can be used to answer many different research questions, caution must also be used when interpreting the data acquired. As Luck (2005) warns, the functional significance of ERP waveforms is not easy to determine. By asking the right questions, however, it is possible to learn a lot about the neural processing of language. Due to their poor spatial resolution, it is not possible to ask where a native language (L1) vs. an L2 is processed, though one can ask whether or not the processing of an L1 and an L2 are similar.

An introduction to ERPs[2]

ERPs reflect the on-line activity of groups of neurons and are therefore a direct measure of electrical neural activity. Specifically, they reflect the large-scale activity of groups of neurons (post-synaptic potentials) that are located near the skull (cortical pyramidal cells); thus ERPs are only able to measure neural activity from a subset of the total neurons in the brain. This is another reason why caution must be taken when interpreting ERP data. ERPs are based on the online electroencephalography which is then time-locked to specific events (in this case linguistic events). These electric potentials that are recorded are averaged over a large number of similar trials to obtain the ERP. Averaging allows the brain activity not directly linked to the event of interest to be reduced while the activity of interest

---

2.   For a more technical introduction to ERPs see Luck (2005). For language specific introductions to ERPs see Stowe and Sabourin (2005) and Kaan (2007).

remains. In this manner, a clear picture of the brain response to a particular event emerges. The emerging waveform consists of a series of positive and negative going deflections. It is these deflections that are considered ERP components when they are consistently time-locked to certain types of stimuli. Some of the most well-known components found to language stimuli are the mismatch negativity (MMN), the P300, the N400, and the P600. These components are considered to represent the underlying neural mechanism involved in certain types of linguistic processing. For each of these components, information such as latency, scalp distribution, and amplitude of the effects are measured and compared across conditions and groups.

ERP experiments have identified a component called the MMN that indicates the detection of a change in an ongoing sequence of similar auditory stimuli. The MMN can be elicited by presenting two sounds following an oddball paradigm during which one of the sounds, called the standard, is played repeatedly and the other, called the oddball (or deviant) intrudes intermittently. This method does not require the participant to do anything. In fact, during an MMN experiment, participants are instructed not to pay attention to the stimuli. This component makes it possible to determine when pairs of phonemes are discriminable to participants. Typically, the MMN is characterised by a negative deflection peaking between 100 and 250ms following stimulus onset in the frontocentral electrodes (Näätänen 2001). Another ERP component that has been interpreted as being a measure of sound discrimination is the P300 (Dalebout & Stack 1999; Tampas, Harkrider & Hedrick 2005). The P300 is a positive deflection that peaks at around 300ms after stimulus onset, with maximum amplitude at the midline, or, more specifically, at the centro-parietal electrodes (Tampas et al. 2005). As opposed to the MMN, which is a pre-attentive component, the P300 is observed when attention is focused on the stimuli.

The most studied language-related ERP component is the N400. The N400 is a negative going wave which peaks at approximately 400ms after the critical stimulus. This component is sensitive to various lexical properties such as word frequency, familiarity, and ease of recognition/integration (within a context). While the N400 component is observed for all content words, it is the N400 effect (the difference between the N400 to lexical items in different conditions) that is of interest. In the first ERP study that investigated language processing, Kutas and Hillyard (1980) found a graded increase in the N400 component to words that were semantically incongruent in sentence-final position. In the example, the pizza was too hot to eat/*drink/*cry, *cry* produced a larger N400 than *drink* which produced a larger N400 than *eat*.

Among the ERP components which can be observed within the grammatical processing domain are the (early) left anterior negativity ((E)LAN) and the P600

(Kaan 2007). The P600 is a positivity which peaks at 600ms following the onset of a critical stimulus. This P600 has been observed in the centroparietal areas in correlation with secondary syntactic processes such as syntactic integration (Elston-Guettler & Friederici 2005), aspects of syntactic complexity (Kaan & Swaab 2003; Osterhout & Holcomb 1992), processes of reanalysis involving garden path sentences (Kaan & Swaab 2003; Osterhout & Holcomb 1992), and reanalysis and repair (Friederici 2004). The (E)LAN, like the P600, has also been observed in grammatical violations. The ELAN typically occurs 100–200ms after the ungrammaticality while the LAN is found between 300 and 500ms. This earlier syntactic component is thought to potentially reflect earlier automatic grammatical processing.

The use of ERPs in second language acquisition (SLA) research

ERPs can be used to establish when different aspects of language are processed and whether there are qualitative and/or quantitative differences in the manner in which they are processed. Comparing different groups of language learners (for example, L1 vs. L2 speakers), it is possible to determine whether there are qualitative differences in processing between groups (e.g., responses of a different type or even absence of a specific component), or whether there are instead quantitative changes (e.g., delays in time or in the size of the signal change). Furthermore, fine grained questions about group differences on the neural processing can be investigated such as the role of AoA or proficiency.

There are several advantages to relying on electrophysiological methods. First of all, the results do not depend on the performance of the individual on a given task. For example, speech discrimination or grammatical processing can be investigated without asking the participants to explicitly make any judgments. This aspect is particularly advantageous for comparing different types of participant groups. Infants, children, and adults can all be tested using the same types of paradigm (Sabourin & Stowe 2008). Some ERP components do not even require the individual to pay attention to stimulation. The MMN, for example, which is a component which does not require attention, is a more objective measure of discrimination abilities than behavioural tasks which are more influenced by voluntary processes (Näätänen & Winkler 1999).

Another major advantage of the online measurements allowed by ERP is the possibility to measure language processing in real time. It is not necessary to wait for a single response that occurs at the end of a sentence or word, as one must do in behavioural testing methods. For example, during a behavioural task judging the acceptability of a sentence, the only data obtained is whether the sentence is accepted or not and how long it takes to do so. In an ERP version of a similar task, besides getting the acceptability judgment and the reaction time, it is also possible to determine at which point during the processing the difficulty has arisen; and in native processing, a biphasal (the (E)LAN and the P600) response is often observed in response to ungrammaticalities.[3] In L2 sentence processing, not only can the acceptability of the sentence be compared, but the opportunity exists to see why differences may have occurred: are they due to the lack of the biphasal response altogether, or is just one part of the response missing or different in L2 processing?

A third advantage of ERPs is that they are often more sensitive than behavioural testing methods alone. Within the field of speech discrimination, one can often see a brain response indicating discrimination before a participant is able to behaviourally show that they can discriminate the sounds. For example, it is sometimes possible to detect a significant MMN to a phonetic change at a younger age than is revealed by behavioural measures (Cheour et al. 1998). Further, in sentence processing, the ERP response can often indicate difficulty of processing ambiguous sentences even when, at a behavioural level, there is no indication of any difficulty.

ERPs and L2 speech perception

Considerable research has been conducted to investigate L1 and L2 speech sound processing. Most speech perception studies have done this by looking at the discrimination of native and non-native speech contrasts. Several patterns have emerged. From these studies, it has now been established, for instance, that, because these contrasts are not found in their phonological system, it is difficult for Japanese speakers to discriminate /r/ vs. /l/ (Golestani & Zatorre 2004) and for French speakers to discriminate /d/ vs. /ð/ (Sundara, Polka & Genessee 2006).

Traditionally, behavioural methods, such as variants of the AX discrimination task and the behavioural oddball paradigm, have been used to investigate speech perception. During an AX task, pairs of sounds are presented and participants indicate whether the sounds were perceived as same or different. In the case of the oddball paradigm, the stimuli are presented such that a standard sound is played repeatedly and an oddball (or deviant) sound intrudes occasionally. Participants are asked to indicate when they perceive a change in the sound sequence. Neurophysiological methods such as ERPs have also provided insightful data about the processing of native and non-native sounds. Studies have shown that

---

3.   For details on this biphasal response see the section below on ERPs and L2 sentence processing.

neurophysiological discrimination can transpire before or without behavioural discrimination (Tremblay 2010; Tremblay, Kraus & McGee 1998. In a study combining a behavioural discrimination task and an ERP experiment, Tremblay (2010) compared monolinguals, bilinguals and multilinguals in their ability to discriminate a non-native contrast before and after receiving training. The results revealed that, while no group differences were found before training at the behavioural level, multilinguals and, to some extent, early bilinguals showed greater neurophysiological discrimination than the monolinguals. At the behavioural level, group differences only became apparent after training. These results suggest that, in order to fully understand L1 and L2 sound processing, speech perception should be studied both at the neurophysiological and the behavioural level.

The MMN is the ERP component that indicates the detection of a change in a string of similar auditory stimuli (Näätänen 2001). The stimuli are presented following an oddball paradigm and an MMN is elicited when the difference between the standard and the oddball is detected. In other words, the presence or absence of the MMN indicates whether or not the contrast has been discriminated. Electrophysiological sound discrimination, as indicated by the MMN, is said to occur at the pre-attentive level, which is at a level that is fully automatic (Näätänen 2001). This ERP component is therefore elicited without any active involvement of participants who are usually instructed not to pay attention to the stimuli. Typically, the MMN is characterised by a negative deflection peaking between 100 and 250ms following stimulus onset in the frontocentral electrodes (Näätänen 2001).

Acoustic vs. Phonetic Discrimination. The MMN can be elicited by both speech and non-speech sound differences such as pure tones (Cowen et al. 1993; Opitz et al. 1999). As a result, the MMN had previously been regarded as an indicator of acoustic discrimination rather than phonetic discrimination. Nevertheless, there are reasons to believe that the MMN can actually signal both acoustic and phonetic discrimination. In fact, the MMN appears to have different characteristics depending on the level at which a sound difference is discriminated. While the acoustic MMN seems to be characterised by an increased negativity that is bilateral, the phonetic MMN is larger in amplitude and is left-lateralised (Näätänen 2001).

In an attempt to explain the differences in MMN effects between the processing of acoustic and phonetic sound differences, Näätänan (2001) suggests that "both speech and complex non-speech sounds activate acoustic sound-analysis mechanisms, but only speech sounds activate the speech-sound traces or recognition models" (p. 8). This claim is supported by MMN experiments that have shown that the increase in negativity is measured at different electrode sites, depending on whether the change is perceived as acoustic or phonetic. Näätänan (2001) attributes the overall larger amplitude and left lateralisation for the phonetic MMN to the double activation in the left auditory cortex for acoustic and speech sound analysis.

MMN for Native and Non-Native Contrasts. There is clear evidence that the brain can detect sound differences which are consciously difficult to perceive. An MMN has indeed been observed in numerous studies that tested contrasts that were poorly discriminated at the behavioural level (Rivera-Gaxiola et al. 2000; Tremblay 2010). Rivera-Gaxiola et al. (2000), for instance, conducted an experiment that investigated the electrophysiological responses to a native and non-native contrast. Their study, which looked at the discrimination of /da/ vs. /ba/ (native contrast) and /da/ vs. /ḍa/ (novel non-native contrast found in Hindi: dental vs. retroflex) by native speakers of English, indicated that an MMN was generated by both types of contrasts, despite the fact that only the native contrast was discriminated behaviourally.

There are, however, quantitative differences between the MMN elicited by native contrasts and the MMN elicited by contrasts that are not phonemic in the participants' L1. Differences have been observed in terms of amplitude, latency, and typology. Compared to the MMN observed for native contrasts, the one evoked by a non-phonemic or unfamiliar non-native contrast is sometimes of smaller amplitude (Dehaene-Lambertz 1997; Sharma & Dorman 1999; Winkler et al. 1999). Dehaene-Lambertz (1997) also suggests that the non-native MMN can appear slightly later and with a different typology on the surface of the scalp.

The differences in electrophysiological responses that signal the discrimination of native and non-native contrasts is reminiscent of the differences between acoustic and phonetic discrimination that were discussed earlier. Variations in the processing of native and non-native contrasts could be due to the fact that they are discriminated at a different level of sound processing. While the electrophysiological response elicited by a native contrast entails both acoustic and phonetic discrimination, the response elicited by a non-native contrast may signal acoustic discrimination only. In other words, while the difference between two sounds in a native contrast is perceived as being linguistically meaningful, the difference between two sounds in a non-native contrast is sometimes perceived as being purely acoustic. It is important to note that not all ERP studies comparing the discrimination of native and non-native contrasts support this view. Several studies have reported a comparable MMN for contrasts differing in phonetic status (Maiste et al. 1995; Sharma et al. 1993). Furthermore, some studies suggest that there are in fact qualitative differences between native and non-native discrimination, such that an MMN is obtained for native contrasts but not for non-native contrasts (Dehaene-Lambertz, 1997).

It is important to point out that the majority of MMN experiments tested contrasts that were totally novel to the participants. Very few studies have looked at how non-native sound changes are processed in the brain of L2 learners. Winkler et al. (1999), for instance, tested Hungarian and Finnish speakers on two vowel contrasts, one contrast that is common to both languages (i.e. /e/ vs. /y/) and one contrast only found in Finnish (i.e. /e/ vs. /æ/). The Hungarian speakers were divided into two groups: fluent L2 learners of Finnish and individuals with no knowledge of that language. The fluent Hungarians were all late learners (i.e. first exposure between 13 and 32 years) and had been living in Finland for a minimum of two years (i.e. 2–13 years). The results revealed that, while the common contrast elicited a comparable MMN in all three groups, the Finnish contrast evoked an MMN in both the Finns and the Hungarians fluent in Finnish, but not in the Hungarians with no knowledge of Finnish. Moreover, the amplitude of the MMN elicited by the Finnish contrast did not differ significantly for the Finns and the fluent Hungarians. These results suggest that, given enough exposure to the language, it is possible for L2 learners to develop new memory traces for L2 sounds even when the acquisition starts later in life.

The P300. As mentioned above, the P300 differs from the MMN in that it is observed when attention is focused on the stimuli. Some studies suggest that a P300 is elicited for contrasts that are easily discriminated behaviourally. The MMN and the P300 could therefore reflect different levels of speech processing (Dalebout & Stack 1999).

The relationship between sound discrimination at the behavioural and the neurophysiological level is still not fully understood. A number of experiments have combined both types of methods in an attempt to determine whether there is a correlation between the ability to discriminate a contrast behaviourally and the MMN or P300. While some researchers have been able to establish a correlation between behavioural and neurophysiological sound discrimination (Dehaene-Lambertz et al. 2005; Lang et al. 1990; Sharma & Dorman 1999; Tampas et al. 2005), others have not (Dalebout and Stack 1999; Pettigrew et al. 2004; Shafer et al. 2004). Among those who did find a relationship between the two levels, it is not clear which ERP component, the MMN or the P300, is the best predictor of behavioural discrimination abilities. On the one hand, some studies indicate that there is a relationship between behavioural discrimination abilities and the amplitude of the MMN (Lang et al. 1990; Sharma & Dorman 1999; Tremblay 2010). Tremblay (2010), for instance, found that better behavioural discrimination abilities are associated with a larger MMN amplitude in left electrode sites. Nevertheless, other studies suggest that the P300 is a better indicator of behavioural discrimination performance (Dalebout & Stack 1999; Tampas et al. 2005).

Future directions and theoretical implications. While considerable research has investigated how native and non-native contrasts are discriminated at the electrophysiological level, to date, very little ERP speech perception research has been done in an SLA context. Most studies involve non-native contrasts that are completely foreign to the participants and, as a result, inform us about how the brain reacts to novel sound changes and not as much on the nature of L2 sound processing. There is an obvious need for ERP research investigating how L2 learners acquire the phonological system of the target language in order to learn more about the changes that occur at the neurophysiological levels throughout the L2 acquisition process, with respect to sound processing.

Some studies have looked at the effect of training on the MMN and there are reasons to believe that the MMN is modulated by learning (Tremblay 2010; Tremblay et al. 1998). For instance, Tremblay (2010) found that training participants to discriminate a novel contrast led to an increase in MMN amplitude. In some cases, this increase was most significant on the left. In Tremblay et al.'s (1998) experiment, the effect of training was manifested by an increase in the duration and area of the MMN as well as a decrease in the onset latency. While this type of experiment provides an idea of how exposure to a contrast affects an ERP component such as the MMN, it is still unknown how proficiency and AoA may affect an individual's potential for the creation of new memory traces to represent L2 sounds. This question is of utmost relevance considering that AoA has a major impact on the acquisition of phonology.

It is clear from the body of literature that the ability to detect changes across phonemic boundaries that are not active in the L1 is not fully lost. Moreover, adults can improve both their behavioural and neurophysiological discrimination abilities for a non-native contrast with very little training. This suggests that the brain does not completely lose its plasticity and that memory traces can be developed in order to encode new phonetic representations (Näätänen 2001; Tremblay et al. 1998). Such findings have important implications since they can inform theories and models of L2 speech perception. For instance, while it is largely accepted that AoA can affect the acquisition of a phonological system, claims vary with respect to the cause. ERP data suggest that the difficulty is not in the development of new representations (i.e. phonetic or phonological categories). This raises the question of what makes it so difficult to learn to speak with a native accent. Future experiments on the effect of AoA and L2 proficiency will provide insightful information on the development of memory traces used for L2 speech processing in advanced learners and will determine the extent to which these new memory traces resemble those of native speakers.

ERPs and L2 lexical processing

Lexical acquisition has long been considered a language skill that is maintained across a lifetime; adults can learn new lexical items (in an L1 or an L2) and this ability may not change in nature across the lifespan (for a discussion on this see Gaskell & Ellis 2011). ERP evidence that is congruent with this claim shows that the L2 processing of anomalous lexical items results in native-like N400 effects with an occasional quantitative difference (i.e., a delay or decrease in the N400 effect likely reflecting the lack of familiarity and/or frequency of these novel items). No matter how late the L2 was learned, an N400 effect is generally seen in L2 lexical semantic processing (e.g., Weber-Fox & Neville 1996). In comparison to L1 speakers, it appears that the only differences with regards to integrating a word into its sentential context are a delay of the N400 peak and a decrease in the amplitude. Thus, there seem to be no major qualitative differences in how lexical semantics are processed in an L1 or an L2.

Testing Bilingual Lexical Organization. Recent research with ERPs have been moving away from a direct comparison between native and L2 processing. This research has started to investigate the organization of the bilingual mental lexicon (e.g., Alvarez, Holcom & Grainger 2003; Geyer et al. 2011; Midgley, Holcomb & Grainger 2009; Schoonbaert et al. 2011). Of interest is whether cross-language lexical items are organized together in one neural representation, or if they are organized in separate, language specific, mental lexicons (e.g., Hernandéz 2002). According to the Revised Hierarchical Model (RHM: Kroll & Stewart 1994), lexical items from each language are stored in their own lexicon but are linked to concepts that are common to both languages. Similarly, the revised Bilingual Interactive Activation Model (BIA$^+$: Dijkstra & van Heuven 2002) assumes that the concepts of both L1 and L2 words are stored together. Silverberg and Samuel's (2004) interactive model, on the other hand, assumes that the L1 and L2 concepts are only stored together for early bilinguals.

These current theories on the organization of the bilingual mental lexicon are based on data from lexical processing studies that are rife with contradictions (see Francis, 2005 for a review). That is, there are data supporting a one-lexicon theory, with both languages organized together (e.g., Dijkstra et al. 2000; Finkbeiner et al. 2004) and data supporting separate lexicons for each of a bilingual's languages (e.g., Ibrahim 2009; Li, et al. 2009).

In order to test where and how the lexicons are linked, one of the experimental procedures used is the (masked) priming paradigm. It is generally believed that words that are semantically related are stored together within the lexicon (Collins & Loftus 1975). This allows one item (e.g., *cold*) to prime the activation of related items (e.g., *snow*, *ice*) within a language. Lexical priming is generally viewed as a spreading activation from prime to target item, although there is some question as to whether this effect occurs at a prelexical level (automatic processing) or if it involves more conceptual-semantic processing. This technique is also widely used in investigating bilingual lexical processing where the presence or absence of cross-language semantic or translation priming is studied (e.g., Neely 1991). When priming effects are found cross-linguistically, it is thought to reflect the links between lexical items of the different languages involved. These findings are then used to support specific models of bilingual lexical organization.

ERPs and Cross-Language Priming. The two main components investigated are the N250 and the N400. As described above, the N400 reflects semantic processing and is thought to reflect conceptual mediation. On the other hand, the N250, which is an earlier ERP component, is thought to reflect prelexical (non-linguistic) processes where, in the visual modality, the orthography is matched onto the lexical representation (Holcomb & Grainger 2006). With the help of ERPs, it is possible to obtain important temporal information about these effects which may help to determine whether the effects are happening at a prelexical level or at a semantic-conceptual level. A previously presented related (or identity) prime serves to reduce the N400 and N250 components to the target (Schoonbaert et al. 2011). The reduction in the N400 is considered to be due to semantic mediation and thus a cross-language reduction found to a translation pair would reflect links at the semantic level. The reduction in the N250, on the other hand, is thought to mostly occur for targets that have been primed by identity primes, a reduction which is diminished as the orthographic overlap decreases between prime and target (Holcomb & Grainger 2006).

In a study by Alvarez et al. (2003) the translation priming effect on the N400 component was larger and started earlier when the prime was presented in the L2 and the target item was in the L1 compared to the opposite direction. This type of result is in agreement with bilingual lexicon models such as the RHM (Kroll & Stewart 1994) which postulates that the L2 lexicon is more directly linked to the corresponding L1 lexical items than vice versa, and that L2 words access their concepts via the L1 words. A recent study by Schoonbaert et al. (2011) investigated the masked translation priming in English L1 and French L2 bilinguals. They found a reduced N250 effect to the translation pairs; however, the effect was larger in the L2 to L1 direction than in the L1 to L2 direction. The authors propose that this differential effect may be due to stronger links that have been created from the L2 word to its L1 translation. This type of interpretation supports the RHM model of bilingual lexical organization.

For the N400 effect, Schoonbaert et al. (2011) found equal priming effects in both directions with an N400 component, though the effect lasted longer in the L1 to L2 direction. The different latency effects of the N400 is interpreted as representing the fact that the L2 target (in the L1 to L2 direction) takes longer to fully process. This longer processing time for L2 targets represents another example of a quantitative (and not qualitative) difference between L1 and L2 processing. These ERP priming results are in contrast with the majority of behavioural cross-language priming effects which show that priming is stronger in the L1-L2 direction (for a review see Duñabeitia, Perea & Carreiras 2010).

Much of this cross-language priming research has been conducted with bilinguals who are dominant in one of their two languages. As such, findings could be due to various other factors, such as the processing time required to fully process an L2 vs. an L1 item. That said, investigating N400 effects while carefully controlling for and testing different proficiency levels and AoA effects seems to be a very promising line of research for the field of bilingual lexical processing. In this vein, Geyer et al. (2011) tested highly proficient L2 speakers of English with L1 Russian. They found that translation priming in both directions (L1 to L2 and L2 to L1) affects the N400 component in the same manner. This result is in line with the BIA$^+$ model (e.g., Dijkstra & van Heuven 2002) as well as with the RHM, where increasing L2 proficiency provides more links from the L2 directly to the conceptual areas.

Future Directions. The use of priming paradigms to investigate bilingual lexicons has slowly been shifting to the use of masked priming paradigms. In masked priming, the prime is presented so briefly that it is not consciously recognized by participants. This improves upon the more traditional priming technique used in testing the bilingual mental lexicon because it can bypass the effects of strategic processing. Given enough processing time, it is possible that participants, in unmasked priming scenarios, are strategically thinking of the translation target. This suggests that, unless masked priming is used, what is being tested is not the organization of the lexicon but strategic top-down effects.

While some cross-language priming studies mentioned above used masked priming, the length of the masked prime (and thus the potential degree of it promoting automatic processing) was not always consistent. For example, while most behavioural and within-language priming studies use a masked prime of approximately 50ms, Schoonbaert et al. (2011) use a prime of 120ms. They claim that, unless the participant is given more time to process the L2 words, they will likely not be processed at all due to the L2 being later learned and therefore less proficient. In order to fully investigate this and other issues, more masked priming ERP studies need to be performed. Furthermore, these studies need to consistently control (or test) such variables as AoA, proficiency, cognate status, script (dis)similarity, and prime exposure.

ERPs and L2 sentence processing

Sentence processing involves not only grammatical analyses but also phrase structure processing. Given the complex nature of sentence processing, the high temporal resolution and distributional measures of ERPs, as described above, are ideal for a precise evaluation of online sentence processing unfolding in real time.

In L1 processing, ELANs have been found in the 300–500ms latency range and appear to be similar in distribution and latency to the standard LAN (Friederici, Hahne & Mecklinger 1996). Although these have been obtained in correlation with early L1 syntactic processes, such as a first-pass structure identification (van Hell & Tokowicz 2010) and detecting phrase structure violations (Ingram 2008), ELAN results for L2 syntactic processing are inconsistent. In a recent study by Pakulak & Neville (2010), native speakers revealed that violations elicited a bilateral and prolonged ELAN with the onset beginning at 100ms, followed by a P600. L2 learners of English, however, did not show violations eliciting an ELAN, although a P600 was elicited, albeit more widespread spatially and temporally compared to the native speakers. In a word category violation task, Rossi and colleagues (2006) found native speakers and high-proficiency L2 learners of both German and Italian eliciting ELANs preceding P600 effects. These results were not duplicated by low-proficiency L2 learners. Similarly, Hahne (2001) did not find ELANs in Russian late learners of German in an auditory phrase structure task, whereas Isel (2007) and Rossi et al. (2006) found ELANs elicited for auditory phrase structure tasks involving German late learners of French, Italian learners of German, and German learners of Italian. These contradictory results demonstrate that further research is needed with regards to ELANs and the type of L2 sentence processing tasks involved.

LANs have been correlated to the areas of the left frontal cortex (i.e., Friederici 2002) and appear as the first part of a biphasal response, that is, they often precede elicited P600s. Tasks involving the processing of grammatical violations (Friederici et al. 1993; Neville et al. 1991), automatic grammatical processing (e.g., Friederici 2002), and outright syntactic violations have elicited LANs preceding elicited P600s (e.g., Angrilli et al. 2002). Compared to outright violations, LANs are not always observed for violations of syntactic preferences, but when evidenced, they are followed by an elicited P600 (e.g., Friederici et al.1996).

The P600 has been observed in the centroparietal areas in correlation with secondary syntactic processes such as syntactic integration (Elston-Guettler & Friederici 2005), aspects of syntactic complexity (Kaan & Swaab 2003; Osterhout & Holcomb 1992), processes of reanalysis involving garden path sentences (Kaan & Swaab 2003; Osterhout & Holcomb 1992), and reanalysis and repair (Friederici 2004).

Age of Acquisition. The critical period hypothesis remains under debate even today, with neuroimaging studies now being utilised in the hopes of resolving the outstanding questions regarding whether or not the age at which one acquires their L2 will have positive or adverse effects on the speaker's attained proficiency. Although many studies have investigated the effects of AoA and proficiency (Golestani et al. 2006; Hernandez et al. 2007), only a few studies to date have specifically investigated the effects of AoA alone, either from infancy (Weber-Fox and

Neville 1996) or from birth (Wartenburger et al. 2003). Weber-Fox and Neville (1996) found native-like performance in participants who had acquired the L2 before the age of one, while Wartenburger and colleagues found no significant neural differences between L1 and L2 processing in participants who had acquired the L2 from birth. These results support the classical hypothesis that the earlier a learner acquires the L2, the more native-like the end-state attainment (Meisel 1991), all of which suggests that this may be true neurologically as well as behaviourally. However, it is important to keep in mind that many of these studies have involved late L2 learners, creating the possibility that there are other critical factors which may affect their performance (e.g., motivation, type of input, learning strategies, anxiety). Hahne and Friederici (2001) investigated phrase structure violations involving late Japanese L2 learners of German, reporting no syntax-related ERP effects. However, in a similar study involving late Russian L2 learners of German, Hahne (2001) reported findings of a P600 effect. Given the similarity in age of L2 acquisition, the contradictory results were explained as due to a difference of proficiency levels between the two learner groups, rather than any effect of age of L2 acquisition. This has led researchers to further investigate the effect of proficiency as well as possible transfer effects on sentence processing.

Proficiency Effects. Recent research utilising ERPs to investigate online L1 and L2 sentence processing has involved verb subcategorization violations (Guo et al. 2009), semantic and syntactic violations (Hahne, 2001), syntactic ambiguity and syntactic anomaly (Kotz et al. 2009), and semantic and morphosyntactic violations (Weber & Lavric 2008). Such studies have revealed proficiency effects in L2 sentence processing compared to native L1 processing. For instance, lower proficiency L2 learners have been found to differ qualitatively from native speakers as LANs have not been found, even though the same grammatical violation elicits a LAN in the L1 of these L2 learners (Hahne 2001; Hahne & Friederici 2001; Weber-Fox & Neville 1996). Alternatively, subjects have shown increased posterior negativities more closely resembling N400s (Ullman 2001; Weber-Fox & Neville 1996). It has been suggested that LANs reflect processing carried out by the grammatical-procedural system (Ullman 2001), which has not been found as commonly with L2 learners as with native speakers. This suggests that this system may be different in L2 learners, where other cognitive systems may be functioning, rather than the grammatical system that is used by native speakers. Elicitation of an N400 in lieu of a LAN may be indicative of such a qualitative difference.

In fact, N400s have been found in very low proficiency L2 learners for grammatical anomalies, even though these anomalies do not elicit LANs or N400s in the L1 (Osterhout et al. 2004). A more recent study by Weber and Lavric (2008) used a sentence reading task containing morphosyntactic violations which were comparable in the L1 and L2. Along with an expected P600 component, an enhanced

N400 was found in conditions containing morphosyntactic violations in the L2 but not the L1. The authors suggest that these findings reflect one of two things: either the resolution of morphosyntactic anomalies in the L2 relies on the lexico-semantic system, or the weaker morphological mechanisms in the L2 lead to greater sentence wrap-up difficulties, something which would be reflected in an N400 enhancement. A similar online sentence processing task which involved reading sentences containing verb subcategorization violations revealed a P600 effect in native English speakers but an N400 effect in L2 learners (Guo et al. 2009). Guo et al. (2009) suggest that these findings are evidence of sentence processing strategies that vary according to language background, and the authors claim that the shallower syntactic ability of L2 learners explains these neural differences. These results support Ullman's (2005) suggestion that such findings are indicative of distinct brain structures for L1 and for lower proficiency L2 grammatical processing.

In contrast, higher proficiency L2 learners have elicited LANs for grammatical violations in natural language (Hahne, Muller & Clahsen 2003) as well as artificial language (Friederici, Steinhauer & Pfeifer 2002). The later positive P600 ERP component has also been found to be elicited by L2 speakers (Hahne 2001; Osterhout et al. 2004; Weber-Fox & Neville 1996). In a study by Kotz, Holcomb and Osterhout (2009), L2 syntactic anomaly detection and syntactic ambiguity resolution were examined using highly proficient L1 Spanish-L2 English readers. Both groups showed a P600 in both conditions, with distribution and latency of the P600 as the only variance in the syntactic anomaly condition for the L2 speakers. Given that the P600 is associated with controlled later syntactic processing in the L1 (Friederici et al. 1996), it has consequently been suggested that the P600 does not depend on procedural processing (Ullman, 2001), a conclusion that has also been supported by the proficiency effects found in the studies presented above.

Transfer Effects. A related issue which has recently been taken into consideration is the effects of transfer. In a task involving syntactically legal sentences in English L2 but not in Spanish L1, Osterhout and Holcomb (1992) found that early learners of L2 English were able to process phrase structure violations on a comparable level to native speakers. The authors suggest this is an effect of positive transfer. Tokowicz and MacWhinney (2005) similarly present evidence of positive transfer effects in late L2 learners. This task involved tense marking, and number and gender agreement. P600 effects were found for sentence structures similar in the L1 and the L2, and for syntax specific to the L2, but not for number agreement differing between the L1 and the L2. Two studies investigating subject-verb agreement in L1 Japanese (Ojima, Nakata & Kakigi 2005) and L1 Chinese (Chen et al. 2007) learners of L2 English found L2 syntactic processing affected by proficiency as well as by structural dissimilarity such as gender, number, or case as morphologically marked syntactic elements. Highly proficient L2 English learners with L1

Japanese revealed a LAN effect, but no P600, whereas intermediate proficiency speakers revealed neither (Ojima et al. 2005). Chen and colleagues (2007) found a LAN but no P600 for intermediate proficient L2 English learners with L1 Chinese. Further, Sabourin and Stowe (2008) found a relatively late P600 effect for ungrammatical conditions in moderately advanced L2 speakers. The authors suggest that the qualitative differences in the native-like nature of responses are dependent on the grammatical structures involved being similar to those of the native language. These findings suggest that languages which share structural similarities allow for positive transfer between L1 and L2, while languages which do not share such similarities only allow for transfer in a more complex manner, with proficiency critically influencing the facilitation of transfer.

Future Directions. The findings of ERP research investigating the complex nature of sentence processing to date suggest that the age at which a learner acquires an L2 may be less significant than previously posited, whereas L2 proficiency and (dis)similarities of the L1 and L2 appear to be crucial factors that influence brain correlates. This new insight into the neurophysiological mechanisms of L2 sentence processing provides a basis for future research to address outstanding issues, such as the correlation of the ELAN and methods being used, and a lack of research involving child L2 learners compared to adult beginning L2 learners. Only with comparable tasks used for online testing and an even quantity of child and adult L2 ERP studies will it be possible to begin to understand the influence that proficiency and transfer might have on sentence processing more fully and the possible interactions they may have with each other.

Conclusions

In this chapter, some of the previous literature on L2 and bilingual processing that has made use of the ERP technique has been summarized. While research within the field of SLA is starting to shed light on how the neural networks for L2 processing are organized, studies with conflicting data are still too numerous to draw any sound conclusions. Initially, one might think that the large amount of conflicting data would make it impossible to figure out. However, by carefully controlling many of the factors that are involved in L2 processing, it should be possible to get a better idea of the factors involved. Researchers need to continue testing different levels of linguistic processes, investigate different pairs of languages and carefully control both AoA and proficiency (furthermore, other factors such as motivation, the type of input, and the role of exposure should be investigated more thoroughly). In addition, rather than comparing distinct groups on their L2 performance, there is an increased need for correlational research. What happens to the ERP responses when a full continuum of proficiency ranges is tested; what about for the full range of possible AoAs? Using ERPs to look at relationships rather than simple differences might be a way to get clearer, more reliable, and more consistent results.

References

Alvarez, R.P., Holcomb, P.J. & Grainger, J. 2003. Accessing word meanings in two languages: An event-related brain potentials study of beginning bilinguals. *Brain and Language* 87: 290–304.

Angrilli, A., Penolazzi, B., Vespignani, F., DeVincenzi, M., Job, R., Ciccarelli, L., Palomba, D. & Stegagno, L. 2002. Cortical brain responses to semantic incongruity and syntactic violation in Italian language: An event-related potential study. *Neuroscience Letters* 322: 5–8.

Chen, L., Shu, H., Liu Zhao, J. & Li, P. 2007. ERP signatures of subject–verb agreement in L2 learning. Bilingualism: *Language and Cognition* 10: 161–174.

Cheour, M., Alho, K., Ceponiene, R., Reinikainen, K., Sainio, K., Pohjavouri, M., Aaltonen, O. & Näätänen, R. 1998. Maturation of mismatch negativity in infants. *International Journal of Psychophysiology* 29: 217–226.

Collins, A.M. & Loftus, E.F. 1975. A spreading activation theory of semantic memory. *Psychological Review* 82(6): 407–428.

Cowen, N., Winkler, I., Teder, W. & Näätänen, R. 1993. Memory prerequisites of mismatch negativity in the auditory event-related potential (ERP). Journal of Experimental Psychology: Learning, *Memory, and Cognition* 19(4): 909–921.

Dalebout, S. D. & Stack, J.W. 1999. Mismatch negativity to acoustic differences not differentiated behaviourally. *Journal of the American Academy of Audiology* 10: 388–399.

Dehaene-Lambertz, G. 1997. Electrophysiological correlates of categorical phoneme perception in adults. *NeuroReport* 8: 919–924.

Dehaene-Lambertz, G., Pallier, C., Serniclaes, W., Sprenger-Charolles, L., Jobert, A. & Dehaene, S. 2005. Neural correlates of switching from auditory to speech perception. *NeuroImage* 24: 21–33.

Dijkstra, T. & van Heuven, W.J.B. 2002. The architecture of the bilingual word recognition system: From identification to system. Bilingualism: *Language and Cognition* 5(3): 175–197.

Dijkstra, A.F.J., Timmermans, M.P.H. & Schriefers, H.J. 2000. On being blinded by your other language: Effects of task demands on interlingual homograph recognition. *Journal of Memory and Language* 42(4): 445–464.

Duñabeitia, J. A., Perea, M. & Carreiras, M. 2010. Masked translation priming effects with highly proficient simultaneous bilinguals. *Experimental Psychology* 57: 98–107.

Elston-Guettler, K. & Friederici, A. 2005. Native and L2 processing of homonyms in sentential context. *Journal of Memory and Language* 52: 256–283.

Finkbeiner, M., Forster, K., Nicol, J. & Nakamura, K. 2004. The role of polysemy in masked semantic and translation priming. *Journal of Memory and Language* 51(1): 1–22.

Francis, W.S. 2005. Bilingual semantic and conceptual representation. In *Handbook of Bilingualism*, J. Kroll & A.M.B. de Groot (eds), 251–267. Oxford: OUP.

Friederici, A. 2002 Towards a neural basis of auditory sentence processing. *Trends in Cognitive Scienc* 6(2): 78–84.

Friederici, A. 2004. Event-related brain potential studies in language. *Current Neurological Neuroscience Report* 4(6): 466–470.

Friederici, A., Hahne, A. & Mecklinger, A. 1996. Temporal structure of syntactic parsing: Early and late event-related brain potential effects elicited by syntactic anomalies. Journal of Experimental Psychology: *Learning, Memory, and Cognition* 22: 1219–1248.

Friederici, A., Pfeifer, E. & Hahne, A. 1993. Event-related brain potentials during natural speech processing: Effects of semantic, morphological and syntactic violations. *Cognitive Brain Research* 1: 183–192.

Friederici, A., Steinhauer, K. & Pfeifer, E. 2002. Brain signatures of artificial language processing: Evidence challenging the critical period hypothesis. Proceedings of the National Academy of Sciences of the USA 99: 529–534.

Gaskell, M.G. & Ellis, A.W. 2011. Word learning and lexical development across the lifespan. *Philosophical Transactions of the Royal Society* 363: 3608–3615.

Geyer, A., Holcomb, P.J., Midgley, K.J. & Grainger, J. 2011. Processing words in two languages: An event-related brain potential study of proficient bilinguals. *Journal of Neurolinguistics* 24: 338–351.

Golestani, N. & Zatorre, R. J. 2004. Learning new sounds of speech: Reallocation of neural substrates. *NeuroImage* 21: 494–506.

Golestani, N., Alario, F., Meriaux, S., LeBihan, D., Dehaene, S. & Pallier, C. 2006. Syntax production in bilinguals. *Neuropsychologia* 44: 1029–1040.

Guo, J., Guo, T., Yan, Y., Jiang, N. & Peng, D. 2009 ERP evidence for different strategies employed by native speakers and L2 learners in sentence processing. *Journal of Neurolinguistics* 22(2): 123–134.

Hahne, A. 2001. What's different in second-language processing? Evidence from event-related brain potentials. *Journal of Psycholinguistic Research* 30: 251–266.

Hahne, A. & Friederici, A. 2001. Processing a second language: late learners' comprehension mechanisms as revealed by event-related brain potentials. Bilingualism: *Language and Cognition* 4: 123–141.

Hahne, A., Muller, J. & Clahsen, H. 2003. Morphological processing in a second language: Behavioural and event-related brain potential evidence for storage and decomposition. *Journal of Cognitive Neuroscience* 18:121–134.

Hernandéz, A. 2002. Exploring language asymmetries in early Spanish-English bilinguas: The role of lexical and sentential context effects. In *Bilingual Sentence Processing*, R.R. Heredia & J. Altarriba (eds), 137–163. Amsterdam: Elsevier.

Hernandez, A., Hoffman, J. & Kotz, S. 2007. Age of acquisition modulates neural activity for both regular and irregular syntactic functions. *NeuroImage* 36: 912–923.

Holcomb, P.J. & Grainger, J. 2006. On the time course of visual word recognition: An event-related potential investigation using masked repetition priming. *Journal of Cognitive Neuroscience* 18(10): 1631–1643.

Ibrahim, R. 2009. Selective deficit of second language: A case of Arabic-Hebrew bilingual brain damaged patient. *Behavioral and Brain Functions* 5(17): 1–10.

Ingram, J. 2008. *Neurolinguistics: An Introduction to Spoken Language Processing and its Disorders*. Cambridge: CUP.

Isel, F. 2007. Syntactic and referential processes in second-language learners: Event-related brain potential evidence. *Neuroreport* 18: 1885–89.

Kaan, E. 2007. Event-related potentials and language processing: A brief overview. *Language & Linguistics Compass* 1(6): 571–591.

Kaan, E. & Swaab, T. 2003. Repair, revision and complexity in syntactic analysis: an electrophysiological investigation. *Journal of Cognitive Neuroscience* 15: 98–110.

Kotz, S., Holcomb, P. & Osterhout, L. 2009. ERPs reveal comparable syntactic sentence processing in native and non-native readers of English. *Acta Psychologia* 128(3): 514–527.

Kroll, J.F. & Stewart, E. 1994. Category interference in translation and picture naming: Evidence for asymmetric connections between bilingual memory representations. *Journal of Memory and Language* 33: 149–174.

Kutas, M. & Hillyard, S.A. 1980. Reading senseless sentences: Brain potentials reflect semantic incongruity. *Science* 207: 203–05.

Lang, H., Nyrke, T., Ek,. M., Aaltonen, O., Raimo, I. & Näätänen, R. 1990. Pitch discrimination performance and auditory event-related potentials. In *Psychophysiological Brain Research*, C.H.M. Brunia, A.W.K. Gaillard, A. Kok, G. Mulder & M.N. Verbaten (eds), 294–298. Tilburg: Tilburg University Press.

Li, L.I., Mo, L.E.I., Wang, R., Luo, X. & Chen, Z. H. E. 2009. Evidence for long-term crosslanguage repetition priming in low fluency Chinese/English bilinguals. Bilingualism: *Language and Cognition* 12(01): 13–21.

Luck, S. 2005. *An Introduction to the Event-Related Potential Technique.* Cambridge MA: The MIT Press.

Maiste, A.C., Wiens, S., Hunt, M.J., Scherg, M. & Picton, T. W. 1995. Event-related potentials and the categorical perception of speech sounds. *Ear and Hearing* 16(1): 68–90.

Meisel, J. 1991 Principles of universal grammar and strategies of language learning: Some similarities and differences between first and second language acquisition. In *Point Counterpoint: Universal Grammar in Second Language Acquisition* [Language Acquisition and Language Disorders 3], L. Eubank (ed.), 231–276. Amsterdam: John Benjamins.

Midgley, K.J., Holcomb, P.J. & Grainger, J. 2009. Masked repetition and translation priming in second language learners: A window on the time-course of form and meaning activation using ERPs. *Psychophysiology* 46: 551–565.

Näätänen, R. 2001. The perception of speech sounds by the human brain as reflected by the mismatch negativity (MMN) and its magnetic equivalent (MMNm). *Psychophysiology* 38: 1–21.

Näätänen, R. & Winkler, I. 1999. The concept of auditory stimulus representation in cognitive neuroscience. *Psychological Bulletin* 125(6): 826–859.

Neely, J.H. 1991. Semantic priming effects in visual word recognition: A selective review of current findings and theories. In *Basic Processes in Reading: Visual Word Recognition,* D. Besner & G.W. Humphreys (eds), 264–336. Hillsdale NJ: Lawrence Erlbaum Associates.

Neville, H., Nicol, J., Barss, A., Forster, K. & Garrett, M. 1991. Syntactically based sentence processing classes: Evidence from event-related brain potentials. *Journal of Cognitive Neuroscience* 3: 151–165.

Ojima, S., Nakata, H. & Kakigi, R. 2005. An ERP study of second language learning after childhood: Effects of proficiency. *Journal of Cognitive Neuroscience* 17: 1212–1228.

Opitz, B., Mecklinger, A., von Cramon, D. Y. & Kruggel, F. 1999. Combining electrophysiological and hemodynamic measures of the auditory oddball. *Psychophysiology* 36: 142–147.

Osterhout, L. & Holcomb, P. 1992. Event-related brain potentials elicited by syntactic anomaly. *Journal of Memory and Language* 31: 785–806.

Osterhout, L., McLaughlin, J., Kim, A., Greenwald, R. & Inoue K. 2004. Sentences in the brain: Event-related potentials as real-time reflections of sentence comprehension and language learning. In *The On-line Study of Sentence Comprehension: Eyetracking, ERPs, and Beyond*, M. Carreiras & C. Clifton, Jr (eds). Hove: Psychology Press.

Pakulak, E. & Neville, H. 2010. Proficiency differences in syntactic processing of monolingual native speakers indexed by event-related potentials. *Journal of Cognitive Neuroscience* 22(12): 2728–2744.

Pettigrew, C.M., Murdoch, B.M., Kei, J., Chenery, H.J., Sockalingam, R., Ponton, C.W., Finningan, S. & Alku, P. 2004. Processing of English words with fine acoustic contrasts and simple tones: A mismatch negativity study. *Journal of the American Academy of Audiology* 15: 47–66.

Rivera-Gaxiola, M., Csibra, G., Johnson, M.H. & Karmiloff-Smith, A. 2000. Electrophysiological correlates of crosslinguistic speech perception in native English speakers. *Behavioral Brain Research* 111: 13–23.

Rossi, S., Gugler, M., Friederici, A. & Hahne, A. 2006. The impact of proficiency on syntactic second-language processing of German and Italian: Evidence from event-related potentials. *Journal of Cognitive Neuroscience* 18(12): 2030–2048.

Sabourin, L. & Stowe, L. 2008. Second language processing: When are first and second languages processed similarly? *Second Language Research* 25: 135–166.

Schoonbaert, S., Holcomb, P.J., Grainger, J. & Hartsuiker, R.J. 2011. Testing asymmetries in non-cognate translation priming: Evidence from RTs and ERPs. *Psychophysiology* 48: 74–81.

Shafer, V.L., Schwartz, R.G. & Kurtzberg, D. 2004. Language-specific memory traces of consonants in the brain. *Cognitive Brain Research* 18: 242–254.

Sharma, A. & Dorman, M. F. 1999. Cortical auditory evoked potential correlates of categorical perception of voice-onset time. *Journal of the Acoustical Society of America* 106(2): 1078–1083.

Sharma, A., Kraus, N., McGee, T., Carrell, T. & Nicol, T. 1993. Acoustic versus phonetic representation of speech as reflected by the mismatch negativity event-related potential. *Electroencephalography and Clinical Neurophysiology* 88: 64–71.

Silverberg, S. & Samuel, A.G. 2004. The effect of age of second language acquisition on the representation and processing of second language words. *Journal of Memory and Language* 51: 381–398.

Stowe, L.A. & Sabourin, L. 2005. Imaging the processing of a second language: Effects of maturation and proficiency on the neural processes involved. *International Review of Applied Linguistics in Language Teaching* 43(4): 329–353.

Sundara, M., Polka, L. & Genesee, F. 2006. Language-experience facilitates discrimination of /d-ð/ in monolingual and bilingual acquisition of English. *Cognition* 100: 369–388.

Swaab, T., Brown, D. & Hagoort, P. 1997. Spoken sentence comprehension in aphasia: Event-related potential evidence for a lexical integration deficit. *Journal of Cognitive Neuroscience* 9(1): 39–66.

Tampas, J. W., Harkrider, A. W. & Hedrick, M. S. 2005. Neurophysiological indices of speech and nonspeech stimulus processing. *Journal of Speech, Language, and Hearing Research* 48: 1147–1164.

Tokowicz, N. & MacWhinney, B. 2005. Implicit and explicit measures of sensitivity to violations in second language grammar. *Studies in Second Language Acquisition* 27:173–204.

Tremblay, K., Kraus, N. & McGee, T. 1998. The time course of auditory perceptual learning: Neurophysiological changes during speech-sound training. *NeuroReport* 9: 3557–3560.

Tremblay, M.-C. 2010. Comparing the Perceptual Abilities of Monolinguals, Bilinguals and Multilinguals: A Combined Behavioural and Event-related Potential Experiment PhD dissertation, University of Ottawa.

Ullman, M. 2005. A Cognitive Neuroscience Perspective on Second Language Acquisition: The Declarative/Procedural Model. In *Mind and Context in Adult Second Language Acquisition: Methods, Theory, and Practice*, C. Sanz (ed.), 141–178. Washington DC: Georgetown University Press.

Ullman, M. 2001. The neural basis of lexicon and grammar in first and second language: The declarative/procedural model. Bilingualism: *Language and Cognition* 4: 105–122.

Van Hell, J., & Tokowicz, N. 2010. Event-related brain potentials and second language learning: syntactic processing in late L2 learners at different L2 proficiency levels. *Second Language Research* 26(1): 43–74.

Wartenburger, L., Heekeren, H., Abutalebi., J., Cappa, S., Villringer, A. & Perani, D. 2003. Early setting of grammatical processing in the bilingual brain. *Neuron* 37: 159–170.

Weber, K. & Lavric, A. 2008. Syntactic anomaly elicits a lexico-semantic (N400) ERP effect in the second language but not the first. *Psychophysiology* 45(6): 920–925.

Weber-Fox, C. & Neville, H. 1996. Maturational constraints on functional specializations for language processing: ERP and behavioural evidence in bilingual speakers. *Journal of Cognitive Neuroscience* 8: 231–256.

Winkler, I., Kujala, T., Tiitinen, H., Sivonen, P., Alku, P., Lehtokoski, A., Czigler, I., Csépe, V., Ilmoniemi, R.J. & Näätänen, R. 1999. Brain responses reveal the learning of foreign language phonemes. *Psychophysiology* 36: 638–642.

Winkler, I., Lehtokoski, A., Alku, P., Vainio, M., Czigler, I., Csépe, V., Aaltonen, O., Raim, L., Alho, K., Lang, H., Iivonen, A. & Näätänen, R.1999. Pre-attentive detection of vowel contrasts utilizes both phonetic and auditory memory representations. *Cognitive Brain Research* 7: 357–369.

On multiplicity and mutual exclusivity

The case for different SLA theories

Jason Rothman and Bill VanPatten

University of Florida and Michigan State University

The field of SLA research is an exciting and energizing enterprise, as the collection of chapters in this volume suggests. Beyond the stimulating nature of the SLA enterprise itself, the scope of its inquiry is even wider than imagined by the pioneers whose work gave rise to what it is today. Nonetheless, SLA is still an emergent area of research and hypothesis creation, which has the consequence of meaning that beyond its current usefulness to scholars and students in the field, the collection of articles in this book embodies a snapshot in time of the historical progression of this enterprise. In other words, this volume provides a glimpse into what the world of SLA research looks like at the beginning of the 21st century. With a future legacy in mind, our goal for the final chapter of this volume is not to be evaluative, but exploratory, taking the approaches and concepts provided in the individual chapters as our point of departure along an epistemological journey of SLA theory.

As noted above, SLA is a discipline still relatively young, if one considers that its contemporary roots are the insights from S. Pit Corder and Larry Selinker dating to the late 1960s and early 1970s. Over these forty-plus years, the field has changed considerably, from first mimicking the research on child L1 (e.g., the morpheme studies, the research on developmental sequences) to being a field that interfaces with other domains (e.g., cognitive science, education). It has moved from a field largely concerned with description to one in search of theories and frameworks that (1) can explain various observed phenomena, and (2) provide the means necessary to articulate research agendas.

The concern for rigorous theories in SLA emerged in the early 1990s, largely as a response to earlier approaches that many deemed inadequate to account for the body of evidence that had then emerged to date (e.g., Contrastive Analysis, Monitory Theory, Acculturation). In the present volume, we get a glimpse of various contemporary approaches to SLA. To be sure, the volume is not exhaustive. Between the various theories currently in existence along with models as well as hypotheses that some tend to treat as theories (e.g., MOGUL, Noticing), there are dozens of accounts that one could entertain in order to understand and research SLA. By their very nature and in light of the sheer volume of approaches to SLA at present, volumes of this sort must be discerningly selective. It is enough to say that the macro-approaches herein cover the core and then some of modern approaches to adult SLA. Because the remit of each chapter is, however, one of holistically representing a particular paradigm while at the same time focusing on some specific aspects, each is inevitably left unable to cover the gamut of relevant research questions, methodologies, debates and hypotheses worthy of discussion. To take one example, Slabakova's chapter represents the generative tradition of L2 acquisition, discussing recent innovations in the modular view of linguistic architecture and how this has translated into more refined proposals regarding how and why L2 competence and performance obtain the way they do. At the micro-level, her chapter focuses on the Bottleneck Hypothesis (Slabakova 2008), which attempts to model, in light of recent proposals of linguistic interface design, how functional morphology and its associated formal features embody the most significant stumbling blocks to acquisition in adulthood. This, of course, does not mean that more traditional questions within Universal Grammar (UG) approaches to SLA have been answered to everyone's satisfaction, such as the extent to which UG remains accessible to adult learners past the so-called critical period and the exact role L1 transfer plays in interlanguage development and ultimate attainment. Instead, the latent goal of her chapter and, to a greater or lesser extent, the goal of all chapters in this volume is to highlight recent advances. The Bottleneck Hypothesis does just that, providing one example of how generative approaches for the past decade or so have moved beyond their traditional core questions, proposing testable models that seek to account for performance variation and issues of L2 learnabilty related to ultimate attainment.

The purpose of the present chapter is rather simple. Although one might expect we would offer some way to evaluate the various approaches in this volume along with an actual evaluation of them, such is not our goal. This has been done elsewhere and we would most likely not offer anything new to the reader (see, for example, VanPatten & Williams, 2007). Instead, we approach this chapter as a series of questions that we think are relevant regarding the current state of theories. Those questions are:

1. Why are there multiple theories in/approaches to SLA (as opposed to convergence on one theory)?
2. How do the various theories and approaches treat the constructs of 'second', 'language' and 'acquisition' within SLA?

3. How does environmental context influence the various theories? (That is, how are theories influenced by particular contexts of learning that may preoccupy particular researchers?)
4. Theories are often said to be in competition. To what extent are the various theories and frameworks in the present volume "in competition"?

We will conclude our chapter with a sketch of a larger picture of SLA, one in which we show how multiple theories in SLA are inevitable and necessary. In so doing, we invite the reader to see how various theories fit into this picture and how they might work to explain different parts of what is the very complex phenomenon of SLA. If successful, our attempt will further underscore the usefulness and importance of collections of this type – collections that present the reader a fair-handed presentation of a variety of theories dealing with the same macro issues.

Question 1. Why are there various theories about adult SLA?

As the present volume suggests – as do other volumes that treat theories and frameworks in SLA – there is a broad spectrum of approaches to understanding how non-primary languages are acquired. This multiplicity of approaches begs a basic question: if SLA is a singular entity, why are there so many theories?

We begin by noting it is not unusual for other disciplines to entertain multiple theories. In physics, for example, there are two broad theories – general relativity and quantum theory, with multiple sub-theories in the latter. In biology, there are theories about evolution/natural selection, cells, bioenergetics, and ecosystems, for example. And in psychology, there are behavioral theories, cognitive theories, and developmental theories, to name three major areas each with sub-theories within them.

Second – and perhaps more importantly – it is illusory that something like SLA is a singular entity. As the various authors in the present volume demonstrate, SLA cannot be a singular entity and thus it is unlikely there can be a singular theory of SLA. Again, let's look at physics for a moment. The reason there are various theories in physics is that most of them attempt to explain different phenomena. The theory of relativity is a theory that works with forces at the macro scale (e.g., gravitational forces in the universe) whereas quantum theory focuses on forces at the micro level (e.g., strong and weak attraction as well as repulsion among sub-atomic particles). As mentioned before, there are sub-theories within quantum theory, involving chromodynamics, electrodynamics, and electromagnetism/weak attraction. As distinct aspects of the forces at the sub-atomic level, each has been isolated and singled out for its own theoretical development within physics. The reason for different theories in biology and psychology stems from similar issues: they generally attempt to explain different things.

As in the sciences and psychology, it is the case that various theories within SLA initially set out to explain different things about SLA. Broadly construed, theories of SLA can explain observations about internal aspects of acquisition (e.g., processing of both input and output, mental representation, storage and retrieval) or they can explain observations about external aspects of acquisition – namely interaction and what factors alter/affect interaction (e.g., context, social roles, identity, communicative intent). Whether or not these theories are in competition is something we take up in another question later in this chapter. For now, it is enough to acknowledge that SLA is complex and consists of different components and processes.

We can illustrate with a very simple example: the acquisition and use of null and overt subject pronouns in Spanish. Spanish allows both null and overt subject pronouns in simple declarative sentences. Thus, both *hablo* and *yo hablo* are grammatically licit sentences equivalent to 'I speak.' First, there is the mental representation underlying these pronouns. The learner's grammar has to license them, meaning that something has to exist within the learner's mind/brain that says both *hablo* and *yo hablo* are licit (in contrast to English, which does not license two versions of the sentence). But we also know that the null and overt subject pronouns are not in free distribution in a language like Spanish; their use is subject to universal constraints (e.g. restrictions on interpretations such as those captured under the Overt Pronoun Constraint) as well as discourse conditions (see Rothman, 2009, and the citations cited therein). Whatever the account of null and overt subject pronouns turns out to be, learners must have this representation somewhere in their minds/brains. Second, there is the question of how this representation gets into the learner's mind/brain. What is the relationship between data in the input and how the mind/brain regulates and organizes language? How are those data processed and used in grammar formation? This question is separate from the mental representation question. In terms of null and overt subject pronouns, the learner has to somehow encounter appropriate data in the language he or she is exposed to (let's call these triggers or cues) in order for the mind/brain to construct a mental representation that is null-subject appropriate. Third, there is the question of how learners get the input they need to construct the system and what that input looks like. How does context (setting, speakers, roles, and so on) affect both the quantity and quality of interactions with language the learner gets? Does context affect the quality of the input, for example? In terms of subject pronouns, how does context affect the data that learners get as well as how they interact with it? Finally, there is the question of how learners put underlying knowledge to use during real time communication. Again, what internal and external factors affect how learners produce and gain skill with the distribution of null and overt subject pronouns in a language like Spanish? Not surprisingly, there are sub-questions within these larger questions (e.g., the role of the L1 in internal hypothesis making, the role of the L1 in processing). The point here is that it is expected that multiple theories and approaches would exist within the field of SLA. This multiplicity reflects the multifaceted and complex nature of SLA.

Question 2. How do the various theories treat the S, the L, and the A of SLA?

As discussed in our answer to Question 1, there are different theories in SLA because they purport to address different aspects of SLA. Nonetheless, all such theories presume to deal with SLA, so it is right to ask how each of the theories treats the main constructs within SLA: 'second', 'language', and 'acquisition.' In examining the theories at this level, we get another glimpse at to what the theories attempt to explain and why they differ from each other.

We believe that all theories essentially assume that 'second' is any non-primary language (i.e., a language learned after acquisition of the first in childhood), so we begin with the nature of language: how does each of the theories conceptualize and treat language? To what extent does each theory or framework specify the nature of language? As we review the theories and frameworks, we find that the different approaches fall into four main groups:

1. Language is a mental construct
   Generative Approach
   Connectionism
   Input Processing
   Processability Theory
2. Language is a socially mediated construct or is rooted in communication
   Systemic-functional Approaches
   Sociocultural Theory (?)
3. Language is a hybrid mental/social-communicative construct
   Spoken Language Grammar
   Sociocultural Theory (?)
4. Language is not specified
   Interactionist Framework
   Skill Acquisition Theory
   Dynamic Systems Theory

In group 1, what distinguishes one approach from another centers on whether language is seen to be something special and modular (the generative approach, input processing) or not (e.g., connectionism). We note that Processability Theory relies on Lexical Functional Grammar (LFG) as its framework for language, which is essentially a generative approach. However, LFG differs from the approach taken in a UG-based account in that LFG attempts to tie underlying competence to performance-related phenomena (e.g., feature unification during real time). In group 4, although the frameworks may not be clear about the precise nature of language, they may be clear about what it isn't. For example, Dynamic Systems Theory rejects a generative view of language, particularly one that is modular and involves an innate component such as UG. Skill Acquisition Theory – because of its focus on the nature of "practice" and "proceduralization" – must also reject any similar generative perspective.

There is also a close relationship between how a theory conceptualizes language and how it construes the causation of change. Within generative theory, parts of the grammar are governed by universals (e.g., Structural Dependency, Locality, Agreement relations of formal features) so these are regulated from within – that is, these formal processes are governed by purely learner-internal mechanisms and not strictly dependent on external variables. Other parts of the grammar – although restricted in terms of alternatives – are indeed sensitive to, if not dependent on, input data. Thus, data from the input could trigger a change in the underlying grammar, in the traditional sense of change being predicated on parsing failures, as when a learner of Japanese L2 with English L1 encounters SOV word order in Japanese. The pervasiveness of OV word is a good candidate to trigger change in head-directionality throughout the grammar (i.e., head-initial to head-final – see Smith & VanPatten in press). With something like connectionism, change is triggered almost exclusively from the environment, that is, from input (e.g., (relative) frequency effects), because unlike a generative perspective, there is nothing universal or internal that "makes language" other than a general learning architecture. Because language is "emergent" within connectionism, all learning is due to input in conjunction with general learning mechanisms. Nothing internal in a purely linguistic sense constrains the grammar as it does within the UG perspective.

Less clear is something like Processability Theory, which claims that learners must acquire output-processing procedures as part of language development. However, it is not specified anywhere within Processing Theory what triggers the learner to move from one processing stage to the next. Because the model is output-oriented and it assumes some kind of grammar is developing in the learner's mind/brain, it does not need to address whether input plays a role or not in linguistic development. What it does need to address is how learners move from one type of output processing procedure to another. We do not find this specification in the current volume or in any other writings on processability theory. The same can be said of some of the other theories and frameworks in the present volume such as input processing, sociocultural theory, and spoken language grammar, for example. Within these frameworks, acquisition as change is not clearly specified (e.g., what exactly changes over time?) and the cause of change remains unspecified. Within input processing, although it is clear what would push a learner to abandon the first-noun strategy, it is not clear what would cause a learner to abandon the lexical preference principle. This does not mean causation in such a case cannot be reasoned out; our claim here is simply that currently this issue is not addressed. In the case of something like sociocultural theory, there is the claim that learners move from other-regulation to more self-regulation. However, this is a behavior about communication and language use rather than a claim about change in language itself. Still, the cause of change from other regulation to self-regulation remains unclear.

To conclude this section, we suggest that theories and frameworks need to be carefully examined for how they construe the nature of language and in turn, how this construal affects the construct of acquisition as well as what causes change during acquisition. To our mind, the better a theory or framework can articulate these constructs, the more likely it is to lead us to a deeper understanding of SLA as well as an account that can lead to testable hypotheses. At the very least, understanding how these theories construct language helps a reader to understand why there are different theories.

Question 3. How does environmental context influence the various theories?

So far, we have highlighted some non-trivial differences between various theories of SLA in an effort to understand why there is a multitude of SLA theories. But as we see it, there is another factor that has encouraged the proliferation of theories. That factor is context, and the issue is the extent to which a theory's questions are related to the degree of emphasis placed on the environmental context. We will argue that this factor must be considered and in doing so sets the stage to better understand that many SLA theories are in less direct competition than some might believe, a point we take up more directly in our fourth section.

We begin by acknowledging, however obvious, that L2 acquisition can occur under different environmental contexts. As is true of all the contributions in the present volume, we focus on adult SLA, given that some if not many of the environmental context variables we will discuss would be different for child L2 acquisition. Considering the extent to which environmental context is deterministic in a macro sense (i.e. contributes to constraining L2 developmental sequencing and ultimate attainment) and how this conceptualization bears upon hypothesis creation for particular theoretical approaches, is an important endeavor. Minimally, highlighting that some SLA theories are primarily or solely concerned with specific types of SLA contexts while other are essentially agnostic to context can help us to understand why they address the questions they do, and ultimately, to what extent the theories are actually in competition for explanatory adequacy. We elucidate this idea in the paragraphs that follow.

Most commonly, SLA takes place, at least in part and especially in its initial stages, in some type of structured environment, usually a classroom. This is not to suggest that SLA does not occur in completely naturalistic settings, just that the instances of such compared to environments of tutored learning are quite disproportional. And, to be sure, advanced learners of a language experience both tutored and untutored environments. How does all of this matter and should it matter?

For theories that see language as primarily a mental construct, the questions they find most appealing deal with how language comes to be represented and/or how processing delimits the instantiation of representation. As such, generative, connectionist, input processing (not to be confused with its corollary Processing Instruction) and processability theory approaches are not focused overtly on the classroom environmental context per se. For such theories, the classroom is in a sense the happenstance locus that provides beginning and intermediate L2 learners with the building blocks needed for acquisition; that is, the input used to create mental linguistic representations. But for these theories, the happenstance locus of acquisition could just as easily be outside the classroom. As such, these theories exist independently of a specific context, seeking to understand what L2 learners do cognitively with the input they have, wherever that input were to come from. In general, they do not assume (or overtly deny the possibility) that specific classroom based interventions will confer necessary differences or advantages for the ways in which grammatical knowledge comes to be represented in the mind/brain. To be sure, none of these theories contends that explicit knowledge of so-called grammatical rules is necessary or even particularly useful for L2 learners with regard to constructing the actual underlying grammatical representations. Essentially, the questions that motivate them involve determining what the mind/brain does with the input available to them in an unconscious sense and how this delimits the processes of interlanguage development and ultimate attainment.

Alternatively, other theories of SLA have been readily applied to classroom situations and in some cases, not at all to non-classroom contexts. These theories include Skill Acquisition Theory and Sociocultural Theory, among others. These kinds of theories are generally concerned with variables unrelated to grammatical representation and processing. Many of these theories examine the roles of "practice", negotiation or interaction, attitude, relationships among participants, aptitude, and others, on the premise that these variables are (1) deterministic in SLA and that (2) (some) of these variables can be manipulated. Some, if not many, of these variables are clearly likely to play a role in explaining why SLA outcomes come to be what they are. If nothing more, these variables may point to how much of the available input can be "taken up" for use by the mind/brain. However, it is not clear that such variables tell us much about the underlying constitution of mental L2 systems or the upper and lower limits of what the mind/brain can achieve for ultimate attainment. Thus, we are back at the issue that different theories look at different aspects of SLA and may be exclusive of domains of inquiry but not in competition for what they explain. We will touch upon this one final time in the last section of this chapter.

The questions and variables researched by various SLA theories, then, are determined in part by the extent to which the researcher emphasizes environmental contexts. As an outcome, it is fair to say that some SLA theories are more immediately practical than others. Theories that have direct implications for or are seemingly predicated on classroom environments are bound to be as popular as they are useful to practitioners of second language instruction. Conversely, theories that have no readily apparent bearing on teaching are likely to be taken as more abstract and, therefore, less practically useful beyond their ability to explicate how the mind/brain constructs a second language. Of course, as SLA scholars we want to know the answers to all questions that come to bear on the processes involved in second language acquisition and this undoubtedly cannot be answered by a single theory. One goal of SLA theorizing should then be to determine which questions of all the ones that need to be addressed and answered are best handled by specific theories. As a result of doing just that, one possible consequence could be that the imagined space of mutual exclusivity between competing SLA theories is more reduced than many believe.

Question 4: To what extent are the various theories and frameworks in the present volume "in competition"?

In posing and addressing question 1 above, we took the position that the existence of multiple theories in SLA is to be expected. This is so precisely because various theories often, although not exclusively, address distinct questions. This does not entail, upon careful consideration, that these theories are in direct competition. Most questions asked in SLA theorizing are ones that should be pondered in a scientific manner, and some questions are simply better answered by the methodologies and under the working assumptions of specific approaches as opposed to others. What we are suggesting, then, is that although various theories may be mutually exclusive in terms of domains of inquiry, this exclusivity does not put them in competition for overall explanatory adequacy. Instead, they actually may be complementary (at least, in some respects). As we will suggest later, there is room for generative, connectionist, processability, and skill theories working together (with others) to account for the complexity of SLA.

To be sure, there are mutually exclusive positions in SLA theorizing. We will take, for example, how second language grammars are represented in the mind/brain of learners. If connectionism is descriptively accurate then surely this must mean that generative approaches and even dynamic system approaches to linguistic representation are patently wrong. However, this is overly simplistic. To be sure, we have our own biases regarding what we believe to be the most explanatory account of linguistic representation, but the whole of connectionism does not have to be incompatible with generative understandings of linguistic representation and vice versa. It is perfectly possible that some domains of grammar are learned in a way described by connectionists. For example, there are the lexicon, and surface morphological inflections. The question is whether or not connectionist models can capture the entirety of linguistic complexities and how these are acquired. In other words, is *everything* really learned by an interaction between simple domain-general learning mechanisms and input frequency alone? Not surprisingly, we don't think so; however, despite our reservations, connectionism presents a good model for how some (if not many) properties of language are learned and stored mentally. So, it might be the case that connectionism is the preferred approach for lexical and morphological acquisition while something like a generative approach is preferred for the acquisition of syntactic computations and representation (e.g., movement and its consequences). Taking this kind of pluralistic position need not threaten any theory of SLA that has a different view of grammatical representation.

Regarding theories other than generative and connectionists accounts that seem to be in direct competition, we note that they do not necessarily have to be viewed as competitive either. A good example of a theory that can be adopted cross-paradigmatically is Input Processing (IP). IP is perfectly compatible with any theory of representation precisely because it focuses on something different in SLA, namely input parsing; that is, the intermediary processes that take the input and "deliver it" to whatever internal system deals with grammatical construction. Although VanPatten's work clearly has a UG understanding of representation, input processing more generally does not need to ally itself with a generative approach. We mentioned previously that Skill Acquisition Theory must assume a domain-general structure building approach of some sort given the tenets of what it claims, but it only needs to do so if no distinction between learning and acquisition is subscribed to. It is possible that explicit knowledge is helpful for advances in output production and that the extent to which this becomes automatic will result in positive effects in learning. For us, however, it will be just that: learning. If one maintains a distinction between learning and acquisition, as we do, then one can accept Skill Acquisition Theory as the process by which a learned system of metalinguistic knowledge independent from the actual competence comes to form a separate usable system for performance for tutored second language learners even if one accepts a generative view of linguistic representation. Proponents of Skill Acquisition Theory largely do not make the distinction between acquisition and learning, and would likely not agree with our characterization here. Our point is not to convince anyone, but rather to point out that such a characterization is possible. As a final example, we offer that the Interactionist Approach as well as Sociocultural Theory – despite being very different themselves – also do not tend to adopt generative approaches to representation. However, we submit that they too are simply looking at such vastly differently questions from what generativists research that they could adopt a generativist type idea of mental representation without changing much if anything to the agendas they push forward. For example, impressive work within Interactionist SLA has been done by one of the editors of this volume, María del Pilar García Mayo, who is at the core a generative SLA researcher. And Susan Gass, in her classic work on interaction and input, explicitly states that she does not see that an interactionist approach is incompatible with a generativist style account of how UG constrains language development in the mind/brain of the learner (Gass 1997).

We anticipate that some readers will disagree with our logic and with some of our specific claims, but the exercise in raising these questions and answering them is useful. Assuming that researchers are all working toward the same goal of understanding SLA, it seems that we will have a greater chance to converge on a more general account of SLA if we work together, when and where possible. The consequence of this enterprise is that we will speak to each other as opposed to at each other. We hope to have problematized the idea that there is pervasive mutual exclusivity across SLA theories. Despite this mutual exclusivity, and acknowledging that it is a necessary outcome of moving the enterprise of understanding SLA forward, the questions remain if exclusivity is irreconcilably detrimental to the overall SLA program of research. As we have pointed out, not all theories of SLA are equally concerned with the same facets of SLA. As such, that various theories have vastly different conceptualizations on what the "S", the "L" and the "A" are even if there is tacit agreement that all facets currently researched are indeed worthy of serious consideration. With this in mind, we submit that the theories represented in this volume all contribute something to the larger puzzle of SLA that is inescapably complex and multifarious.

Getting the bigger picture

In this section, we sketch out how we view acquisition more generally. In so doing, we hope to better situate the various theories and frameworks. Parts of this discussion are based on VanPatten (2010, forthcoming) and the reader is referred to these publications for more detail. First, we separate the acquisition and development of a mental representation (i.e., a linguistic system) from skill development (i.e., the ability to use oral or written language in communicative situations).

Although we make this initial separation, this does not mean the two necessarily act independently of each other – something that will emerge in this discussion.

We take mental representation to be an abstract, interactive, and implicit system of a generative nature. It is abstract because it consists not of rules and paradigms familiar to many teachers but of principles and abstract rules/parameters such as the Overt Pronoun Constraint, Structure Dependency, Head-Directionality, Null-subject Parameter, and so on. This system defines not only what is possible in a given language but what is also prohibited. It is interactive because the various components of language such as syntax, semantics, lexicon/morphology, phonology, and pragmatics interact to yield the surface structures that we hear, read, and speak. It is implicit because it exists outside of awareness, even for second language learners with formal exposure, and is available only for introspection and articulation with training *after* the system is in place. The question becomes "How does this mental representation come to exist?" We see its development due to a complex interaction of input, Universal Grammar, and processing mechanisms that mediate between input and UG.

Skill development, on the other hand, consists of the real-time use of language involving both speed and accuracy. The relative contributions of speed and accuracy are context dependent, as they would be for any skill (e.g., making an omelet, tying a tie, wrapping gifts). Skill development evolves in only one way: through transfer appropriate behaviors – that is, behaviors that are similar to if not the same as those that make up the skill. Thus, speaking develops by engaging in actual communicative speech (not, for example, by repetition and imitation). To be clear, skill development depends on some kind of underlying representation; that is, skill requires that learners know language in some way, regardless of the relative degree of that knowledge on a scale in which native-likeness is one extreme. To put this another way, learners can't put language to use if they don't have language.

How theories fit into this larger scheme of things should begin to be apparent to the reader. For example, as we alluded to above, both generative and connectionist approaches can be used to sketch out the nature of mental representation. Connectionism can be used to address some aspects of acquisition as could Input Processing. Processability Theory provides insights into the initial stages of skill development (i.e., how things emerge in speech over time) while Skill Theory itself is useful to talk about how the procedures sketched out by Processability Theory come under control by the learner. Theories such as Sociocultural Theory and Interactionist theories have a good deal to say about the nature and quality of interactions, which in turn imply how both input and skill are affected. That is, these two approaches can help us understand more about the nature of the external environment and how that environment is conducive or not to (1) getting high quality and appropriate input, and (2) the types of things that learners do to communicate that allow skill to develop.

We are being necessarily sketchy here as it is not our goal to lay out an all-encompassing model of how SLA works from beginning to end. Our goal is more modest but just as important: to point out the complexity of SLA and to underscore that different theories tackle different issues that – when viewed in the broader context of factors known to be implicated in SLA (e.g., input, processing, UG) – provide the bigger picture. In so doing, we also underscore the necessity of the different theories working out the details of their particular domains before there is assembly of these smaller theories into a larger account of SLA.

Any attempt, such as the present one, at drawing SLA researchers' attention to the idea that multiple theories have roles to play in the overall enterprise of understanding SLA will inevitably meet resistance. Like other SLA researchers, we are the byproducts of our training and paradigmatic biases. What is more, we are interested in and motivated by specifically narrow questions. The fact that both of us are aligned with generative theories as they relate to grammatical representation should not be taken to mean that we thus believe other approaches do not make important or necessary contributions to the entirety of the SLA enterprise, even when they appear to qualify as "diametrically opposed" to our approach. At a minimum, any emergent field that adopts a scientific methodology a priori, such as SLA, must consider what the history of science has shown: every theory must believe itself to be correct if only to have the fairest of chances to develop and become articulated. And almost every theory in science, or subparts of it, is eventually proven wrong. Take, for example, what was known as a virtual fact 700 years ago as it pertains to what the center of the universe was. There was little question that the earth was the center and that the sun literally rose and set each day. However, we know this to be patently wrong centuries later. What is important about scientific statements and research agendas is that in hindsight, these statements may seem to be unscientific and in some cases, laughable. Still, they provided the point of departure for the evolution of thought about some observable phenomenon, a point against which to argue; that is, they provided a claim that could be investigated empirically. This is what modernity tells us, and a crucial aspect of modernity is that it is in a constant state of change. We maintain that no one is arrogant enough to believe that future L2 researchers, within their own modernities, will not look back on at least some of what we take to be near truths now and – while applying the same respect we give to our pioneers – smile like we do now about how wrong they seemingly were. Yet, the foundations we pave today shall always be remembered as the road that brought scholars closer to descriptive and explanatory adequacy.

References

Gass, S.M. 1997. *Input, Interaction, and the Second Language Learner.* Mahwah NJ: Lawrence Erlbaum Associates.

Rothman, J. 2009. Pragmatic deficitis with syntactic consequences: L2 pronominal subjects and the syntax-pragmatics interface. *Journal of Pragmatics* 41: 951–973.

Slabakova, R. 2008. *Meaning in the Second Language.* Berlin: Mouton de Gruyter.

Smith, M.C. & VanPatten, B. in press. Instructed SLA as parameter setting: Evidence from the earliest-stage learners of Japanese as L2. In *The Grammar Dimension in Instructed SLA: Theory, Research, and Practice*, C. Laval & M. J. Arche (eds.). London: Continuum Press.

VanPatten, B. 2010. The two faces of SLA: Mental representation and skills. *International Journal of English Language Studies* 10: 1–18.

VanPatten, B. Forthcoming. Mental Representation and Skill in Instructed SLA. In *Innovations in SLA, Bilingualism, and Cognition: Research and Practice*, J. Schwieter (ed.). Amsterdam: John Benjamins.

VanPatten, B. & Williams, J. 2007. *Theories in Second Language Acquisition.* Mahwah NJ: Lawrence Erlbaum Associates.

List of contributors

María Basterrechea
Departamento de Didáctica de la
Lengua y la Literatura
Escuela Universitaria de Magisterio
Universidad del País Vasco
(UPV/EHU)
Juan Ibáñez de Sto. Domingo, 1
01006 Vitoria-Gasteiz
SPAIN
maria.basterrechea@ehu.es

Alessandro Benati
Professor of Applied Linguistics and
Second Language Studies
Director of Research and Enterprise
School of Humanities and Social
Sciences
Greenwich Campus, SE10 9LS
UNITED KINDGOM
A.Benati@gre.ac.uk

C.L.J. de Bot (Kees de Bot)
Department of Applied Linguistics,
University of Groningen and
Department of English, The University
of the Free State
PO Box 716
9700AS Groningen
THE NETHERLANDS
c.l.j.de.bot@rug.nl

Christie Brien
Department of Linguistics
University of Ottawa
Arts Hall
70 Laurier Ave East
Ottawa, Ontario
K1N6A5 CANADA
christiebrien@hotmail.com

Adela Gánem-Gutiérrez
Graduate Programmes Director
Department of Language and
Linguistics
University of Essex
Wivenhoe Park
Colchester CO4 3SQ
UK
aganem@essex.ac.uk

María del Pilar García Mayo
Departamento de Filología Inglesa y
Alemana
Facultad de Letras
Universidad del País Vasco (UPV/
EHU)
Paseo de la Universidad 5
01006 Vitoria-Gasteiz
SPAIN
mariapilar.garciamayo@ehu.es

Junkal Gutierrez Mangado
Departamento de Filología Inglesa y
Alemana
Facultad de Letras
Universidad del País Vasco (UPV/
EHU)
Paseo de la Universidad 5
01006 Vitoria-Gasteiz
SPAIN
junkal.gutierrez@ehu.es

Gisela Håkansson
Department of Linguistics
Center for Language and Literature
Lund University, Box 201
S-221 00 Lund
SWEDEN
Gisela.Hakansson@ling.lu.se

Ping Li
Department of Psychology
Pennsylvania State University
University Park PA 16082
USA
pul8@psu.edu

Ana Llinares
Dpto. de Filología Inglesa
Facultad de Filosofía y Letras
Universidad Autónoma de Madrid
Cantoblanco 28049 Madrid
SPAIN
ana.llinares@uam.es

Wander Lowie
Department of Applied Linguistics,
University of Groningen and
Department of English, The University
of the Free State
Faculty of Arts
University of Groningen
PO Box 716, 9700 AS Groningen
THE NETHERLANDS
w.m.lowie@rug.nl

Roy Lyster
Department of Integrated Studies in
Education
McGill Univeristy
3700 McTavish St.
Montreal, Québec
CANADA H3A 1Y2
roy.lyster@mcgill.ca

María Martínez Adrián
Departamento de Filología Inglesa y
Alemana
Facultad de Letras
Universidad del País Vasco (UPV/
EHU)
Paseo de la Universidad 5
01006 Vitoria-Gasteiz
SPAIN
maria.martineza@ehu.es

Florence Myles
Department of Language and
Linguistics
University of Essex
Wivenhoe Park
Colchester CO4 3SQ, UK
tel: +44(0)1206 87 2228
fmyles@essex.ac.uk

†Teresa Pica
Graduate School of Education
University of Pennsylvania
3700 Walnut Street
Philadelphia, PA 19104
USA

Jason Rothman
170 Dauer Hall
P.O. Box 117405
University of Florida
Gainesville, FL 32611-7405
USA
jrothman@ufl.edu

Laura Sabourin
Department of Linguistics
University of Ottawa
70 Laurier Ave. E., Rm. 401
Ottawa, ON K1N 6N5
Laura.Sabourin@uottawa.ca

Masatoshi Sato
Fernández Concha 700
Las Condes
Departamento de Inglés
Universidad Andrés Bello
Santiago
CHILE
masatoshi.sato@unab.cl

Roumyana Slabakova
Department of Linguistics
557 English Philosophy Building
University of Iowa
Iowa City, IA 52242
USA
roumyana-slabakova@uiowa.edu

Steven L. Thorne
Department of Applied Linguistics,
University of Groningen and Portland
State University
PO Box 751
Portland, OR 97207
USA
stevenlthorne@gmail.com

Marie-Claude Tremblay
School of Modern Languages
Newcastle University
Old Library Building
Newcastle upon Tyne, United Kingdom
NE1 7RU
marie-claude.tremblay@ncl.ac.uk

Bill VanPatten
Department of Romance and Classical
Studies & Dpt. of Second Language
Studies
Michigan State University
USA
bvp@msu.edu

Marjolijn Verspoor
Department of Applied Linguistics,
University of Groningen and
Department of English, The University
of the Free State
PO Box 716
9700AS Groningen
THE NETHERLANDS
m.h.verspoor@rug.nl

Regina Weinert
Department of Humanities
School of Arts and Social Sciences
Northumbria University
Lipman Building
Sandyford Road
Newcastle upon Tyne
NE1 8ST
regina.weinert@northumbria.ac.uk

Xiaowei Zhao
Department of Psychology
Emmanuel College
400 The Fenway
Boston, MA 02115
USA
zhaox@emmanuel.edu

Index